Collective Labour Rights for Self-Employed Workers

Bulletin of Comparative Labour Relations

VOLUME 116

Founding Editor

The series started in 1970 under the dynamic editorship of Professor Roger Blanpain (Belgium), former President of the International Industrial Relations Association. Professor Blanpain, Professor Emeritus of Labour Law, Universities of Leuven and Tilburg, was also General Editor of the International Encyclopedia of Laws (with more than 1,600 collaborators worldwide) and President of the Association of Educative and Scientific Authors Authors. He passed away in October 2016.

General Editor

In 2015 Frank Hendrickx, Professor of labour law at the Faculty of Law of the University of Leuven (Belgium) joined as a co-Editor. Frank Hendrickx has published numerous articles and books and regularly advises governments, international institutions and private organisations in the area of labour law as well as in sports law. He is the Editor-in-Chief of the European Labour Law Journal and General Editor of the International Encyclopaedia of Laws.

Introduction

The Bulletins constitute a unique source of information and thought-provoking discussion, laying the groundwork for studies of employment relations in the 21st century, involving among much else the effects of globalization, new technologies, migration, and the greying of the population.

Contents/Subjects

Amongst other subjects the Bulletins frequently include the proceedings of international or regional conferences; reports from comparative projects devoted to salient issues in industrial relations, human resources management, and/or labour law; and specific issues underlying the multicultural aspects of our industrial societies.

Objective

The Bulletins offer a platform of expression and discussion on labour relations to scholars and practitioners worldwide, often featuring special guest editors.

The titles published in this series are listed at the end of this volume.

Collective Labour Rights for Self-Employed Workers

A Human Rights-Based Approach of Platform Work

Charalampos Stylogiannis

General Editor
Frank Hendrickx

Founding Editor
Roger Blanpain

Wolters Kluwer

Published by:
Kluwer Law International B.V.
PO Box 316
2400 AH Alphen aan den Rijn
The Netherlands
E-mail: lrs-sales@wolterskluwer.com
Website: www.wolterskluwer.com/en/solutions/kluwerlawinternational

Sold and distributed by:
Wolters Kluwer Legal & Regulatory U.S.
920 Links Avenue
Landisville, PA 17538
United States of America
E-mail: customer.service@wolterskluwer.com

Printed on acid-free paper.

ISBN 978-94-035-0667-8

e-Book: ISBN 978-94-035-0687-6
web-PDF: ISBN 978-94-035-0677-7

Notes on Author

Charalampos Stylogiannis is a postdoctoral researcher at the Institute for Labour Law, University of KU Leuven, Belgium, where he also obtained his Doctor of Laws (PhD). He holds a BSc from the Kapodistrian University of Athens, Greece, in the field of Political Science and Public Administration. He also obtained an LLB from the University of Sussex and his LLM from the University College London (UCL), in the United Kingdom. He worked as an intern in the Office of the High Commissioner for Human Rights (OHCHR), Human Rights and Social Issues Section and in the International Labour Organization (ILO), Labour Law and Reform Unit, in Geneva. He has worked as an external consultant for the ILO, as well as other organisations. His main publications include a book on *Gig Economy* published by *Edward Elgar*, which he has co-edited and authored, a book chapter in the *Oxford Handbook of the Law of Work* (forthcoming), two ILO Working Papers, as well as articles published with international journals, such as the *International Labour Review Journal*.

Funder Acknowledgement

This is the submitted manuscript for obtaining the doctoral degree at KU Leuven which was successfully defended on 27 February 2023. This work has been made possible thanks to the funding provided by the Research Foundation Flanders (FWO) under the Odysseus programme on 'employment rights and labour protection in the on-demand economy' (Ref. 179461/G0H8118N), coordinated by Professor Frank Hendrickx and Professor Valerio De Stefano.

Table of Contents

Preface

This research examines the challenges (dependent) self-employed platform workers are facing with respect to their collective labour rights. It, more particularly, focuses on the exercise of the rights to freedom of association and collective bargaining of platform workers. Reference is also made to the right to strike.

In doing so, the research refers to a number of important experiences of platform workers' collective organisation around the world, as well as the very nature of such rights as human rights. It is contended that the changing context of work has prompted changes in modern workplaces, which in turn, *inter alia*, have generated a novel interest in the need to adopt a human rights-based approach (HRBA) regarding labour protection. Such an approach identifies workers, regardless of their employment status, as rights-holders that are entitled to rights, like the right to collective bargaining, derived from international human rights instruments. A HRBA, moreover, does not aim at forcing the requalification of workers who find themselves in a 'grey' zone between employment and self-employment, including many platform workers. It rather seeks to establish a protection floor for all workers, who, by exercising their fundamental collective rights, will be able to ameliorate their working conditions and produce adequate labour standards that will be dependent upon their employment status.

In light of this, this doctoral dissertation identifies some of the positive ramifications of a HRBA towards collective labour rights. For example, this approach moves away from a strict dichotomy between employment and self-employment. This is also important for the field of labour law as a whole, as the allocation of fundamental collective labour rights to those who need it the most can assist the field in maintaining its normative coherence and integrity. Moreover, a HRBA can be utilised to re-establish the relationship between labour and competition laws. The nature of collective labour rights as human rights should guide this interplay. A HRBA towards collective labour rights can also be used as a shield of protection for the enjoyment of other human rights at work, like discrimination-related entitlements; it can, furthermore, help workers in solving some of the practical challenges they are currently facing, such as the lack of a common identity.

As the last part of this research illustrates though, the effective application of a HRBA is still away from being guaranteed in practice. This is to say that even if someone was placing competition-related issues on the side, there are still challenges stemming from complexions within national systems of industrial relations. On many occasions, existing legal apparatuses for collective bargaining seem outdated and do not match the realities within the new world of work and the increase of self-employed workers dependent upon their principals. By considering such complications, this research comes up with some requirements capable of facilitating in practice the exercise of collective bargaining for self-employed, including many platform workers.

Acknowledgements

The completion of this manuscript would not be possible without the unconditional support of a wonderful group of people.

First of all, I would like to single out two outstanding individuals who have unreservedly supported me throughout this process, my promoters – Prof Frank Hendrickx and Prof Valerio De Stefano – their support not only helped me to develop my academic and research skills but also helped me to grow as a person more in general. Your love, values and kindness will always guide me. I am, moreover, grateful to my promoters for putting together an excellent jury, without the support and encouragement of whom, my journey to writing this book would not have been so smooth and pleasant. Particularly, I would like to sincerely thank Prof. Dr Filip Dorssemont (UCLouvain), Prof. Dr Koen Lemmens (KU Leuven), Prof. Dr Evelyne Terryn (KU Leuven), as well as Prof. Dr Frank Hutsebaut (Chair, KU Leuven). It was a privilege to collaborate with you for the completion of this project.

I would also like to deeply thank my colleagues at the Institute for Labour Law, namely, Mathias, Silvia, Stan, Simon, Sara, Frea, Christina, Bettina, Margot, Josephine, Miet, and Pieter for their academic support and friendship. A sincere thank you to my beloved colleague Dr Ilda Durri, who has been next to me since day one of this journey.

Finally, I would like to acknowledge with gratitude the support and love of my family – my parents, Alexandra and Costas; my grandma, Chariklia. I owe you everything, I owe you all of me. And of course, I am particularly grateful to Irini. Thank you for bringing 'peace' in my thoughts.

Introduction

1 SUBJECT

This is the submitted manuscript for obtaining the doctoral degree at KU Leuven which was successfully defended on 27 February 2023. This work has been made possible thanks to the funding provided by the Research Foundation Flanders (FWO) under the Odysseus programme on 'employment rights and labour protection in the on-demand economy' (Ref. 179461/G0H8118N), coordinated by Professor Frank Hendrickx and Professor Valerio De Stefano.

This research focuses on the protection of collective labour rights of self-employed workers, with a particular emphasis on the so-called platform-based economy, or gig economy. It is proposed that the changing context of work has prompted changes in the function of labour markets, which in turn, *inter alia*, have generated a novel interest in the need to adopt a human rights-based approach (HRBA) vis-à-vis labour protection. Concretely, such an approach identifies workers, regardless of their employment status, as rights-holders entitled to rights derived from international human rights and labour rights treaties.

Platform-based work constitutes a type of non-standard work,[1] facilitated through technology and digital markets, on-demand and it shares important features of flexibility and precariousness with other casual work arrangements that are on the rise around the world.[2] Having said that, a large portion of workers engaged in such occupations often remain in a legal 'grey zone' between traditional employment and

1. According to the International Labour Office, non-standard-forms of employment comprises four different employment arrangements ((1) temporary employment; (2) part-time work; (3) temporary agency work; and (4) other forms of employment), which fall out of the realm of the 'standard employment relationship', understood as work that is full time, indefinite, as well as part of a subordinate and bilateral employment relationship (International Labour Office (ILO), (2016), *Non-standard employment around the world: Understanding challenges, shaping prospects*, Geneva, ILO, 7).
2. De Stefano, V., *The Rise of the 'Just-in-Time Workforce': On-demand Work, Crowdwork, and Labor Protection in the 'Gig-economy'*, 37 Comparative Labor Law & Policy Journal 476-477 476 (2016).

self-employment, in which the scope of labour regulation is traditionally limited to the bare minimum. The majority of platform businesses tend to 'enlist' casual workers and label them as independent contractors, even though the real nature of the job may indicate a disguised employment relationship, often concealed behind a *façade* of organisational and economic independence. As a result, they are frequently excluded from the protective framework of employment and labour laws, including the effective exercise of their collective labour rights. The major reason for the occurrence of this phenomenon is inextricably linked to the existing limitations of the labour law framework. This is to say that labour protection(s) still, and by large, remain concentrated within 'subordinate' wage employment, particularly of a full-time and open-ended nature. Self-employed workers, instead, have historically been assumed to be able to 'defend' themselves on the market without the need for State intervention and, therefore, have generally been excluded from the scope of labour protection. It has been argued, for instance, that within the European Union's (EU) legal framework, the adoption of several instruments against discrimination of self-employed persons[3] is still far from guaranteeing the application of the full range of anti-discriminatory measures to self-employed.[4]

Thus far, the vast majority of the literature identified with respect to platform work and other atypical forms of work is broadly focusing on the classification of workers between employment and self-employment, and the need to redefine the scope of labour protection, as well as on discussions related to individual employment rights and working conditions (e.g., protection against discrimination).[5] Concomitantly though, less attention has been paid to the field of industrial relations, particularly to the fact that the extensive use of freelance jobs entails the risk of excluding a significant portion of workers from the protection of fundamental collective labour rights, including their coverage from collective agreements. Therefore, this research puts forward the idea that a reflection is urgently needed on the collective labour front. Such a discussion becomes all the more relevant considering the ever-increasing

3. *See*, for instance, Council Directive 2000/78/EC of 27 November 2000 establishing a general framework for equal treatment in employment and occupation; Council Directive 2000/43/EC of 29 June 2000 implementing the principle of equal treatment between persons irrespective of racial or ethnic origin; Directive 2010/41/EU of the European Parliament and of the Council of 7 July 2010 on the application of the principle of equal treatment between men and women engaged in an activity in a self-employed capacity and repealing Council Directive 86/613/EEC.
4. For instance, *see* Barnard, C., *Discrimination Law, Self-Employment and the Liberal Professions*, 12 European Anti-discrimination Law Review 21-31 n. 21 (2011); Garben, S. (2017), *Protecting Workers in the Online Platform Economy: An Overview of Regulatory and Policy Developments in the EU*, European Risk Observatory Discussion Paper, Luxembourg, Publications Office of the European Union, available at: https://osha.europa.eu/sites/default/files/publications/documents/Protecting_Workers_in_Online_Platform Economy.pdf (accessed 26 February 2019); *supra* ILO (2016).
5. For instance, *see* Prassl, J., Risak, M., *The Legal Protection of Crowdworkers: Four Avenues for Workers' Rights in the Virtual Realm* (Pamela Meil and Vassil Kirov eds, *Policy Implications of Vitrual Work*, Palgrave Macmillan 2017), 273-293; Schoukens, P., Barrio, A., *The Changing Concept of Work: When Does Typical Work Become Atypical?*, 8 European Labour Law Journal 306 n. 4 (2017), 306-332; Freedland, M., Prassl, J., *Employees, Workers and the 'Sharing Economy', Changing Practices and Changing Concepts in the UK*, 6 Spanish Labour Law and Employment Relations Journal 16 n. 1-2 (2017), 16-29.

interest of trade unions in representing platform workers, along with several initiatives to force platform businesses into collective agreements, irrespective of workers' employment status.

That said, limitations on collective labour rights can also occur, in situations where workers' activities come into clash with another area of law, namely, competition law. Indeed, self-employed workers are often restricted from joining trade unions and they – de facto – fall outside the scope of collective agreements, as the latter largely rely on employment status for coverage. This is due to not only the traditional approach of labour law but also the existence of strict antitrust laws, which consider self-employed workers as undertakings; hence, collective agreements are in breach of competition law. In this respect, there are certain occasions where national legal systems have attempted to resolve such issues. In Ireland, for example, the national competition law was recently amended to include two categories of workers beyond 'employees' that may be allowed to engage in collective bargaining.[6] Still, albeit a positive development, the national amendment has not gone without criticism. For instance, the explicit reference of the Act to an income derived from not more than two principals can be tricky, particularly as far as platform workers are concerned, as they often work for more than two platforms. Discussions on the interaction between labour law and competition law have also taken place in other countries, like the Netherlands.[7] Moreover, in 2022, at an EU level, the Commission officially published its long-awaited Guidelines on the application of EU competition law to collective agreements concerning the working conditions of solo self-employed persons, including platform workers.[8] The adequacy of these kinds of initiatives will be further elaborated as this research unfolds.

At this point, it should be stressed that platform work does not constitute '*a parallel and watertight dimension of the labour market with structurally separated feature and needs*'.[9] It is rather, part of the overall phenomenon of an increased number of weak self-employed dependent upon their principals, for whom labour protection and employment regulation are assumed not to apply by default.[10] A special focus on platform workers seems to constitute a good illustration of the issues related to this

6. Competition (Amendment) Act 2017. Some specific categories of self-employed workers were specifically exempted from competition law under Schedule 4 of the Act. These are: '(1) actors engaged as voiceover actors; (2) musicians engaged as session musicians; (3) journalists engaged as freelance journalists'.
7. For instance, *see* Laagland, F.G., *The Netherlands* (Bernd Waas and Christina Hießl eds, *Collective Bargaining for Self-employed Workers in Europe: Approaches to Reconcile Competition Law and Labour Rights*, Kluwer Law International 2021), 177-197.
8. European Commission, (2022), 'Communication from the commission Guidelines on the application of Union competition law to collective agreements regarding the working conditions of solo self-employed persons 2022/C 374/02', available at: https://eur-lex.europa.eu/legal-content/EN/TXT/?uri=CELEX%3A52022XC0930%2802%29 (accessed 14 October 2022); A solo self-employed is defined as a person '*who does not have an employment contract or who is not in an employment relationship and who rely primarily on his or her own personal labour for the provision of the services concerned*', para. 2(a) of the Guidelines.
9. *Supra*, De Stefano (2016), 2.
10. *Supra*, ILO, (2016); OECD, (2019), *Policy Responses to New Forms of Work*, OECD Publishing, Paris, available at: https://doi.org/10.1787/0763f1b7-en (accessed 29 April 2022).

trend. The particular focus is also justified by the rise in the numbers of such workers, along with increased attention in terms of visibility and policymaking around the world.[11] For example, in 2018, in Australia, the Report of the Inquiry into the Victorian On-Demand Workforce was released. It is the first extended national inquiry that attempts to address and tackle some of the main problems that many workers in the platform economy are dealing with.[12] Moreover, at an EU level, a proposed EU Directive on improving working conditions in platform work has become available to the public.[13] As some commentators have already argued, this is the most comprehensive response to platform work thus far.[14]

Due to their weak position compared to the platform operators, as well as the clients using the platforms, workers often experience a genuine need for protection, as it is shown by a growing number of socioeconomic studies.[15] Such issues, as noted, have also made social partners around the world to become active in seeking to organise and represent platform workers and in turn, provide them with better working conditions.[16] As mentioned, however, due to the friction between labour rights and other laws, such as in the case of collective bargaining and competition law, the efforts of trade unions to protect these workers risk being unreasonably restricted before the law, by also considering the weak economic and bargaining position of such workers. Thus, the very limitations of labour law, along with its conflict with competition law, prompt the need to thoroughly investigate the adoption of an approach within labour law capable of tackling the issues experienced by such workers. As it will be examined, this can be done through a sound framework which perceives fundamental labour rights as human rights.

The International Labour Organization (ILO) acknowledges five categories of Fundamental Principles and Rights at Work, namely, (1) the freedom of association and the effective recognition of the right to collective bargaining, (2) elimination of all forms of forced or compulsory labour, (3) effective abolition of child labour, (4) elimination of discrimination in respect of employment and occupation, and finally (5)

11. Lenaerts, K., Belbavy, M., Kilhoffer, (2017), *Government Responses to the Platform Economy: Where do we stand?*, CEPS Policy Insights, 27 July 2017, available at: https://www.ceps.eu/system/files/PI201730_Government%20Responses%20to%20the%20Platform%20Economy.pdf (accessed 29 April 2019).
12. Forsyth, A. (2020). *Collectivising the Gig Economy in Australia*. 27 *Journal of the International Centre for Trade Union Rights*, 18 n. 3.
13. European Commission, Proposal for a Directive of the European Parialment and of the Council on improving working conditions in platform work COM(2021) 762 final.
14. De Stefano, V., Aloisi, A. (2021), 'The EU Commission Takes the Lead in Regulating Platform Work', *Social Europe* (blog), 9 December 2021, available at: https://socialeurope.eu/european-commission-takes-the-lead-in-regulating-platform-work (accessed 29 April 2022).
15. For instance, *see* ILO, *Digital Labour Platforms and the Future of Work: Towards Decent Work in the Online World*, Geneva, ILO, 2018; Huws, U., Spencer, N.H., Syrdal, D.S., Holts, K. (2017), *Work in the European Gig Economy: Research Results From the UK, Sweden, Germany, Austria, the Netherlands, Switzerland, and Italy*, Foundation for European Progressive Studies Report, available at: (accessed 20 March 2019).
16. Forsyth, A. (2018), 'What Does Collective Representation Look like in Australia's Gig Economy?', *Labour Law Down Under* (blog), 27 October 2018, available at: https://labourlawdownunder.wordpress.com/2018/10/27/what-does-collective-representation-look-like-in-australias-gig-economy/ (accessed 25 February 2019).

occupational health and safety at work.[17] These are perceived as having a universal application upon all workers,[18] and Member States of the ILO are expected to promote and realise them. In the case of many self-employed persons, including platform workers, nevertheless, their enjoyment is at risk.

Accordingly, this research predominately focuses on the collective labour rights of self-employed workers, i.e., the right to freedom of association, including the right to form a trade union and the right to collective bargaining. Reference to the right to strike takes place as well. This selection does not mean that other rights and principles, such as elimination of all forms of forced or compulsory labour, are of less importance. Nonetheless, as this research will mainly focus on legal developments within advanced economies, the emphasis given to these particular rights seems to be more relevant to the problems faced by self-employed persons within the given context.

Importantly, collective labour rights have also been incorporated in a vast number of international law treaties, regional instruments, as well as various national constitutions, and they have acquired the status of fundamental human rights.[19] Any restriction on their application, therefore, should be justified under law and it should be considered necessary in a democratic society. This has arguably not been thoroughly evaluated for current exclusions. Thus, an investigation is needed to assess whether certain limitations can be justified. The examination will also take place in light of developments in competition law, which attempt to address current issues about the protection of self-employed workers (e.g., the Competition (Amendment) Act 2017 in Ireland). Finally, such an endeavour can be also particularly relevant and beneficial from a business perspective, as an effective protection of these rights can level the plain field between companies on ensuring respect for minimum labour standards.

2 CONTEXT AND BACKGROUND

2.1 Platform Work

Platform-based work represents one of the most recent and debated labour market trends and an expression of technological advancement in the 21st century. According to a joint ILO-Eurofound report, information and communication technologies (ICTs)

17. ILO Declaration on Fundamental Principles and Rights at Work, 1998; In June 2022, at its 110th Session, the International Labour Conference decided to amend para. 2 of the ILO Declaration on Fundamental Principles and Rights at Work (1998) to also incorporate 'a safe and healthy working environment' as a fundamental principle and right at work.
18. They are included in the eight fundamental Conventions of the ILO: (1) Forced Labour Convention, 1930 (No. 29), (2) the Abolition of Forced Labour Convention, 1957 (No. 105), (3) the Freedom of Association and Protection of the Right to Organise Convention, 1948 (No. 87), (4) the Right to Organise and Collective Bargaining Convention, 1949 (No. 98), (5) the Equal Remuneration Convention, 1951 (No. 100), (6) the Discrimination (Employment and Occupation) Convention, 1958 (No. 111), (7) the Minimum Age Convention, 1973 (No. 138), and (8) the Worst Forms of Child Labour Convention, 1999 (No. 182).
19. For instance, *see* the European Convention on Human Rights (ECHR); European Social Charter (ESC); The Charter of Fundamental Rights of the European Union (CFEU).

have radically transformed daily work and life arrangements, enabling people to undertake work anytime and anywhere.[20] This phenomenon, *inter alia*, can be attributed to the increased demand for flexibility on the part of employers, better labour market efficiency and, in some cases, the desire for greater flexibility on the part of workers.[21]

The tasks offered through platform economy can be skilled or unskilled; they can be the main source of income, or they can just offer supplementary earnings to the workers involved, and they expand to a wide variety of services and industries, ranging from transportation (e.g., Uber) to domestic services industry (e.g., TaskRabbit), to work entirely done online (e.g., Amazon Mechanical Turk). Platform-based work is usually understood to include two forms of work, namely, crowdwork and work-on-demand through applications.[22] The former category includes tasks, which are carried out via online platforms bringing together clients and workers from potentially all around the world. The nature of these tasks varies, including micro-tasks, such as completing surveys or tagging photos, and bigger projects, like the creation of a web page. These types of work arrangements can indeed occur anytime and anywhere. Work-on-demand, instead, includes activities that are executed offline and are matched via applications that are controlled by businesses which are establishing minimum quality standards of services.[23] The location and timeframe of such activities, therefore, are more limited in comparison to tasks undertaken by crowdworkers. The differences between these two forms of work, as they will be examined, are of particular importance when considering the application of fundamental collective labour rights.[24]

2.2 Fundamental (Collective) Labour Rights of Platform Workers

Undoubtedly, work provided through platforms has the potential to offer new and more flexible – mostly in terms of time and location – opportunities to people that are seeking employment. In some cases, it also seems to match better the needs of those who have duties of a special nature, such as care responsibilities, or those who are homebound because of health problems or disabilities.

At the same time though, issues faced by those working in the platform economy not only reflect but also contribute to the emergence of broader labour market trends towards casualisation, triangulated work relationships, the demutualisation of the

20. Eurofound & International Labour Organization, (2017), *Working Anytime, Anywhere: The Effects on the World of Work* 3, Geneva, Publications Office of the European Union and the International Labour Office.
21. Aloisi, A., *Commoditized Workers: Case Study Research on Labour Law Issues Arising from a Set of 'On-demand/gig economy' Platforms*, 37 Comparative Labor Law & Policy Journal, 653 n. 3 (2016), 653-690.
22. *Supra*, De Stefano (2016), 3.
23. *Ibid.*, 2.
24. For instance, the application of collective rights for crowdworkers is much more complicated due to the fact that they are spread around the world. Workers-on-demand, instead, are located to a specific area; hence, for instance, trade union participation can be easier for them in practical terms.

risks of employment, the globalisation of work, and the move to non-standard work.[25] As noted, the majority of platform workers are considered as independent contractors, rather than employees of these platforms,[26] despite evidence, such as work surveillance and control mechanisms, which undercut this designation.[27] Their classification as independent contractors is profitable for platforms, as it limits their liability and nullifies the vast majority of protections afforded by employment and labour laws. Consequently, many of these workers find themselves in a precarious situation where the enjoyment of their fundamental human rights is at risk. This situation is particularly apparent concerning restrictions on collective labour rights. That said, to better grasp the issues that platform work can generate for the effective exercise of such rights, this research (mainly in Chapter 4) focuses on the collective experiences of platform workers, regardless of their status, in practice. Such a discussion will assist this research to come up with crucial observations for the particular challenges self-employed platform workers are currently facing regarding their labour protection, including the enjoyment of their fundamental collective labour rights.

As far as the right to freedom of association is concerned, for example, the very nature of platform work can impose significant constraints in the enjoyment of the right at issue, in many instances, irrespective of workers' employment status. Work arrangements, where reputation and rating systems play a key role for workers to maintain their employment, or access better-paid jobs, may prevent workers from freely associating, including their right to join a trade union. This can occur because of the fear that their reputation will be negatively affected.[28] Platforms can punish 'unwanted activism' by simply erasing the profile of workers from their database without any proper justification. Both crowdworkers and workers-on-demand can be affected by this fear. Furthermore, platform workers often have low chances to unionise due to their frequent turnovers, little attachment to a single workplace and fissured workplaces; consequently, it can be significantly challenging to create a common collective identity and organise themselves. As noted, and will be further demonstrated below, such challenges can negatively affect both self-employed platform workers and platform workers who are considered employees, albeit the former are considerably more exposed to the risks stemming from these issues.

The limits to the protection of fundamental labour rights for platform workers are also apparent in relation to other collective labour rights, such as the right to collective bargaining, on which this research will mainly focus. These restrictions are relevant for self-employed platform workers. Indeed, as most national legislation do not exclude

25. Blackham, A., *We are All Entrepreneurs Now': Options and New Approaches for Adapting Equality Law for the 'Gig Economy'*, 34 International Journal of Comparative Labour Law and Industrial Relations 413 n. 4 (2018), 415-416.
26. European Commission, (2016), *Communication from the Commission to the Council. A European Agenda for the Collaborative Economy*, COM 356 final, Luxembourg:, 2016, available at: https://ec.europa.eu/transparency/regdoc/rep/1/2016/EN/1-2016-356-EN-F1-1.PDF (accessed 29 April 2019).
27. Newlands, G., Lutz, C., Fieseler, C., *Collective Action and Provider Classification in the Sharing Economy*, 33 New Technology, Work and Employment 250 n. 3 (2018), 251.
28. Dagino, E., *Uber law: prospettive giuslavoristiche sulla sharing/on-demand economy*, 26 Diritto delle relazioni industriali 137 n. 1 (2016), 137-163.

collective bargaining agreements from the scope of competition law, antitrust authorities have been using their influence to target certain categories of workers – platform workers are among them – who have concluded collective bargaining agreements on the grounds that these are price-fixing agreements between undertakings; hence, they hamper competition. The interpretation given by courts in cases of conflict between competition law and collective bargaining can be also problematic and lead to severe restrictions on collective labour rights. That said, the problems do not end here. Indeed, even if someone was placing competition-related challenges on the side, as this research explains, it soon becomes apparent that national industrial systems seem currently incapable of enabling the effective exercise of the right to bargain collectively for self-employed workers, including platform workers. Both of the aforementioned challenges can, in turn, cause conflicts between different sources of supranational and international law, e.g., between EU regulation on the one side and ILO and Council of Europe (CoE) instruments on the other.[29]

As will be further explained, restrictions on fundamental collective rights can also be associated with additional limitations on human rights at work. For instance, important challenges can be identified with respect to non-discrimination rights. Indeed, the fact that a great portion of platform workers are often excluded from collective bargaining schemes and other collective initiatives, can further exacerbate incidences of discrimination. This remark is supported by research that observes that workplaces with a substantial degree of organisation of social partners are associated with a lower incidence of various forms of intimidation and discrimination.[30] In many occasions, such discriminatory practices reflect already existing problems regarding discrimination in employment. Some empirical studies investigating 'global online platforms', for example, have shown a pay disparity between male and female workers, as women's hourly rates are significantly lower than men's.[31] Concerns have been additionally raised with respect to the ability crowdwork platforms offer to providers in limiting the geographical areas from where online tasks can be undertaken by platform workers. Restrictions of this nature, especially when they take place without a proper justification, can lead to the exclusion of entire countries or regions from access to work; hence, they can lead to discriminatory practices.[32] Concomitantly, there are views highlighting the substantial lack of transparency in relation to the functioning of algorithms which platforms use in order to assess and rank their workers.[33] Algorithms are created by humans, thus, they can be the carriers of inherent

29. De Stefano, V., Aloisi, A., *Fundamental Labour Rights, Platform Work and Human Rights Protection of Non-standard Workers* (Janice R. Bellace and Beryl ter Haar eds, *Research Handbook on Labour, Business and Human Rights Law*, Elgar Publishing 2019), 372-378; For case law for instance: Case 413/13 *FNV Kunsten Informatie en Media* (2014) ECLI: EU:C:2014:2411.
30. OECD, (2019), *Negotiating Our Way Up: Collective Bargaining in a Changing World of Work*, OECD Publishing, Paris.
31. Kullmann, M., *Platform Work, Algorithmic Decision-Making, and EU Gender Equality Law*, 34 International Journal of Comparative Labour Law and Industrial Relations 1 n. 1 (2018), 3.
32. *Supra*, De Stefano and Aloisi, (2019), 366-367.
33. *See*, for instance, Rani, U., Furrer, M., *Digital Labour Platforms and New Forms of Flexible Work in Developing Countries: Algorithmic Management of Work and Workers*, 25 Competition &

biases or discrimination. Inadequacy of transparency of how they actually operate can be detrimental in addressing these issues, and it can also perpetuate deep-rooted stereotypes in workplaces and in society more broadly.

Therefore, due to the increasing number of problems, challenges, or questions related to new forms of casualised work arrangements via the existing approaches of labour law, there is a need to reassess labour protection for self-employed workers by having platform workers as a point of reference. In this regard, this research undertakes a new approach through a human rights analytical legal framework.

It will be advanced that labour rights are human rights, '*even though the human rights movement and the labour movement run on tracks that are sometimes parallel and scarcely meet*'.[34] Still, such tracks, through the inclusion of fundamental labour rights within international instruments and human rights treaties, as well as through the rulings of international and national supreme courts, have now converged.[35] As a consequence, labour issues have increasingly been examined from the standpoint of human rights law. The UN Guiding Principles on Business and Human Rights, and the vast ongoing discussion over corporate responsibility for human rights, constitute an additional illustration of the increased convergence of the two fields.[36] It can be claimed though that this formal recognition is not always adequate to prevent restrictions on workers' protection of fundamental labour rights. As noted, this is particularly evident with platform workers and the enjoyment of their fundamental collective labour rights.

2.3 'False' Allegations, Policy Responses and Platform Workers' Over-Increasing Mobilisation

Platform work has attracted much attention from lawmakers and courts around the world. Since the advent of the so-called gig economy platform colossuses, such as Uber, Deliveroo and Amazon, often hiding under the 'cloak' of technological innovation have been passionately defending the 'independent' ability of technology to establish unprecedented organisational alterations within modern workplaces. Allegedly, due to these new technologies, people can work for themselves as self-employed persons, away from any supervision, or control. This is why digital labour platforms and other businesses with similar features are often described as disruptors of established markets and firms.[37] Of course, it is by now well-established that such allegations solely represent a small part of what is happening in practice. Many of the

Change 212 n. 2 (2021), 222-230; Schubert, C., Hütt, M.T., *Economy-on-demand and the Fairness of Algorithms*, 10 European Labour Law Journal 3 n. 1 (2019), 3-16.

34. Leary, V., *The Paradox of Worker's Rights as Human Rights* (Lance Compa, L., Stephen F. Diamond eds, *Human Rights, Labor Rights and International Trade,* Philadelphia, University of Pennsylvania Press 1996), 22.
35. *See,* for instance, Alston, P., *Labour Rights as Human Rights* (Oxford University Press 2005).
36. UN Guiding Principles on Business and Human Rights: https://www.ohchr.org/documents/publications/GuidingprinciplesBusinesshr_eN.pdf.
37. ILO, (2021), *World Employment and Social Outlook 2021: The role of digital labour platforms in transforming the world of work*, ILO, Geneva, 43-44, referring to Clewlow, R. & Mishra, G.,

adverse effects of platform work have already become apparent. In this respect, this research comes at a moment when the disruptors have, indeed, started to be 'disrupted', by both seminal court decisions and regulatory initiatives, which aim at tackling the challenges in the realm of the platform economy.[38] A considerable part of these developments is scrutinised in Chapter 3 of the research.

As argued in earlier work, the recent changes in rhetoric and practice are not coincidental or a simple realisation on the part of regulators and courts of the poor working conditions faced by many platform workers.[39] It is rather the pressure of an ever-increasing collective organisation, lobbying and action of workers that contributed to, or even brought up, these changes, often supported by external actors, such as the international academic community.[40] Simultaneously, what is arresting constitutes a mounting deployment of institutional unions in representing the interests of platform workers, as well as a proliferation of workers' associations, that do not automatically fit the traditional model of trade unions. Such processes, filtered with solidaristic characteristics and a human rights rhetoric in certain instances, are indicative of the existence of closer cooperation between organised labour and workers in non-standard forms of employment (NSFE). That being said, an essential prerequisite concerning this motion is that fundamental collective labour rights, such as the right to freedom of association and the right to bargain collectively, should be effectively protected. As will be examined in Chapter 4, despite any restrictions, both legal and practical, platform workers, regardless of their employment status, by exercising these rights have already achieved some important victories. Of course, as will be demonstrated in this research, the situation for self-employed platform workers can be much more challenging compared to platform workers who find themselves in an employment relationship. The latter mainly have to deal with obstacles of a practical nature (e.g., fissured workplaces), whereas self-employed platform workers have also to face severe legal exclusions. For instance, the majority of collective agreements signed in the context of the platform economy cover only employees and there are only a few occasions where self-employed workers are covered by such agreements. Moreover, even when collective agreements for self-employed platform workers exist, as will be discussed, these usually take the form of 'soft' or 'diluted version(s)' of collective bargaining.

This research investigates the aforementioned issues in an attempt to assess the gaps within the current protective framework related to platform workers. In turn, it thoroughly explores whether the adoption of a HRBA can ensure, at least to a certain degree, a better framework for construing collective labour rights for platform workers.

Disruptive Transportation: The Adoption, Utilization, and Impacts of Ride-Hailing in the United States, Research Report (2017) UCD-ITS-RR-17-07, Institute of Transportation Studies, University of California, Davis.

38. De Stefano, V., Durri, I., Stylogiannis, C., Wouters, M., *Introduction* (De Stefano V., et. al. eds, *A Research Agenda for the Gig-Economy and Society*, Edward Elgar Publishing, 2022), forthcoming.
39. Stylogiannis, C., '*Freedom of Association and Collective Bargaining in the Platform Economy: A Human Rights-Based Approach and an ever increasing mobilization of workers*', 162 International Labour Review 1 n. 1 (2021).
40. For instance, *see* Austrian Chamber of Labour et al. (2016), *Frankfurt Paper on Platform Based Work*, Frankfurt.

3 OBJECTIVE AND RESEARCH QUESTION(S)

Despite the limitations of the traditional scope of labour law regarding the enjoyment of platform workers' fundamental collective labour rights, very limited literature exists on taking a HRBA as a possible way to overcome this gap in labour law protection. This research departs from the fact that some platform workers are particularly vulnerable workers due to their typical labelling as independent contractors. As such, they are excluded from labour protection despite being weak in terms of bargaining and economic powers. To this extent, this research forwards the idea that fundamental collective labour rights should be considered human rights. Hence, based on international requirements, they should be applied to such people, regardless of their employment status.

The central research question in this work is:

> Can a human rights-based approach (HRBA) towards collective labour rights bridge the labour protection gap of self-employed platform workers?

The aim of this main research question is to assess if and how a HRBA in the labour protection for self-employed platform workers can offer a novel basis of protection for those who, due to their employment status, are currently excluded from labour law protections, and more specifically from the enjoyment of their fundamental collective labour rights. It will be shown that international labour and human rights law can indeed offer useful guidance in solving the conflict between labour law and other areas of law, such as competition law. Other possible benefits of a HRBA towards collective labour rights will be also examined. That said, as will be illustrated, its effective application, together with its potential benefits, regardless of the existence of competition law, is dependent upon other factors, like the current structure of national industrial systems. As such, the assessment of the HRBA can also be pertinent to other categories of self-employed workers. As it will be discussed, for instance, merely permitting collective bargaining for self-employed persons, including platform workers, as it currently happens in several countries (albeit with some limitations), may not be enough to enable substantial bargaining activities in practice. Among other things, the lack, or decline of multi-employer collective bargaining systems, the absence of statutory rights to compel employers to recognise collective agreements for self-employed workers, along with high representation thresholds for unions' recognition, are only some of the impediments self-employed workers and other self-employed persons have to deal with when they attempt to exercise their right to collective bargaining.

With a view to providing a comprehensive answer to the main research question in relation to the collective labour rights of self-employed platform workers, this research is subdivided into six sub-questions, addressed in six respective chapters:

> *RQ1*: What are the key features of platform work and how can the latter be linked to the current challenges in the world of work?
> The analysis of the very phenomenon of platform-mediated work, along with the examination of its particularities, is essential in grasping the overall

challenges with respect to the existing legal gaps in workers' labour protection. Equally important is also to understand how platform work can be related to broader challenges within modern labour markets.

RQ2: To what extent do platform work's specific features influence the labour protection of platform workers, including the exercise of collective labour rights?
Such an examination is necessary in order to identify the major (legal) problems stemming from platform work in relation to working conditions, together with the exercise of workers' fundamental collective labour rights. Identifying these challenges, including the obstacles deriving from competition law, is important not only for platform workers per se but also for the field of labour law more broadly. The latter's inability to address the needs of some of the most vulnerable workers, in particular, self-employed workers, can have deeper foundational implications, which can threaten its whole edifice.

RQ3: What are the existing legal responses toward the protection of platform workers?
A global overview of responses related to challenges stemming from platform work arrangements is essential to identify the limitations and, or the lack of adequate solutions related to the labour protection of these workers. In particular, responses relate to the issue of employment status and the scope of labour protection. Such responses can be found both in legislation and the verdict of labour and administrative courts, ruling on the employment classification of platform workers. These findings can are significant for self-employed workers in the platform economy.

RQ4: What is the potential of collective labour rights and what do the experiences of platform workers and other workers in NSFE show about their exercise of such rights in practice?
The answer to this question is vital in order to understand the value of such rights in practice and identify trends and developments in the collective mobilisation of platform workers and other atypical workers. At the same time, such a discussion is important to realise the limitations on the exercise of collective labour rights; an exercise that, in turn, will lead us to the suggestion that a possible way forward can derive from the adoption of a HRBA towards fundamental collective labour rights.

RQ5: What are the legal basis and possible benefits of a HRBA towards fundamental collective labour rights for self-employed platform workers?
The findings of this discussion will enable this research, from a positive law perspective, to rely on a sound legal framework so as to establish the concept that collective labour rights should be applied to all workers, irrespective of their status (including self-employed workers), based on the requirements of international labour and human rights law. A human rights legal framework,

as well as rhetoric, can potentially have beneficial implications for both workers' overall protection and for the field of labour law in general.

RQ6: What are the implications of a HRBA for industrial relations?
The examination of this question aims to lead this research to a nuanced series of debates, related to a future agenda of industrial relations systems. First, it is important to summarise what the findings on the collective mobilisation of the platform can tell us about the future of unionisationf. Second, it is essential to understand whether a HRBA towards collective labour rights, implying collective rights for self-employed workers, can practically take place under the existing structure(s) of national industrial systems, and if not, what would they be at least some of the requirements to make its application effective in practice.

4 METHODOLOGY AND STRUCTURE

4.1 Legal Research

This research is, first and foremost, a legal research. In this regard, the main sources that it uses are legal sources, such as international human rights and labour rights treaties and conventions, such as the ILO, the European Convention on Human Rights (ECHR) and the European Social Charter (ESC), domestic legislation and regulations, rulings from international and national courts, as well as interpretative and authoritative sources, including legal literature the decisions of bodies that supervise international standards. Moreover, theoretical literature in relation to the foundations of labour law is also included, as an understanding of principles and values underpinning labour law is considered important in assessing whether the field in question fulfils its normative basis on the protection of workers. Finally, further literature beyond the legal discipline is used as a complimentary source as this is essential in order to assess the working conditions of platform workers. Therefore, this research includes an interdisciplinary analysis by mainly, using the outcomes of social-sciences studies related to the platform economy. As such, a better insight is given into the research with respect to the particular features of platforms and the working conditions of platform workers.

4.2 Comparativism

Writing about the importance of comparativism in labour law and industrial relations, Roger Blanpain, by also referring to the work of Manfred Weiss, explains:

> Due to new challenges labour law no longer can be treated merely as a phenomenon within national borders. No country any longer can escape the impacts of international norm-setting and the consequences of globalisation, Therefore,

> comparative labour law has become more important than ever before and will become even more important in the future.[41]

By following this observation, in certain parts of this research (e.g., Chapters 3, 4 and 6) a 'functionalist' comparative approach is followed.[42] The latter is not solely confined to a purely legal comparative exercise. It also includes a comparison with respect to current realities within industrial relations. This is done, for instance, by focusing on the collective representation of platform workers in a number of countries (Chapter 4), or by assessing the implications of the HRBA towards collective labour rights for self-employed (platform) workers within existing national frameworks of industrial relations (Chapter 6). An interdisciplinary comparative approach and the integration of 'extra-legal' factors (i.e., looking at the law, but also in industrial relations), has been described as being of '*utmost importance*' in exploring the challenges around labour law.[43]

That said, considering that collective labour rights for self-employed (platform) workers are a fundamental issue for labour law and industrial relations in more general terms, this doctoral research is not focusing on an in-depth positive law analysis of a particular national legal system. It rather provides a helicopter view related to both the legal developments within the context of the platform economy, as well as to issues that touch upon the field of industrial relations, including platform workers' collective mobilisation (Chapter 4), and an assessment of industrial systems' ability to enable an effective application of a HRBA in practice (Chapter 6).[44] Such a comparative analysis will, thus, enable this research to identify certain trends, developments and complexities with respect to platform work and the exercise of collective labour rights for self-employed persons. As Zweigert and Kötz explain, if national (legal) systems experience similar problems, then, at least to a certain degree, a given answer to such

---

41. Blanpain, R., *Comparativism in Labor Law and Industrial Relations* (Roger Blanpain ed., *Comparative Labour Law and Industrial Relations in Industrialized Market Economies,* Wolters Kluwer 2014), 3. The author refers to: Weiss, M., *The Future of Comparative Labor Law as an Academic Discipline and as a Practical Tool,* 25 Comparative Labor Law & Policy Journal 169 n. 1 (2003), 169-182.
42. There is a diversity of approaches and interpretations of the 'functionalism' method in comparative law. *See* for instance: Zweigert, K., and Kötz, H., *An Introduction to Comparative Law,* (Oxford University Press 1997); Michaels, R., *The Functional Method of Comparative Law,* (Mathias Reimann, and Zimmermann, Reinhard eds, *The Oxford Handbook of Comparative Law,* Oxford University Press 2006), 340-380; Brand, O., *Conceptual Comparisons: Towards a Coherent Methodology of Comparative Legal Studies,* 32 Brooklyn Journal of International Law 405 n. 2 (2007), 405-466; Adams, M. and Griffiths, J., *Against 'Comparative Method': Explaining Similarities and Differences* (Maurice Adams, M. and Jacco A. Bomhoff eds, *Practice and Theory in Comparative Law,* Cambridge University Press 2012), 279-301; Frankenberg, G., *Critical Comparisons: Re-Thinking Comparative Law,* 26 Harvard International Law Journal 411 (1985), 411-455.
43. *Supra,* Blanpain (2014), 4.
44. The selection of countries in Chapter 6 includes examples from both common law (the UK) and civil law (Belgium and Poland) legal context. This selection can help the reader to better grasp the subject matter under analysis, that is, the assessment of a HRBA within existing frameworks of industrial relations. Chapter 6 does not proceed with an in depth positive law analysis, but it is rather used as an overview of the obstacles that a HRBA can face in practice.

problems can be similar too.[45] This observation, nonetheless, does not intend to suggest that a 'one-size-fits-all' method is adopted in this research. Considering the diversity of legal and industrial systems around the world, the perils of a 'one-size-fits-all' approach have already been identified by the seminal work of Otto Kahn-Freund.[46] Concomitantly though, the existence of a diverse landscape should not be seen as an impediment in proceeding with some crucial observations, which can inform future discussions on the field of industrial labour relations and the application of fundamental human rights.

4.3 Structure and Methodological Steps

As noted, this research engages with the central research question and the three sub-questions throughout six chapters.

Chapter 1 aims at analysing the phenomenon of platform work, including its terminology[47] and main particularities. This exercise will take place through a descriptive and analytical approach.[48] Before dealing with platform work arrangements per se though, via the same methodological approach(es), the chapter in question refers to the current challenges and threats protective labour law(s) are facing within the new world of work and the way in which, platform work is connected to these very issues. This examination is considered justified because labour law was built by having as a point of reference models of production that relied on vertically integrated workplaces and standard employment relationships (e.g., full-time work in fixed workplaces). Such realities, nonetheless, are no longer the rule. Among other things, the vertical disintegration of firms, along with the digital outsourcing of working tasks, have made the distinction between salaried workers and autonomous workers an extremely complicated task. Such an analysis is essential in order to understand the existing gaps in the existing framework of labour law.

After discussing the specificities of platform work, *Chapter 2* focuses on the implications that these types of work arrangements have on working conditions, including the enjoyment of workers' fundamental collective labour rights, also acknowledged as human rights. The analysis of this chapter can be considered as being analytical and evaluative at the same time. The observations made regarding the working conditions of platform workers are based on empirical findings and socioeconomic studies. To this extent, the latter highlight the precarious nature of platform work, which is often associated with problematic employment practices, poor working conditions and overall job insecurity. Moreover, platform workers, due to their 'obscure' employment status, are also facing serious obstacles towards their collective rights, such as the right to freely associate and bargain collectively. Restrictions can be both of a legal and practical nature. As far as the legal impediments are concerned, this

45. *Supra*, Zweigert, K., and Kötz (1997), 40.
46. Kahn-Freund, O.O., *On Uses and Misuses of Comparative Law*, 37 Modern Law Review 27 n. 1 (1974), 1-27.
47. This research departs from already established definitions of platform work.
48. Kestemont, L., *Handbook on Legal Methodology. From Objective to Method* (Intersentia 2018).

chapter mainly focuses on the conflict between labour law and competition law. As will be, moreover, discussed, hurdles to the enjoyment of collective rights can also have adverse ramifications on the exercise of other human rights at work, like non-discrimination and privacy rights. Finally, via an evaluative analysis that is based on a foundational approach to labour law, it will be shown that platform work on top of human rights-related concerns, can also generate deeper foundational implications for labour law. Such implications derive from the latter's current inability to address and combat platform workers' precariousness.

Chapter 3 through an analytical and simultaneously evaluative approach(es), discusses the limitations, as well as the potentials of the existing regulatory responses towards platform work. It will be discussed that, as far as labour law is concerned, such responses mainly derive from the courts and legislation. As such, this part first refers to a number of legislative responses, which aim at regulating the labour protection of platform workers. In turn, reference is made to several jurisprudential developments and how labour courts and tribunals have responded to the emergence of platform work. The chapter concludes with legal responses related to the clash between labour law and competition law, a conflict which is inextricably linked to challenges stemming from platform work arrangements.

Chapter 4 looks at the experiences and potentials with respect to the exercise of fundamental collective labour rights in practice. To this extent, initially, a reference is made to the important role of the right to collective bargaining. It then discusses the relationship between traditional trade unions and workers in atypical work arrangements. It is observed that trade unions are showing a vivid interest in representing such workers. In turn, various major developments and achievements of collective mobilisation within the platform economy are indicated. Such activities derive from both self-employed platform workers, as well as platform workers who are considered employees. As will be demonstrated in this respect, most of the collective agreements in the context of the platform economy have been concluded for platform workers situated within an employment relationship. Some collective agreements now also include self-employed platform workers; however, these agreements have adopted a more 'diluted' version of collective bargaining. Many of these initiatives have already been proven beneficial for platform workers, however, as will be illustrated, legal obstacles continue to restrict workers' rights to freedom of association and collective bargaining. Once again, a combination of analytical and evaluative approach(es) will be used in this chapter. A comparative approach is also taking place when comparing the collective experiences of platform workers around the world.

Chapter 5 espouses a normative approach. It is suggested that a possible way to bridge the gap in labour protection of self-employed platform workers can derive from a HRBA towards fundamental collective labour rights. An approach as such can be also relevant for other atypical workers (mostly dependent self-employed workers). More specifically, this chapter explores the nature of collective labour rights as human rights from a positive law angle. Via this analysis, it is suggested that such rights should be afforded to all workers, regardless of their status, including self-employed persons. In this regard, reference is made to various international legal instruments, such as the ILO and the European Social Charter (ESC), as well as to the language of their supervisory bodies. Then mainly from a legal perspective, the Chapter examines why a HRBA within labour policy can be advantageous for the overall protection of workers in the platform economy and other workers in NSFE. Of course, as it is argued below, the effective application of such an approach is conditional on additional factors, such as the legal structure of national systems of industrial relations.

Finally, *Chapter 6*, via the prism of a HRBA, summarises and evaluates (evaluative approach) the main findings regarding the mobilisation and unionisation of platform workers and explores what such observations entail for the future of trade unions. In turn, the implications of a HRBA for industrial relations are discussed. Based on some national examples (comparative approach), it will be claimed that, at least to a certain extent, the existing structures of national industrial systems fall short of enabling an effective application of a HRBA in practice. For this reason, some suggestions are made in order to facilitate its application, in line with the requirements of international labour and human rights instruments.

5 NORMATIVE FRAMEWORK

This research has a normative dimension, as an evaluation is being made regarding the challenges platform work can pose on the very issue of workers' labour protection, including the effective exercise of their collective labour rights. To this extent, three normative layers are identified.

5.1 Labour Protection Gap(s)

The first normative dimension, as this will be developed in Chapter 2, touches upon the problem of the lack of labour protection experienced by a considerable portion of platform workers. This is done through the description and evaluation of the latter's working conditions. Such an analysis will not be merely theoretical, but it will also be based upon a series of empirical and socioeconomic studies, which highlight the often precarious nature of platform work.[49] As it will be examined, regardless of their on-line or off-line nature, these types of work arrangements, can be, *inter alia*, associated with problematic employment practices, poor working conditions and job uncertainty.[50] For instance, a survey commissioned by KU Leuven in the framework of the Odysseus

49. DE Groen, W. P., Kilhoffer, Z., Lenaerts, K., Mandl, I. (2018), *Employment and Working Conditions of Selected Types of Platform Work*. Luxembourg, Publications Office of the European Union. European Commission (2020), '*Study to gather evidence on the working conditions of platform workers*', available at: https://ec.europa.eu/social/main.jsp?catId=738&langId=en&pubId=8280 (accessed 20 March 2021); Pesole A., Urzí Brancati M.C., Fernández-Macías E., Biagi, F., *González Vázquez* I. (2018), *Platform Workers in Europe: Evidence from the COLLEEM Survey*, Luxembourg, Publications Office of the European Union.
50. For instance *see* CIPD, (2017), *To Gig or Not to Gig? Stories from the Modern Economy*, Chartered Institute of Personnel and Development, London; *supra* HUWS, et al. (2017); *supra*, BERG (2016), 554-555.

project and executed by Ipsos in three European countries[51] identifies income insecurity as one of the main challenges platform workers are facing.[52] Further research conducted on selected types of platform work, also suggests that many workers have to deal with poor career prospects and limited training opportunities that will enable them to enhance their chances to adjust to the new realities of modern labour markets.[53] Important concerns have been also raised in relation to the risks such workers are facing regarding health and safety-related issues, as well as discriminatory practices.[54]

Having said that, it will be contented that much of these challenges, as empirical research also confirms,[55] derive from the fact that the overwhelming majority of platform workers are considered self-employed workers, despite evidence that may suggest the existence of employment status.[56]As a consequence, they are automatically excluded from a wide range of employment and collective bargaining regulations. As already mentioned and will be further analysed, the vast majority of labour protection(s) still and by large, remain concentrated within 'subordinate' wage employment. Thus, platform businesses are usually not legally bound to comply with labour regulations in areas, such as health and safety regulations, a minimum wage, limitations in working hours, sick pay, and annual leave. These gaps in labour protection can be especially problematic considering that platform workers are often situated in a comparable predicament to that of employees, where their weak negotiating position and economic dependency towards their principals make for a precarious situation. As noted though, in the case of (weak) self-employed workers, the protection afforded to them is traditionally limited to the bare minimum. In light of this, the problem of precariousness faced by these types of workers is also linked to the narrow scope of labour law.

5.2 Foundational Considerations

The second normative layer in this research relates to a foundational, value-oriented approach to labour law. This normativity will further be developed and critically discussed in Chapter 2, departing from the position that the aforementioned labour protection-related challenges can have a negative impact on workers' dignity at work.

51. These are: Belgium, France and Italy (IPSOS, (2020), 'High level summary of key findings', *Surveys commissioned by KU Leuven*).
52. *Ibid.*, 12.
53. *Supra*, De Groen, et al. (2018); *Supra* Huws, et al. (2017).
54. For instance, *see* Cefaliello, A., Inversi, C., *The Impact of the Gig-economy on Occupational Health and Safety: Just an Occupation Hazard?* (Valerio De Stefano, Ilda Durri, Charalampos Stylogiannis and Mathias Wouters eds, *A Research Agenda for the Gig-Economy and Society*, Edward Elgar Publishing 2022), 33-51.
55. For instance, *see* Fairwork, (2019) *The Five Pillars of Fairwork: Labour Standards in the Platform Economy*, Fairwork Foundation, Oxford, UK, available at: https://fair.work/wpcontent/uploads/sites/97/2019/10/Fairwork-Y1-Report.pdf (assessed 9 December 2020); Fredman S., du Toit D., Graham, M., Howson K., Heeks R., van Belle J.P., Mungai P., Osiki A., *Thinking Out of the Box: Fair Work for Platform Workers*, 31 King's Law Journal 236 n. 2 (2020), 236-249.
56. For instance, platform operators adopt a digital payment system, where a commission fee is deducted for the service, with the amount determinable by each platform. Moreover, via new technological tools, platforms are able to supervise the execution of the work performed.

It will be suggested that this situation goes hand in hand with the commodification of work often observed within the context of the platform economy. This is because new types of casual work, such as platform work, seem to give a '*normative priority*' to considerations of efficiency, flexibility and economic competitiveness.[57] What is often missing, nevertheless, are considerations that touch upon workers' protection of human dignity. As it will be developed below, the commodification of workers is also inextricably associated with the severe restrictions platform workers are facing in the enjoyment of their fundamental (collective) labour rights. These observations, lead us to the second normative layer of this research that is platform work's deeper foundational implications for labour law. More specifically, it will be explained that labour law's inability to address the needs of some of the most vulnerable workers can have deeper foundational implications, as its whole edifice can be put into question. In this regard, this research puts forward the idea that platform work can directly challenge the main, or at least one of the main foundations that labour law was based on, namely, the notion that '*labour is not a commodity*'; hence, labour should not be exchanged in the markets for the lowest price, as workers are human beings with dignity and rights. This maxim can be traced in the ILO Declaration of Philadelphia in its first principle, in Article 1(a), which explicitly enshrines that '*labour is not a commodity*'.[58] It is also reaffirmed in the 2008 ILO Declaration on Social Justice for a Fair Globalization and in the 2019 ILO Centenary Declaration for the Future of Work.[59]

5.3 Human Rights-Based Approach (HRBA)

The third normative layer relates to the construction and application of a human rights-based approach towards (collective) labour rights. This theoretical framework will be extensively developed in Chapter 5. Considering (self-employed) platform workers' genuine need for protection, as well as the challenges that arise for the field of labour law as a whole, this doctoral research in Chapter 5 puts forward a legal and theoretical framework capable of bridging some of the gaps in the labour protection of platform workers and other atypical workers. This framework is grounded in the adoption of a HRBA towards collective labour rights, whereby workers (including self-employed) can enjoy such rights, also recognised as human rights, irrespective of their employment status.[60] Such an approach does not aim at forcing the requalification of workers who find themselves in a 'grey' zone between employment and self-employment, including many platform workers. It rather intends to generate a

57. Rittich, K., *Between Workers' Rights and Flexibility: Labor Law in an Uncertain World*, 54 Saint Luis University Law Journal 565 n. 2 (2010), 579.
58. The ILO Declaration of Philadelphia, 1944.
59. The ILO Declaration on Social Justice for a Fair Globalization, 2008; Article 1(a), the ILO Centenary Declaration for the Future of Work, 2019.
60. The importance and potential of the exercise of collective labour rights in practice is developed in Chapter 4.

protection floor for all workers who, by exercising their collective labour rights will be able to ameliorate their working conditions and produce adequate labour standards that will not depend on their employment status. As will be developed in Chapter 5, the legal framework for a HRBA derives from a positive law perspective, which is based on the verdict and principles traced in human rights and international labour rights instruments, such as the ILO, the ECHR and the ESC. To this extent, it will be explained that there is a broad consensus that collective labour rights are human rights with universal application; hence, they should not only be enjoyed within the realm of an employment relationship.[61] In other words, among other supervisory bodies, both the ILO Committee of Experts and the European Social Committee, have multiple times pointed out that all workers should be eligible to exercise their right to freedom of association and collective bargaining. As it will be explained, an alike observation can be also made as far as the right to industrial action, including the right to strike, is concerned. At a theoretical level, moreover, there is also a growing number of views that acknowledge the categorisation of (collective) labour rights as human rights.[62]

That being said, as this research will illustrate in Chapter 5, a HRBA towards collective labour rights can generate a number of positive implications for the labour protection of platform workers and other atypical workers with similar characteristics, including self-employed persons (e.g., a HRBA can be beneficial in moving away from a strict dichotomy between employment and self-employment). An approach as such, moreover, can be important for the field of labour law as a whole, as the allocation of fundamental collective labour rights to those who need it the most, can assist the field to maintain its normative coherence and integrity.

6 SOCIETAL AND ACADEMIC RELEVANCE

The main academic relevance of this research comes down to the challenges the platform economy poses to fundamental labour rights that are protected as human rights. As noted, these problems are also relevant in relation to other self-employed workers dependent upon their principals. Most of the existing literature focuses on considerations around the employment status of these types of workers, and whether they can be classified as employees and, therefore, their ability to have access to the whole of labour protection in national jurisdictions. Nonetheless, there is a lack of an analysis that thoroughly touches upon the possibility of protecting such workers at national and international levels from a fundamental and human rights perspective.

61. *Irish Congress of Trade Unions v. Ireland*, No. 123/2016; ILO CFA, (2018), *Freedom of Association. Compilation of decisions of the Committee on Freedom of Association*, Geneva, ILO; ILO CFA, (2010) Report no. 363, Case no. 2786, para. 349; ILO CFA, (2012) Report no. 363, Case no. 2602, para. 461. For an in-depth analysis, *see* Chapter 5.3.1.

62. For instance, *see* Hepple, B., *Rights at Work* (Ghai, D. ed., *Decent Work: Objectives and Strategies* Geneva: ILO, International Institute for Labour Studies 2006), 33-73; Fenwick, C. and Novitz, T. eds, *Human Rights at Work, Perspectives on Law and Regulation* (Hart Publishing 2010); Gearty, C. and Mantouvalou, V. eds, *Debating Social Rights* (Hart Publishing 2011); Mantouvalou, V., *Labour Law and Human Rights*, 41 New Zealand Journal of Employment Relations 3 n. 2 (2016), 3-20; Bellace, J., ter Haar, B. (eds), *Research Handbook on Labour, Business and Human Rights Law, Cheltenham and Northampton*, Elgar Publishing 2019.

This research, therefore, responds to a genuine need for in-depth research with respect to the protection of the human rights of platform workers, and other self-employed workers through the adoption of an analytical framework that attempts to ensure their adequate protection. The analysis at issue can also help in resolving conflicts arising regarding the status of some labour rights as human rights.

From a societal point of view, this research is important due to the ongoing growth of dependent and disguised self-employment, including platform work. It has been estimated, for instance, that 4.3 per cent of total employment in the EU28 is dependent on self-employment.[63] The majority of such workers do not have access to the entitlements of those within a recognised employment relationship. An immediate result of this phenomenon is that the enjoyment of their fundamental labour rights is at risk.

As stated, platform work is illustrative in relation to the situation of other dependent self-employed persons. That said, it is difficult to estimate the exact number of workers in the platform economy.[64] According to some existing data, those engaged in the platform economy represent a small but still significant portion of the workforce in various countries. In the US and UK for example, evaluations suggest that 1 per cent-2 per cent of the national labour force is engaging with platforms every week.[65] In Australia, it is estimated that less than 0.5 per cent of adult Australians work on peer-to-peer platforms more than once per month.[66] The numbers are small in overall terms, but there has been very rapid growth in this sector in a fairly short time. Another reason for the societal relevance of this research constitutes the increased political and regulatory interest in the role of digital labour platforms.[67] The need for a system of protection for platform workers, for instance, has been demonstrated by the Global Commission on the Future of Work. It is highlighted that:

> as the organization of work continues to change, social protection systems will need to evolve to deliver continued protection for workers who move between wage employment and self-employment [...] ensuring that rights and benefits are accessible and portable, including for those working on digital platforms.[68]

63. Williams, C.C., Lapeyre, F. (2017), *Dependent Self-Employment: Trends, Challenges and Policy Responses in the EU*, Employment Working Paper 228, Geneva, ILO, 5.
64. This difficulty, among other reasons, can be attributed to the fact that enterprises are often not willing to reveal that information.
65. Codagnone, C., Abadie, F., Federico, B. (2016), *The Future of Work in the 'Sharing Economy': Market Efficiency and Equitable Opportunities or Unfair Precarisation?*, JRC Science for Policy Report EUR 27913 EN, Institute for Prospective Technological Studies, 5, available at: http://publications.jrc.ec.europa.eu/repository/bitstream/JRC101280/jrc101280.pdf (accessed 29 April 2019).
66. Australian Government Productivity Commission, (2016), *Digital Disruption: What Do Governments Need to Do?*, Productivity Commission Research Paper, 140-143, 77, available at: https://www.pc.gov.au/research/completed/digital-disruption/digital-disruption-research-paper.pdf (accessed 31 April 2022).
67. *See*, for instance, *supra*, Lenaerts, Belbavy and Kilhoffer (2017).
68. Global Commission on the Future of Work, (2019), *Work for a brighter future*, Geneva, ILO, 2019, p. 13. https://www.ilo.org/wcmsp5/groups/public/---dgreports/---cabinet/documents/publication/wcms_662410.pdf (consultation: 28 February 2019).

A human rights approach in this respect could lay the foundations for an effective system of protection, especially in relation to fundamental collective labour rights. At the EU level, there is also an acknowledgement of the precarious situation of platform workers, as well as proposals for safeguarding their fundamental labour rights.[69]

69. *See* European Commission, 'Proposal for a regulation of the European parliament and of the council on promoting fairness and transparency for business users of online intermediation services', Brussels, 26 March 2018.

CHAPTER 1
Platform Work and Challenges in the World of Work

1.1 INTRODUCTION

Platform-mediated work has gained precedence over the past decade.[70] Among other things, it is often associated with remarkable technological innovation and the promise of the creation of new and more flexible jobs. By now, however, it is well-documented that platform work can, if not properly regulated, pose serious risks to the enjoyment of a wide range of fundamental labour rights, which are also recognised as human rights within international instruments and human rights treaties. This point is particularly apparent as far as the exercise of fundamental collective labour rights, such as the right to freedom of association and the right to collective bargaining, is concerned.

At the same time, platform-mediated work can also expose the very limitations of labour regulations around the globe by leaving a considerable amount of workers with limited, or even without any access to labour protection, let alone social security benefits.[71] Also, its emergence reveals how, in many instances, technological innovation can be exceptionally problematic within the context of modern workplaces, as well as for future developments in the world of work.[72] Indeed, as this research shows, an

70. *See*, for instance, Global Commission on the Future of Work, *Work for a brighter future*, Geneva, ILO, 2019; European Commission, *Questions and Answers: First stage social partners consultation on improving the working conditions in platform work*, Brussels, European Commission, 2021, available at: https://ec.europa.eu/commission/presscorner/detail/en/qanda_21_656 (accessed 1 March 2021).
71. For issues in relation to social security protections *see*: Schoukens, P., Barrio, A., De Becker, E., *Platform Economy and the Risk of In-work Poverty: A Research Agenda for Social Security Lawyers* (Valerio De Stefano, Ilda Durri, Charalampos Stylogiannis and Mathias Wouters eds, *A Research Agenda for the Gig-Economy and Society*, Edward Elgar Publishing 2022), 93-111.
72. *See*, for instance, European Parliament, (2020). *Data subjects, digital surveillance, AI and the future of work*, Panel for the Future of Science and Technology, European Union, Brussels,

overview of the academic literature related to the topic demonstrates the potential risks stemming from these types of work arrangements. Further investigation of numerous articles published in mainstream newspapers and tabloids, as well as research conducted by trade unions and international and regional institutions, all give evidence of the problematic characteristics associated with platform work. These themes have even found their way into the art world, with the movie *'Sorry We Missed You'*, produced by Ken Loach, vividly portraying how platform workers can be trapped in a precarious existence, where their human dignity is threatened.

It can be claimed, therefore, that platform work is of particular interest from both a human rights law perspective, as well as a labour law angle. This is not only due to the possible restrictions on platform workers' human rights, or their limited coverage from labour protections. It is also important for the reason that platform work, which as a phenomenon encompasses many of the characteristics of modern labour markets, can contribute to a more general discussion in relation to the future of labour law and its connection with the realm of human rights.

Globalisation, the relationship between capital and labour, different regulatory approaches with respect to labour law and new forms of employment followed by new technological developments are just some of the realities which can be inextricably linked to platform work. These are also some of the features which have positioned 'labour law in defence'.[73] As noted, they have exposed, maybe like never before, the existing limitations of labour law frameworks around the world, where protections still and by large remain concentrated within 'subordinate' wage employment, particularly of a full-time and open-ended nature. As such, workers engaged in non-standard work arrangements, including many workers in the platform economy, often remain in a legal 'grey zone' between traditional employment and self-employment, whereby the scope of labour regulation is traditionally limited to the bare minimum.[74] As explained throughout this research, this phenomenon takes place despite the fact that the real nature of the job performed by a number of workers may indicate a disguised employment relationship.

Due to the changing context of work, therefore, mainly within advanced economies, a debate has been brought to the fore on the foundations and functions of labour law, with many advocating for the need for the modernisation of the field.[75] How the term modernisation can be interpreted, however? Does it refer to a debate that puts into

---

available at: https://www.europarl.europa.eu/RegData/etudes/STUD/2020/656305/EPRS_STU(2020)656305_EN.pdf (accessed 9 December 2020).

73. Hendrickx, F., *Foundations and Functions of Contemporary Labour Law*, 3 European Labour Law Journal 108 n. 2 (2012), 108; *supra*, Codagnone, C., Abadie, F., Federico, B. (2016).
74. According to the International Labour Office, non-standard-forms of employment comprises four different employment arrangements ((1) temporary employment; (2) part-time work; (3) temporary agency work; and (4) other forms of employment), which fall out of the realm of the 'standard employment relationship', understood as work that is full time, indefinite, as well as part of a subordinate and bilateral employment relationship (International Labour Office (ILO), (2016), *Non-standard Employment Around the World: Understanding Challenges, Shaping Prospects*, Geneva, ILO, 7).
75. Sciarra, S. (2007), *Modernization of Labour Law: A Current European Debate: a Public Lecture*. International Institute for Labour Studies.

question the very foundations of labour law, or does bring up a discussion that labour law needs to be integrated into a larger project that will enable the field to expand its scope of protection to workers that are currently outside of it?

It has been stressed that the role of 'intellectuals' is to keep ideas alive and available at the moment in which their actual existence is in immediate danger. It is an irony that this proposition derives from Milton Friedman, an economist that strongly espoused the idea of labour market deregulation.[76] Still, his suggestion can be equally used by those who powerfully believe that the idea, or at least some of the ideas,[77] of labour law should remain unchanged: protecting workers' dignity and enabling them to seek justice at the workplace and the labour market, in general. Unchanged, however, does not necessarily mean 'static' and disconnected from contemporary concerns.

The purpose of Chapter 1 is to introduce the phenomenon of platform work by relying on already established concepts and identify its main particularities and issues towards labour protection. In doing so, the chapter in question begins by exploring some of the main challenges that labour law is currently facing. Globalisation, the vertical disintegration of firms, and new technologies have put into question some of the certainties under which labour law was developed. In this context, the lines between employment and self-employment have become all the more obscure. That said, as it will be further explained, those challenges are now apparent within the realm of the platform economy. Not only this, but the latter can also raise novel concerns in relation to labour protection.

1.2 LABOUR LAW(S) UNDER ATTACK

For decades now, labour laws around the world have been under constant attack. On many different occasions, they are seen as an obstacle to competition, flexibility, efficiency, as well as overall economic growth.[78] Indeed, from the 1980s onwards, some of the certainties under which labour law was conceived, meaning, *inter alia*, to compensate for the inequality of bargaining power inherent in the employment relationship, have started to fade away.[79] This situation has been going hand in hand with the slow decay of the social and economic realities which led to such certainty, together with a developed body of legislation that aimed, in a rather 'rigid' manner, at protecting workers, while reducing employers' freedom(s).[80] As some authors explain,

76. Friedman, M., *Capitalism and Freedom* (University of Chicago Press 1962), xiv.
77. There is no single idea behind the foundations of labour law. Different approaches will be discussed in Chapter 2.
78. *See*, for instance, Collins, H., *Regulating the Employment Relation for Competitiveness*, 30 *Industrial Law Journal* 17 n. 1 (2001), 17-48; Stone, K.W., *Flexibilisation, Globalization and Privatization: Three Challenges to Labour Rights in Out Time*, 44 Osgoode Hall Law Journal 79 n. 1 (2006), 79-104; Weiss, M., *Re-Inventing Labour Law?* (Guy Davidov and Brian Langille eds, *The Idea of Labour Law*, Oxford, Oxford University Press 2011), 43-56.
79. *Ibid.*, Weiss (2011), 43-44.
80. Rainone, S., *Labour Law Beyond Its Emancipatory Nature: What Is Left?* (Stafano Bellomo and Antonio Preteroti A. eds, *Recent Labour Law: Issues a Multilevel Perspective*, G. Giappichelli Editore 2019), 26-27.

the most apparent outcomes of the societal changes that took place during this period are to be associated with the embrace of neoclassical economic labour market strategies and anti-welfare state politics.[81] The adoption of this theory, which identifies labour regulation as an external intervention, or interference with market self-regulation, has come along with the intensification of global competition and monetarist policies, often in tandem with the deregulation of labour markets.[82]

Consequently, many governments have opted to dismantle labour regulations, which restricted the negotiation autonomy and power of the parties within an employment relationship, in an attempt to cut off labour-related costs. A point of caution should be added here. Deregulation is often described as a process that regulation is non-existent or extremely limited. As Bob Hepple rightly puts it though, '*in fact, it means leaving regulation to ordinary market rules, to the private law of property and contract*';[83] hence, labour laws, through the lenses of a regulatory theory as such, are perceived as costs that obstruct competition and in turn hamper efficiency.[84] Furthermore, deregulation can be also adopted by national authorities due to their failure to modify and bring up-to-date labour and employment policies, which aim at adequately safeguarding workers '*in the type of work, and under the work relations, in which they currently find themselves and extend real – as opposed to theoretical – opportunities to bargain collectively and influence the terms and conditions of work*'.[85] This is something that Guy Standing has described as the 'implicit-deregulation'.[86] In light of this discussion, it can be argued, as some have expressed it, that the labour market tends to be treated like a market of any kind; a rationale that it can equally treat labour, as any other commodity.[87] As it is explained below, some of the CEOs of the most powerful digital platform businesses seem to openly promote this idea.

In more recent times, likewise, the fact that labour laws are under a continuous threat becomes even more evident when someone attempts to look at the recent economic and financial crisis of 2008. During that period, for many countries in which austerity has been '*the only game in the town*',[88] hostile reforms towards workers'

81. Fudge, J., *Labour as a 'Fictive Commodity': Radically Reconceptualizing Labour Law* (Guy Davidov and Brian Langille eds, *The Idea of Labour Law*, Oxford University Press 2011), 121; Fudge, J., *The Future of the Standard Employment Relationship: Labour Law, New Institutional Economics and Old Power Resource Theory*, 59 Journal of Industrial Relations 374 n. 3 (2017), 374-392; Harvey, D., *A Brief History of Neo-liberalism* (Oxford University Press 2005).
82. Arthurs, H.W., *Labour Law after Labour* (Guy Davidov and Brian Langille eds, *The Idea of Labour Law*, Oxford University Press 2011),15; *see also* Heinemann, F., *The Drivers of Deregulation in the Era of Globalization* (Peter Bernholz and Roland Vaubel eds, *Political Competition and Economic Regulation*, Routledge 2007), 245-266.
83. Hepple, B., *Factors Influencing the Making and Transformation of Labour Law in Europe* (Guy Davidov and Brian Langille eds, *The Idea of Labour Law*, Oxford University Press 2011), 33.
84. *See*, for instance, Deakin, S., Wilkinaon, F., *Rights vs Efficiency the Economic Case for Transnational Labour Standards*, 23 Industrial Law Journal 289 n. 4 (1994), 289-310.
85. Rittich, K. (2010), '"Between Workers" Rights and Flexibility: Labor Law in an Uncertain World', 54 Saint Luis University Law Journal, 572 n. 2.
86. Standing, G., *Global Labour Flexibility: Seeking Distributive Justice* (Macmillan 1999), 75-76.
87. *Supra*, Fudge, (2011), 121-122.
88. Van Kersbergen, K., Vis, B., Hemerijck, A., *The Great Recession and Welfare State Reform: Is Retrenchment Really the Only Game Left in Town?*, 48 Social Policy & Administration 883 n. 7 (2014), 884.

protection and fundamental social rights have contributed to a 'deconstruction' of national labour laws, not to mention the erosion of collective bargaining procedures.[89] Notably, as has been pointed out by the previous Director-General of the ILO, Juan Somovia, many of these reforms preceded the economic crisis and the imposed austerity has been used multiple times as '*an excuse to disregard internationally agreed labour standards*'.[90]

What Somovia describes appears to be also true within the contemporary world of work. Even though the post-effects from the residues of the economic crisis are still considerably apparent in a number of countries,[91] the aggression towards labour laws, as well as the evasion of their protective function, is something that is not solely limited to periods of economic stagnation. Among other reasons, the ongoing prioritisation of 'free market' values, along with the pressures of global competition have led to, or permitted the proliferation of, forms of work that are specially designed to escape from formal regulation and save labour costs. As noted in the introduction, the present-day displays of casual work, as these, for instance, have been manifested through platform work, have 'pushed' a great portion of workers who enjoy a limited bargaining power away from the realm of labour law and its associated benefits. Instead, they are now positioned in a situation they are expected to defend themselves in the market, without, to a great extent, any intervention from the state. As the following sections examine, such a phenomenon can considerably be attributed to the existing limitations of labour law's protective framework.

1.3 THE CHANGING ORGANISATIONAL STRUCTURES OF BUSINESSES

The fact that labour law is a product deriving from industrialisation is something that has been stated multiple times in literature.[92] It was built on a social and economic reality, where its main point of reference was the Fordist model of production, which had as a typical feature the development of centralised technologies of mass production. The workforce was characterised by a relatively homogeneous group of potential members, comprised of workers - mainly blue-collar and only to a small extent white-collar - in their majority male, working full-time, in relatively secure occupations and within a vertically integrated workplace.[93] Furthermore, workplace

89. Clauwaert, S., Schomann, I. (2012), *The Crisis and National Labour Law Reforms: A mapping exercise*, ETUI Working Paper 2012.04, Brussels.
90. Somovia, J. 'ILO Director-General address to the European Parliament', 14 September 2011, available at: https://www.ilo.org/global/about-the-ilo/newsroom/statements-and-speeches/WCMS_162828/lang--nl/index.htm (accessed 13 October 2020).
91. For instance, *see* Brandl, B. Bechter, B., *The Hybridization of National Collective Bargaining Systems: The Impact of the Economic Crisis on the Transformation of Collective Bargaining in the European Union*, 40 Economic and Industrial Democracy 469 n. 3 (2019), 469-489.
92. For instance, *see* Deakin, S. Lele, P. and Siems, M., *The Evolution of Labour Law: Calibrating and Comparing Regulatory Regimes*, 146 International Labour Review 133 n. 3-4 (2007), 133-162; Davidov, G. and Langille, B. eds, *The Idea of Labour Law* (Oxford University Press 2011).
93. Gumbrell-McCormick, R., *European Trade Unions and 'Atypical' Workers*, 42 Industrial Relations Journal 293 n. 3 (2011), 297.

relationships were defined by rather strict hierarchical control. The latter, as Casale has argued, consisted of the authority of the employers to give orders, supervise compliance with them and penalise workers in situations where the work is not performed according to the orders given.[94]

Workers in standard employment relationships, therefore, were seen as the main actors on the stage of social and political affairs.[95] At the same time, solo self-employed and other workers in dependent self-employment were historically positioned outside the scope of the employment protection into less well-defined categories, including service contacts, workers engaged in liberal professions, such as lawyers and auditors and workers in 'grey areas' between employment and self-employment.

The Fordist model of production was prevalent in the US, as well as throughout Europe, and had taken various forms. According to Supiot, at least within a European context, all these diverse forms of production were mirrored in certain differences in the legal and institutional structures of various countries.[96] Any differentiation, however, hardly negated the fact that to a great extent, the core features of this model were present everywhere.[97] For that reason, as noted, and due to the overwhelming numerical superiority of workers engaged in wage employment, labour laws were shaped in a way that accommodated the specific characteristics of the Fordist model of production. For instance, Stone observes that the framework of American labour law was developed on the assumption of a long-term attachment to the same place of work.[98] The legal framework around collective bargaining, individual employment rights, as well as a number of social security rights, were all provided on the basis of a stable and continuous relationship between the worker and the employer.

Having said that, much of the reality just described is hardly the case today. In recent years, as Judy Fudge puts it: '*the nation state, the vertically integrated firm, the standard employment relationship, the male breadwinner and female housewife gender contract … have either weakened or been transformed*'.[99] The composition of the workforce has become much more diverse, while forms of standard employment relationships are no longer necessarily the norm. This is of course not to say that standard forms of employment arrangements do not remain dominant.[100] Still, the decline of jobs that barely fit the paradigm form of a vertically integrated business

94. Schoukens, P., Barrio, A., *The Changing Concept of Work: When Does Typical Work Become Atypical?*, 8 European Labour Law Journal 306 n. 4 (2017), 309, citing Casale, G., *The Employment Relationship: A General Introduction* (Giuseppe Casale G. ed., *The Employment Relationship: A Comparative Overview*, Hart Publishing 2011), 1-34.
95. Ojeda Avilés, A., *The 'Externalization' of Labour Law*, 148 International Labour Review, 47 n. 1-2 (2009), 55.
96. Supiot, A., *Beyond Employment: Challenges in Work and the Future of Labour Law in Europe* (Oxford University Press 2001), 1-22.
97. *Ibid.*
98. Stone, V.W. K., *Legal Protections for Atypical Employees: Employment Law for Workers Without Workplaces and Employees Without Employers*, 27 Berkley Journal of Employment and Labor Law 253 n. 2 (2006), 254.
99. *Supra*, Fudge (2011), 120.
100. Eurofound, (2020), *Labour market change: Trends and policy approaches towards flexibilisation*, Challenges and prospects in the EU series, Publications Office of the European Union, Luxembourg; *Supra*, ILO (2016).

model has exposed the existing limitations in the structure of labour protections, as a great portion of workers now falls outside of labour law's protective framework. Transformations are observed both in the contexts of developed and developing economies, even though significant differences are detected within the literature.[101] In the Global South, for example, the emergence of a wide variety of 'non-standard' and contingent forms of work is often associated with the move of a significant number of workers towards the informal sector.[102]

As is highlighted throughout this research, the rise of NSFE is by no means a natural evolution or process. It can be rather attributed to a variety of interrelated factors, such as the strive towards flexibility and an over-increased global competition. These phenomena have considerably altered the organisational structures of businesses. Since the 1970s, more specifically, what is observed has been a trend towards a vertical disintegration of firms by arranging many of the aspects of production through, *inter alia*, subcontracting, outsourcing and offshoring.[103] In other words, production activities have been moving outside the premises of the employer's firm. By externalising various facets of production and servicing, businesses have attempted to eliminate certain expenses, such as the risk of costs of labour and compliance with employment law(s). This situation has, as a result, that the distribution of managerial prerogatives traditionally concentrated into the hands of one employer, to be now circulated into multiple entities; something that, as is discussed below, has '*strained the narrow readings of the notion of subordination*'.[104]

From a business perspective, vertical disintegration and external contracting can often lead to long-range advantages, which, as noted, are mostly related to the saving of labour costs. Collins, for example, in one of his early works at the beginning of the 1990s, pointed out that employers can avoid spending their resources on quasi-fixed costs associated with employment, such as training and hiring.[105] Businesses, furthermore, can circumvent the expenses linked to employment protection rights, as well as refrain from committing to long-term contractual relations; the latter factor can also enable employers to impose stricter contractual terms in relation to the expected performance of workers.[106] Empirical evidence also suggests that the avoidance of long-term commitments and the use of flexible work arrangements by employers can further boost the resilience of businesses in the event of fluctuations in demand for goods or services, due to seasonality, or other unforeseen reasons.[107]

---

101. Fudge, J., McCrystal, S. and Sankaran K. eds, *Challenging the Legal Boundaries of Work Regulation* (Hart Publishing 2012).
102. Sankaran, K., *Flexibility and Informalisation of Employment Relationships* (Judy Fudge, Shae McCrystal and Kamala Sankaran eds, *Challenging the Legal Boundaries of Work Regulation*, Hart Publishing 2012), 29-48.
103. Collins, H., *Independent Contractors and the Challenge of Vertical Disintegration to Employment Protection Laws*, 10 Oxford Journal of Legal Studies 353 n. 3 (1990), 353-380.
104. Countouris, N., *The Employment Relationship: A Comparative Analysis of National Judicial Approaches* (Giuseppe Casale ed., *The Employment Relationship: A Comparative Overview*, Hart Publishing 2011), 51.
105. *Supra*, Collins (1990), 360.
106. *Ibid.*
107. *Supra*, ILO (2016), 159.

It should be mentioned at this point that the drivers for the vertical disintegration of firms can also include considerations that are not necessarily attributed to the reduction of costs, albeit a potential profit may occur.[108] The purpose of outsourcing, for instance, can benefit businesses in terms of avoiding spending precious management time on activities, which are not central to expanding their competitive advantage. In other words, they can exclusively focus on functions that are central to the core operations of the business.[109] The outsourcing of tasks to external suppliers can also assist the latter in increasing the quality of their services with respect to areas that require greater expertise than the one they can provide.

In recent times, the diffusion of activities has been expedited by new technologies, especially advances in information and communication technologies and the overall digitalisation of work.[110] The introduction of algorithms, for instance, into labour production has given a chance to big firms, such as those operating in the platform economy, to minimise the transaction costs of labour outsourcing and temporary access to assets. In this respect, Drahokoupil and Fabo indicate that algorithms allow these types of businesses to effectively match a large pool of labour providers and users, while at the same time, transaction costs are limited insofar as these platforms can also facilitate micro-transactions.[111] Moreover, the use of new technological tools also assists platforms to reduce or manage risks involved in market transactions, like features of incomplete information about the labour provider, or the risk of cheating; therefore, market failures can be addressed in a better way and of course faster than ever before. According to the European Trade Union Confederation (ETUC), the use of online platforms that aims at the reduction of costs is capable of establishing '*a new spiraling trend towards externalisation and outsourcing of work to subcontractors*'.[112] This, in turn, can put further pressure on businesses that are still committed to '*regular in-house work*' to change their organisational structure(s).[113]

As explained, the rationales behind the fragmentation of enterprises, along with the decline of vertical hierarchical structures in the organisation of work can vary. It can be claimed, however, that at least a key reason, of greater or lesser force in particular situations, is the desire of businesses to lower their costs through avoiding liability under labour and employment laws. As research, furthermore, confirms, on many occasions, national policies can and have indeed facilitated businesses' endeavour towards greater flexibility and the diffusion of tasks, expediting in this way the

108. *Ibid.*, 160.
109. Prahalad, C.K. and Hamel, G., *The Core Competence of the Corporation*, 68 Harvard Business Review 79 n. 3(1990), 79-91.
110. *Supra*, Aloisi, (2020).
111. Drahokoupil, J., Fabo, B., *Outsourcing, Offshoring and the Deconstruction of Employment: New and Old Challenges* (Amparo Serrano-Pascual and Maria Jepsen eds, *The Deconstruction of Employment as a Political Question: 'Employment' as a Floating Signifier*, Springer 2018), 33-61.
112. ETUC, (November 2017), *ETUC Resolution on tackling new digital challenges to the world of labour, in particular crowdwork*, available at: https://www.etuc.org/en/document/etuc-resolution-tackling-new-digitalchallenges-world-labour-particular-crowdwork (assessed 9 December 2020).
113. *Ibid.*

proliferation of workers in atypical jobs.[114] In this regard, as is further discussed below, the spread of these types of work arrangements can be further attributed to specific policies enacted by national authorities, which by following ideas of a general labour market deregulation, can indeed increase the opportunities given to employers, such as digital labour platforms, '*to deny or curtail the protection of labour law's regulation to working people*'.[115] It is, therefore, observed that there is a combination of different drivers behind the occurrence of such phenomena.

Still, whatever the reasons may be, the manner in which many business enterprises are now organising themselves has led to what some authors call the '*commercialisation*' of work.[116] This concept refers to the breakdown of the boundary between commercial activities and employment. In this context, the lines between employment and self-employment are getting blurry, while the limitations of labour law, on many occasions, are getting 'crystal' clear.

1.4 OBSCURE LINES BETWEEN EMPLOYMENT AND SELF-EMPLOYMENT

Having as a point of reference models of production that relied on vertically integrated workplaces, the standard employment relationship as a concept, according to the ILO, is '*understood as work that is full time, indefinite, as well as part of a subordinate and bilateral employment relationship*'.[117] The latter, in the entirety of legal systems, is regulated through the contract of employment. There are three key elements of particular importance in this respect, namely, subordination, continuity and bilateralism.[118] More specifically, as a matter of law, both in common law and civil law countries, the employment relationship has been 'conceptualised' as a personal relationship between two parties, in which the notion of subordination serves as the core element.[119] In broad terms, as Countouris argues, this notion is recognised as a '*manifestation of the power of control and direction over a worker*'.[120] It has been consistently used by courts around the world in cases related to the legal classification of workers. Indicative, for instance, has been the application of the 'control test' by courts in the UK, or the use of the concept of *lien de subordination juridique* in the French legal system and other civil law countries.[121] In addition, interrelated to the notion of subordination, there are two additional elements, which appear to be

114. Adams, Z., Deakin, S., *Institutional Solutions to Precariousness and Inequality in Labour Markets*, 52 British Journal of Industrial Relations 779 n. 4 (2014), 779-809.
115. *Supra*, Freedland (2019), 181.
116. Fudge, J., *Blurring Legal Boundaries: Regulating for Decent Work* (Judy Fudge, Shae McCrystal and Kamala Sankaran eds, *Challenging the Legal Boundaries of Work Regulation*, Hart Publishing 2012), 1.
117. *Supra*, ILO (2016), 7.
118. *See also* the analysis of Countouris, *supra*, Countouris (2019), 6-10.
119. Fudge, J. (2006). '*Fragmenting Work and Fragmenting Organizations: The Contract of Employment and the Scope of Labour Regulation*', 44 Osgoode Hall Law Journal, 618-619 n. 4.
120. Countouris, N. *Defining and Regulating Work Relations for the Future of Work*, ILO, Geneva, (2019) 8.
121. *Supra*, ILO (2016), 11.

prominent for the existence of an employment relationship. First, the continuity of work performance, a requirement that has been often used for drawing the line between employment and self-employment.[122] Second, associated with subordination is the conception that the employment relationship has a strictly bilateral character, as it takes place between a worker and an employer.

Thus, matured alongside the growth of industrialisation, at least in the context of industrialised democracies, key legal elements, such as the notion of subordination and bilateralism, have been historically used to define the scope of employment protection and social security benefits.[123] The problems start to arise, nonetheless, when considering the changing organisational structure of workplaces, as was described in the previous section. Indeed, the vertical disintegration of businesses together with, *inter alia*, the proliferation of non-standard jobs with a particular emphasis on entrepreneurship, as well as the introduction of new technologies, have as an immediate outcome what Countouris calls the '*erosion of the subordinate contract of employment*'.[124] This, in turn, has resulted in alterations in, and a polarisation of, employment relations, where the legal concepts of the employee and employer have been put into question.

More specifically, as we are steadily moving away from the paradigm of a vertically integrated firm, a strict interpretation of the notion of subordination cannot be applied in a relatively 'straightforward' manner. The externalisation of tasks outside the premises of the business has changed the manner in which traditional hierarchical control and direction are exercised by the employer. To this extent, as early as 2001, the so-called Supiot Report pointed out the growing similarities with respect to the working conditions and the performance of work of many employees and those in self-employment.[125] Furthermore, as previously noted, the progress of technology and more specifically the introduction of algorithms within modern workplaces has further altered the way that those elements are applied.[126] Reflecting on such developments, De Stefano argues that employers, in many instances, are able to give detailed instructions and direct the work via the use of digital applications, which rely on artificial intelligence, as well as other technological tools.[127] The shifting apparatus of subordination exercised by some employers, therefore, is capable of conferring on workers the alleged autonomy necessary for them to fall into the category of self-employed workers – an area in which the scope of labour regulation is traditionally limited to the bare minimum.

In a similar vein, the application of rigid bilateralism in the context of an employment relationship (one employer and one worker), inextricably linked to subordination, can be also really challenging, as in many cases, it fails to address the

122. *Supra*, Countouris (2019), 9.
123. Nicola Countouris reminds us the contract of employment should not be seen as a single 'monolith' that has taken a single formulation. The shape of this concept can vary across different regions or countries with different legal traditions (*supra*, Countouris (2019), 2-3).
124. *Ibid.*, 9.
125. *Supra*, SUPIOT (2001), 1-46.
126. *Supra*, De Stefano (2017), 1-17.
127. *Supra*, De Stefano (2018), 7-16.

real number of parties engaged in the exercise of different functions for the same employer.[128] According to Fudge, the strict bilateral distinction within employment relationships has resulted in two problems. As she puts it:

> First, it assumes that there is a conceptual and normative salience to the distinction between employees and independent contractors for the purpose of determining the scope of employment and labour protection. Second, it anthropomorphizes or personalizes the employer by assuming that the employer is a unitary entity.[129]

Taking once more into consideration the developments in the world of work, such as the occurrence of trends towards greater flexibility of work arrangements, what Fudge describes is becoming particularly apparent. Undeniably, the rise of market-mediated forms of work, like outsourced and temporary work, has blurred the lines between contracts of services and contracts for services. The complications in this regard can be further aggravated due to the existence of contractual terms that allow workers to be substituted by other workers. Substitution clauses in some legal systems, such as in the UK, have become multiple times the object of judicial interpretation,[130] as they are giving the chance to (possible) employers, such as platform businesses, to argue that their inclusion into the contractual agreement is indeed suggestive of workers' status as independent contractors.[131] At the same time, this can occur despite the fact that such clauses, in reality, were never, or marginally used by the workers in question. Their existence, therefore, as has also been confirmed by various national courts, has only served so as to preclude the latter from claiming the personal performance of work and their status as employees.[132]

Furthermore, as noted, the continuity in work relations constitutes another quintessential condition for the existence of an employment relationship. As in the cases of subordination and bilateralism, in an era where flexible work arrangements are on the rise, a narrow and strict interpretation of this requirement can, as Countouris suggests, lead to significant exclusionary outcomes.[133] For example, by relying on research conducted by the ILO, he argues that the provision of qualification periods within contractual arrangements has the potential of denying many workers, particularly those in short and fixed-term contracts, access to a number of labour rights, even in situations where the performance of tasks for the same employer continues for a considerable amount of time, albeit on an intermittent basis.[134] The same thing can be

128. For a comprehensive discussion on this issue *see*: Prassl, J., *The Concept of the Employer* (Oxford University Press 2015).
129. Supra, Fudge, J. (2006), 631.
130. *Supra*, Countouris (2019), 9. The author, for instance, refers to the cases of *Pimlico Plumbers v. Smith* [2018] and *Stringfellows v. Quashie* [2012]).
131. For instance, *see* High Court of Justice 5 December 2018, Case No. CO/810/2018, *IWGB v. Central Arbitration Committee.*, in the UK; 37ª Vara do Trabalho de Belo Horizonte, 30 de janeiro de 2017, N° 0011863-62.2016.5.03.0137, in Brazil.
132. Juzgado de lo Social Madrid 22 de julio de 2019, Case No. ECLI: ES:JSO:2019:2952; Juzgado de lo Social de Valencia 10 de junio de 2019, Case No. ECLI: ES:JSO:2019:2892. Both rulings coming from Spain.
133. *Supra*, Countouris (2019), 8.
134. *Ibid.*, 8-9, citing *supra*, ILO (2016), 256.

also said in relation to platform work, where, in many instances, the flexibility in working schedules offered by platform operators is capable of depriving workers of various employment protections.[135] In this respect, the ILO Committee of Experts has recently called attention to the fact '*that the use of casual work on a regular basis, to carry on activities that concern the main business of the enterprise is a form of disguised employment relationship and contributes to the natural precariousness of this type of work*'.[136]

Overall, as a consequence of the aforementioned complexities, a considerable number of workers find themselves in a grey zone between employment and self-employment, including many platform workers. This is not to claim that the existence of these types of workers constitutes a novel phenomenon. Still, as the ILO Committee of Experts recently observed, the contemporary changes in the organisation of work, combined with technological developments, have increased the number of workers who are positioned in a grey legal zone.[137] Such workers, according to the ILO, are classified into two categories, namely, those who are engaged in disguised employment relationships[138] and those who find themselves in dependent-self-employment.[139]

Individuals, therefore, who may once have fallen into the category of employees, have been gradually transformed and treated as self-employed. It should be argued at this point though, that self-employed workers do not constitute a homogeneous category. At the high end of the spectrum, organisational changes in the way that businesses function, in a number of instances, have 'created' high-skilled and high-income entrepreneurs who have the ability to defend themselves in the market. At the lower end of the spectrum, however, as Collins contends, such changes have created workers who '[despite their self-employment status] *appear to be in an equivalent position of social subordination and economic dependence to that of ordinary employees*'.[140]

Platform work arrangements illustrate many of the challenges just explained. To this extent, they are often characterised as a '*conspicuous example of compound*

135. For instance, *see* De Stefano, V. (2018) 'Platform work and labour protection', Flexibility is not enough, *Regulating Globalization* (blog), 23 May 2018 available at: http://regulatingforglobalization.com/2018/05/23/platform-work-labour-protection-flexibility-not-enough/ (accessed 10 July 2022).
136. ILO Committee of Experts, (2020), *Promoting employment and decent work in a changing landscape*, Geneva, ILO, 127.
137. *Ibid.*, 117.
138. '*A disguised employment relationship is one which is lent an appearance that is different from the underlying reality, with the intention of nullifying or attenuating the protection afforded by the law. It is thus an attempt to conceal or distort the employment relationship, either by cloaking it in another legal guise or by giving it another form in which the worker enjoys less protection*' (ILO, (2003). *Report V The scope of the employment relationship*, Geneva, ILO, 24-25).
139. These are: '*working relationships where workers perform services for a business under a contract different from a contract of employment but depend on one or a small number of clients for their income and receive direct guidelines regarding how the work is to be done. Dependent self-employed workers are typically not covered by the provisions of labour or social security laws*' (*supra*, ILO (2016), 36).
140. *Supra*, Collins (1990), 354.

non-standard employment'.[141] Having said that, the remaining part of this chapter focuses on the very phenomenon of platform work and aims at exploring its particular features, as well as its often adverse impact on working conditions.

1.5 PLATFORM WORK: DEFINITION AND TERMINOLOGY

Platform-based work represents one of the most recent and debated labour market trends and an expression of technological advancement in the 21st century. According to a joint ILO-Eurofound report, information and communication technologies have radically transformed daily work and living arrangements, enabling people to undertake work anytime and anywhere.[142] This phenomenon, *inter alia*, can be attributed to the increased demand for flexibility on the part of employers, better labour market efficiency and in some cases, the desire for greater flexibility on the part of workers.[143] Despite the current attention that platform work has attracted both in relation to literature and regulation, there is not a unified 'label' that characterises this type of work. Instead, multiple labels have been recently used in an attempt to capture the phenomenon in question. These, for instance, among others, include the terms 'gig economy', 'collaborative economy', 'sharing economy' and 'on-demand economy'.

It can be argued that the problem with these terminologies is that some instances can lead, intentionally or unintentionally, to demeaning connotations, or interpretations that do not necessarily depict the reality of the work per se.[144] Take, for example, the label 'gig economy, or work'. According to the Cambridge dictionary, the term gig refers either to '*a public performance by pop, rock, or jazz musicians or by a comedian*', or to '*a job, especially a temporary one*'.[145] The main element in these definitions is that the act performed is of a temporary nature, like on the occasion of a concert. This interpretation, however, comes in contrast with the real nature of the work of many platform workers where their main source of income derives from such an activity, which is far from something temporary.[146] Confusion can be also generated when it comes to the label of the 'sharing economy', which as a term in its initial digital form, refers to the facilitation of real sharing that often takes the form of lending, in the

141. De Stefano, V., Durri, I., Stylogiannis, C., Wouters, M., '*Exclusion by Default: Platform Workers' Quest for Labour Protections*' (De Stefano V., Durri, I., Stylogiannis, C., Wouters, M. eds, *A Research Agenda for the Gig-Economy and Society*, Edward Elgar Publishing 2022), 17.
142. Eurofound & International Labour Organization, (2017), *Working Anytime, Anywhere: The Effects on the World of Work 3*, Geneva, Publications Office of the European Union and the International Labour Office.
143. Aloisi, A., *Commoditized Workers: Case Study Research on Labour Law Issues Arising from a Set of 'on-demand/gig economy' Platforms*, 37 Comparative Labor Law & Policy Journal, 653 n. 3 (2016), 653-690.
144. Pesole A., Urzí Brancati M.C., Fernández-Macías E., Biagi, F. & González Vázquez I. (2018), *Platform Workers in Europe: Evidence from the COLLEEM Survey*, Luxembourg, Publications Office of the European Union, 7.
145. Cambridge Dictionary, available at: https://dictionary.cambridge.org/dictionary/english-french/gig (accessed 2 October 2020).
146. For instance, *see* BERG, J., *Income Security in the On-Demand Economy: Findings and Policy Lessons from a Survey of Crowdworkers*, 37 Comparative Labor Law & Policy Journal 554 n. 3 (2016), 554-555.

absence of barter or payment.[147] Again, this is not what defines the majority of work relationships between platform businesses and their workers. For this reason, some authors have argued that this particular label has been used to normalise precarious types of work arrangements.[148] In order to avoid any misinterpretations, therefore, this research uses relatively neutral terms, such as platform economy and platform workers.

Having said that, the lack of a unified label has not prevented supranational institutions and scholars from pursuing a definition of the phenomenon of platform work. For instance, research conducted by the ILO describes digital labour platforms as including '*both web-based platforms, where work is outsourced through an open call to a geographically dispersed crowd ("crowdwork"), and location-based applications (apps) which allocate work to individuals in a specific geographical area*'.[149] Furthermore, the Organisation for Economic Co-operation and Development (OECD) refers to platform work as '*transactions mediated by an app (i.e., a specific purpose software program, often designed for use on a mobile device) or a website, which matches customers and clients, by means of an algorithm, with workers who provide services in return for money*'.[150] Lastly, Eurofound describes platform work as '*an employment form in which organisations or individuals use an online platform to access an indefinite and unknown group of other organisations or individuals to solve specific problems or to provide specific services or products in exchange for payment*'.[151]

The tasks offered through the platform economy can be skilled or unskilled; they can be the main source of income, or they can just offer supplementary earnings to the workers involved; and, they expand to a wide variety of services and industries, ranging from transportation (e.g., Uber) to domestic services industry (e.g., TaskRabbit), to work that takes place entirely online (e.g., Amazon Mechanical Turk). Platform-based work is usually understood to include two forms of work, namely, crowdwork and work-on-demand through applications.[152] This separation can also be observed within the definition provided by the ILO. The former category includes tasks, which are carried out via online platforms that bring together clients and workers from potentially all around the world. The nature of these tasks varies, including micro-tasks, such as completing surveys or tagging photos, and more extensive projects, such as the creation of a web page. Crowdworkers have the ability to provide their online services from wherever they are based and at any time. Work-on-demand, instead, includes activities that are executed offline and are matched via applications

147. Eurofound, (2018) *Non-standard forms of employment: Recent trends and future prospects*, Dublin, Eurofound, 21.
148. Cockayne, D.G., *Sharing and Neoliberal Discourse: The Economic Function of Sharing in the Digital On-demand Economy*, 77 Geoforum n. 73 (2016), 73-82.
149. Berg J., Furrer M., Harmon E., Rani, U., Six Silberman M. (2018), *Digital Labour Platforms and the Future of Work: Towards Decent Work in the Online World*, Geneva, ILO, xv (2019).
150. OECD, (2019), *Policy Responses to New Forms of Work*, OECD Publishing, Paris, 14.
151. Rasche M. (2019), *Literature Review – Online Moderately Skilled Click-work: Employment and Working Conditions*, Dublin, Eurofound, 2.
152. De Stefano, V., *The Rise of the 'Just-in-time Workforce': On-demand Work, Crowdwork, and Labor Protection in the 'Gig-Economy'*, 37 Comparative Labor Law & Policy Journal 476 n. 3 (2016), 476-477.

that are controlled by businesses which are establishing minimum quality standards of services that workers have to comply with.[153] Thus, the location and timeframe of such activities are more limited in comparison to work that takes place online.

The differences between these two forms of work, as it is argued below, are of particular importance when considering the application of some fundamental labour rights and, specifically collective labour rights. For instance, for crowdworkers, the enjoyment of their rights to freely associate and bargain collectively can be restricted due to the fact that they are spread around the world and there is the absence of a transnational framework that rules their online activities.[154] Workers-on-demand, instead, are located in a specific area. Therefore, it can be easier for them to freely join a trade union both in practical terms, as well as from a legal perspective as they fall under the same national regulatory structure(s).[155] That said, the majority of the enacted legislation around the world regarding platform workers is touching upon the issue of work-on-demand. These kinds of issues have made some scholars, such as De Stefano and Aloisi, point out that this very differentiation is important and perhaps a distinct regulatory approach is indeed necessary.[156]

1.6 OLD PRACTICES HIDDEN UNDER THE CLOAK OF TECHNOLOGICAL INNOVATION

In the 2020 World Economic Forum's Annual Meeting in Davos, Mr Daniel Zhang, the Chairman and CEO of Alibaba Group, the '*alter ego*' of Amazon in China, noted:

> We create the business, we create demand. Then, because of demand, [businesses] need to hire more people ... when you grow the platform, when you have so many packages developed from this business, you need delivery guys, last-mile guys. So, I think that's the evolution of the platform.[157]

According to Mr Zhang and many other CEOs of some of the most powerful platform businesses, the main driver behind this 'evolution' is the continuous development of new technologies. Indeed, this is exactly the rhetoric that many platform operators, such as Uber and Amazon Mechanical Turk, have been using in order to preach for the emergence of the platform economy, which represents a new way of organising economic activities, capable of offering new and more flexible opportunities for those who are seeking employment. These schemes are perceived as moving away from the hierarchical business organisation towards a structure that makes it possible

153. *Ibid.*, 2.
154. Johnston H., *Labour Geographies of the Platform Economy: Understanding Collective Organizing Strategies in the Context of Digitally Mediated Work*, 159 International Labour Review 25 n. 1 (2020), 29.
155. *Ibid.*
156. *Supra*, Aloisi, 660-664; De Stefano, V., Aloisi, A. (2018), *European Legal Framework for Digital Labour Platforms*, Luxembourg, Publications Office of the European Union (2016).
157. Brennan, T., 'Alibaba CEO talks 'power of the platform' at Davos' 2020, 23 January 2020, available at: https://www.alizila.com/alibaba-ceo-talks-power-of-the-platform-at-davos-2020/(accessed 2 October 2020).

for people to become free independent suppliers, flexible to move from one job to another and connect with purchasers of their services.[158]

In line with the aforementioned perspective, digital innovation is presented as the core element for these developments, or in other words, a 'natural' force, which by itself is capable of bringing about a series of structural changes in the way that labour markets are functioning. Importantly, as Prassl explains, some platforms, as well as economists seem to suggest that it is not solely the organisation or the creation of new businesses that are entirely changing, but also everything about the concept of work itself.[159] In this respect, labels such as '*paradigm shift*' from McKinsey[160] and '*fourth industrial revolution*'[161] from the executive chairman of the World Economic Forum have been employed in order to describe this phenomenon. It can be observed, therefore, that there is a strong emphasis on the technological, rather than the social causes that lead to new organisational structures and other work-related developments more broadly. The inquiry that arises, nonetheless, is whether such work arrangements represent a novel aspect in labour markets. Two elements are of particular interest in this regard: first, the role of technology as a 'natural' force of change, and second, the alleged novelty of the very organisational model of platform businesses.

1.6.1 Technology as a Natural Force of Change, or Not?

To begin with, in his book, *Toward a Rational Society*, Jürgen Habermas rejects the claims of other important theorists, such as Helmut Schelsky, who suggest a model of change in which technology is an '*independent force*'.[162] According to Habermas, the question that someone should rather ask is whether (or not) technological conditions are dominated by society in general. In this respect, he recognises that 'social interests determine the direction, functions, and pace of technical progress'.[163] This means that technological progress as a fundamentally human activity should not be seen as something detached from wider societal developments. Such an activity is, moreover, informed by '*goals and explicit judgements with respect to public and private goods, and it is also informed by norms and practice*'.[164] Now, if someone attempts to apply this logic to modern labour markets within a capitalist system of production, it can be argued that these norms and practices, as far as the direction of technological

158. Stanford, J., *The Resurgence of Gig Work: Historical and Theoretical Perspectives*, 28 The Economic and Labour Relations Review 382 n. 3 (2017), 383-388.
159. Prassl, J., *Humans as a Service* (Oxford University Press 2018), 73-74.
160. Loffler, M., Tschiesner, (2013), 'The Internet of Things and the Future of Manufacturing'. 1 June 2013, available at: https://www.mckinsey.com/business-functions/mckinsey-digital/our-insights/the-internet-of-things-and-the-future-of-manufacturing (accessed 2 October 2020).
161. Kaminska, I. (2016), 'Davos: Historians Dream of Fourth Industrial Revolutions', 20 January 2016, available at: http://ftalphaville.ft.com/2016/01/20/2150720/davos-historians-dream-offourth-industrial-revolutions (accessed 2 October 2020).
162. Bimber, B., *Karl Marx and the Three Faces of Technological Determination*, 20 Social Studies of Science 333 n. 2 (1990), 336.
163. *Ibid.*
164. Habermas, J., *Toward a Rational Society* (Beacon Press 1970), 105.

innovation is concerned, are exceedingly dependent upon certain elements, such as the ones of high efficiency and productivity.[165] For instance, as Mangan observes, already since the early half of the 20th century, business models, like Fordism and Taylorism, used technological innovation in a manner that focused on getting the most out of the efforts of workers, as constituent elements of the enterprise.[166] Of course, as the same author, as well as further literature, confirms, the application of technology under these business models had as an ultimate goal the maximisation of productivity and reduction of costs.[167] This approach seems to continue in recent times. In this regard, within modern workplaces, as De Stefano contends, the use of artificial intelligence and a number of other technological tools have been employed in digital business models in order to ensure productivity and the performance of their workers.[168] As the same author explains, this phenomenon is not strictly confined to the platform economy, but it can be also applied across various modern workplaces.[169]

That being said, arguments against 'techno-deterministic' assumptions and the very nature of technology as a driver of change, are not something new. Karl Marx, back in 1857, in the seminal *Grundrisse*, discusses the role of technology and more particularly, of automation under industrial capitalism.[170] As other authors confirm, albeit Marx acknowledged that the introduction of new machinery constituted an important requirement for the advent of the first Industrial Revolution, this very fact did not automatically mean that technology was the source or the cause of it.[171] According to Marx, the introduction into the labour process was and will continue to be dependent upon foregoing social organisation, specialisation and accumulation of wealth.[172]

At the same time though, there are voices that opt to recognise the role that technology can play as a driver of change. Hughes, for example, mentions that a technological system can be both a cause and an effect: it can shape or be shaped by society.[173] As he explains, more complex technological systems are capable of shaping society rather than being shaped by it; hence, the momentum of novel technological

165. For instance *see* Chandler, A.D.J., *Scale and Scope: the dynamics of industrial capitalism* (Harvard University Press 1994).
166. Mangan, D., *Ford, Taylor and the Gig: Workplaces in Transition* (Valeria Pulignano and Frank Hendrickx eds, *Employment Relations in the 21st Century: Challenge for Theory and Research in a Changing World of Work*, Kluwer Law International 2020), 23-28.
167. For instance, *see* Srnicek, N., *Platform Capitalism* (Polity Press 2017).
168. Aloisi, A. and De Stefano, V., *Your Boss Is an Algorithm: Artificial Intelligence, Platform Work and Labour* (Bloomsbury Publishing 2022); De Stefano, V. (2018), '"*Negotiating the Algorithm": Automation, Artificial Intelligence and Labour Protection*', 41(1), ILO Employment Working Paper N. 246, Geneva, ILO.
169. *Ibid.*
170. Marx, K., *Grundrisse: Foundations of the critique of political economy* (Penguin 2005).
171. *Supra*, Bimber (1990), 344-345; *see also* Gartman, D., *Marx and the Labor Process: An Interpretation*, 8 Insurgent Sociologist 97 n. 2-3 (1978), 97-108.
172. *Ibid.*
173. Hughes, T.P., *Technological Momentum* (Merritt R. Smith, M.R. and Leo Marx, L. eds, *Does Technology Drive History?: The Dilemma of Technological Determinism*, The MIT Press 1994), 112.

systems is a concept that can be positioned somewhere between the poles of technological determinism and social constructivism.[174] Following the same line of thought, Misa argues that views, which deny the significant material force that technology has on the direction of society are not solely inconsistent with everyday experience, but they also seem '*especially undesirable in an age of pervasive socio-technical problems*'.[175] Other authors, such as Rice and Emery, by rejecting arguments in favour of technological determinism, also seem to promote the idea of a mutual relationship between technology and societal structures.[176]

Overall, there was a time that technology was considered an 'independent force', insulated from other social developments. This rationale, likewise, seems to revive through the language used by many platform businesses. Still, especially within recent literature, such views seem to fade away. Technological innovation cannot be seen in isolation from other societal changes, something that of course is equally applicable within the world of work. This is the case not solely in terms of the creation of new businesses and occupations, but also in relation to the organisation of work itself. It does not come as a surprise, therefore, when some authors argue that innovation does not directly determine the organisational work structures or practices of businesses. Instead, the changes that new technologies bring about are inextricably linked with societal dynamics that can vary from one context to the other. This suggestion brings us to the second enquiry of this section, namely, as to whether the very organisational model of platform businesses represents a novel aspect in the world of work.

1.6.2 Old Practices in a New Wrapper

As noted and will be further discussed below, platform-mediated work is part of the overall phenomenon of NSFE, including the rise of an increased number of weak self-employed workers dependent upon their principals.[177] New technological tools, such as digital apps relying on algorithmic management, have enabled platforms businesses to engage with a large pool of workers that share different characteristics and needs.[178] In this digital environment, the link between demand and supply of different activities, which extend to multiple sectors of the labour market, takes place

174. *Ibid.*
175. Misa, T. J., *Retrieving Sociotechnical Change from Technological Determinism* (Merritt R. Smith, M.R. and Leo Marx, L. eds, *Does Technology Drive History?: The Dilemma of Technological Determinism*, The MIT Press 1994), 115-141.
176. Rice, A.K., *Productivity and Social Organization in an Indian Weaving Shed: An Examination of Some Aspects of the Socio-Technical System of an Experimental Automatic Loom Shed*, 6 Human Relations 297 n. 4 (1953), 297-329; Emery, F., *Characteristics of Sociotechnical Systems* (Tavistock Institute 1959).
177. Trends towards the casualisation of labour can be observed both within the context of developed and developing economies: For instance, *see* Eurofound, *Casual Work: Characteristics and Implications*, Luxembourg, Publications Office of the European Union, 2019; Van Der Linden, M., *Workers of the World: Essays Toward a Global Labor History* (Brill Academic Publishers 2008); De Stefano, V., *Casual Work Beyond Casual Work in the EU: The Underground Casualization of the European Workforce – and What to Do About It*, 7 European Labour Law Journal 421 n. 3 (2016), 421-441.
178. *See* the analysis below in Chapter 4.

at an enormously high speed that few could imagine in the past. To this extent, digital labour platforms and other businesses with alike characteristics are often described as 'disruptors' of established markets and firms.[179] It has been argued, for instance, that geographically tethered platforms, like taxi platforms, '*have disrupted established transportation business models by harnessing data and algorithms to match passengers with drivers in real time*'.[180]

Matching tasks as the ones just described, usually occur at a very low cost and '*without the need to abide by the protections associated with an employment relationship*',[181] despite the fact that much evidence suggests that such workers are subject to different forms of supervision and control, comparable to the ones that traditional employers exercise. Indeed, platforms can impose '*minimum acceptable standards*'[182] on workers and apply them via various disciplinary measures. They can, for instance, set the minimum wages for platform workers.[183] In addition, jobs may be posted on apps chiefly at certain times of the day; hence, to a certain extent, hours of work are dictated by platforms. On top of that, if the performance of work does not meet the requirements found within the terms and conditions of the contract in question, then platforms have the ability to expel anyone who did not meet the performance benchmarks.

Furthermore, most of the time, such working arrangements take place in a casual manner and more precisely in a '*"just-in-time" fashion and* [they are] *compensated on a "pay-as-you-go" basis*'.[184] In this regard, jobs offered via digital labour platforms, both crowdwork and work-on-demand via applications, are often referred to as '*the casual work of the 21st century*',[185] or as '*internet-enabled casual work*'.[186] At this point, it should be mentioned that, thus far, there is the absence of a unified definition of 'casual work', both at the European and international levels. Still, for the purposes of this research and by drawing on existing definitions within the literature, it suffices to say that casual work arrangements amount to jobs of a short-term, often intermediated and intermittent nature.[187] For example, the ILO defines them as '*work that is executed for a very short period, or occasionally and intermittently, often for a specific number of*

179. Vandaele, K. (2018), *Will Trade Unions Survive in the Platform Economy? Emerging Patterns of Platform Workers' Collective Voice and Representation in Europe*, ETUI Research Paper, Brussels, 8.
180. *World Employment and Social Outlook 2021: The Role of Digital Labour Platforms in Transforming the World of Work*, ILO, (2021) Geneva, 43, referring to Clewlow, R. Mishra, G., *Disruptive Transportation: The Adoption, Utilization, and Impacts of Ride-Hailing in the United States*, Research Report UCD-ITS-RR-17-07, Institute of Transportation Studies, University of California, Davis.
181. *Ibid.*, 8.
182. Healy, J., Nicholson, D., Pekarek, A., *Should We Take the Gig Economy Seriously?*, 27 Labour and Industry 232 n. 3 (2017), 232-248.
183. IPSOS, (2020), *High level summary of key findings*, Surveys commissioned by KU Leuven, 15.
184. Aloisi, A. (2020), *Hierarchies Without Firms? Vertical Disintegration, Outsourcing and the Nature of the Platform*, E-book 'Quaderni 8th Giorgio Rota Best Paper Award' 2020, 12.
185. De Stefano, V., *Labour Is Not a Technology: Reasserting the Declaration of Philadelphia in Times of Platform-Work and Gig-Economy*, 2 IUSLabor 1 (2017), 9.
186. Eurofound, (2015), *New forms of employment*, Publications Office of the European Union, Luxembourg, 47.
187. *Supra*, Freedland (2019), 100.

hours, days or weeks'.[188] In a similar vein, a study conducted by the European Parliament refers to such engagements as '*work which is irregular or intermittent with no expectation of continuous employment*'.[189] That said, as noted, many platforms, such as Deliveroo, Uber and Amazon Mechanical Turk, appear to reject the idea that they can be considered companies which rely their business model on these types of jobs. After all, as a study that was conducted for the ILO by the Institute for Labour Law at KU Leuven explains, most of the platform companies around the world offer contracts, which according to their terms and conditions are under no legal obligation to ever provide any work to the persons that are making use of the digital app.[190]

Indeed, hiding under the cloak of technological innovation, platform operators tend to defend the 'independent' ability of technology to bring about unprecedented organisational alterations within workplaces. They argue that as a result of these developments, people can work for themselves as self-employed persons, away from any supervision, or control. The question that arises, nonetheless, as Aloisi and De Stefano put it, is whether these forms of work along with the proliferation of self-employed workers '*correspond to truly "new" and "liberating" business models* [or they do constitute] *a rebrand of casualised forms of work*' that existed in the past.[191] A simple overview of literature related to this topic seems to suggest the latter argument.

More precisely, '*nothing new under the sun*',[192] '*as old as the hills*'[193] and '*old wine in new bottles*',[194] are just some of the phrases which have been utilised by labour lawyers and academics to portray the organisation of work practices of digitally mediated businesses. As Stanford contends, drawing on the work of others, these forms of work arrangements are characterised by five broad organisational elements.[195] First, work is taking place on an on-demand basis, and there is an absence of a guarantee for further provision of work. Second, payment for the work provided occurs on a piecework basis and not for the time spent in order to complete the task. Third, workers are required to supply their own tools and equipment. Fourth, the entity responsible for the work organisation is separate from the end-user, or the final consumer of the 'product' that results in a triangular relationship between the producer, the end-user and the intermediary. Finally, through the use of digital means, platform businesses are able to assign and outsource the work, supervise it, and facilitate payment. According to Stanford, the last feature is the only one that can be

188. *Supra*, ILO (2016), 22.
189. European Parliament, (2000), *Atypical Work in the EU*, Working Paper, Social Affairs Series, Luxembourg, 66, available at: https://ec.europa.eu/social/BlobServlet?docId=2440&langId=en (accessed 26 May 2021).
190. De Stefano, V., Durri, I., Stylogiannis C., Wouters, M. (2021), *Platform Work and the Employment Relationship*, ILO Working Paper, Geneva, ILO, 12-15.
191. *Supra*, De Stefano and Aloisi (2019), 361.
192. *Supra*, PRASSL (2018), 73-84.
193. Freedland, M., *New Trade Union Strategies for New Forms of Employment: A Brief Analytical and Normative Foreword*, 10 European Labour Law Journal 180 n. 3 (2019), 180.
194. *Supra*, Vandaele, (2018), 9.
195. *Supra*, Stanford (2017), 384-385.

said to be connected with recent technological developments.[196] Multiple other scholars seem to concur with this observation. For example, along the same lines, De Ruyter, Brown and Burgess have pointed out that platform work arrangements are solely '*novel in the sense that labor supply is matched to labor demand by an online platform*'.[197] As explained above though, these changes are neither neutral nor exogenous, as, at least to a certain extent, reflect the decisions and interests of competing constituencies.

That said, all the other features with respect to the organisation of work, as the aforementioned quotes indicate, are far from novelties. Work-related characteristics, such as short-term and often low-skilled jobs, on-demand, frequently intermediated and outsourced, even date back to the pre-industrial period and the putting-out system of home-based production, that was common in the manufacture of products, such as textile, clothing and footwear.[198] This system was comprised of merchants that were subcontracting various jobs to workers who in turn had to complete their tasks at home by using their own tools; there was no promise of re-engagement. A number of intermediaries were in charge of the selection and termination of workers and setting of payment, always on a piece basis. They were, moreover, responsible to provide the workers with the initial material necessary to accomplish their task, as well as to deliver detailed instructions as to how the job needs to be performed.[199] Directing the execution of tasks was a key responsibility for the intermediaries, as they were directly accountable to the merchants. In order to achieve this, they were exercising indirect control over the work of the so-called task force, either via economic pressures or through the threat of not offering a future assignment to those workers who were not following the instructions or complaining about their payments.[200] Upon the completion of the task, the goods were returned to the merchant or were passed on to the next worker. Furthermore, as historical evidence confirms the intermediaries in question used to retain a considerable amount from the wages of workers.[201] Do all these sound familiar? According to scholars, such as Prassl, absolutely:

> Technology apart, the essential features of most intermediaries' business models were identical to platforms' and apps' digital work intermediation in the on-demand economy: they acted as a broker for a set of tasks, exercised tight control, and took a cut of workers' earnings.[202]

Similar business models were also widespread in the post-industrial era with the emergence of 'task economies' that adopted a Tayloristic mode of production, moving away from the Fordist model that was characterised by the development of centralised technologies of mass production. Importantly, as the literature indicates, the working conditions of this 'older task force', in many cases, were characterised by poor conditions, low wages and general uncertainty for future work engagement. As

196. *Ibid.*
197. De Ruyter, M. Brown & Burgess J., *Gig Work and the Fourth Industrial Revolution: Conceptual and Regulatory Challenges*, 72 Journal of International Affairs 37 n. 1 (2019), 39.
198. *Supra*, Prassl (2018), 74-77.
199. *Ibid.*
200. *Ibid.*, 80.
201. *Ibid.*
202. *Ibid.*, 79.

Chapter 2 discusses, many of these characteristics can be also found within the context of platform work.

1.6.3 Platform Work and (Some of) Its Novel Complexities

It was argued that while much attention has been concentrated on the new digital technologies behind platform work, the majority of the elements observed regarding the organisation of work practices of digital labour platforms are far from novelties. They can be detected in the pre-industrial systems of production, as well as in the early stages of the Industrial Revolution.[203] This remark, nonetheless, by no means aims at suggesting that platform work is not capable of generating a number of new complexities and considerations in the world of work. This is a claim that can be accurate both as a matter of law, as labour law's existing protective framework can be put into question, and as a matter of fact, regarding the impact that platform work per se can have on workers more in general, albeit these two considerations can be inextricably linked. These novel complexities can justify the reference by some authors and institutions and in turn the inclusion of these types of work within the typology of what is often called 'new forms of work'.[204] Another inquiry that comes to the fore, therefore, is: which are the elements (or at least some of them) that distinguish platform work from earlier formats of casual work, such as those described above?

To begin with, as a matter of legal concern, the main difference between new forms of casual work and their pre-existing versions can be found when someone attempts to examine the specific period in time when these types of work have actually taken place. As Freedland suggests, earlier forms of casual work occurred in a time when labour laws and other workplace regulations, such as collective bargaining processes, were not that much concerned with the protection and prioritisation of secure and stable jobs over casual ones.[205] This 'omission', according to the same author, had permitted employers in previous eras to '*propose and implement casual work arrangements without special regard to the question of whether or not they came within the scope of such regulation as then existed*'.[206]

However, with the coming of the 20th century, the situation started to change. This is to say that to a great extent, labour law regulations and collective bargaining, at least within the context of Western economies, were developed on the premise of a long-term attachment to the same place of work, a feature that, as previously noted, constitutes a main characteristic of standard employment relationships.[207] Thus,

203. *See also* Wood, E.M., *The Origin of Capitalism: A Longer View* (Verso Books 2002).
204. *Supra*, Freedland (2019), 179-182; OECD, *Issues note: The emergence of new forms of work and their implications* for labour relations, 2018, available at: https://www.oecd.org/g20/topics/employment-education-and-social-policies/OECD-Note-on-The-emergence-of-new-forms-of-work.pdf (accessed 26 May 2021).
205. *Ibid.*, Freedland, 181.
206. *Ibid.*
207. As it is argued throughout this research, the vast majority of individual employment rights still remain within a stable and continuous relationship between the worker and the employer.

labour legislation and collective bargaining functioned with the intention of guaranteeing that standard employment arrangements normally prevailed over casual and precarious jobs.[208] This also elucidates the stunning, at least up until recently, numerical superiority of workers engaged in subordinated employment in a big number of national systems.

Still, in recent decades, what is observed and despite the existence of the aforementioned 'legal armoury', conceived to secure standard forms of employment, is the resurgence and re-deployment of casual work arrangements that are designed to circumvent existing legal regulations and institutions within modern labour markets. In other words, many of these arrangements, which are also expressed through platform work, are deliberately designed in such a way as to fall outside the protective scope of labour law. As noted, such trends occur in spite of the fact that the actual production process is largely not much diverse from production methods within subordinated forms of employment. It should be mentioned, moreover, that these issues have arisen not solely due to the efforts of many employers, like a large number of platform businesses, to evade and curtail the protections emanating from labour laws. They have also come to the surface due to the existence of specific regulations which have enabled their proliferation.

More specifically, as Adams and Deakin, among others, have pointed out, there is a plethora of deliberate policy decisions at various national levels, which have prioritised and facilitated the casualisation of work relationships and decline of wages over secure work and a living wage.[209] These policies can take the form of specific regulations that purposely, or unintentionally, give incentives to employers to utilise flexible work arrangements. For instance, this can occur when temporary workers are disqualified from severance payments.[210] In a similar vein, it can also be the absence of any regulatory environment that equally paves the way for the use of these types of jobs.[211]

Concluding with the legal concerns, it can be argued that modern casual forms of work, including platform work, have resurfaced in a manner that poses new challenges to regulations of labour law, which were construed with the aim of promoting secure employment. This is also the reason that, on many occasions, they have been perceived as having a disruptive effect on well-established regulatory approaches to the labour market.[212] As claimed, these complexities were not apparent with respect to earlier forms of casual work arrangements.

In addition to legal complexities, it should also be noted that platform work also has the potential to generate novel challenges when it comes to the operation of the work itself. Such an argument is inextricably related to what Stanford and other scholars have recognised as one of the 'cutting-edge' features of platform businesses,

208. *Supra*, Freedland, 181-182.
209. Adams, Z., Deakin, S., *Institutional Solutions to Precariousness and Inequality in Labour Markets*, 52 British Journal of Industrial Relations 779 n. 4 (2014), 780.
210. *Supra*, ILO (2016), 161.
211. *Ibid.*, citing Gleason, S.E. ed., *The Shadow Workforce: Perspectives on Contingent Work in the United States, Japan, and Europe* (Upjohn Institute for Employment Research 2006).
212. *Supra*, ILO, (2021), 29-101.

namely, the use of new technological tools to supervise the performance of work activities. Algorithms and Artificial intelligence (AI)enabled means have permitted platforms to monitor workers using their app, in an 'automated' manner that can be compared to that in factories, or office-based jobs, albeit platform workers lack close proximity due to the fact that they are geographically dispersed.[213] Of course, as some authors have pointed out, contemporary methods of the so-called digital Taylorism are far more advanced and pervasive than employers' physical methods of the past, where they used to rely on people's eyes and ears.[214] Thus, they 'pale' in comparison to certain contemporary techniques of surveillance, which can systematically direct, track and compare employee performance. Within this digital work environment, managerial prerogatives and powers can be magnified and extended.[215]

Indeed, digital reputation systems, such as those that exist via the Uber and Deliveroo apps, have replaced the old-style command and control approach in deciding the selection of platform workers and the quality of the completed task(s). More specifically, workers are assigned to the next job by the app's algorithm, which is programmed to assess the completing tasks based on the reviews of the customers, as well as by other factors, such as the speed of the work performed.[216] Quality control, therefore, not only can be crow-sourced by platforms but it is also left to algorithms to decide whether the tasks are completed according to the terms and conditions of the contract in question. As previously noted, workers who consistently get bad ratings are at risk of being excluded from the service.

Moreover, as De Stefano and Taes have recently observed, one of the chief ingredients necessary for algorithms to operate well is an enormous amount of data collected from workers' different activities via monitoring and tracking systems.[217] Valuable data gathering can literally take place every second of the day that workers are logged in to the app, for instance, even in the so-called dead miles, namely, moments when on-demand couriers moving around the streets while waiting for the next task to appear without getting paid to do so.[218] Such data are in turn '*processed by software to assess, among other purposes, their productivity and engagement*', thereby enhancing the functioning of algorithms through 'machine-learning' technologies.[219] In this regard, concerns have been expressed as, on many occasions, it seems to be a

213. Adams-Prassl J., *What If Your Boss Was an Algorithm? Economic Incentives, Legal Challenges, and the Rise of Artificial Intelligence at Work*, 41 Comparative Labor Law & Policy Journal 123 n. 1 (2019), 123-146.
214. Manokha, I., *The Implications of Digital Employee Monitoring and People Analytics for Power Relations in the Workplace*, 18 Surveillance & Society 540 n. 4 (2020), 540-554.
215. *Supra*, De Stefano (2018), 13-17.
216. Prassl, J. (2018), *Collective Voice in the Platform Economy: Challenges, Opportunities, Solutions*, ETUC Report, 12.
217. De Stefano, V., Taes, S. (2021), *Algorithmic Management and Collective Bargaining*, ETUI Research Paper, Brussels, 3; DAGNINO, E., *People Analytics: lavoro e tutele al tempo del management tramite big data*, 3 Labour & Law Issues 1 n. 1 (2017), 1-31; Bodie M.T., Cherry M.A., McCormick M.L., Tang J., *The Law and Policy of People Analytics*, 88 University of Colorado Law Review 961 n. 4 (2017), 961-1042.
218. Thomas, C., *Ride Oversharing: Privacy Regulation Within the Gig Economy*, 36 Cardozo Arts & Entertainment Law Journal 247 n. 1 (2018), 247-276.
219. *Ibid.*, De Stefano and Taes (2021).

lack of transparency and limited access to information on how exactly algorithms are programmed, by whom, under whose instructions and what is their exact aim.[220] For instance, an algorithm which is designed with the ultimate purpose of achieving the highest possible profitability will function in a different way compared to an algorithm that is intended to mitigate biases or disparities in parallel.[221] On top of that, the assembly of 'big data' can be also extended beyond workers' activities to '*the actions of ordinary people, consumers and small economic actors that use digital platforms*'.[222] As a consequence, both workers and consumers contribute, without any remuneration and in some instances, without their informed consent, to the stock of impalpable capital of platform companies. The latter, therefore, through the use of digital means and the subsequent creation of user-generated content, have to a considerable degree, the capacity to shape in their own terms, various aspects of the labour market and society in general. These, in the words of Drahokoupil and Jepsen, *inter alia*, include:

> how labour is being exchanged on digital platforms, how consumers are becoming producers (so-called prosumers), [...] how underused asset capacity can be shared at close to zero marginal cost [...] [and] how new monopolies are emerging.[223]

All in all, there are varied opinions vis-à-vis the peculiar challenges that 'new forms' of work, including platform work, can have with respect to the world of work and how the recent developments are shaping the future of labour relations. Often enough, a considerable number of these views are based on quantitative analysis, that is, discussions on the number of jobs which are likely to be vanished due to technological developments.[224] As seen, nonetheless, increased attention should be

220. Duggan, J., Sherman, U., Carbery, R., McDonnell, A., *Algorithmic Management and App-work in the Gig Economy: A Research Agenda for Employment Relations and HRM*, 30 Human Resources Management Journal 114 n. 1 (2020), 126.
221. Problems can also stem when data are used for purposes that are different than the initial aim of collecting such information. In this respect, the 'Working Party on the Protection of Individuals with regard to the Processing of Personal Data', a former advisory body of the EU set up under Article 29 of Directive 95/46/EC, had pointed out that: '*The increase of the amount of data generated by the IoT* [internet of Things] *in combination with modern techniques related to data analysis and cross-matching may lend this data to secondary uses, whether related or not to the purpose assigned to the original processing. Third parties requesting access to data collected by other parties may thus want to make use of this data for totally different purposes*'. Article 29 data protection working party, (2014), *Opinion 8/2014 on the on Recent Developments on the Internet of Things*, 14/ENWP 223, 16 September 2014, available at: https://www.pdpjournals.com/docs/88440.pdf. (accessed 24 June 2021).
222. Parminder, J.S. (2020), *Economic rights in a data-based society Collective Data Ownership, Workers' Rights, and the Role of the Public Sector*, Friedrich-Ebert-Stiftung, Global Policy and Development, 7, available at: http://library.fes.de/pdf-files/iez/16034.pdf (accessed 23 June 2021).
223. Drahokoupil J., Jepsen M., *The Digital Economy and Its Implications for Labour. 1. The Platform Economy*, 23 Transfer 103 n. 2 (2017), 104.
224. For instance, *see* Frey, C.B., Osborne, M.A., *The Future of Employment: How Susceptible Are Jobs to Computerisation*, 144 Technological Forecasting and Social Change 280 (2013), available at: https://www.oxfordmartin.ox.ac.uk/downloads/academic/The_Future_of_Employment.pdf (accessed 24 June 2021); Cellan-Jones, R. (2019), 'Robots "to replace up to 20 million factory jobs" by 2030', *BBC News*, 26 June 2019, available at: https://www.bbc.com/news/business-48760799 (accessed 24 June 2021).

also consecrated on the qualitative issues that platform work and alike job arrangements are posing to modern workplaces. Novel legal complexities, as well as practical problems, constitute important factors that need to be taken into serious consideration. The increased control over workers, data and 'digital intelligence' are chief components of power within the context of platform work by, as Parminder explains, '*increasingly shaping the global economic, social and political order*'.[225] As the following chapter discusses, such work arrangements can have severe implications in relation to the working conditions of workers and the overall enjoyment of their fundamental labour rights.

1.7 PLATFORM WORKERS: NOT SO INDEPENDENT AFTER ALL

For quite some time now, alterations in society and the economy, along with unprecedented technological advancements, have led to the rise of new employment arrangements, which are frequently positioned between traditional employment and self-employment. Many employers, through the decentralisation of working activities to subcontractors, freelancers, or the use of temporary employment agencies, have succeeded in escaping labour regulations and reducing their costs related to employment and social protection. As a consequence, the binary distinction between salaried workers and self-employed seems incapable of adequately depicting the economic and social reality of work.[226]

Many of these atypical categories of workers are engaged either in disguised employment relationships or find themselves in dependent-self-employment. Since the early months of the new millennium, the OECD raised a number of concerns regarding self-employment; such concerns, *inter alia*, touched upon the working conditions of these workers, including income insecurity, as well as the emergence of self-employment as a form of disguised employment.[227] As noted, around the same period, the so-called Supiot Report pointed out the existence of workers who cannot be regarded as employees, and yet are economically dependent on a single principal.[228] Since then, there is an abundance of evidence, which suggests that a considerable number of self-employed persons, particularly those who do not employ others, are resembling much more employees rather than genuine entrepreneurs.[229] Also, more and more people engaged in these types of atypical arrangements are facing a risk of in-work poverty.[230] As will be further discussed in Chapter 3, policymakers and courts

225. *Supra*, Parminder (2020), 1.
226. Rosioru, F., *The Changing Concept of Subordination* (György Kiss ed., *Recent Developments Labour Law*, Akadémiai Kiadó 2013), 150-185.
227. OECD, (2000), *OECD Employment Outlook*, Paris, OECD, 155-199.
228. *Supra*, Supiot (2001), 220.
229. For instance, *see* European Economic and Social Committee, (2010), *Opinion of the European Economic and Social Committee on new trends in self-employed work: the specific case of economically dependent self-employed work*, 29 April 2010, available at: https://www.eesc.europa.eu/en/our-work/opinions-information-reports/opinions/new-trends-self-employed-work-specific-case-economically-dependent-self-employed-work (accessed 5 April 2022).
230. For instance, *see* Ratti, L., *In-Work Poverty in Europe: Vulnerable and Under-Represented Persons in a Comparative Perspective* (Kluwer Law International 2022).

around the world, at least to a certain extent, have recognised the issues surrounding such workers. For instance, an intermediate category of workers, between employees and the self-employed, has been established in some countries; hence, some national legislations give dependent self-employed persons a set of protections without (re-)classifying them as employees. In other words, economic dependence is not used as proof of employment status (at least in the majority of the situations), but rather as a condition that necessitates some sort of protection.[231] The adequacy of intermediate categories will also be examined below.

As seen, platform work arrangements are inextricably linked to the current conversations on self-employment and more specifically, on weak self-employed workers. Since the advent of the platform economy, there has been a powerful narrative of labour platforms unleashing autonomy and independence, capable of leading to a new generation of entrepreneurs. Certainly, there are cases, especially when it comes to high-skilled platform workers, in which such a description can be accurate.[232] Still, as explained above and will be further discussed below, this is not the case for a considerable part of workers in the platform economy. Often enough, as many studies also indicate, many of these workers are not possessing the levels of professional independence, let alone the absence of any entrepreneurial opportunities.[233] To this extent, work arrangements of this kind can exhibit a comparable degree of economic and operational dependence on employees. For instance, many platform operators determine the work schedule and the manner in which the work needs to be performed. They can also determine prices algorithmically, with no input from or without the knowledge of the parties involved.[234] On top of that, as seen, the supervision of work can be also outsourced to the customers of the platforms through the use of rating systems. It can be argued, therefore, that in a number of instances, many platform workers who are considered self-employed do not conform to the ideal of entrepreneurship that is marked by ownership, control over production, and autonomy.

Platform businesses have emerged as dominant players in modern labour markets. Their powers are often associated with monopolistic and monopsonistic tendencies.[235] While their success has some potential benefits for consumers, for example, through the provision of services at low prices, their dominance has also led to '*winner-take-all dynamics*'; thus, granting them powerful monopolies by precluding

231. For an analysis, *see* Perulli, A. (2003), *Study on Economically Dependent Work/Parasub ordinate (Quasi-Subordinate) Work*, Brussels, European Parliament.
232. Hauben, H., Lenaerts, K., Waeyaert, W., (2020), *The Platform Economy and Precarious Work*, Publication for the committee on Employment and Social Affairs, Policy Department for Economic, Scientific and Quality of Life Policies, Luxembourg, European Parliament.
233. Todoí-Signes, A., *The Gig Economy: Employee, Self-Employed or the Need for a Special Employment Regulation?*, Transfer: European Review of Labour and Research, 23, 193-205 (2017), 199.
234. For instance, *see* Rosenblat, A., Stark, L., *Algorithmic Labor and Information Asymmetries: A Case Study of Uber's Drivers*, 10 International Journal of Communication 3758 (2016), 3758-3784.
235. For instance, *see* Howson, K., Ferrari, F., Ustek-Spilda, F., Salem, N., Johnston, H., Katta, S., Heeks, R., Graham, M., *Driving the Digital Value Network: Economic Geographies of Global Platform Capitalism*, 22 Global Networks 631 n. 4 (2022), 631-648.

new entrants from coming in.[236] The examples of Uber and Lyft, for instance, and their attempts to become monopolies in their respective industry, are illustrative of such tendencies. Not only this but the sectors and businesses likely to be subjugated by platform operators are constantly growing.[237] The latter's capacity to monopolise, control and sell data ('data-opolies') gives such businesses another distinguished advantage compared to 'old business models'.[238] Such an ability also enables them to provide cheap services.

All in all, the concertation of labour market power has allowed platform operators to exercise a tremendously high degree of economic and bargaining power that, as noted, has been illustrated in their ability to fix wages, control their workforce, and often escape labour and employment laws. On the other side of the spectrum, many self-employed platform workers, who possess a considerably weak bargaining position compared to their principals, still face exclusions from labour law protections, including the effective exercise of their collective labour rights.

1.8 INTERMEDIATE CONCLUSIONS

As the first Chapter initially demonstrated, many of the problems in respect of labour law's protective framework are not novel. The vertical disintegration of firms, along with the reduction of labour costs, the blurring lines between employment and self-employment and the proliferation of atypical work arrangements, are all issues which have been present for quite some time. This is not to say that new and more complex issues are not arising within the context of modern workplaces. As seen, for instance, new digital technologies, like the use of algorithms, have, in a number of instances, replaced the old-style command and control that used to be exercised by traditional employers. As a result, as will be further elaborated in Chapter 3, some of the legal tests for the determination of the existence of an employment relationship may fail in offering firm answers to modern challenges, especially if interpreted in a rather narrow way.

That being said, the majority of current challenges within modern workplaces can also be observed through the lens of platform work, which constitutes an important 'case study' of what is actually happening in the world of work in the 21st century. Its importance lies in both quantitative and qualitative considerations. Concerning the former, the number of platform workers is increasing at a rapid pace year by year. Some commentators even suggest that in the next few years, one in three

236. Platform Revolution, (2014) 'The Dark Side of Platform Monopoly', *Online Blog*, available at: https://platformthinkinglabs.com/materials/the-dark-side-of-platform-monopoly/ (accessed 2 November 2022).

237. Parker, G., Van Alstyne, M., Jiang, X., *Platform Ecosystems: How Developers Invert the Firm*, 41 Management Information Systems Quarterly 255 n. 1 (2017), 255-266. A monopsony is a market condition that takes place when in a given market there are only a few buyers of labour services or even only one. This situation can negatively affect the services of service providers.

238. Stucke, M., Maurice E., *Should We Be Concerned About Data-Opolies?*, 2 Georgetown Law Technology Review 275 n. 2 (2018), 275-324.

labour transactions will be mediated by digital labour platforms.[239] Such an estimation, if accurate, shows that the demand for such workers will be even higher in the near future than nowadays. What is more, from a qualitative perspective, as Chapter 2 discusses, the situation can be particularly problematic with respect to the working conditions of platform workers, including the enjoyment of their fundamental collective labour rights. Against this background, platform work should not be seen in isolation from the problems other atypical workers face with respect to their labour protection. On top of that, as will further be developed below, some of these issues can also be pertinent for workers in standard employment relationships, such as concerns in relation to mechanisms of pervasive surveillance and privacy at work.[240]

239. *See*, for instance, Standing, G., *The Corruption of Capitalism: Why Rentiers Thrive and Work Does Not Pay London* (Biteback Publishing 2016).
240. For instance, *see* Hendrickxx, F., *From Digits to Robots: The Privacy-Autonomy Nexus in New Labor Law Machinery*, 40 Comparative Labor Law & Policy Journal 365 n. 3 (2019), 365-388.

CHAPTER 2

The Effect(s) of Platform Work on Working Conditions and Collective Labour Rights and the Overall Impact on the Field of Labour Law

2.1 INTRODUCTION

After having identified the particular features of platform work, Chapter 2 delves into the implications that such characteristics have on the labour protection of platform workers, including the exercise of their collective labour rights. In doing so, Chapter 2 initially focuses on the working conditions of platform workers, which, as will be shown, are often associated with the concept of precariousness. Such a discussion will take place based on the findings of socioeconomic and empirical studies. In turn, this chapter will refer to both the legal and practical obstacles platform workers are facing with respect to the enjoyment of their collective labour rights, such as the rights to freely associate and bargain collectively. In relation to the legal impediments, an extensive reference will be made to the challenges which arise from the clash between labour law and competition law. Finally, Chapter 2, based on a foundational approach to labour law, will evaluate the possible implications that platform work can have on the very field of labour law and the main foundation(s) upon which the latter was developed.

2.2 WORKING CONDITIONS OF PLATFORM WORKERS

2.2.1 Precarious Work: Terminological Considerations

Within academic literature which attempts to illustrate the working conditions of platform workers, the reader often encounters the terms precariousness[241] and precarity.[242]These nouns, at least among Western scholars, are often employed interchangeably in order to depict the insecure and vulnerable position that platform workers often find themselves in. What can also be observed is that in many instances, '*the term "precarity" might have replaced "precariousness" with the advantage of a prompt neologism*'.[243] Before further engaging in more detail with the actual working conditions of platform workers, it is worth mentioning the main differences between these two terms. The reason behind this endeavour lies in the fact that precarity as a concept is often associated with Western conceptions of precarious work arrangements.

Precarity, or *precarité* in its current expression, emerged in the language of French sociologists and their efforts to comprehend the convergence of struggles by unemployed and intermittent workers in the late 1990s.[244] In recent academic literature, one of the most influential analyses of this term stems from the work of Guy Standing, who is considering that under neoliberalism and the construction of a globalised market economy, workers are no longer having a fair share in the gains from economic growth.[245] Such gains are going to those who own physical, financial and intellectual property. As a result, the emergence of a new working class can be observed, the so-called precariat.[246] This 'new' social class, according to the author, is formed by people being habituated to a life of unstable and insecure labour. Moreover, these workers along with the lack of several forms of secure labour, such as their exclusion from health and safety regulations, also have to deal with an insufficient social income, the absence of various community benefits and the lack of an occupational identity.[247] Therefore, as it has been argued, the notion of precarity assumes two claims. First, the fact that precarity is a relatively new concept that indicates a distinctive phase of the evolution of capitalism and more specifically the neoliberal

241. For instance, *see* Berg, J., *Protecting Workers in the Digital Age: Technology, Outsourcing, and the Growing Precariousness of Work*, 41 Comparative Labor Law & Policy Journal 69 n. 1 (2019), 69-94.
242. For instance, Sutherland, W., Jarrahi, M.H., Dunn, M., Nelson, S.B., *Work Precarity and Gig Literacies in Online Freelancing*, 34 Work, Employment and Society 457 n. 4 (2020), 457-475.
243. Mitropoulos, A. (2005), 'Precari-US?', *Tranversal* (blog), 3 March 2005, available at: https://transversal.at/transversal/0704/mitropoulos/en (accessed 2 October 2020).
244. *Ibid.*
245. Standing, G., *The Precariat: The New Dangerous Class* (Bloomsbury Academic 2014).
246. *Ibid.*
247. This idea of precarity as a rather political concept that does not solely touches upon the working conditions of precarious workers, has been also embarrassed by some authors: For instance, *see* Neilson, B., Rossiter, N., *Precarity as a Political Concept, or, Fordism as Exception*, 25 Theory, Culture & Society 51 n. 7-8 (2008), 51-72.

era.[248] Second, it refers to the precaritisation that takes place within neoliberalism, a system that is capable of bringing about class alterations that in turn transform collective identities and politics.[249]

Though really influential, Standing's approach as well as the general inclination in Western scholarship to add *'an aura of newness to the precarity'*[250] that certain types of workers are facing, has not escaped critique(s) by some scholars. Scully, for instance, opposes the view of Standing that precarity constitutes a 'novel' universal phenomenon, as within the context of the global South, precarity, has for a long time constituted a condition that characterises the working conditions of many workers, especially in low and main income regions.[251] Or, as Munck put it: *'the Southern experience of precarity is marked by the nature of the postcolonial state and, later, by the developmental state where this has emerged'*.[252]

Moving on to the concept of precariousness, it has also been employed in literature to *'confer general, pervasive ontological condition of vulnerability, displacement, and insecurity'*.[253] The main difference between this term to precarity lies in the fact that it is not principally tied to the contemporary system of neoliberalism and its tendency to generate a new social class, characterised by insecure and poor working conditions for workers. Precariousness, instead, as a term, is tied to more generic characteristics that have been formed throughout history.[254] Even though it can have multiple definitions, precariousness at work, as the ILO confirms by adopting a broad description, is typically conceived as work poorly paid, insecure in terms of the continuation of employment and unprotected, where workers have no say about their working conditions, wages and the hours of work.[255] According to the ILO, moreover, precariousness is not something that is exclusive to NSFE; it can also be found in standard employment relationships.[256] Following the same rationale, it would be an overstatement to argue that all non-standard jobs are precarious.

Debates on the differences between precarity and precariousness and as to whether a distinct and new global precariat in fact exists have not yet been resolved. On many occasions within the literature, such terms continue to be used interchangeably. In this research, however, as a matter of coherence, the term preciousness (or, the expression precarious work) is preferred, as it seems to be a more universally accepted

248. Kasmir, S. (2018), 'Precarity', *The Cambridge Encyclopedia of Anthropology*, 13 March 2018, available at: https://www.anthroencyclopedia.com/entry/precarity (accessed 26 October 2020).
249. *Ibid.*
250. Soriano, C.R., Cabanes, J.V., *Entrepreneurial Solidarities: Social Media Collectives and Filipino Digital Platform Workers*, 6 Social Media and Society n. 2 (2020), 2, available at: 2056305120926484 (accessed 5 May 2021).
251. Scully, B., *From the Shop Floor to the Kitchen Table: The Shifting Centre of Precarious Workers' Politics in South Africa*, 42 Review of African Political Economy 295 n. 128 (2016), 295-311.
252. Munck, R., *The Precariat: A View from the South*, 34 Third World Quarterly 247 n. 5 (2013), 273.
253. *Supra*, Kasmir (2018).
254. *Ibid.*
255. *Supra*, ILO (2016), 18.
256. *Ibid.*

term. This is important, especially when reference is made to a global phenomenon, such as platform work.

2.2.2 General Working Conditions of Platform Workers Around the World

Undoubtedly, work facilitated via platforms has the potential to offer new and more flexible – mostly in terms of time and location – opportunities to people that are seeking employment. Indeed, as a survey commissioned by KU Leuven and prepared by IPSOS confirms, a considerable number of the 72 respondents valued the flexibility associated with platform work.[257] In some cases, this type of work also seems to match better the needs of those who have duties of a special nature, such as care responsibilities, or those who are homebound because of health problems, or disabilities.[258] Moreover, it has been argued that the factor of 'anonymity' which is regularly observed in these types of work arrangements, especially with respect to crowdwork, is capable of reducing phenomena of occupational-related prejudice(s), by facilitating the access to either local or global labour markets for groups of workers that are often the victims of discrimination.[259]

Concomitantly though, platform work, irrespective of its online or offline nature, is often associated with problematic employment practices, poor working conditions, and job insecurity.[260] Furthermore, as Blackham mentions, issues faced by a plethora of platform workers mirror but also contribute to the emergence of broader labour market trends towards casualisation, triangulated work relationships, the demutualisation of the risks of employment, the globalisation of work, and the move to non-standard work.[261] To this extent, as recent research conducted to inform the Committee on Employment and Social Affairs of the European Parliament points out, platform-mediated work may encourage undeclared work that is difficult to be detected by enforcement agencies, especially when it takes place online.[262]

That said, there are not a few occasions that the human labour provided via platforms is perceived as a commodity that can be sold to the markets like any other article of commerce. This position does not constitute a personal opinion but rather the views of the CEOs of some of the biggest platforms globally. For example, it was back in 2006 when Jeff Bezos, the CEO of Amazon's 'crowdworking' marketplace Mechanical Turk, famously noted that humans could be used as services through the assistance

257. IPSOS, (2020), *High level summary of key findings*, Surveys commissioned by KU Leuven, 5.
258. *Supra* OECD (2019), 31; *supra*, Codagnone *et al.* (2016).
259. Graham, M., Hjorth, I., Lehdonvirta, V., *Digital Labour and Development: Impacts of Global Digital Labour Platforms and the Gig Economy on Worker Livelihoods*, 23 Transfer: European Review of Labour and Research 146 n. 2 (2017), 146-147.
260. *Supra*, Berg J. (2016); CIPD, (2017), *To Gig or Not to Gig? Stories from the Modern Economy*, Chartered Institute of Personnel and Development, London.
261. Blackham, A., *We are All Entrepreneurs Now': Options and New Approaches for Adapting Equality Law for the 'Gig Economy'*, 34 International Journal of Comparative Labour Law and Industrial Relations 413 n. 4 (2018), 415-416; *see also* Rubery, J., Grimshaw, D., Keizer, A., Johnson. M., *Challenges and Contradictions in the 'Normalising' of Precarious Work*, 32 Employment and Society 509 n. 3 (2018), 509-527.
262. *Supra*, Pesole *et al.* (2018).

of technology.[263] Lukas Biewald, one of the two founders of Figure Eight, likewise stressed that:

> Before the Internet, it would be really difficult to find someone, sit them down for ten minutes and get them to work for you, and then fire them after those ten minutes. But with technology, you can actually find them, pay them a tiny amount of money, and then get rid of them when you don't need them anymore.[264]

It does not come as a surprise therefore that these views, to a great extent, reflect the reality with respect to the working conditions within platform work arrangements around the world. As noted, the emergence of platform work is not a phenomenon that only occurs within the so-called advanced economies. Studies conducted in 2017 revealed that there were approximately 70 million registered digital workers globally, with a significant portion of them to be located in the Global South.[265] As an illustration, Insight2Impact, a global research centre, relying on available data collected from just seven African countries, found that 4.8 workers have earned an income via platform work.[266] The latter, in some instances, is not solely perceived as an attractive choice by individual workers in terms of income and lifestyle in general, but it can be also seen as a driver of development by governments.[267] In the Philippines, for example, Soriano and Cabañes, by reflecting on the work of others, contend that many workers find in platform work the opportunities they want to earn a better salary and access the global labour market in relatively better working conditions compared to other sectors.[268] Research also indicates that in some cases, Indian platform workers have managed to successfully supplement their income through working with platforms.[269] Of course, the reference to better salaries and conditions at work is taking place in a national context and the position of these workers cannot be contrasted to their counterparts in Western societies. It can be argued though that indeed for some people, especially in the context of the Global South, platform work can offer some opportunities to elevate their living standards. However, this bright side is only a limited approach to the overall emergence of these types of economic activities. Academic literature and further research conducted on the topic reveal some more problematic aspects.[270]

263. Irani, L., *The Cultural Work of Microwork*, 17 New Media & Society 720 n. 5 (2013), 720.
264. Kalleberg, A.L. and Dunn, M., *Good Jobs, Bad Jobs in the Gig Economy*, 20 Perspectives on Work 10 (2016), 1.
265. Graham, M. and Anwar, M. A., *The Global Gig Economy: Towards a Planetary Labour Market*, 24 First Monday 1 n. 4 (2019), 3.
266. Insight2impact. (2019), *Africa's Digital Platforms and Financial Services: An Eight-Country Overview*, Johannesburg.
267. Graham, M. and Anwar, M. A., *Between a Rock and a Hard Place: Freedom, Flexibility, Precarity and Vulnerability in the Gig Economy in Africa*, 25 Competition & Change 237 n. 2 (2020), 240.
268. *Supra*, Soriano and Cabanes (2020), 2-7.
269. Beerepoot, N. and Lambregts, B., *Competition in Online Job Marketplaces: Towards a Global Labour Market for Outsourcing Services?*, 15 Global Networks 236 n. 2 (2015), 236-255.
270. For instance, *see* Rani, U., Gobel, N., Rishabh K.D., *Is Flexibility and Autonomy a Myth or Reality on Taxi Platforms? Comparison Between Traditional and App-Based Taxi Drivers in Developing* Countries (Valerio De Stefano, Ilda Durri, Charalampos Stylogiannis and Mathias Wouters eds, *A Research Agenda for the Gig-Economy and Society*, Edward Elgar Publishing 2022), 167-192.

For example, in relation to the aforementioned hopes for economic development and better working conditions, empirical evidence suggests that such optimism can be misleading. According to the ILO, as far as the Asia-Pacific region is concerned, access to work mediated via platform businesses continues to be unequally distributed.[271] This is because, in many countries, there is a significant division between rural and urban populations. People working in rural areas have much less chances to get a job in the platform economy, especially when platform work occurs offline, in sectors such as transportation and delivery, or other services that are designed to take place in specific locations.[272] As such, the elimination of poverty and the bridge of wealth inequalities is not something that should be taken for granted. The same can also be argued regarding many African countries. As Graham and Amir Anwar argue, despite hopes that platform work has the potential to constitute a pathway out of poverty as well as out of the informal economy (at least as the World Bank indicated),[273] until now, there is no empirical evidence to prove this.[274] What exists, contrariwise, is the documentation of the poor working conditions for many workers engaged with platform work in these regions, let alone, the unchanging rates of informality.[275]

The main reason behind this phenomenon, as empirical research also confirms,[276] is the fact that the overwhelming majority of platform workers are considered independent contractors; a factor that automatically excludes them from a wide range of employment and collective bargaining regulations -the latter issue will be further discussed in subsequent chapters. In other words, the self-employment status, or in many instances the lack of formal employment status of workers means that most of the platform businesses are not legally bound to comply with labour regulations that touch upon areas such as health and safety regulations, a minimum wage,[277] limitations in working hours, sick pay and annual leave. Workers, moreover, engaged with crowdwork, face intense competition as they have to compete with other crowdworkers from all over the world. It has been observed, for instance, that Kenyan and Nigerian workers have experienced situations of being outcompeted due to lower bids offered by Indian, Bangladeshi and Filipino workers who have a reputation for bidding

271. ILO, *World Employment and Social Outlook: Trends 2020*, Geneva, ILO (2020).
272. *Ibid.*, 57.
273. World Bank, (2016), *World Development Report 2016: Digital Dividends*. Washington D.C, World Bank.
274. *Supra*, Graham and Anwar (2020), 3-6.
275. *Ibid.*, 1-22.
276. For instance, *see* Fairwork, (2019), *The Five Pillars of Fairwork: Labour Standards in the Platform Economy*, Fairwork Foundation, Oxford, UK, available at: https://fair.work/wpcontent/uploads/sites/97/2019/10/Fairwork-Y1-Report.pdf (assessed 9 December 2020); Fredman S., du Toit D., Graham, M., Howson K., Heeks R., van Belle J.P., Mungai P., Osiki A., *Thinking Out of the Box: Fair Work for Platform Workers*, 31 King's Law Journal 236 n. 2 (2020), 236-249.
277. Despite the fact that in some countries like South Africa, some platform workers are gaining more than the average minimum wage, the fact that they are responsible to both provide and maintain the equipment necessary to perform their work has as a result that their salary falls below it. (Fairwork, (2020) *Fairwork South Africa Ratings 2020: Labour Standards in the Gig Economy*, Cape Town, South Africa; Oxford, UK; Manchester, UK, available at: https://fair.work/wpcontent/uploads/sites/97/2020/03/Fairwork-South-Africa-2020-report.pdf (assessed 9 December 2020).

at particularly low prices.[278] Moreover, there are some cases, especially in relation to crowdworkers, where even if they complete their job, clients refuse to pay them if they decide that they are not satisfied with the final result.[279] Many workers, as a consequence, due to the lack of labour-related protections, remain unpaid, notwithstanding their effort and time spent on specific tasks. Despite the fact that in some countries like South Africa, a small number of platforms have started taking steps towards ameliorating the working conditions of their workers; such instances are limited.[280]

The inherent precariousness that often characterises platform work in emerging economies is also apparent in the Global North. Of course, once again, someone should be mindful when comparing the working conditions in different regions and contexts, as the threshold of 'decent' working conditions can vary. Moreover, also in the context of advanced economies, platform workers do not constitute a homogeneous category. In this respect, there is a number of workers, especially the ones with high skills, who can benefit through their engagement in the platform economy or workers who have gained access to labour markets that were not possible before. These jobs, as noted, can also be a good option for people who desire a more flexible work schedule.

Still, multiple studies conducted by official institutions, accompanied by disaggregated data on selected types of platform workers in different European countries, reveal a variety of problems in relation to the working conditions of a great portion of workers engaged in the platform economy.[281] The same can also be argued for the US, despite the fact that there is not the same amount of disaggregated information available.[282] In both contexts, the main problems can be attributed to the fact that the vast majority of such workers are hired and labelled as independent contractors, despite the fact, as is also explained in other parts of this research, that the real nature of the job may indicate a disguised employment relationship that hides the true legal status of these workers. As a consequence, they are often facing low and insecure incomes with unpredictable working hours. An ILO research, for instance, indicates that approximately 75 per cent of American workers surveyed on Amazon Mechanical Turk, earned less than the federal minimum wage.[283] On top of that, platform workers and especially crowdworkers can spend a significant amount of time on work that is

278. *Supra*, Graham and Anwar (2020), 13.
279. *Ibid.*, 15.
280. *Supra*, Fairwork (2020).
281. De Groen, W. P., Kilhoffer, Z., Lenaerts, K., and Mandl, I. (2018), *Employment and working conditions of selected types of platform work*. Luxembourg, Publications Office of the European Union; European Commission (2020), *Study to gather evidence on the working conditions of platform workers*, available at: https://ec.europa.eu/social/main.jsp?catId = 738&langId = en&pubId = 8280 (accessed 20 March 2020); *Supra*, Pesole *et al.*, (2018); IPSOS, (2020), 'High level summary of key findings', *Surveys commissioned by KU Leuven*.
282. Ravenelle, J.A., *Hustle and Gig: Struggling and Surviving in the Sharing Economy* (University of California Press 2019); DeVault, I., Figueroa, M., Kotler, FB., and Maffie MD. (2019), *On-Demand Platform Workers in New York State: The Challenges for Public Policy*, Report from the Worker Institute at Cornell University.
283. ILO. *Digital labour platforms and the future of work: Towards decent work in the online world*, ILO, (2018) Geneva.

not compensated, such as looking for tasks and researching the profiles of possible clients in order to make sure that their work will be paid upon its completion.

Research supported by surveys on selected types of platform work, furthermore, suggests that many workers have to deal with poor career prospects and limited training opportunities that will enhance their chances to adjust to the new realities of modern labour markets.[284] Concerns have also been expressed with respect to the risks they are facing regarding health and safety-related problems.[285] For example, the absence of annual leave and limited rest breaks for workers engaged with delivery apps and in general on-location platforms could generate health and safety issues. Fatigue, especially for riders and drivers, can contribute to a higher risk of accidents. These workers, in the majority of cases, are also responsible for providing and maintaining their own equipment and tools needed to perform the job. Besides the fact that such a responsibility can further reduce their income, it can also be dangerous. This is due to the fact that the increased competition that characterises platform work may push workers to undertake tasks for which they do not have the right equipment or have no experience to take on, even in instances they are actually sick.[286]

2.2.3 The COVID-19 Impact on Platform Workers

At the time of writing this research, a pandemic is on the rise. Up until September 2020, more than 87 million have been infected worldwide, with more than a million deaths occurring.[287] The global outbreak of COVID-19 and the restriction measures as a result of it have profoundly affected workers around the world, as well as the economy as a whole.[288] According to ILO estimates, labour income losses reveal a global decline of 10.7 per cent during the first three quarters of 2020 compared to last year; this amounts to USD 3.5 trillion, or 5.5 per cent of global gross domestic product (GDP) for the first

284. *Supra*, DE Groen, *et al.*, (2018); Huws, U., Spencer, N.H., Syrdal, D.S., Holts, K. (2017), *Work in the European Gig Economy: Research Results From the UK, Sweden, Germany, Austria, the Netherlands, Switzerland, and Italy*, Foundation for European Progressive Studies Report (2017), available at: http://unieuropaprojects.org/content/uploads/europeagigeconomy-longversionpdf.pdf (accessed 20 March 2019).
285. Cefaliello, A., Inversi, C., *The Impact of the Gig-Economy on Occupational Health and Safety: Just an Occupation Hazard?* (Valerio De Stefano, Ilda Durri, Charalampos Stylogiannis and Mathias Wouters eds, *A Research Agenda for the Gig-Economy and Society*, Edward Elgar Publishing 2022), 33-51.
286. *Supra*, Pesole et al., (2018); Garben, S. (2017), *Protecting Workers in the Online Platform Economy: An Overview of Regulatory and Policy Developments in the EU*, European Risk Observatory Discussion Paper 2017, Luxembourg, Publications Office of the European Union, available at: https://osha.europa.eu/sites/default/files/publications/documents/Protecting_Workers_in_Online_Platform Economy.pdf (accessed 26 February 2019).
287. Worldometer, *Covid-19 Coronavirus Pandemic*, available at: https://www.worldometers.info/coronavirus/ (accessed 7 January 2021).
288. World Bank, (2020), *The Global Economic Outlook During the COVID-19 Pandemic: A Changed World*, 8 June 2020, Feature Story, available at: https://www.worldbank.org/en/news/feature/2020/06/08/the-global-economicoutlookduringthecovid19pandemicachangedworld#: ~ :text =Businesses%20might%20find%20it%20hard,by%20almost%208%25%20in%202020 (accessed 9 September 2020).

three quarters of 2019.[289] In addition, hundreds of millions of jobs have been lost, with the numbers expected to grow as the virus persists.[290]

It makes no surprise, therefore, as a recent OECD analysis points out, that many workers in NSFE, including platform workers, are at a particularly high risk as they are especially vulnerable to income or job losses.[291] In a similar vein, research followed by a survey that was conducted by the Appjobs Institute[292] found that platform workers are among the hardest hit economically by the COVID-19 pandemic.[293] As the same research highlights, while the health crisis has resulted in an increase in global demand with respect to specific jobs, such as the provision of delivery services, the demand for other occupations, including cleaning and housesitting, has been considerably affected.[294] Moreover, according to the Online Labour Index,[295] freelance jobs provided via online labour platforms have also been reduced to a great extent.[296] Furthermore, on many occasions, platform workers are not receiving any form of sickness or income support. Thus, the current situation is also capable of increasing existing inequalities between standard and non-standard employment, as the welfare policies addressed to workers in the latter category are, by comparison, more limited, and they require more time to be implemented.[297]

A series of comprehensive studies conducted by the Fairwork Foundation, focusing solely on geographically tethered platforms, constitutes a useful guide as to how the COVID-19 crisis has exacerbated the already vulnerable position of platform workers around the globe. Only in March 2020, reports suggested that half of platform workers lost their jobs and many had to face the harsh choice between destitution and

289. *ILO Monitor: COVID-19 and the world of work,* sixth edition, Geneva, ILO (2020), 1.
290. *Ibid.*
291. OECD, (2020), *Distributional risks associated with non-standard work: Stylised facts and policy considerations,* OECD Policy Responses to Coronavirus (COVID-19), OECD Publishing, Paris, available at: http://www.oecd.org/coronavirus/policy-responses/distributional-risks-associated-with-non-standard-work-stylised-facts-and-policy-considerations-68fa7d61/ (accessed 6 January 2021).
292. The survey conducted through an online platform to compare app-based jobs around the world. The survey can be found at: https://www.appjobs.com/blog/coronavirus-effect-on-gig-economy (accessed 6 January 2021).
293. Moulds, J. (2020), 'Gig workers among the hardest hit by coronavirus pandemic', *World Economic Forum,* 21 April 2020, available at: https://www.weforum.org/agenda/2020/04/gig-workers-hardest-hit-coronavirus-pandemic/ (accessed 6 January 2021); the negative effects of the pandemic on platform workers' payments can be also observed in the surveys prepared by IPSOS (*Supra*, IPSOS (2020).
294. *Ibid.*
295. '*The Online Labour Index (OLI) is the first economic indicator that provides an online gig economy equivalent of conventional labour market statistics. It measures the supply and demand of online freelance labour across countries and occupations by tracking the number of projects and tasks across platforms in real time*', available at: https://ilabour.oii.ox.ac.uk/online-labour-index/ (accessed 6 January 2021).
296. Fabian, S. (2020), 'Pandemic's effects on online freelance work: distancing dividend or downscaling loss?', *On-line Labour Index: Covid-19,* 2 April 2020, available at: https://ilabour.oii.ox.ac.uk/pandemics-effects-on-online-freelance-work-distancing-dividend-or-downscaling-loss/ (accessed 6 January 2021).
297. OECD, (2020), *Organisation for Economic Co-operation and Development,* COVID-19: Protecting people and societies, available at: https://read.oecd-ilibrary.org/view/?ref=126_126985-nv145m3l96&title=COVID-19-Protecting-people-and-societies (accessed 6 January 2021).

infection.[298] They have also been facing a considerable loss of income. In the US, for instance, during the pandemic, salaries continue to shrink due to increased competition, with many unemployed workers seeking a source of income through the platform economy.[299] The situation does not seem to be better in the Global South. Drivers in countries such as Indonesia, Vietnam, and Thailand have reported a significant loss in revenue from ride-hailing services, while there is no evidence that platform businesses have taken any steps to compensate workers for their loss of income.[300]

Particularly challenging, moreover, is the situation as far as health and safety regulations are concerned. Recent studies indicate that even though a bigger number of platforms have started to offer sick pay – especially in countries like the UK and Germany – such schemes still remain largely unavailable to workers, especially in the context of emerging economies.[301] It has also been observed that not all platform workers have access to preventive measures, including the provision of disinfectants and protective masks. Even in situations where they actually do have access to such equipment, then these distributions are often one-off and despite the fact that personal protective equipment should be continuously replaced and maintained, as it is one of the most effective ways for workers to protect themselves against the virus.[302]

Various platform companies have adopted specific measures in order to mitigate the risks stemming from the pandemic. As noted, in some instances, such initiatives have taken the form of financial aid directed to assist platform workers. Uber, for example, has offered approximately 50,000 delivery riders and drivers the amount of USD 19 million as a financial boost.[303] Considering, however, that Uber has almost 4 million registered drivers and riders, many workers remain excluded from some sort of support. In the UK, Hermes, a courier platform company, has established a fund with the purpose of providing sick pay for its millions of couriers.[304] Importantly, the platform has also pledged to assist its workers '*in finding a substitute driver to cover their shift while guaranteeing that roles are left open for them when they return*'.[305] Likewise, ProntoPro, an Italian freelance platform, has provided its workers with a one-off 'convalescence allowance' of EUR 1500 in the event of hospitalisation and a one-off payment of EUR 350 in case of a compulsory quarantine.[306] Similar policies

298. Fairwork, (2020), *The Gig Economy and Covid-19: Looking Ahead*, Fairwork Foundation, Oxford, UK, available at: https://fair.work/en/fw/publications/the-gig-economy-and-covid-19-looking-ahead/ (accessed 6 January 2021).
299. *Ibid.*, 15.
300. *Ibid.*
301. *Ibid.*, 21.
302. *Ibid.*
303. Bellon, T. (2020), 'Uber Has Spent $19 Million on Coronavirus Financial Assistance for Drivers', *Reuters*, 21 May 2020, available at: https://uk.reuters.com/article/uk-health-coronavirus-uber/uber-has-spent-19-million-on-coronavirus-financial-assistance-for-drivers-idUKKBN22X1XQ (accessed 9 September 2020).
304. Gilbert, S. (2020), 'COVID-19: A unique challenge for gig-sector businesses', *Lexology*, available at: https://www.lexology.com/library/detail.aspx?g=d401d8ef-ffce-4769-b750-65bf7f18b627 (accessed 6 January 2021).
305. *Ibid.*
306. OECD, (2020), *What have platforms done to protect workers during the coronavirus (COVID-19) crisis?*, OECD Publishing, Paris, 2020, 6.

have also been taken by other platforms around the world, especially the ones that are experiencing a greater demand during the crisis.[307]

In addition to financial support, a number of platform businesses have also adopted different measures which attempt to address health and safety-related concerns. To this extent, the majority of them worldwide have proceeded with the introduction of 'contact-free services', or on some occasions, 'cash-free services', in order for the physical distance with clients to be reduced to the bare minimum.[308] For example, in Dubai, Quiqup, a logistics company that provides on-demand delivery services, published a step-by-step instructional video to guide its workers as to how to perform a contactless delivery.[309] It has been noticed, however, that these kinds of services are mostly directed at the protection of the customers instead of workers' well-being.[310] It is difficult for couriers, for instance, to avoid close contact with the personnel that prepares the food in restaurants. That said, a data collection exercise that the OECD carried out in collaboration with the AppJobs Institute suggests that a small amount of platform businesses have allowed their workers to have greater control over which tasks they need to undertake. In this way, they are able to accept less risky and/or better-paid tasks. Illustrative in this regard is the policy assumed by Shipt, a labour platform in the US, which has allowed its workers to preview the shopping list for an order before accepting it so that they could choose the orders they think are dangerous in such circumstances. As the same research also observes, only a limited number of platforms have reported offering or reimbursing the costs of purchasing personal protective equipment, such as masks and hand sanitisers.[311]

In light of the risks that arise from COVID-19, some governments have also adopted exceptional protective strategies aimed at pertaining to the platform economy. Such policies, *inter alia*, encompass the extension of financial relief packages. In Finland, for instance, the national authorities have announced that self-employed and freelance workers, including platform workers, are eligible for unemployment benefits until the pandemic comes to an end.[312] In Denmark, the government introduced a temporary compensation scheme which captures, among others, platform workers who expect a loss of income; through this initiative, they will be able to receive '*75% of the expected loss of turnover in the period compared to the average turnover in the latest fiscal year*'.[313] Analogous developments can be observed in countries, like the UK and Italy.[314] Still, as the Fairwork Foundation highlights, the accessibility to these types

307. *Ibid.*, 6-7.
308. *Supra*, Fairwork (2020), 19-20.
309. *Supra*, OECD (2020), 5.
310. *Supra*, Fairwork (2020), 16.
311. *Supra*, OECD (2020), 6.
312. ETUC, (2020), *National measures to protect non-standard workers including workers in the platform economy*, ETUC Briefing Note.
313. Eurofound, 'Temporary compensation scheme for self-employed persons – measures in Denmark', 15 April 2020, available at: https://static.eurofound.europa.eu/covid19db/cases/DK-2020-11_624.html (accessed 3 March 2020).
314. Eurofound, (2020), 'Platform economy: Developments in the COVID-19 crisis', 3 July 2020, available at: https://www.eurofound.europa.eu/el/data/platform-economy/dossiers/developments-in-the-covid-19-crisis (accessed 3 March 2020).

of schemes remains unknown.[315] Finally, along with the provision of financial support, some governments and health authorities have also made it compulsory for platforms to offer certain types of protection to their workers, such as the disinfection of vehicles and the provision of personal equipment against the virus.[316]

Overall, it can be argued that the existing poor working conditions of many platform workers, especially the ones engaged with location-based apps, have further deteriorated due to the negative impacts of COVID-19. Platforms initiatives, such as the provision of sick pay, as well as government actions with financial relief packages, have increased, providing some workers with additional support. Nonetheless, in a global context, such efforts do not seem to be enough, neither in quantity nor coverage. Job losses, reduction of income, and exposure to occupational hazards are just some of the issues that platform workers have to come across on a daily basis. Ironically enough, it is the pandemic itself that made many people realise that these workers perform crucial to society functions, as during this period, they have maintained essential public services, including delivering food and household essentials to those self-isolating or practising social distancing and providing care services to those in need.

2.3 THE IMPACT OF PLATFORM WORK ON COLLECTIVE LABOUR RIGHTS

Within the context of modern labour markets, platform-mediated work can be indeed beneficial for a variety of reasons, including, among others, the creation of new jobs and the choice of flexibility when workers consider that the latter matches better their personal needs. Still, as the first Chapter discussed, such work arrangements can be particularly problematic from a labour law perspective. Their dark side is often comprised of low wages, irregular hours, short-term and often low-skilled tasks, on-demand, frequently intermediated and outsourced, and of course, an often obscure employment status. The latter aspect is indeed the source of many of the issues that platform workers are facing.

As new forms of work are becoming more diverse and self-employment continues to be on the rise, especially as far as platform work is concerned, the problems in relation to labour protection are becoming perceptible to an even greater extent. As noted, the majority of platform businesses tend to 'enlist' workers and label them as independent contractors, even though the real nature of the job may indicate a disguised employment relationship. Simultaneously, as it is illustrated within the literature, the amount of digital labour platforms that allow their workforce to perform services under a contract of employment and therefore enjoy employee status is very limited.[317] Not only this, but most of the platform operators, by unilaterally

315. *Supra*, Fairwork (2020), 26.
316. *Ibid.*
317. *Supra*, De Stefano, V., Durri, I., Stylogiannis, C., Wouters, M. (2021), 12.

determining the terms and conditions of their engagement, also seem to suggest that the relationship of the worker with the client remains one of self-employment.[318]

It makes no surprise that workers' classification as self-employed (or, independent contractors) is profitable for many platforms. This is to say that it limits their liability and nullifies all protections afforded by collective bargaining and employment laws. A source from New York Times, for instance, indicates that for platform businesses, it would cost an average of 20 per cent to 30 per cent more if they were to classify platform workers as employees rather than as independent contractors.[319] Despite any repercussions this tactic may have for taxpayers and societies at large, its effects are particularly challenging for workers themselves.

Indeed, due to this treatment, a great portion of platform workers are facing severe difficulties, both practical and legal, in the exercise of their fundamental collective labour rights, such as the rights to freedom of association and collective bargaining.[320] As a matter of law, the mixture of legal and practical obstacles may seem strange at first. However, as this research explains, practical impediments can, at least to a certain extent, cause problems as serious as legal obstacles. Moreover, omissions to prevent practical challenges may also interfere with the positive obligations national systems have in promoting the effective application of such rights.[321]

The rights to freely associate and bargain collectively are enshrined in a number of constitutions around the world.[322] Such rights are inextricably linked. As the ILO Committee on Freedom of Association (CFA) has multiple times indicated, the right to collective bargaining constitutes an essential element of the right to freedom of association.[323] Among other supervisory bodies, this is also confirmed by the European Court of Human Rights (ECtHR) in the seminal case of the landmark case of *Demir and Baykara*.[324] At the international level, those rights have also been included in the 1998 ILO Declaration on Fundamental Principles and Rights at Work.[325] The rights and principles enshrined in the Declaration are considered to be universal and therefore should be applicable to all workers in all ILO Member States, by the very fact of their

318. *Ibid.*
319. Meneghello, R. (2018), 'Gig Economy Business Model Dealt a Blow in California Ruling', *The New York Times*, 30 April 2018, available at: https://www.nytimes.com/2018/04/30/business/economy/gig-economy-ruling.html (accessed 8 October 2021).
320. For instance, *see* Stylogiannis, C., '*Freedom of Association and Collective Bargaining in the Platform Economy: A human Rights-Based Approach and an Over Increasing Mobilization of Workers*', 162 International Labour Review 1 n. 1 (2021).
321. *See* discussion in Chapters 5 and 6.
322. For instance, *see* Fudge, J., *Constitutionalizing Labour Rights in Europe* (Tom Campbell, Keith D. Ewing and Adam Tomkins eds, *The Legal Protection of Human Rights: Sceptical Essays*, Oxford University Press 2011), 244-267. Fudge, J., *The New Discourse of Labour Rights: From Social to Fundamental Rights?*, 29 Comparative Labour Law & Policy Journal 29 (2007), 29-66; Tucker, E., *The Constitutional Right to Bargain Collectively: The Ironies of Labour History in the Supreme Court of Canada*, 61 Labour/Le Travail 151 (2008), 151-180.
323. ILO CFA (2018), *Freedom of Association. Compilation of decisions of the Committee on Freedom of Association*, Geneva, ILO, para. 1232.
324. *Demir and Baykara v. Turkey*, App. no. 34503/97 [2008].
325. ILO Declaration on Fundamental Principles and Rights at Work, 1998. Specifically, the Freedom of Association and Protection of the Right to Organise Convention, 1948 (No. 87), the Right to Organise and Collective Bargaining Convention, 1949 (No. 98).

membership and irrespective of ratification of the relevant conventions. As will be further discussed below, such rights are also part of the 'universal list' of human rights, as they have been incorporated into a number of international human rights instruments.[326] This is also something that is confirmed by many judgments, or international and national supreme courts.[327] Platform work, therefore, can be particularly challenging from a human rights law angle as well.

Many of the restrictions that platform workers are facing are inextricably associated with the existing limitations of the labour law framework, where labour protection, including the enjoyment of collective labour rights, still and by large, remains concentrated within 'subordinate' wage employment and more specifically of a full-time and open-ended nature. In this respect, as Dorssemont points out *'the employment contract is often seen to be gateway to the application of labour law'*.[328] At the same time, as noted, self-employed workers are usually excluded from the majority of the existing labour protections, as they are conceived as being capable of defending themselves in the market. Moreover, there are still some national jurisdictions in which the majority of self-employed workers are prevented from being members of trade unions, or there is no clear right for them to become members of a union.[329]

On top of that, such rights can also be restricted, in instances where platform workers' working activities come into clash with another area of law, namely, competition law. In this respect, such workers are often restricted from joining trade unions, and they - de facto - fall outside the scope of collective agreements, which largely rely on employment status for coverage. This occurs because of the existence of strict antitrust laws, which consider self-employed workers (including many workers in the 'grey zone') as undertakings. Specifically, the introduction of minimum employment terms and conditions can be considered as price-fixing to the detriment of consumers and fair competition; hence, collective agreements as such can infringe competition law.[330] As it is examined below, when the discussion focuses on a number of practical examples of platform workers' mobilisation, a strict application of these rules has already excluded a considerable portion of the workforce engaged in the platform economy from the coverage of collective agreements.[331]

It should also be claimed that in addition to legal obstacles, platform workers also have to deal with practical hurdles upon attempting to exercise their collective rights. This can be the case even if they are considered employees of the platform in question. Of course, as Aloisi observes, such practical issues are widespread within the realm of

326. *See* discussion in Chapter 5.
327. For instance, *see* ECtHR, *Demir and Baykara v. Turkey* (2008) ECHR 1345; Supreme Court of Canada, *Dunmore v. Ontario (AG)*, [2001] 3 S.C.R. 1016, 2001 SCC 94; Supreme Court of Canada, *Ontario (AG) v. Fraser*, [2011] SCC 20.
328. Dorssemont, F., *Collective Workers' Rights for Workers in the Gig Economy* (Maria T. Carinci and Filip Dorssemont eds, *Platform Work in Europe: Towards Harmonisation?*, Intersentia 2021), 209.
329. Fulton L. (2018), *Trade Unions Protecting self-Employed Workers*, ETUC, Brussels, 30.
330. Lianos, I., Countouris, N., De Stefano, V., *Re-thinking the Competition Law/Labour Law Interaction: Promoting a Fairer Labour Market*, 10 European Labour Law Journal 291 n. 3 (2019), 291-333.
331. *See* discussion in Chapter 4.4.1.

NSFE in the sense that '*non-standard workers are barely in physical, temporal and linguistic proximity and may have multiple and conflicting agendas as well as opposite needs and preferences*'.[332] These realities can indeed render the exercise of collective labour rights, like the right to the freedom of association, less attractive. It is, therefore, an amalgamation of the limitations of labour law's current framework, the latter's clash with competition law and the very nature of platform work per se that can impede the enjoyment of the rights at issue.

2.3.1 Restrictions on the Right to Freely Associate

Two important bodies in charge of supervising the application of ILO standards by Member States, namely, the ILO CFA and the CEACR, have both observed that there are many occasions in which workers in non-standard work arrangements are finding serious impediments in their attempt to exercise their rights to freedom of association and bargain collectively.[333] As De Stefano argues, in some instances, the restrictions are going '*as far as* [completely] *denying access of non-standard workers to collective rights*'.[334] Indeed, in some national legal orders, such workers due to their employment status as self-employed persons may be prohibited from joining trade unions or, trade unions of their choice.[335] Platform workers represent an illustrative example of these issues.

To begin with, in relation to the right to freely associate, the very nature of platform work can impose significant constraints on the enjoyment of the right at issue. One of the main reasons behind this phenomenon can be attributed to the way that platforms' rating systems are functioning. As the literature indicates, work arrangements, such as those found in the context of platform work, where reputation and rating systems play a key role for workers to maintain their employment, or access better-paid jobs, may prevent workers from freely associating, including their right to join a trade union.[336] As it has been argued elsewhere, such a restriction can occur as workers in temporary contracts, irrespective of their employment status, can be exposed to what De Stefano names '*an implicit-threat mechanism*'.[337] According to the author, this notion underlines their hesitation to properly exercise their contractual and labour rights due to a fear that their contract will not be renewed, or lengthened.[338] They also fear that their reputation may be negatively affected for future engagements,

332. Aloisi, A. (2019), *Negotiating the Digital Transformation of Work: Non-standard Workers' Voice, Collective Rights and Mobilisation Practices in the Platform Economy*, EUI Working Paper No. 3. San Domenico di Fiesole, European University Institute, 2.
333. *Supra*, ILO, 2016.
334. De Stefano, V., *Non-Standard Work and Limits on Freedom of Association: a Human- Rights Based Approach*, 46 Industrial Law Journal 185 n. 2 (2017), 185.
335. *Supra*, ILO (2016), 209.
336. De Stefano, V., Aloisi, A. (2019), *Fundamental labour rights, platform work and human rights protection of non-standard workers* (Bellace, J. and Ter Haar, B. eds, *Research Handbook on Labour, Business and Human Rights Law*, Research Handbooks in Human Rights Series, Elgar Publishing), 369.
337. *Ibid.*
338. *Ibid.*

thereby, in some instances, leaving them outside of the labour market. As previously explained, these issues are particularly pertinent for platform workers. This is to say that digital labour platforms have the capacity to punish 'unwanted activism' by simply erasing the profile of workers from their database without any further justification. Both crowdworkers and workers-on-demand can be affected by this fear irrespective of their employment status. It can be argued though that workers who are not considered employees, can be even more unprotected from these risks, as they lack access to protective employment and labour laws, such as protections against unfair dismissals.

Furthermore, on top of the so-called implicit-threat mechanism, there are additional reasons why platform workers and other workers in NSFE can face difficulties in properly exercising their right to freedom of association. Once more, such problems can be connected to the nature of their job. More specifically, they have a lower probability to unionise due to a variety of practical reasons which, *inter alia*, include frequent turnovers, a limited attachment to a single workplace, and fissured workplaces; as a result, it can be considerably difficult to create a common collective identity.[339] Moreover, many traditional trade unions, at least up until recently, were also hesitant to engage these types of workers in their actions.[340] To this extent, literature also indicates that some unions were of the opinion that the inclusion of non-standard workers and especially those in self-employment in their policies, could cause friction with the interests of their existing members.[341] Concomitantly, workers in NSFE, on many occasions, are of the opinion that their particular interests cannot be properly represented through traditional unions.[342]

Moreover, and in relation to platform workers' attempts to freely associate, someone should not omit to make a reference to another significant restriction that is often uninvestigated. Such a constraint stems from the very resistance of digital labour platforms to facilitate collective efforts by workers to organise themselves. In this regard, as Prassl points out, platforms' resistance can take different forms, including among other things, instant rejections of unionisation efforts, setting up of alternative representation arrangements to compete with traditional worker representatives, and putting forth arguments that collective bargaining would not be appropriate for flexible work arrangements of this kind.[343] These issues will be further discussed below in more detail, together with the specific challenges related to the unionisation of platform workers.

Finally, as noted, there are still some countries in which self-employed workers are still prohibited from joining trade unions, or vice versa trade unions are not allowed to incorporate such workers. According to a report conducted for the ETUC, Bulgaria,

339. *See* discussion in Chapter 4.
340. Heery, E., *Unions and the Organizing Turn: Reflections after 20 Years of Organising Works*, 26 The Economic and Labour Relations Review 545 n. 4 (2015), 545-560; Gumbrell-McCormick, R., *European Trade Unions and 'Atypical' Workers*, 42 Industrial Relations Journal 293 n. 3 (2011).
341. *Ibid.*
342. *See* the discussion in Chapter 4.
343. Prassl J., *Collective Voice in the Platform Economy: Challenges, Opportunities, Solutions*, ETUC Report (2018), 14-16.

Hungary and Romania are illustrative of this phenomenon.[344] It should be mentioned, however, that this is not the case for the majority of countries. In this regard, some domestic jurisdictions have recently amended their legislation, also at the constitutional level, in order to ensure that all workers have the right to freedom of association.[345]

2.3.2 Restrictions on the Right to Collective Bargaining

The limits to the protection of fundamental labour rights for platform workers are also evident with respect to the right to collective bargaining. As noted, the extension of such a right to workers who are classified as self-employed, including sham self-employed persons - platform workers are often among these workers - may be seen as breaching competition law. In one of his most recent contributions, Alan Bogg recalls an early essay written by Lord Wedderburn back in 1995, in which the latter investigated the relationship between labour law and competition law.[346] He prophesied that within the European legal order, competition law would generate an immense danger towards the functions of autonomous trade unions and the exercise of collective bargaining across the continent.[347] Lord Wedderburn could not be more precise in what he was writing back in the 1990s. His prediction, moreover, is relevant not only for Europe but also in relation to other parts of the world, such as the US.[348] As Cengiz observes, on both sides of the Atlantic, '*competition laws have become a disciplining mechanism against collective worker action*'.[349]

Indeed, competition authorities around the world have been using their influence to target certain categories of workers, including platform workers, who have concluded collective bargaining agreements on the ground that these are price-fixing agreements between undertakings; hence, these agreements are capable of hampering competition, a phenomenon that in turn can negatively impact the overall welfare of consumers.[350] Under this perspective, the protection of consumers' welfare from anti-competitive practices by sellers is perceived as the chief objective of competition law. According to some scholars, nonetheless, what is often overlooked is the '*process that takes place before consumers meet products and services, and the position of*

344. *Supra*, Fulton (2018), 6.
345. According to an ILO research these countries are: Chile, El Salvador and Kenya. *Supra*, ILO (2016), 257.
346. Bogg, A., *Economic Coordination as Freedom of Association* (Shae McCrystal, Ewan McGaughey and Sanjukta Paul eds, *The Cambridge Handbook of Labor in Competition Law*, Cambridge University Press 2022), 27-56.
347. *Ibid.*
348. For instance, *see* Paul, S.M., *The Enduring Ambiguities of Antitrust Liability for Worker Collective Action*, 47 Loyola University Chicago Law Journal 969 n. 3 (2016), 969-1048.
349. Cengiz, F., *The Conflict Between Market Competition and Worker Solidarity: Moving from Consumer to a Citizen Welfare Standard in Competition Law*, 41 *Legal Studies* 73 (2020), 87.
350. *Ibid.*, 73-90; *see also* Biasi, M., '*We Will All Laugh at Gilded Butterflies*'. *The Shadow of Antitrust Law on the Collective Negotiation of Fair Fees for Self-Employed Workers*, 9 European Labour Law Journal 354 n. 4 (2018), 354-373.

workers within it'.[351] Additionally, the interpretation given by courts in cases of conflict between competition law and collective bargaining can be also problematic and lead to severe restrictions on collective labour rights; this is something that, in turn, can also cause conflicts between different sources of supranational and international law, e.g., between EU regulation on the one side and ILO and CoE instruments on the other.[352]

Under EU law, the rules relevant to our discussion thus far are to be traced in Articles 101 and 102 of the Treaty on the Functioning of the European Union (TFEU). They respectively forbid agreements of an anti-competitive nature and abuses of dominance by one, or more undertakings, which can be the only entities subject to these regulatory instruments.[353] EU competition rules, therefore, can apply to collective activities of workers if the latter are to be regarded as 'undertakings'. In this respect, the jurisprudence of EU courts has also confirmed that the concept of an undertaking under Article 101(1) TFEU includes an association that acts on behalf of self-employed workers.[354] At the same time, in accordance with EU competition law, the conclusion of collective agreements is permitted under two antitrust exemptions, which stem from the 1999 ruling of the Court of Justice of the European Union (CJEU) in the seminal case of *Albany*.[355] More precisely, the famous Albany exception takes place when collective agreements constitute: '(1) *the outcome of collective negotiations between organisations representing employers and workers*'[356] and (2) *have the purpose to 'jointly adopt measures to improve conditions of work and employment*'.[357] In other words, the CJEU held that collective bargaining for employees should fall outside the scope of competition law. It has been argued that this decision was not reached due to the status of collective bargaining as a fundamental labour right, but rather for reasons that were, *inter alia*, related to the promotion of social dialogue in the EU.[358] It is important to recall that back in 1999, the right in question was neither recognised as a fundamental right under Article 28 of the EU Charter of Fundamental Rights (CFREU), nor the latter had acquired the same legal value as an EU Treaty,[359] something that it actually happened in 2009 with the Treaty of Lisbon.

351. *Ibid.*, 74; *see also* Davidov, G., *Collective Bargaining Laws: Purpose and Scope*, 1 International Journal of Comparative Labour Law and Industrial Relations 81 (2004), 1-20.
352. *Supra*, De Stefano and Aloisi (2019), 378.
353. This notion of what constitutes an undertaking was first established in Case C-41/90 *Höfner and Elser*; For a thorough analysis of the concept of undertaking, *see*: Daskalova, V., *Regulating the New Self-Employed in the Uber Economy: What Role for EU Competition Law?*, 19 German Law Journal 461 n. 3 (2018), 461-508.
354. *Supra*, Lianos, Countouris and De Stefano (2019), 301.
355. Case C-67/96 *Albany International BV v. Stichting Bedrijfspensioenfonds Textielindustrie* [1999] ECR I-5751.
356. *Ibid.*, para., 62.
357. *Ibid.*, para., 59. For an analysis, *see* Monti, G., *Collective Labour Agreements and EU Competition Law: Five Reconfigurations*, 17 European Competition Journal 714 n. 3 (2021), 715-716.
358. *Supra*, Bogg (2022), 51-52.
359. The CFREU, since 2009 and the adoption of the Lisbon Treaty, obtained a direct effect, as provided for by Article 6(1) TEU; hence, it became a binding source of EU primary law.

In a more recent development, the so-called *Albany* exception was upheld and extended in the famous judgment of the CJEU in *FNV Kunsten*.[360] In this case, the CJEU had to rule on the validity of a collective agreement concluded in the Netherlands. Negotiated by the Dutch FNV Union, the agreement aimed at addressing the working conditions of both employed and self-employed substitute orchestra players, including beneficial provisions with respect to their compensation. By relying on the previous case law of the CJEU, the antitrust authorities in the Netherlands issued an opinion according to which the conclusion of the agreement was not supposed to be exempted from antitrust laws, as it was negotiated in favour of self-employed orchestra workers. As a consequence, the agreement was declared null and void by the Dutch authorities. This decision was not accepted by the FNV Union. The latter initiated judicial proceedings in order to defend the validity of the collective agreement. The domestic procedures eventually led to a referral to the CJEU.

The Court reinstated its previous position that collective bargaining agreements in favour of self-employed workers cannot be exempted from the scope of competition law. It points out, however, that '*in today's economy it is not always easy to establish the status of some self-employed contractors as "undertakings", such as the substitutes at issue in the main proceedings*'.[361] As such, it went on to introduce a new element to the *Albany* exemption so that in addition to 'employees', it also incorporated the category of 'false self-employed' persons, whose situation is 'comparable to that of employees.[362] As far as the term 'employee' is concerned, the CJEU noted that '*for the purpose of EU law must itself be defined according to objective criteria that characterise the employment relationship*'.[363] In this regard, the judgment indicates that according to well-established jurisprudence of EU courts, the '*essential feature of that relationship is that for a certain period of time one person performs services for and under the direction of another person in return for which he receives remuneration*'.[364]

Commenting on this very paragraph, as well as the overall assessment made by the CJEU, De Stefano and Aloisi have expressed their concern with respect to the interpretation of the 'direction' criterion.[365] In relation to the latter, they argue that as it stands may '*limit the right to collective bargaining only to workers in an employment relationship defined under a strict test of control and subordination*'.[366] What is therefore problematic with an approach as such is the emphasis given by the CJEU on criteria traditionally used to establish an employment relationship. As noted, and it will be further elaborated below, within modern labour markets, work has become considerably more heterogeneous than in the past, and the lines which divide self-employed and employed persons are much less apparent. The digitalisation of workplaces has exposed such realities to an even greater extent. In light of these

360. Case C-413/13 *FNV Kunsten Informatie en Media v. Staat der Nederlanden* [2014] EUECJ C-413/13 (*FNV Knusten*).
361. *Ibid.*, para. 32.
362. *Ibid.*, para. 31.
363. *Ibid.*, para. 34.
364. *Ibid.*
365. *Supra*, De Stefano and Aloisi (2019), 373.
366. *Ibid.*

developments, a strict reliance on control and direction as the one that the Luxembourg Court expressed in the *FNV Kunsten* case is indeed possible to leave a big portion of weak self-employed workers, such as many platform workers, without any protection against the attacks of competition law. Concomitantly, the 'niche' element of the *FNV Kunsten* judgment to the *Albany* exemption towards antitrust laws, namely, the inclusion of the 'false self-employed' category, is likely to be applicable solely '*to blatant cases of employment misclassification*'.[367] This is also the reason why Alan Bogg refers to this case as a missed '*golden opportunity*' for a more inclusionary approach and arguments which would also be based upon the recognition of the right to collective bargaining as a fundamental right under EU law.[368]

A more inclusionary method, for instance, could have derived from Advocate General Wahl's Opinion. He, more specifically, argued for a wider interpretation of the *Albany* exemption by permitting collective agreements to cover (genuine) self-employed workers if their goal is to prevent social dumbing; a situation that can also negatively affect employees in specific sectors of the labour market.[369] In the case at issue, applying the terms and conditions of the collective agreement to self-employed musicians could avert '*social dumping in the form of replacement by less paid workforce and thus it could secure the collectively agreed wage settings for the employees*'.[370] Arguably, the merit of such an approach is extremely important considering the constant efforts of powerful businesses within modern workplaces, like digital labour platforms, to avoid labour expenses, by relying on precarious self-employed workers. After all, as AG Wahl underlined, it is the CJEU itself, which has previously ruled in more than one case that '*the objective of preventing social dumping may, in principle, constitute an overriding requirement in the public interest which is capable of justifying a restriction on the fundamental freedoms*'.[371] The Court though, in the FNV Knusten decision, appeared to neglect the AG's Opinion and his view that the prevention of social dumping constitutes '*an objective that can be legitimately pursued by a collective agreement*'.[372]

The legal developments within the EU legal framework illustrate only one of the examples concerning the inherent tension between competition law on the one hand and labour law and the enjoyment of collective labour rights on the other hand. Leaving EU law on the side for a moment, this can also be observed in the US. More precisely, the 1914 Clayton Antitrust Act explicitly states that: '[t]*he labor of a human being is not a commodity or article of commerce*'. As such, '[n]*othing contained in the antitrust laws shall be construed to forbid the existence and operation of labor* [...] *organizations, instituted for the purposes of mutual help,* [should not] *be held or*

367. *Ibid.*, 373.
368. *Supra*, Bogg (2022), 52.
369. Opinion of Advocate General Wahl in Case *C-413/13 FNV Kunsten*, 77-79; *see* analysis from Doherty, M., Franca, V. (2020), 'Solving the "Gig-saw"? Collective Rights and Platform Work', 49 *Industrial Law Journal*, 3, 352-376; *Supra*, Lianos, Countouris, and De Stefano, V. (2019), 300-321.
370. *Supra* Biasi (2018), 368.
371. Opinion of Advocate General Wahl in Case *C-413/13 FNV Kunsten* (delivered on 11 September 2014), 80.
372. *Ibid.*, 79.

construed to be illegal combinations or conspiracies in restraint of trade, under the antitrust laws'.[373] The Clayton Act came as a response to the Sherman Act of 1890, through which employers by invoking its sections I and II used to attack collective actions by workers.[374] That said and despite an explicit reference to the motto: 'labour is not a commodity', as Cengiz observes, antitrust laws on the other side of the Atlantic can be especially severe towards workers. According to the author, as well as further academic literature, this situation can be attributed to the rather restrictive judicial test(s) adopted by both the US Supreme Court and Federal courts in applying the exemptions towards antitrust laws, an approach that can indeed commodify labour.[375] In this regard, Sanjukta Paul argues that the interpretation given to antitrust laws in the US has espoused a trajectory of neoclassical economics, which perceives '*market actors as black boxes: they are just "firms", whether they are massive corporations or a single truck driver*', whose salary and overall bargaining power are considerably low.[376]

On top of that, different courts also have extended labour exemptions to protect collective actions by employers from the intervention of antitrust authorities; this is something, that as some have explained, comes into contrast with '*the explicit intention of Congress to protect workers and not employers*'.[377] It is not within the scope of this section, or research to further engage in the legal developments regarding the conflict between labour law and competition law in the US. A reference as such though, constitutes another illustrative paradigm of the difficulties that many low-wage workers, who may not meet the legal test for employee status, can face in the enjoyment of their collective labour rights.

2.3.3 Platform Work and Human Rights Risks in a Nutshell

Based on the above discussion, it can be claimed that platform work has the potential to impose serious restrictions on the enjoyment of fundamental collective labour rights that, as noted and will be further analysed below, have also been recognised as human rights. It should be also added that the exclusive focus of this research on such rights does not intend to imply that platform work cannot equally impede the exercise of other (individual) human rights. Once again, such restrictions can be attributed to the particularities of platform work, along with issues related to workers' employment status. Workers falling outside the protective framework of an employment relationship can be exposed to certain dangers to an even greater extent when compared to employees. It has been argued, for instance, that the very nature of platform work has generated a growing concern in relation to incidences of discrimination that are linked

373. Clayton Antitrust Act 1914 15 US Code § 17.
374. *Supra*, CENGIZ (2020), 82-85; *supra*, PAUL (2016), 969-1048.
375. *Ibid.*, CENGIZ 82; *see also* Evans, D.S., Padilla, A.J., *Designing Antitrust Rules for Assessing Unilateral Practices: A Neo-Chicago Approach*, 72 University of Chicago Law Review 73 (2005), 73-98.
376. *Supra*, Paul (2016), 977.
377. *Ibid.*, 87.

to algorithmic decision-making.[378] The severe implications that new technological tools can have on workers' privacy rights and the collection of big data have been another matter of concern.[379] Research, moreover, indicates that rating or scoring systems are not trustworthy with respect to their main function of distinguishing high-quality, or reliable offerings from lower-quality or untrustworthy offerings.[380] Algorithms are created by humans. As such, they can be the carriers of inherent biases or discrimination. In this regard, limited transparency of how they actually function can be detrimental to addressing these issues, and it can also perpetuate deep-rooted stereotypes in workplaces and in society in general.

The possible misuse of new technologies does not represent the only source of potential risks for platform workers. In some occasions, such work arrangements reflect already existing problems regarding occurrences of discrimination in employment. For example, a number of empirical studies which aim at investigating 'global online platforms', have shown a pay disparity between male and female workers, as women's hourly rates are significantly lower than the ones received their male counterparts are enjoying.[381] Concerns have been additionally raised with respect to the ability that crowdwork platforms offer to their providers in limiting the geographical areas from where online tasks can be undertaken by platform workers. The restrictions in question, especially when they take place without a proper justification, can lead to the exclusion of entire countries or regions from access to work; hence, they can lead to discriminatory practices.[382]

Even though this research does not aim at focusing on these issues in much detail, it can be, nonetheless, argued that possible violations of individual human rights can be closely linked to restrictions observed in relation to fundamental collective labour rights. As it is explained below, for instance, workplaces with effective structures of collective bargaining can be associated with lower instances of discriminatory practices.

To conclude, the purpose of this section was to demonstrate that platform-mediated work constitutes a phenomenon that can be particularly challenging from both a human rights law angle as well as a labour law perspective. As seen, on a practical level, platform workers, regardless of whether they perform their job on a bike or behind a computer screen, can be individually or collectively restricted from exercising their fundamental labour rights, recognised as human rights. For labour law, on a theoretical level, as the next section shows, the manner in which many platform businesses treat the labour of their workers, can be especially problematic, as it can challenge the field's *raison d'être*.

---

378. For instance, *see* Kullmann, M., *Platform Work, Algorithmic Decision-Making, and EU Gender Equality Law*, 34 International Journal of Comparative Labour Law and Industrial Relations 1 n. 1 (2018), 1-22; *supra*, Blackham, A. (2018).
379. *Supra*, De Stefano (2018), 9-16.
380. *Ibid.*, citing Slee, T., *What's Yours Is Mine – Against the Sharing Economy* (O/R Books 2015).
381. *Supra* Kullmann (2018), 3, relying on Katz, L.F., Krueger, A.B. (2016), *The Rise and Nature of Alternative Work Arrangements in the United States, 1995-2015*, NBER Working Paper No. 22667.
382. *Supra*, De Stefano and Aloisi (2019), 366-367.

2.4 THE OVERALL IMPACT OF PLATFORM WORK IN THE WORLD OF WORK: AN IMMINENT THREAT FOR LABOUR LAWS' (MAIN) FOUNDATION(S)?

Considering the discussion thus far, it becomes evident that platform work constitutes a good illustration of the reality many workers in NSFE are experiencing. As noted, some of these issues can also be particularly relevant for workers in standard employment relationships, such as those stemming from the often misuse of new technological tools within modern workplaces. Such observations will be further evaluated as this research unfolds. That being said, let us conclude Chapter 2 by reflecting on the impact platform work can have on labour law's theoretical framework. A point of caution should be added here. It is not within the scope of this research to proceed with a full account of all the different lines of thought with respect to the justifications of labour law and its correlated functions. What needs to be assessed, however, is whether some of the main 'features' that platform work represents can indeed interfere with perhaps the most well-known and most-discussed justification of labour law. That is the idea that human labour should not be treated as a commodity, a notion that, at least on a theoretical basis, has attracted a wide consensus, both in academic literature and international law, mainly through the language of the ILO that represents 186 Member States. If platform work that, as noted, constitutes a phenomenon that includes many of the characteristics of modern labour markets can put into question this very notion, then we run the risk of deviating from labour law's initial conception(s); as a result, its whole edifice could be jeopardised.

2.4.1 Labour Law's Principal Foundation

If someone attempts to engage in a discussion on the purposes behind the creation of labour law in the traditional sense, then the question that someone should ask is: what is the source of the problem? A discussion in that term(s) can be rather limited compared to today's considerations, which, arguably, have multiplied. It is by now well-documented, both in literature and international legal documents, that labour law's main justifications appealed to considerations around the protection of workers, through a fair distribution of power and wealth at work; a claim that in turn was considered to bring about socioeconomic implications in the society at large.[383] More specifically, the traditional theory regarding labour law was profoundly based on the regulation of subordinate labour that takes place via the existence of an employment contract. This original idea was mainly expressed by Hugo Sinzheimer, one of the most prominent fathers of labour law.[384] Sinzheimer pointed out that the contract of

383. For a discussion on the justifications of labour law, *see*: ZEKIC, N., *The Normative Framework of Labour Law*, Law and Method 1 (2019), 1-17; BOGG, A., *Labour, Love and Futility: Philosophical Perspectives on Labour Law*, 33 *International Journal of Comparative Labour Law and Industrial Relations* 7 n. 1 (2017), 7-37.

384. *See* DUKES R., *Hugo Sinzheimer and the Constitutional Function of Labour Law* (Guy Davidov and Brian Langille eds, *The Idea of Labour Law*, Oxford University Press 2011), 57-68.

employment was nothing different than a '[in]voluntary' submission to conditions that cannot be altered by the worker.[385] This act of submission is also accepted by the great student of Sinzheimer, namely, Otto Kahn-Freund.[386] A body of rules and laws, thus, had to intervene in order to remedy the uneven contractual power of employers vis-à-vis workers, in a way that as Collins notices, attempts to alleviate a major social and economic problem in modern societies, that is, the subordination of workers to the capital, or of employees to employers.[387]

This idea became particularly apparent after the dawn of the First Industrial Revolution, where the ever-increasing gap between those who owned the means of production, such as machinery and factory buildings, and those working to produce, was established as a dominant characteristic of labour relations. The need to improve what was just described has been based upon certain facts and values. In particular, the main idea was that labour does not constitute a commodity. It cannot be detached from the person performing the work, as labour power is embodied in human beings.[388] Under this view, labour cannot be exchanged in the markets for the lowest price because workers are human beings with dignity and rights. In other words, as Judy Fudge suggests: '*unlike other commodities, human beings have the capacity to act individually and collectively to resist the dull compulsion of supply and demand*'.[389]

It is precisely the existence of human dignity, as Weiss highlights, that led Sinzheimer to contend that a special value as such can be endangered within the realm of an employment relationship, where one person becomes dependent on someone else's desires.[390] Furthermore, the fact that labour should not be conceived as a commodity made Sinzheimer bring forth the claim that the economy becomes not just a private matter, but also a matter of state interest.[391] Concomitantly, as it has been multiple times claimed in the literature, it is difficult to compare labour markets to any other market, or it would be even problematic to do so, as the human element attached to labour would be undermined.[392] As noted, the perception that labour should not be seen as a commodity has been reflected in the language of international instruments. The Declaration of Philadelphia, in its first principle, in Article 1(a), explicitly enshrines that 'labour is not a commodity'.[393] This *maxim* is reaffirmed in the text of the

385. Rodgers, L. (2014), *Labour Law and Kantian Ideas of Legality and Citizenship*, University of Leicester School of Law Research Paper No. 14-07, 4, referring to Sinzheimer, H. *Democracy and the Employment Relationship* (1928) quoted in Lord Wedderburn, (2000), *Collective Bargaining or Legal Enactment: The 1999 Act and Union Recognition, Industrial Law Journal*, 29 n. 1, 3.
386. Davies, P. and Freedland, M., *Kahn-Freund's Labour and the Law*, (Stevens & Sons 1983), 18.
387. Collins, H., *Labour Law as a Vocation*, 105 Law Quarterly Review 468 (July 1989), 469.
388. For instance, *see* Paton, J., *Labour as a (Fictitious) Commodity: Polanyi and the Capitalist 'Market Economy'*, 21 The Economic and Labour Relations Review 77 n. 1 (2010), 120-136.
389. *Ibid.*, Fudge (2011), 130.
390. *Supra*, Weiss (2011), 44.
391. *Ibid.*
392. *Supra*, Paton (2010), *Supra*, Fudge (2011); Hendrickx (2012).
393. The ILO Declaration of Philadelphia, 1944.

2008 ILO Declaration on Social Justice for a Fair Globalization[394] and more recently in the 2019 ILO Centenary Declaration for the Future of Work.[395]

It should be mentioned at this point, however, that there are views in the literature, which bring forth the argument that even though labour should not be perceived as a complete commodity, it could be, nevertheless, apprehended as an 'incomplete' commodity. This, as Frank Hendrickx, one of the scholars who examine this narrative, argues, might sound disturbing for some advocates of labour rights.[396] Still, as he explains, labour is not solely but also a function of the market, as it has both an economic value and an exchange value that are subject to market regulations.[397] Whether someone agrees or disagrees, it can be said that this approach reflects the concrete reality within labour markets, rather than an idealistic construction with respect to the concept of labour law, as well as the function of the economy. An interesting analysis in this respect is coming from the seminal work of Karl Polanyi in his book *The Great Transformation*, in which he refers to labour as a 'fictive commodity'.[398] According to the author, commodities are produced for sale on the market. For that reason, labour, money, and land should be differentiated from simple commodities as none of them is created for sale. He goes on to point out:

> Nevertheless, it is with the help of this fiction that the actual markets or labor, land, and money are organized; ... their demand and supply are real magnitudes ... Undoubtedly, [therefore], they are essential to a market economy. But no society could stand the effects of such a system of crude ... [unless] its human and natural substance ... was protected.[399]

In light of this claim, labour is an essential feature within an economic process that is applied through a commodity exchange system. Still, labour also encompasses '*a purpose and value extraneous to the market*',[400] unlike any other article of commerce. In this regard, as Radin explains, the existence of regulatory structures, which are intended to safeguard the supply of labour can constitute another valid reason further demonstrating its 'incomplete commodification'.[401]

Importantly enough, the conversation around the nature of 'human labour' has intrigued some scholars to examine further justifications for labour law that touch upon exactly this issue. Hendrickx, for instance, explores the idea of the market economy as a supplementary foundation of the field, at least within a Western context.[402] Once more, actual reality, rather than idealism, and the role of the (free) market in modern capitalist societies seem to inform his views. As a way of example, he uses the application of the *collective laissez-faire* principle that can also be found to

394. The ILO Declaration on Social Justice for a Fair Globalization, 2008.
395. Article 1(a), The ILO Centenary Declaration for the Future of Work, 2019.
396. *Supra*, Hendrickx. (2012), 112.
397. *Ibid.*
398. Polanyi, K., *The Great Transformation: The Political and Economic Origins of Our Time* (2nd ed. Beacon Press 2001).
399. *Ibid* 76.
400. *Supra*, Paton (2010), 82.
401. *Ibid.*, 83: quoting Radin, M. J., *Contested Commodities* (Harvard University Press 1996), 109.
402. *Supra*, Hendrickx (2012), 117-118.

refer to the principles of the market.[403] After all, as Fugde points out, quoting the work of Polanyi, '[labour] *regulation and market...grew up together*'.[404] Despite their alleged coexistence, however, it is difficult to be claimed with certainty that the existence of labour law is dependent upon the presence of the market economy, as labour is brought into being and exists quite independently of any particular economic system. Therefore, in the words of Hendrickx, '*the market seems to be a reason of existence rather, than a condition of existence of labour law in abstracto*';[405] thus, it would be an overstatement for someone to argue that it indeed constitutes a fundamental justification for the creation of labour law. Thus, the labour market should not be treated in the same way as any other kind of existing market. This conception also explains why the plurality of the labour law's chief objectives and goals,[406] like its function as a countervailing force to counteract the inequality of bargaining power inherent in the employment relationship, have been constructed around this understanding.

2.4.2 The Transposition of Human Dignity into Labour Law

It can be stated that the discussion as to whether labour should be seen as a complete or incomplete commodity cannot put into question labour's social aspect and the embodiment of human dignity within it. As such, the latter's existence has been articulated as constituting the most, or at least one of the most fundamental justifications for the creation of labour law.[407] This is why De Stefano, by also relying on the work of others, describes the history of labour protection in modern times as an era of a de-commodification of labour.[408] Of course, what the author describes implies the existence of certain rights, which aim at protecting the very essence of the human factor within workplaces. In other words, what began as a recognition of the human dignity of every worker gradually transposed into the law with the inclusion of a number of labour rights in several constitutional texts, which put human dignity at the epicentre of their legal system, thereby, elevating those rights to the status of fundamental rights.[409]

403. *Ibid.*, 117.
404. *Supra*, Fudge (2011), 121: referring to Polanyi, K. (1944). *The Great Transformation: Origins of Our Time* Victor Gollancz, Ch. 6.
405. *Supra*, Hendrickx (2012), 118.
406. Within literature, there is a big number of functions attributed to labour law. Hendrickx, for instance, identifies four functions, namely, the ordering function, the well-being function, the integrative function and the intermediary function (*Supra*, Hendrickx (2012), 119-129.
407. *See* Dukes, R. (2014), *The Labour Constitution. The Enduring Idea of Labour Law*, Oxford, Oxford University Press, 198; *Supra*, Zekić (2019), 7-10.
408. De Stefano, V., *Labour Is Not a Technology: Reasserting the Declaration of Philadelphia in Times of Platform-Work and Gig-Economy*, 2 IUSLabor 1 (2017), 11.
409. For instance, Articles 36 and 41 of the Italian Constitution are illustrative of how dignity can be integrated at the heart of labour law; CARACCIOLO, A. (2015), *Right to Dignity into Contemporary New Humanism*, Conference Paper, 1957; moreover, as previously explained, the rights to freedom of association and collective bargaining have become part of the constitutional order in a number of countries around the world.

Thus, as Habermas nicely puts it: '*human dignity forms the "portal" through which the egalitarian and universalistic substance of morality is imported*'.[410] In order for this substance to be secured, as Comparato, among others, has stated, dignity must be treated as an end in itself and not as a means.[411] In this sense, the way in which the latter is to be protected lies in the rights surrounding the very notion of human dignity. This is something that has also been pointed out by Michel Hansenne, the ILO's former Director-General, when he referred to the function of the Organisation's standards:

> [they] are not an end in themselves; they are one of the means undeniably the most important – that the Organization has at its disposal to attain its objectives and ensure that the values enshrined in its Constitution and the Declaration of Philadelphia are put into practice. These values are those of the dignity of the human person, in particular the dignity of human beings at work and through work, which is expressed in the solemn affirmation of the principle that labour is not a commodity.[412]

Notably, such a statement took place a year before some of these standards were elevated to the status of fundamental labour rights through the adoption of the 1998 ILO Declaration on Fundamental Principles and Rights at Work. Since then, at least on a theoretical level, the rights enshrined in the 1998 Declaration have been endorsed by corporations and other actors in the global labour market and have been integrated into corporate codes of conduct and industry standards.[413] Of course, in practice, as was also illustrated by the poor working conditions faced by many platform workers and other workers in NSFE, the reality can be considerably different. What is often observed is an army of vulnerable workers, who, due to their often insecure position, find themselves in a situation where their human dignity can be at risk.

2.4.3 Platform Work's Deeper Foundational Implications for Labour Law

'Commoditised Workers': this is the term that Antonio Aloisi uses in one of his articles to describe on-demand platform workers.[414] This description, according to his analysis, can be attributed to the multiple challenges many of these workers are facing with respect to their limited labour protection. The threat of the commodification of platform

---

410. Habermas, J., *The Concept of Human Dignity: A Realistic Utopia*, 41 Metaphilosophy 462 n. 4 (2010), 469.
411. The reference was found in, Mezzaroba, O., Silveira, V.O.D., *The Principle of the Dignity of Human Person: A Reading of the Effectiveness of Citizenship and Human Rights Through the Challenges Put Forward by Globalization*, 5 Revista de Investigações Constitucionais 273 (2018), 274. The authors refer to: Comparato, F.K., *A afirmação histórica dos direitos humanos* (Saraiva 1999), 20.
412. ILO Director-General, (1997), *The ILO, Standard Setting and Globalization*, 3, ILO Doc. 2941/M (1997).
413. For instance, *see* Hassel, A., *The Evolution of a Global Labor Governance Regime*, 21 Governance 231 n. 2(2008), 231-251; Swepston, L. (2019), *How the ILO Embraced Human Rights*, (Bellace, J. and Ter Haar, B. eds, *Research Handbook on Labour, Business and Human Rights Law*, Research Handbooks in Human Rights Series, Elgar Publishing), 295-313.
414. Aloisi, A., *Commoditized Workers: Case Study Research on Labour Law Issues Arising from a Set of 'On-demand/Gig Economy' Platforms*, 37 Comparative Labor Law & Policy Journal, 653 n. 3 (2016), 653-690.

workers' labour, both in relation to online and offline jobs, has been also highlighted by other authors.[415] Ironically enough, as previously noted, such a claim can be based not solely on an in-depth analysis of platform workers' working conditions, but also on the views that some platform operators' representatives have expressed from time to time. To use another example, a CEO of a very important global labour platform at some point said: '*as an entrepreneur, I had this army of people I can hire on demand to do things for me ... So I then thought to myself, why isn't there an eBay of jobs?*'[416] Of course, eBay is a well-known e-commerce corporation for the exchange of products. Thus, such a claim, along with other statements of a similar nature, underscore the rationale of some platform businesses in relation to workers' commodification.

A considerable number of platform workers around the world are facing both legal and practical exclusions from protective labour frameworks. As a direct consequence, they are usually excluded from fundamental principles and rights at work, such as the right to bargain collectively or protection against incidences of discrimination. Moreover, they are often associated with poor working conditions of an insecure, precarious, and low-income nature. Certainly, these challenges are also present for other persons in NSFE. Still, as De Stefano, among others, observes, compared to other forms of atypical work arrangements, in the case of platform workers, one of the differences, *inter alia*, lies in the fact that '*periods of paid employment are even shorter and normally go by fraction of hours and minutes*'.[417] To this extent, platform operators have the ability to end workers' contracts without prior notice and without clearly explaining the reasons behind this decision. In a similar vein, the ability to terminate a contract on the spot can also be transferred to the platform's clients without the latter having a strict obligation to justify their actions. Furthermore, on some occasions, the problems go as far as denying certain workers their payment if the clients in question decide that they are not satisfied with the outcome of the service. As Wood and Graham inform us, this is an issue that is particularly relevant for a number of 'online freelancers' and 'contractors' in the Global South.[418] That said, the phenomenon of unpaid work, as noted, can be equally expanded to the whole spectrum of platform work, also in the Global North. Illustrative in this regard is that for both offline and online platform workers, the consumption of time for work-related activities, such as breaks and mandatory training, goes without payment, not to mention the absence of compensations when such workers are unable to work, for instance, due to sickness.[419] Moreover, as was previously discussed, many of these issues have been exacerbated

---

415. From an interdisciplinary perspective, *see*, for instance, Durlauf, M., *The Commodification of Digital Labor in the Gig Economy: Online Outsourcing, Insecure Employment, and Platform-Based Rating and Ranking Systems*, 7 Psychosociological Issues in Human Resource Management 54 n. 1 (2019), 54-59; *Supra*, De Stefano, V. (2017), 11-14; Wood, A.J., Graham, M., Lehdonvirta V., Hjorth, I., *Networked but Commodified: The (Dis)Embeddedness of Digital Labour in the Gig Economy*, 53 Sociology 931 n. 5 (2019), 931-950.
416. *Ibid.*, Wood et al. (2019), 942.
417. *Supra*, De Stefano (2017), 8; *see also supra*, Berg (2016).
418. Wood, A.J., Graham, M. (2019), 'Networked but commodified: digital labour in the remote gig economy', *New Internationalist*, 28 February 2019, available at: https://newint.org/features/2019/02/28/networked-commodified-digital-labour-remote-gig-economy (13 January 2021).
419. *Ibid.*, *supra* De Stefano, 10.

during COVID-19. The pandemic, for example, has exposed, to an even greater extent, the risks platform workers, especially in delivery and transportation services, are facing in relation to their health and safety entitlements, or even better, the lack of such entitlements.

It can be, therefore, suggested that many platform businesses have attempted to generate an army of extremely commodified workers through the generation of unregulated global competition. To this extent, they have managed to avoid labour and employment regulations by relying on labelling their workers as self-employed, or a new breed of entrepreneurs who take advantage of new technologies in order to create their own jobs. As previously examined though, instead of a new class of self-employed persons who manage their own work and have no bosses, it would be more accurate to perceive platform work (or, at least its main aspects) as a '*twenty-first-century casual work rebranded*', to use the description of Berg and De Stefano.[420] As it has been claimed elsewhere, in the context of labour markets, these new types of casual work seem to give a '*normative priority*' to considerations of efficiency, flexibility, and economic competitiveness.[421] What they lack, nonetheless, is a focus, if any, on one of the most essential justifications for labour law, namely, the protection of workers' human dignity. Such a phenomenon goes hand in hand with the commodification of work as it is observed in the context of platform work. It is also inextricably linked to the severe restrictions platform workers are facing in the enjoyment of their fundamental (collective) labour rights. As noted, the latter constitutes the means through which human dignity at work can be safeguarded. Therefore, it can be stated that platform work can indeed obstruct the effective transposition of human dignity into the law; thereby, it can indeed have deeper foundational implications for the field of labour law as a whole.

2.5 INTERMEDIATE CONCLUSIONS

Thus far, this doctoral research has pointed out that to a great degree, the challenges platform workers are facing with respect to their labour protection can be attributed to the very limitations of labour law, where the main protections, including the enjoyment of collective labour rights, still and by large, remain concentrated within subordinate wage employment. At the beginning of Chapter 1, some of the main reasons behind such limitations were discussed. In turn, as discussed in Chapter 2, the exclusion from labour law's protective framework can indeed negatively impact the lives of workers in the platform economy. Against this background, this chapter highlighted the often precarious nature of platform work. Problematic employment practices, poor working conditions and overall job uncertainty are just some of the problems that many platform workers are dealing with on a daily basis. Not only this

420. Berg. J., De Stefano, V. (2017), 'It's time to regulate the gig economy', *Sheffield Political Economy Research Institute* (Blog), 18 April 2017, available at: http://speri.dept.shef.ac.uk/2017/04/18/its-time-to-regulate-the-gigeconomy/. (accessed 14 January 2021).
421. Rittich, K. (2010), *Between Workers' Rights and Flexibility: Labor Law in an Uncertain World*, Saint Luis University Law Journal, 54 n. 2, 579.

but due to their often 'obscure' employment status, they are also facing serious obstacles towards the exercise of their collective rights, such as the right to bargain collectively. To this extent, as a matter of law, it was mentioned that such impediments can also be attributed to the conflicting relationship between labour law and competition law and the existence of strict antitrust law. Consequently, many workers with weak economic and bargaining power are left unprotected towards hostile competition rules and regulations. As finally discussed, the aforementioned phenomena are not only problematic for workers per se, but they can also have deeper foundational implications for labour law.

Problems of this kind have not gone unnoticed by lawmakers and the courts. The next chapter explores several judicial and legislative responses, which aim at regulating the phenomenon of platform work and the issue of labour protection for platform workers.

CHAPTER 3
Responses Towards the Regulation of Platform Work

3.1 INTRODUCTION

An employee or a self-employed worker? As already discussed, this question is certainly not novel for the purposes of labour law protection.[422] In the context of platform work and other atypical forms of employment, such an inquiry can be characterised as a 'million-dollar question'. It remains extremely important, at the same time though, its answer can be rather complicated at first. As seen, among other reasons, the vertical disintegration of firms, along with the digital outsourcing of working tasks, have contributed to the difficulties in answering this question. Indeed, work arrangements that take place within a zone, where the work performed is frequently defined by increased flexibility, 'multilaterality' and fragmentation of tasks, are difficult to be categorised for employment status purposes.[423] As a result, a considerable number of workers with weak economic and bargaining power remain without or with limited labour protection. Developments in the context of the platform economy constitute an illustrative example of these phenomena.

It comes as no surprise that both legislators and judges around the globe have attempted to offer solutions to such difficulties. Their attempts predate the advent of platform work. For example, as far as legislative responses are concerned, it is often believed that the introduction of an intermediate category between employment and self-employment can offer adequate protections to these types of workers, including

422. *See also* Davies, P., Freedland, M., *Employees, Workers and the Autonomy of Labour Law* (Dieter Simon and Manfred Weiss ed., *Zur Autonomie des Individuums (Liber Amoricum Spiros Simitis)*, Nomos 2000), 31-46.
423. Pichault, F., McKeown, T., *Autonomy at Work in the Gig Economy: Analysing Work Status, Work Content and Working Conditions of Independent Professionals*, 34 New Technology, Work and Employment 59 n. 1 (2019), 59.

the enjoyment of their fundamental collective rights.[424] Moreover, in relation to judicial responses, there are also views that seek for solutions in a broad interpretation of the notion of subordination, when courts are ruling on the existence of employment relationships. That said, it is not in the scope of this chapter to argue which of these actors is in fact in a better position to provide better solutions to current challenges related to atypical workers, including platform workers. A brief discussion on some of these views, nonetheless, will better assist us in assessing whether the present responses towards platform workers are enough to adequately address their problems, including the exercise of their collective labour rights; something that constitutes the aim of this chapter. To that end, this part first focuses on some of the most important legislative developments related to the protection of platform workers and other atypical workers. Subsequently, the discussion turns to some of the most important legislative developments related to the protection of platform workers. Finally, an assessment is taking place in relation to the policy responses advanced in order to tackle the longstanding clash between labour law on the one hand and competition law on the other.

3.2 LABOUR LAW RESPONSES: LEGISLATIVE DEVELOPMENTS

3.2.1 The Case of a 'Third Category' of Workers

As noted, legislative attempts that aim at offering solutions in relation to the labour protection of workers, who find themselves between employment and self-employment, are not novel, and certainly, some of them predate the advent of the platform economy. In some countries, for instance, this is the case with the introduction of a 'third category' of workers; a measure that some commentators believe can also assist platform workers.[425] Thus, before engaging with other legislative initiatives on platform work per se, let us briefly discuss the case of the 'third category' of workers.

Indeed, for some time now, a number of national legislations have introduced an intermediate category of workers who are positioned between employees and self-employed. Labour protection is partially applicable to these persons, as they are considered to be in need of it, despite the fact that they do not legally qualify to possess employee status. As has been argued, therefore, quasi-subordinate categories of workers in all the countries that exist have borrowed some of their important contractual elements from the model of the contract of employment.[426] In Germany, for example, the so-called *arbeitnehmerähnliche Personen* (employee-like persons) are able to have access to labour protections, such as annual leave rights, protection

424. Harris, D., Krueger, A.B. (2015), *A Proposal for Modernizing Labor Laws for Twenty-First-Century Work: The 'Independent Worker'*, The Hamilton Project, Discussion Paper, available at: http://www.hamiltonproject.org/assets/files/modernizing_labor_laws_for_twenty_first_century_work_kruegharris.pdf (accessed 10 December 2019).
425. *Supra* Harris and Krueger (2015).
426. *Supra*, Countouris, N. (2019), 12.

against unfair dismissal and the right to collectively bargain.[427] Similar categories can be traced in Austria, Italy (*lavoratori parasubordinati*), the UK (limb-b workers), Spain (*autónomos económicamente dependientes*) and Canada, while there have been several discussions for this category to be introduced in other legal systems, like in Brazil and Uruguay.[428]

Albeit definitions in relation to the third category of workers may vary from one country to the other, some common criteria have been identified in the literature.[429] These, *inter alia*, include the requirement to receive a certain amount of income mainly from a single client, or the condition that the activity must include mainly personal work that is performed in a continuous manner. As Mathias Wouters observes in his analysis, the percentage of income required for a worker to be considered dependent can range around 75 per cent-80 per cent in some countries, while in others, such as Germany and Canada, a 50 per cent threshold (or, even less in some occasions) exists.[430]

In some cases, the introduction of an intermediate category of workers has also been considered an appropriate solution for regulating work arrangements within the context of the platform economy. For example, in 2019, in Colombia, a bill was introduced with the purpose of tackling some of the issues related to economically dependent platform workers.[431] In doing so, the draft law suggests the creation of a new legal category, through which platform workers who are falling into it, will be able to have access to a number of important labour rights, such as the right to the freedom of association and the right to collective bargaining. In the US, there have also been some voices which put forward the view that an intermediate category can possibly benefit those who are working in the platform economy.[432] For the time being, however, there are no developments as such with respect to both of the aforementioned examples.

Having said that, the third category of workers can indeed expand the scope of labour protection coverage and enable workers who find themselves in a grey legal zone to gain access to a number of fundamental labour rights, such as the right to collective bargaining. In a similar vein, workers falling into this category can also enjoy some civil rights entitlements, mostly related to anti-discrimination regulations.[433] Yet, as many authors argue, the negative effects stemming from the existence of an intermediate status should not be disregarded. First of all, in countries such as the UK, the presence of 'limb-b' workers has not prevented the exclusion of casual and

427. *Supra*, ILO (2016), 37.
428. *Ibid.*, 37-38.
429. Perulli, A. (2003), 'Study on economically dependent work/parasubordinate (quasi-subordinate) work', Brussels, European Parliament.
430. Wouters, M., *International Labour Standards and Platform Work: An Analysis of Digital Labour Platforms Based on the Instruments on Private Employment Agencies, Home Work and Domestic Work* (Wolters Kluwer 2022), 219.
431. Proyecto de Ley No, de 2019, Por medio de la cual se regula el trabajo digital económicamente dependiente realizado a través de empresas de intermediación digital que hacen uso de plataformas digitales en Colombia.
432. *Supra*, Harris and Krueger (2015).
433. *Ibid.*

intermittent workers, including those in the platform economy,[434] from the scope of important labour entitlements, like those of minimum wage and working time regulations.[435] Adams and Deakin, moreover, have contended that one of the risks entailed in the intermediate category is the creation of '*new forms of dualism and division, with the boundary between protected and unprotected forms of work reappearing in a new form*'.[436] This situation can lead to further complications for national lawmakers regarding the amount of labour protection attributed to persons falling into this category, as well as an overall legal uncertainty which is often reflected in occasions where courts have to rule on workers' reclassification. The several legislative reforms, which took place in Italy from the mid-1970s up until 2016 and led to the revaluation of the parasubordinate category in the country, can constitute an illustration in this respect.[437]

Furthermore, as Countouris argues, in some countries where a third category has been introduced, it makes it easier for employers to rely on these types of workers, avoiding that way responsibilities and costs that derive from standard employment relationships, even though the latter may exist in reality; the risks of misclassification, therefore, can be particularly high.[438] This situation, in turn, can lead to a race to the bottom in terms of the overall labour protection of workers, who are indeed in need of such coverage. Finally, as a matter of law, Countouris and De Stefano have pointed out that it is much easier for courts to be convinced that a person is qualified to be included in the quasi-subordinate category of workers, even if, in reality, the person in question should have been tread as an employee; instances of worker's misclassification, therefore, can be proliferated, rather than regulated.[439]

Thus, despite the existence of an intermediate status in some countries, many workers in highly flexible work arrangements appear to be still missing adequate legal protection. Not only this but as some authors indicate, in the context of modern workplaces, a number of them might fail to satisfy some of the current criteria for the existence of dependent self-employment, even if, in reality, they lack the autonomy necessary to be considered genuine self-employed.[440] For instance, the common requirement under national legislation that a major source of income should derive from a main principal or client, can indeed prevent some workers from falling into the definition of a quasi-subordinate category of workers. This situation particularly reflects the reality of some platform workers. Wouters, for example, contends that

434. For instance, *see* Freedland, M., Prassl, J., *Employees, Workers and the 'Sharing Economy', Changing Practices and Changing Concepts in the UK*, 6 Spanish Labour Law and Employment Relations Journal 16 n. 1-2 (2017), 16-29.
435. *Supra*, Adams and Deakin (2014).
436. *Ibid.*, 797.
437. For instance, *see supra* De Stefano (2016), 30-31; Perulli, A., *Subordinate, Autonomous and Economically Dependent Work: A Comparative Analysis of Selected European Countries* (Giuseppe Casale ed., *The Employment Relationship: A Comparative Overview*, Hart Publishing 2011), 137-188; Gramano, E., Gaudio, G., *'New Trade Union Strategies for New Forms of Employment': Focus on Italy*, 10 European Labour Law Journal 242 n. 3 (2019), 242-245.
438. Countouris, N. (2019), 12-13.
439. Countouris, N., De Stefano, V. (2019), *New Trade Union Strategies for New forms of Employment*. ETUC. Brussels, 58-59.
440. *Ibid.*

albeit some crowdworkers or domestic workers have multiple sources of income, '*they* [still] *operate like a casual cog in the machine of other businesses*' under conditions of control and economic dependency.[441]

3.2.2 Platform Work and Legislation

The problems related to the labour protection of platform workers have, unsurprisingly, attracted much of the attention of both legislators, as well as supranational institutions.[442] Thus far, multiple approaches have emerged around the world. As is explained in a Working Paper conducted for the ILO by the Institute for Labour Law, KU Leuven, such developments considerably vary from each other.[443] These differences are due to the particularities of every domestic legal order, albeit approaches in foreign countries may inform domestic changes in the law. That said, a number of regulatory measures that have already been implemented are designed to specifically tackle issues related to platform work per se. To this extent, it is observed that 'platform-specific' legal developments may serve very diverse regulatory aims.[444] In some countries, for instance, certain protections have been granted to self-employed workers who provide their services via a digital platform;[445] while in other legal jurisdictions, laws, regulations, or collective agreements have been put in place, which explicitly apply to certain categories of platform workers, on the condition that they are already considered as employees.[446]

To be more specific, some legal systems have intensified their efforts in including specific categories of platform workers within the protective framework of an employment relationship. Indeed, as noted in the previous section, in Spain, in 2021, the so-called Riders law[447] was adopted, which brings forth an 'employee unless' presumption. According to the law at issue, unless the employer can prove the opposite, an employment relationship is presumed to exist:

> for those who provide, in exchange for remuneration, the services of delivering and distributing products for employers who exercise the business powers of organization, direction and control indirectly or implicitly through a digital

441. *Supra*, Wouters (2022), 225.
442. For instance, *see* Article 1 Regulation 2019/1150 of the European Parliament and of the Council of 20 June 2019 on promoting fairness and transparency for business users of online intermediation services.
443. *See* De Stefano, V., Durri, I., Stylogiannis, C., Wouters, M. (2021), *Platform Work and the Employment Relationship*, ILO Working Paper, Geneva, ILO.
444. *Ibid.*
445. For instance, *see* the legal developments in France with Loi n° 2016-1088 du 8 août 2016 relative au travail, à la modernisation du dialogue social et à la sécurisation des parcours professionnels (1).
446. *Supra* DE Stefano, V., Durri, I., Stylogiannis, C., and Wouters, M. (2021), 23: A collective agreement as such can be, for instance, traced in Austria. This agreement will be further analysed in Chapter 4.4.1.
447. Real Decreto-ley 9/2021, de 11 de mayo, por el que se modifica el texto refundido de la Ley del Estatuto de los Trabajadores, aprobado por el Real Decreto Legislativo 2/2015, de 23 de octubre, para garantizar los derechos laborales de las personas dedicadas al reparto en el ámbito de plataformas digitales.

platform, or through the algorithmic management of the service or the conditions of work.[448]

Furthermore, another piece of legislation that adopts an 'employee unless' presumption can be traced in Portugal, where in 2018, the government adopted what is now known as the 'Uber Law'.[449] Its purpose, *inter alia,* is to include at least a number of platform workers under the scope of employment protection. Similar to the Spanish example above, the law in question also establishes a presumption that is applicable to the contract between drivers and the platform they are using. Moreover, under section 13 of the law, it is enshrined that drivers should not operate a vehicle for more than 10 hours per day, irrespective of the number of platforms a driver works for. Section 14 also provides for a complaint mechanism that needs to be offered to the drivers by digital platforms in the sector of transportation.

Initiatives that share a similar aim - although the scope might be different - namely, to enhance the protection of certain platform workers, have also taken place in other EU countries, such as Italy and France.[450] With respect to France, for instance, Act No. 2016-1088, known as the Loi Travail, was introduced into the Labour Code.[451] The Act in question enshrines a protective framework applicable to self-employed platform workers, who offer their services to a platform that decides the service's features and determines each task's price.[452] The protective scheme includes the exercise of the right to strike[453] (employment status is not an obstacle) and the freedom to become a member of a union. Platform operators should also pay insurance against workers' occupational accidents.

Furthermore, interesting developments have also emerged in other parts of the world. In Argentina, for example, in 2020, a law was introduced which offers a number of protections to on-demand platform workers. These, among others, include a minimum wage, limitations in working hours, an annual leave, as well as the existence of a mechanism to calculate the compensation in the event of unjustified dismissals.[454]

448. Pérez Del Prado, D. (2021), *The Legal Framework of Platform Work in Spain: The New Spanish 'Riders' Law'*, Comparative Labor Law & Policy Dispatch No. 36., Champaign, University of Illinois College of Law.
449. Lei n.° 45/2018 de 10 de agosto 2018. Regime jurídico da atividade de transporte individual e remunerado de passageiros em veículos descaracterizados a partir de plataforma eletrónica.
450. *Supra*, De Stefano, V., Durri, I., Stylogiannis, C., and Wouters, M. (2021), 18-22.
451. Section L7342-1 Code du travail. 'Platforms matching "traditional gigs" (Task-Rabbit, Helping, Fiverr, Upwork) and externalising micro-tasks (like mTurk) are not covered by the law' (Haipeter, T., Owczarek, D., Faioli, M., Iudicone, F. (2020), *Don't Gig Up*, Final Report, 24, available at: http://www.dontgigup.eu/wp-content/uploads/2020/04/Final-Report-3.pdf (accessed 9 February 2021).
452. *Ibid.*, 20.
453. Article L 7342-5 enshrines that platform workers' refusal to offer their services should not lead to a contractual liability, nor an immediate termination of the employment relation, nor a reason for retaliation. The analysis was found in Carinci, M. T., Dorssemont, F. (2021), *A Comparative Analysis*, (CARINCI, M.T. and Dorssemont, F. eds *Platform Work in Europe: Towards Harmonisation?*, Cambridge - Antwerp - Chicago, Intersentia), 241.
454. Estatuto del Trabajador de Plataformas Digitales Bajo Demanda, 6 de Mayo de 2020; *see* also developments in Colombia, Proyecto de Ley No, de 2019, Por medio de la cual se regula el trabajo digital económicamente dependiente realizado a través de empresas de intermediación

Contrary to the aforementioned examples, other domestic legal orders have espoused totally different approaches that instead aim at excluding platform workers from the scope of an employment relationship and, as a consequence, from all, or at least the majority of the related protections deriving from it. The drivers behind the adoption of such measures can considerably defer from one country to another, albeit the promotion and fostering of 'entrepreneurship' can be considered one of the chief reasons towards this direction.[455]

Illustrative in this respect are some recent legislative developments in the US, which 'by default' reject the possibility that such workers can, in reality, be the employees of digital labour platforms. Indicative are the words of a policy brief conducted by the National Employment Law Project: '[o]*ver the 2018 legislative session, nearly identical bills have been introduced in states including Alabama, California, Colorado, Florida, Georgia, Indiana, Iowa, Kentucky, Tennessee and Utah that deem all workers on so-called "marketplace platforms", (such as Uber and Handy) independent businesses, and not the employees of the companies*'.[456] Indeed, a number of these bills have already come into force in different states, like Iowa and Utah. According to the local law of Iowa, for example, platform workers are defined as 'marketplace contractors' and should be classified as independent contractors.[457] In a similar vein, in Utah, the local labour code creates a presumption that a '*building service contractor*', or in other words, a platform worker, is an independent contractor.[458]

Furthermore, legislative attempts through which countries have attempted to constrain platform workers' chances of obtaining employment rights can also be traced within a European context. In Belgium for instance, the Act of 18 July 2018, by replacing the 2016 '*Loi De Croo*', among other things,[459] provided for the exemption of persons performing work via digital labour platforms from the application of most protections found in labour and social security legislation; hence, the law created a de facto status for platform workers, under which the latter by no means could be considered as employees. The Act at issue was later found to be unconstitutional, as it

digital que hacen uso de plataformas digitales en Colombia (*supra*, De Stefano, V., Durri, I., Stylogiannis, C., and Wouters, M. (2021), 21).

455. De Stefano, V., Durri, I., Stylogiannis, C., Wouters, M. (2022), *Exclusion by Default: Platform Workers' Quest for Labour Protections*, (De Stefano V., Durri, I., Stylogiannis, C., Wouters, M. eds, *A Research Agenda for the Gig-Economy and Society*, Edward Elgar Publishing), 25; *see also* the developments in Ukraine: **Закон України Про стимулювання розвитку цифрової економіки в Україні**, No. 1667-IX from 15 July 2021.

456. Smith, R., *Marketplace Platforms and 'Employers' Under State Law – Why We Should Reject Corporate Solutions and Support Worker-Led Innovation*, (New York, NELP 2018); *see also* Pinto, M., Smith, R. and Tung, I., *Rights at Risk: Gig companies' Campaign to Upend Employment as We Know It* (NELP 2019).

457. Section 93.2 Iowa Code.

458. Section 34-53-201 Utah Code.

459. The Act '*framed platform work as one of the three forms of work of which the generated income is considered "auxiliary" and is tax-exempt. As long as the worker does not earn more than 6.340 euro a year – in addition to a monthly threshold – through recognised platforms, this income is exempted from regular taxes and social security contributions. The law also specifies the conditions to fall under this beneficial tax status*'. (*Supra* De Stefano, V., Durri, I., Stylogiannis, C., and Wouters, M. (2021), 19.

violated the principle of equality under Belgian law.[460] As a consequence, platform workers are now able to offer their work under the previous Act of 2016, which does not include any provisions that preclude domestic courts from ruling, always on a case-by-case basis, that some of these workers can indeed be employees of the platform for which they are providing services.

3.2.3 Tacking the Problems of Platform Work Through Legislation: A More 'Holistic' Approach

Besides a number of regulatory measures shaped in a manner to specifically address issues related to platform-mediated work, some countries have taken a more 'holistic approach'. To this extent, it can be claimed that these initiatives aim at offering more clarity to the concept of the employment relationship, as well as to the very elements which distinguish employees from self-employed workers.[461] Along the same lines, a number of national policies have been put in force with the purpose of combating misclassification at workplaces, more in general.[462]

Arguably, one of the most illustrative examples of what was just described as a 'holistic approach', can be found in the adoption of Assembly Bill 5 (hereinafter, 'AB5 law') in California, US. The latter was developed on the basis of the seminal ruling in *Dynamex Operations W. v. Superior Court*.[463] In this case, it was established that courts should start using the so-called ABC test in determining the employment status of workers. The transposition of this test into statutory law attempts to create a broad scope of application for labour law in general by permitting a wide range of elements for the determination of an employment relationship. In this respect, workers will no longer have the burden of showing they are employees of a business; instead, they would be presumed legally employed, except if the hiring entity manages to demonstrate that all three conditions of the ABC test are satisfied.[464] Such an approach can be compared to the 'employee-unless' paradigms, as explained in the cases of Spain and Portugal above. Still, the scope of application of the AB5 law is much broader and does

460. Wouters, M. (2021), *Cheap and Flexible Labor for Non-Profits: How the Belgian 'Act On Auxiliary Income' Evolved Into An 'Act On Association Work'*, Comparative Labor Law & Policy Dispatch No. 36. Champaign: University of Illinois College of Law, 5.
461. *Supra, Supra* De Stefano, V., Durri, I., Stylogiannis, C., and Wouters, M. (2021), 23.
462. For example, one of the regulatory approaches that national policymakers have adopted in order to combat issues related to workers' misclassification constitutes the active involvement of labour inspectorates and in some cases the even greater increase of their responsibilities. In Slovenia, for instance, after the amendment of the law in 2017, labour inspectorates were conferred with special powers to compel employers to enter into an employment relationship with a person illegally working under a contract for services. Of course, the decisions of the labour inspectorate can subsequently be reviewed by domestic labour courts (section 19, *Zakon o inšpekciji dela (ZID-1) št. 19/14 z dne 17. 3. 2014*).
463. Supreme Court of California 30 April 2018, Case No. S222732, *Dynamex Operations West, Inc. v. Superior Court of Los Angeles County*.
464. '*[A] person providing labor or services for remuneration shall be considered an employee rather than an independent contractor unless the hiring entity demonstrates that all of the following conditions are satisfied: (A) The person is free from the control and direction of the hiring entity in connection with the performance of the work, both under the contract for the performance of the work and in fact. (B) The person performs work that is outside the usual course of the hiring*

not only concern workers in the platform economy, even though, at an early stage, its adoption made some authors optimistic that a considerable number of platform workers would most likely be benefited by the law's provisions.[465]

Having said that, soon after the law came into effect in California, the aforementioned optimism started to evaporate. This can be attributed to the intensified attempts, including a political campaign, of platform operators in order to neutralise the new Bill.[466] Uber and Postmates took the lead in these initiatives by arguing that the AB5 law violates the Federal and State Constitutions.[467] After failing to impose a preliminary injunction against the enforcement of the law at issue,[468] they went on to introduce a referendum proposition, which is now known as Prop 22. In doing so, they spent an enormous amount of money in advertising their objections regarding the AB5 Law in an attempt to convince their users, as well as the general public, to support this ballot initiative and maintain the '*flexibility that drivers value so much while adding protections that all gig workers deserve*'.[469] The platform operators, eventually, won and as a consequence platform workers will continue to be classified as independent contractors with certain specific protections applying to them, such as non-discrimination safeguards and minimum earnings while performing rides, a guarantee that applies to workers in the transportation sector.[470]

Moreover, apart from the US, the holistic approach towards the employment protection of certain types of workers can also be observed in other national jurisdictions. This is the case, for instance, in Italy, where the legislation of 2015, as amended in 2019, was enacted with the purpose of expanding the scope of employment protection beyond the existence of an employment relationship. Therefore, the law in question provides for the extension of employment rights, as well as social protections

---

entity's business. (C) The person is customarily engaged in an independently established trade, occupation, or business of the same nature as that involved in the work performed.' § 2775 California Labor Code.

465. Sachs, B. (2018), 'Looks like the gig is up for Uber in California', *onlabor*, 1 May 2018, available at: https://onlabor.org/looks-like-the-gig-is-up-for-uber-in-california/ (accessed 12 October 2021). This optimism though, as other scholars have argued, does not preclude the possibility that in some instances platform operators would be successful in meeting the criteria necessary to establish the absence of an employment relationship, *See* Lianos, I., Countouris, N., De Stefano, V., *Re-thinking the Competition Law/Labour Law Interaction: Promoting a Fairer Labour Market*, 10 European Labour Law Journal 291 n. 3 (2019), 291-333.
466. De Stefano, V. (2020), '"I now pronounce you contractor": Prop22, labour platforms and legislative doublespeak', *UK Labour Law Blog*, 13 November 2020, available at: https://uklabourlawblog.com/2020/11/13/i-now-pronounce-you-contractor-prop22-labour-platforms-and-legislative-doublespeak-by-valerio-de-stefano/ (accessed 16 November 2022).
467. Marshall, A. (2020), 'Now the Courts Will Decide Whether Uber Drivers Are Employees', Wired, 1 March 2020, available at: https://www.wired.com/story/courts-decide-uber-drivers-employees/ (accessed 12 October 2021).
468. Schaedel, J., Boughton, R., XU, J. (2020), 'California brings action against Uber and Lyft for misclassifying drivers', *Lexology*, 20 May 2020, available at: https://www.lexology.com/library/detail.aspx?g=b3b8b983-13b7- 4e61-99b8-8bdeb5962126 (accessed October 2021).
469. White, B.J. (2020), 'Uber CEO sees California ballot initiative as a model for other states', *Politico*, 11 May 2020, available at: https://www.politico.com/states/california/story/2020/11/05/uber-ceo-sees-california-ballot-initiative-as-a-model-for-other-states-9424660 (accessed 12 October 2021).
470. *Supra* DE STEFANO, V., DURRI, I., STYLOGIANNIS, C., and WOUTERS, M. (2021).

enjoyed by employees to all workers whose work is organised by another party (these workers are known as *lavoratori etero-organizzati*), including through labour digital platforms.[471] As will be also discussed below, the law will not be applicable for such workers solely in cases where a collective agreement provides otherwise.[472]

3.2.4 EU Regulatory Approaches on Platform Work

Even with a slight delay, the sharp increase in the number of atypical workers represents a challenge that has not gone unnoticed by policymakers at the EU level. Such an observation can be equally applied to the phenomenon of platform work. In this regard, some legislative developments that contain protections for workers with unpredictable work arrangements, of often 'casual', 'short-term' and 'on-demand' nature, might also impact platform workers. A seminal development of this kind can be traced back to 2019, with the adoption of the EU Directive on Transparent and Predictable Working Conditions (TPWCD).[473] The latter constitutes one of the legal instruments adopted in that period with the purpose of delivering on the strong commitments stemming from the European Pillar of Social Rights.[474] The TPWCD, furthermore, came to correct the shortcomings of the previous Written Statement Directive (WSD),[475] which as literature, as well as an assessment initiated by the EU Commission itself pointed out, could not address the challenges deriving from new forms of casual work arrangements due to its considerably narrow scope of application.[476]

Some authors have characterised the adoption of the TPWCD as a positive development in the sense that it provides some minimum predictability to workers with unpredictable work schedules.[477] Among other things, the instrument at issue enshrines the right to request a transition to more stable employment, a pre-established reference with respect to working hours and days and a reasonable notice period for the assignment and cancellation of shifts. In relation to the latter provision, moreover, workers might be eligible for compensation in situations related to a late cancellation

471. *Ibid.*
472. *See* discussion in Chapter 4.
473. Directive (EU) 2019/1152 of the European Parliament and of the Council of 20 June 2019 on transparent and predictable working conditions in the European Union.
474. The other legal instruments are: Directive (EU) 2019/1158 of the European Parliament and of the Council of 20 June 2019 on work-life balance for parents and carers and repealing Council Directive 2010/18/EU.
475. Council Directive of 14 October 1991 on an employer's obligation to inform employees of the conditions applicable to the contract or employment relationship (91/533/EEC); Council Recommendation of 8 November 2019 on access to social protection for workers and the self-employed 2019/C 387/01.
476. European Commission (2017), *REFIT Evaluation of the 'Written Statement Directive' (91/533/EEC)*, SWD 205 final. Brussels: European Commission; For an analysis, *see also* Georgiou, D., *The New EU Directive on Transparent and Predictable Working Conditions in the Context of New Forms of Employment*, European Journal of Industrial Relations 1 (2022), 2-5.
477. Aloisi, A., De Stefano, V., Six Silberman, M. (2019), 'A manifesto to reform the Gig Economy', *Regulating for Globalization* (blog), 1 May 2019, available at: http://regulatingforglobalization.com/2019/05/01/a-manifesto-to-reform-the-gig-economy/ (accessed 26 January 2022).

of a pre-booked task.[478] Another worth-mentioning aspect of the Directive is the inclusion of a provision that prohibits the extensive use of exclusivity, or non-competition clauses.[479] As noted, all these provisions, which, as has been pointed out elsewhere, have a wider material scope compared to the previous WSD,[480] attempt to address some of the main vulnerabilities that casual workers, including platform workers, are facing. In fact, paragraph 8 of the Directive's preamble makes an explicit reference to platform workers as possible beneficiaries of its provisions if they fall within the notion of 'worker' under its Article 1. Such a clear reference, though, does not automatically mean that the majority of these workers can indeed be benefited from the TPWCD. As Bednarowicz, among others, has highlighted, the chief reason behind this claim lies in the personal scope of the instrument at issue.[481]

More precisely, under Article 1(2), the TPWCD applies to '*every worker in the Union who has an employment contract or employment relationship as defined by the law, collective agreements or practice in force in each Member State with consideration to the case-law of the Court of Justice*'.[482] As seen at the beginning of this chapter, the concept of 'worker' (or, employee) and the overall interpretation of what constitutes an employment relationship under national laws, can be construed in a rather narrow manner, which is predominately based on features, such as those of 'subordination' and 'control'. As a result, many misclassified platform workers and other workers in NSFE risk being excluded from the protective framework of the Directive. This can the case despite the latter's reference to the jurisprudence of the CJEU that, in some instances, has espoused a rather broader understanding of 'employment', compared to national legislation.[483]

It is, therefore, problematic that the Directive fails to take under consideration issues stemming from workers' misclassification and how these very issues can actually position some vulnerable workers, including platform workers, outside the ambit of EU labour and social protection legislation.[484] On top of that, as Georgiou observes in her analysis, there can be some situations in the future, where some workers will fail to utilise the protections granted by the TPWCD, even if, in principle, they satisfy the criteria set by the CJEU for them to be considered as falling within an employment relationship.[485] As the author explains, the Directive provides for derogations that Member States can rely on, with the purpose of excluding, always on objective grounds, certain types of workers from the instrument's protective scope. According to Article 1(7), these derogations can also be introduced in relation to

478. Article 10(3) of the TPWCD.
479. *Supra* Georgiou (2022), 11. The author refers to Article 9(1) of the TPWCD, which reads as follows: '*MS shall ensure that an employer neither prohibits a worker from taking up employment with other employers nor subjects a worker to adverse treatment for doing so*'.
480. *Supra* Georgiou (2022), 1-18.
481. Bednarowicz, B., *Delivering on the European Pillar of Social Rights: the New Directive on Transparent and Predictable Working Conditions in the European Union*, 48 Industrial Law Journal 604 n. 4 (2019), 604-623.
482. Article 1(2) of the TPWCD.
483. De Stefano et al. (2021), 28.
484. *Supra*, Bednarowicz (2019), 607.
485. *Supra*, Georgiou (2022), 10.

domestic work, tackling in this way the particular nature of these arrangements. To this extent, Member States can exclude individuals who are employing domestic workers from obligations arising under the Directive, which, among other things, provides for free-of-charge training and a redress mechanism in occasions where some information is missing from the provided documents.[486] As noted though, these derogations are only applicable to individual employers and not to big businesses hiring domestic workers. This is because individuals may not have the financial capacity to undertake all the related costs that the Directive stipulates.[487] Still, it can be argued that in the context of platform work, this exemption can be challenging in certain cases. These might be situations in which a household uses a platform to hire a domestic worker, by accepting to be the legal employer of this worker, according to the terms and conditions prescribed by the platform in question.[488] This is a business structure that some digital labour platforms have relied on in the past. Such situations constitute the exception rather than the rule, but this does not mean that the aforementioned derogations cannot be used by the platforms themselves in order to once more avoid labour-related costs.

Overall, as a study conducted as part of the Impact Assessment of the TPWCD[489] reveals, the 'fear(s)' of platform workers' exclusion from the instrument's protective framework has actually materialised. It is highlighted that only 3 per cent of platform workers can be actually covered by the Directive; thereby, an extremely low percentage of such workers and an indication that further actions were indeed necessary.[490] That said, only a couple of years after the adoption of the TPWCD, the Commission announced, undeniably, the most important legal initiative on the regulation of platform work in Europe thus far. That is the proposed Directive on improving the conditions of platform work.[491]

The new legal instrument, as De Stefano and Aloisi argue, has the potential to '*materially reshape work through digital platforms*'.[492] It touches upon three key areas of concern, namely: (a) the employment status of platform workers; (b) fairness, transparency and accountability in algorithmic management; and (c) enforcement of the applicable rules. Before further engaging with the proposed Directive, it should be mentioned that many of the latter's provisions reflect, but also espouse, much of the developments observed within EU Member States' legal orders, both at the legislative

486. Paragraph 14 of the TPWCD.
487. *Supra*, Georgiou (2022), 10.
488. *Supra*, Wouters (2022), 243.
489. European Commission, 'Commission Staff Working Document Impact Assessment Accompanying the Document Proposal for a Directive of the European Parliament and of the Council on Transparent and Predictable Working Conditions in the European Union' SWD (2017) 478 final.
490. European Commission, (2019), 'Towards transparent and predictable working conditions', *EU Commission Factsheet*, 9 April 2019, 2, available at: https://ec.europa.eu/social/main.jsp?langId=en&catId=1313 (accessed 3 November 2022).
491. European Commission, Proposal for a Directive of the European Parliament and of the Council on improving working conditions in platform work COM(2021) 762 final.
492. De Stefano, V., Aloisi, A. (2021), 'European Commission takes the lead in regulating platform work', *Social Europe*, 9 December 2021, available at: https://socialeurope.eu/european-commission-takes-the-lead-in-regulating-platform-work (accessed 27 January 2021).

and judicial levels. This is, for instance, apparent with respect to the first set of concerns on platform workers' employment status. Contrary, nonetheless, to legal initiatives at a national level as those explained above, the new legal instrument adopts an 'all-encompassing approach' to platform work, meaning that it captures all the different types of platform workers, including both on-demand workers and crowd-workers.[493] In other words, in contrast to national legislative developments, which, as seen, only touch upon specific segments of platform work (e.g., the 'Riders law' in Spain), the new proposed Directive enshrines protections for sectors that until now enjoyed little attention from policymakers, such as domestic platform workers and 'on-line' workers, like those working for Amazon Mechanical Turk.[494] Importantly, the 'all-encompassing' approach does not end here. Under Article 1(2), the minimum rights contained in the Directive should be applicable, not only to persons who are employed by a platform but also to those persons '*who based on an assessment of facts may be deemed to have, an employment contract or employment relationship*'.[495] The inclusion of this wording, as it stands, clearly attempts to include all these platform workers who are now excluded by protective legislation and regulations, due to their misclassification as self-employed, or because they find themselves in a 'grey zone' between employment and self-employment. In doing so, the article at issue makes an explicit reference to the so-called primacy of facts principle,[496] a tool that courts around the world are broadly using in the determination of the employment relationship[497] and '*it is arguably one of the most important contributions of* [ILO] *Recommendation No. 198 to the already pre-existing body of international labour standards*'.[498] More specifically, Article 3 enshrines that '[t]*he determination of the existence of an employment relationship shall be guided primarily by the facts relating to the actual performance of work*'; such a determination, moreover, shall be taking into consideration '*the use of algorithms in the organisation of platform work, irrespective of how the relationship is classified in any contractual arrangement*'.[499] Thus, not only substance should overcome the formal description of the relationship chosen by the parties, but also this very substance should be interpreted by taking into account novel aspects of work; an exercise that, as examined, has already started to be undertaken by national judges.

Having said that, the most promising feature of the new Directive can be traced in the manner in which it attempts to address the first set of concerns, namely, the

493. Article 1(2) of the proposed Platform Work Directive.
494. *Supra*, De Stefano and Aloisi (2021), referring to Article 2 of the proposed Platform Work Directive.
495. Article 1(2) of the proposed Platform Work Directive.
496. '*For the purposes of the national policy of protection for workers in an employment relationship, the determination of the existence of such a relationship should be guided primarily by the facts relating to the performance of work and the remuneration of the worker, notwithstanding how the relationship is characterized in any contrary arrangement, contractual or otherwise, that may have been agreed between the parties.*' Employment Relationship Recommendation, 2006 (No. 198).
497. *See Supra*, ILO (2016), 262.
498. *Supra*, De Stefano et al. (2021), 31.
499. Article 3(2) of the proposed Platform Work Directive.

employment status of platform workers. It does so, by inserting a rebuttable legal presumption[500] for platform workers' employment status in situations where a '*digital labour platform controls certain elements of the performance of work*'.[501] According to the Directive, the burden of proof that no employment exists will lie on the platform business in question. In order for the presumption to be triggered, platform workers would need to meet at least two out of the five criteria set out in the Directive. In a few words, these are: (a) the setting of wages to specific levels by the platform; (b) workers' obligation to follow certain rules, *inter alia*, with respect to the performance of work and conduct towards clients; (c) the work and its quality need to be supervised, including via electronic means; (d) the platform efficiently restricts, also through sanctions, the freedom to organise one's work, including, the choice of working hours and periods of absence, or the right of workers to be substituted; and finally (e) the platform effectively limiting workers' ability to have their own clientele.[502]

As it has been argued elsewhere, these criteria not only reflect many of the features identified within the business model of many digital labour platforms, but they also mirror key findings from several European courts, ruling in favour of an employee status for platform workers, including, among others, the Supreme courts of France, Spain and the UK.[503] It can therefore be claimed that the existence of such a rebuttable presumption can be extremely valuable for workers' status.[504] That said, albeit with its possible rewards, the inclusion of a legal presumption in the new EU Directive, by no means, as Miriam Kullmann also points out, should be seen as a panacea for platform workers.[505]

As the text of the new instrument stands at the moment, platform workers will still have to go in front of their national courts in order to rip the benefits of the rebuttable legal presumption. There, in a case-by-case scenario, they will have to prove that two out of five criteria are satisfied; as such, they should qualify as employees. This '*moderate*' type of presumption, to use Aloisi's terminology,[506] may still generate difficulties for some workers to establish an employment relationship with the platform, as some of the criteria '*are still drafted in a very stringent way*',[507] let alone the

500. A legal presumption can be also found in the TPWCD, as well as in para. 11(b) of the ILO Employment Relationship Recommendation, 2006 (No. 198).
501. Article 4 of the proposed Platform Work Directive.
502. Article 4 the proposed Platform Work Directive.
503. *Supra*, De Stefano and Aloisi (2021).
504. *See also* Kullmann, M., *'Platformisation' of Work: An EU Perspective on Introducing a Legal Presumption*, European Labour Law Journal, Online 1 (2021), 7, available at: https://journals.sagepub.com/doi/10.1177/20319525211063112 (accessed 30 January 2022).
505. *Supra*, Kukkmann (2021), 7-8.
506. Aloisi in his analysis identifies two main types of presumptions, namely, a 'radical' presumption and a 'moderate' one. The former presumes that all relationships constitute employment relationships and thus, the burden of proof lies entirely on the principal. The latter mitigates the burden of proof by containing one, or several criteria capable of proving the existence of an employment relationship. ALOISI, A., P*latform work in Europe: Lessons learned, legal developments and challenges ahead*, European Labour Law Journal Online Article (2022), 23-24, available at: https://journals.sagepub.com/doi/pdf/10.1177/20319525211062557 (accessed 1 February 2022).
507. *Supra*, De Stefano, Durri, Stylogiannis and Wouters (2022), 24.

costs related to judicial proceedings. The possibly '*burdensome*' nature of the aforementioned criteria, in practice, has also been highlighted by press communication(s), released by the ETUC, as well as some political actors in the EU, soon after the Commission's proposal.[508] On top of this, someone should not underestimate the capacity of a number of platform operators to modify the terms and conditions of their contracts with workers, so as to avoid falling within the ambit of these criteria. This is something that has happened in the past, and further attempts of this kind are expected to take place in the near future. Therefore, as noted, albeit beneficial, the existence of a rebuttable legal presumption cannot be seen as a remedy for all issues platform workers are facing regarding their classification. At a national level, this can also be illustrated by the above-mentioned case against Deliveroo, in Belgium, a country in which a rebuttable presumption of employment applicable to road transport and logistics already exists.[509] In this case, despite the fact that Deliveroo workers managed to meet six out of the eight specific criteria contained in the presumption, the Court ruled the absence of a legal link of subordination, *inter alia*, because of the couriers' unrestricted ability to organise their working time or the absence of a hierarchical relationship with the platform. It is worth mentioning that according to Belgian law, in order for courts to determine whether the presumption is rebutted, they have to examine four (different) general criteria enshrined in the Labour Relations Act.[510] This is a 'structure'('eight' plus 'four') that considerably varies from what the new proposed Directive suggests. This can be an additional challenge to be solved when it comes to EU Member States, which have already included a general presumption in their legal armoury. Should they redefine their general presumptions, or should they create a rebuttable presumption specifically created for platform workers? These rhetorical questions are expected to be answered as the consultations at an EU level proceed.

Moving on, the new Directive also includes other important provisions. In a nutshell, these are meant to capture the specific characteristics emerging from platform work arrangements. To this extent, the proposed instrument acknowledges that risks derive from algorithmic management and, therefore the pressing need for transparency, fairness, and accountability with respect to the use of artificial intelligence and automated systems in the process of work. For instance, workers should have the right to obtain information on automated monitoring systems and decisions made by the platforms themselves '*that significantly affect those platform workers' working conditions*'; such information, among other things, should include their remuneration, their access to work assignments and the suspension, or termination of their contract.[511] The

508. The Greens/Efa, (2021), 'New EU Proposal Makes 4 Million Platform Porkers Eligible for Better Working Conditions', *Press Release*, 9 December 2021, available at: https://www.greens-efa.eu/en/article/press/new-eu-proposal-makes-4-million-platform-workers-eligible-for-better-working-conditions (accessed 1 February 2022); ETUC, (2021), *EU ends free ride for platforms*, Press Release, 9 December 2021, available at: https://www.etuc.org/en/pressrelease/eu-ends-free-ride-platforms (accessed 1 February 2022).
509. As provided for by the Royal Decree of 29 October 2013.
510. Labour Relations Act 2006. These are: (i) the will of the parties; (ii) the freedom to organise the work schedule; (iii) the freedom to organise the manner in which work is performed; and (iv) the existence of hierarchical control.
511. Article 6(1) of the Proposed Directive.

Directive also provides for human monitoring of automated systems and their effect on working conditions; the human resources costs related to this task shall lie on platform operators.[512] Workers, furthermore, are granted the right to due process, as platforms via a written statement of reasons need to make available to them, any significant '*decision taken or supported by an automated decision-making system*', like decisions to suspend a worker's account or refuse payment for work accomplished.[513] Importantly, all these protections should apply to all platform workers, irrespective of their employment status; hence, they also capture self-employed persons.[514] Moreover, these provisions as Kelly-Lyth and Prassl observe, not only built on the already existing framework of the 2016 General Data Protection Regulation (GDPR), but they also complement and expand the latter's protections by, *inter alia*, restricting the ability of platforms to process data that are not directly required by the performance of work.[515]

Furthermore, the proposed Directive does not say much in relation to fundamental collective labour rights and especially with respect to the rights to freedom of association and collective bargaining. Nor it does recognise the fundamental nature of such rights in accordance with international standards and, of course, under the CFREU. Article 9 solely mentions that platform workers' representatives should have the right to information and consultation on '*decisions likely to lead to the introduction of or substantial changes in the use of automated monitoring and decision-making systems*'.[516] In cases there are no such representatives, then information and consultation procedures should take place with platform workers themselves.[517] In addition, the instrument acknowledges the complications these workers can experience in communicating with one another, due to the dispersed nature of their work. To this end, the proposal calls for the Member States to ensure that platform operators will enable the creation of communication channels which will tackle such issues; by doing so, the digital labour platforms should abstain from interfering with those communication mechanisms.[518] Still, the Directive does not go any further than these provisions. As some commentators have already pointed out, there is nothing in this instrument that attempts to enhance social dialogue or to 'push' platforms to actively engage in collective bargaining negotiations with works councils, worker collectives, and unions.[519] Along those lines, no reference is made to the threats that strict antitrust laws can pose for platform workers' collective bargaining rights; something that will be discussed below was left up to the issues EU Guidelines on the application of Union

512. Articles 7(1) and 7(3) of the Proposed Directive.
513. Article 8 of the Proposed Directive.
514. Article 10 of the Proposed Directive.
515. Kelly-Lyth, A., Prassl, J. (2021), 'The EU's Proposed Platform Work Directive: A Promising Step', *VERFASSUNGS* (Blog), 14 December 2021, available at: https://verfassungsblog.de/work-directive/ (accessed 2 February 2022); *see also supra*, De Stefano and Aloisi (2021).
516. Article 9 of the Proposed Directive.
517. *Ibid.*
518. *Ibid.*, Article 15.
519. Fairwork, (2021), 'Fairwork Response to the European Commission's Proposal for a Directive on Platform Work', *Fairwork* (website), 9 January 2021, available at: https://fair.work/en/fw/blog/fairwork-response-to-the-european-commissions-proposal-for-a-directive-on-platform-work/ (accessed 2 February 2022).

competition law to collective agreements regarding the working conditions of solo self-employed persons. Such an absence can possibly limit the effectiveness of this very instrument, as a number of workers will continue to be denied direct access to raise their concerns vis-à-vis platforms.[520]

Overall, without a doubt, the new proposed Directive constitutes a step towards the right direction. According to the Commission's projections, approximately 4 million workers will be eligible for better working conditions. As such, in addition to recent domestic developments attempting to regulate the phenomenon of platform work, the time of the latter's exceptionalism has also started to fade away at a supranational level. This does not mean, however, that the Commission could not go further, either by introducing a less 'moderate' legal presumption or by explicitly recognising the nature of rights, like the right to collective bargaining, as a fundamental one. Therefore, as Rainone contents, '*more needs to be done to decouple workers' access to fundamental labour rights from the "subordination vs autonomy" dichotomy*'.[521] It remains to be seen whether the Directive will maintain its current form after the final consultation stage.

3.2.5 The Impact of Legislation on Platform Workers: An Overall Assessment

The aforementioned examples constitute only some of the legal initiatives which have been taking place around the world with respect to the legal protection of platform workers. Arguably, at the point of writing this research, it would be difficult for someone to assess the actual impact these developments may have in practice. Not only this endeavour can be challenging due to the fact that many of the enacted laws are relatively new,[522] but it can also be very ambitious, as on many occasions, there is a lack of aggravated information on the actual number of workers offering their services via digital labour platforms. Of course, such a statement can considerably vary from one country to another and from one region to the next. Moreover, no matter where they operate, many of these businesses are usually under no legal obligation to reveal the actual number of workers using their apps, or any other relevant information on their workforce. After all, as usually happens with legislative measures, a lot depends and will always depend on the very implementation of these laws in practice.

520. *Ibid.*
521. Rainone, S. (2022), 'Digital Transition: An Opportunity to Advance Labour Rights', *Global Workplace Law & Policy* (blog), 1 February 2022, available at: http://global-workplace-law-and policy.kluwerlawonline.com/2022/02/01/digital-transition-an-opportunity-to-advance-labour -rights/ (accessed 2 February 2022).
522. It has to be argued though that some information is already available regarding the impact of recently enacted laws within the context of platform work. In Spain, for example, shortly after the 'Riders law' came into force, some platforms started to comply with the new law. Moreover, another platform operator, namely, Stuart Delivery, has promised to directly hire an important part of its workers, as well as to negotiate a future collective agreement (the information was found in: Aranguiz, A. (2021), 'Platforms put a spoke in the wheels of Spain's 'riders' law', 2 September 2021, *Social Europe*, available at: https://socialeurope.eu/platforms-put-a-spoke-in -the-wheels-of-spains-riders-law (accessed 12 December 2022)).

Still, for the purposes of this chapter, some general observations need to be made. These, in broad terms, will assist us in evaluating whether the existing legal armoury suffices for the adequate protection of workers within the context of the platform economy, including the protections related to collective labour rights.

To begin with, it can be argued that depending upon the national legal system in question, laws and other forms of regulations might take a considerable amount of time in order to come into force. For instance, regarding the new proposed EU Directive on improving the conditions of platform work, Member States will have up to two years to transpose it into national law. On top of that, at the domestic level, some of the draft bills aiming at the protection of platform workers might be temporarily blocked or not even make it into the law; this is already the reality with respect to some proposed initiatives.[523] As a result, many workers in these occupations need to work for a long period of time under no employment and labour protections, let alone social security entitlements. In addition to that, as explained, some of the *lex specialis* measures adopted in the context of platform work have attempted to deny such workers the possibility of being included within the protective realm of an employment relationship. Of course, some of these laws, like in the case of Belgium, are not in force anymore.[524] Still, in other countries, such as the US, these legislative developments are still in place, and their effect can be detrimental to those who provide their services via a digital platform.

Furthermore, it can be claimed that, up until now, platform-specific measures which aim at extending labour and employment protections to certain categories of platform workers, like in Spain (Riders law), have a rather narrow scope of application. This is to point out that such laws solely concern the protection of workers in the transport and delivery areas. Yet, this is only a small segment of platform-mediated work, and those legislative acts do not necessarily assist the self-employed workers toiling on platforms that, for instance, offer cleaning and care services. Nor do they necessarily ameliorate the working conditions of online crowdworkers. Indeed, both domestic platform workers and crowdworkers have different needs from Uber drivers or Deliveroo riders; therefore, a special treatment for them would be essential.[525] That said, the new Proposed Directive apparently deviates from this narrow scope of application, as it adopts an all-encompassing approach, by covering all the different types of platform workers, including both on-demand workers and crowdworkers. Some commentators though, argue that the instrument could have gone even further, as it risks coving '*only those platforms that organise the work performed by individuals*

523. For instance, *see* the developments in Seattle, US, where a proposed legislation (2015) allowing Uber drivers in the city to organise irrespective of their independent contractor status, was blocked due to a temporary injunction requested by the National Chamber of Commerce (Collier, R.B., Dubal, V. Carter, C. (2017), *Labor Platforms and Gig Work: The Failure to Regulate*, IRLE Working Paper, 21).
524. Similar developments can be also observed in France, with the decision of the Conseil constitutionnel, *Conseil constitutionnel du 20 décembre 2019, décision n° 2019-794*. For an analysis, *see supra*, De Stefano, V., Durri, I., Stylogiannis, C., and Wouters, M (2021), 20.
525. *Supra*, De Stefano, Durri, Stylogiannis and Wouters (2022), 16.

(Article 2), thus potentially excluding some crowdworkers'.[526] Add to this, the instrument's 'failure' to recognise that all platform workers, irrespective of employment classification, should enjoy some basic labour standards in accordance with international standards.

Finally, another point of caution stems from the resistance that platform businesses exert against the implementation of protective legislation, which to a certain extent, 'pushes' them to hand employment contracts to their workforce. This type of legislation, for instance, can derive through the existence of an 'employee unless' presumption. In this respect, in Spain, soon after the 'Riders Law' was adopted, Deliveroo declared that it will stop operating in the country; as a consequence, approximately 3,000 riders could possibly lose their job.[527] Moreover, another big delivery platform, namely Glovo, announced that will only hire a small portion of the workers using its app. In order to justify its decision, the '*company has incorporated changes to its algorithm formula: riders will be able to log in "freely" without selecting time-slots and adjust the price of the delivery slightly* [...] *well as being able to refuse deliveries and subcontract to other workers*'.[528] Undoubtedly, the changes in Glovo's terms and conditions, aim at rebutting the presumption that the new law in Spain establishes, hence, escaping labour-related costs.

Another example with respect to platforms' resistance towards the adoption of new protective legislation can also be observed in the US. As noted, shortly after the enactment of the so-called AB5 law in California, some platform giants, like Uber, by winning a direct ballot initiative, managed to keep their workers away from being subject to the law in question; therefore, their chances of obtaining the employee status faded away. In this regard, Californian voters, by approving Prop 22, were able to undo the work of the legislature, something that the public considered beneficial for these types of workers, as the latter could keep their flexibility and status as independent contractors. It is one of these instances, therefore, that the general public, including platforms' clients, can be proven '*a formidable source of opposition to regulations that threaten these platforms*'.[529] Of course, such an opinion was highly influenced by the massive campaign the platforms themselves initiated. This development also illustrates the political power that such businesses possess in the market. Indeed, As Culpepper and Thelen put it: '*Companies with platform power* [...] *benefit from the tacit allegiance of consumers, who can prove a formidable source of opposition to regulations that threaten these platforms.*'[530] It remains to be seen whether new episodes will be added to the saga of the AB5 law. Until then, many workers in the platform economy will remain unprotected from the protective framework of the employment relationship.

526. *Supra*, Rainone (2022).
527. *Supra*, Aranguiz (2021).
528. *Ibid.*
529. Culpepper, P.D., Thelen, K., *Are We All Amazon Primed? Consumers and the Politics of Platform Power*, 53 Comparative Political Studies 288 n. 2 (2020), 288.
530. *Ibid.*, 294.

3.3 LABOUR LAW RESPONSES: JUDICIAL DEVELOPMENTS

3.3.1 Solutions Through Courts' Interpretation?

In addition to legislative efforts, national courts, in a number of instances, have also attempted to tackle the difficulties stemming from a strict interpretation of subordinate labour. In this regard, it has been observed that several countries have adopted a variety of criteria and tests that are more far-reaching than 'older' tests for the determination of an employment relationship, such as the 'control test', which relied on the mere exercise of control by the employer over the activities of the worker. For instance, courts in the US, through the development of the 'economic-realities' test, can rely on a variety of factors that focus on the economic dependency of workers on their employers, rather than putting an emphasis on the power to control the working activities.[531] Moreover, in South Africa, the courts, by following the 'dominant impression test', are able to look at all the aspects of the contract and not rely on a single factor, such as the right of supervision or control, which is an important consideration, but not a conclusive proof of the existence of an employment relationship.[532] Other multi-factor tests (e.g., integration test, mutuality of obligations) have also been adopted in a number of common law countries, such as the UK, India and Australia, as well as in some civil law countries, like Greece; such tests can include different considerations, depending on the legal framework of the national jurisdiction in question.[533] In a similar vein, the Dutch Supreme Court has clarified that for the assessment of the existence of an employment relationship, a number of indicators should be taken under consideration (holistic approach), including, *inter alia*, the freedom of workers to refuse work, who bares the economic risks and who possesses the materials to perform the work and whether the work is performed for a living.[534]

At this point, it should be mentioned, however, that the development of a wide variety of criteria and tests for the determination of an employment relationship does not constitute a panacea in terms of problems related to labour classification. The 'mutuality of obligations' test in the UK, for instance, has been used in a way that, on many occasions, short-term and intermittent workers in precarious jobs have been excluded from the protections of labour law.[535] Likewise, the 'dominant impression' test in South Africa has been heavily criticised by some scholars, as it fails to give a

531. *Supra*, ILO (2016), 263.
532. For instance, *see Smit v. Workmen's Compensation Commissioner* 1979 (1) SA 51 (A).
533. *Supra*, ILO (2016), 264.
534. Digennaro, P., *Subordination or Subjection? A Study About the Dividing Line Between Subordinate Work and Self-Employment in Six European Legal Systems*, 6 Labour & Law Issues 1 n. 1 (2020), 18, citing the rulings: Dutch Supreme Court, 11 February 2011, *JAR 2011/75*; Dutch Supreme Court, 17 November, 1978 1979, 140 and 5 November, 1982, NJ 1983, 231; Dutch Supreme Court, 8 May, 1998, *JAR 1998/168*.
535. Countouris, N., *Uses and Misuses of 'Mutuality of Obligations' and the Autonomy of Labour Law* (Alan Bogg, Cathryn Costello, Anne C.L. Davies, Jeremias Prassl eds, *The Autonomy of Labour Law*, Hart Publishing 2015), 169-188.

clear definition of who is an employee and offers no assistance in cases of classification for workers between employment and self-employment.[536] In some cases, as Deakin has pointed out, this problematic aspect can be, in part, attributed to the fact that some courts in determining the existence of an employment relationship have rigorously interpreted legal tests, which, although more recent, they are no more than a modified form of more traditional legal tests that have resurfaced.[537]

Furthermore, another way that courts have attempted to broaden the scope of the employment relationship or employment protection, is by adopting a more 'expansive' interpretation of the concept of subordinated labour. For example, as Adams and Deakin indicate, since the 1980s, the French courts have also taken a broad purposive approach to the issue of the personal scope of protective legislation.[538] This development, as the authors contend and by relying on the work of others, has been abetted by legislative reforms that have shifted the burden of proof on the employer in situations where a person finds herself or himself in the 'grey zone' between employment and self-employment.[539] Some courts, moreover, have adopted looser criteria when applying the control test in a way that its criteria can be satisfied, even in cases where the elements of direction and control with respect to all the aspects of work are not exerted by the employer.[540] This, for instance, is observed in some civil law jurisdictions, such as Italy. In this respect, the Italian Supreme Court has, on various occasions, pointed out that the threshold of subordination can also be satisfied in cases where the employer did not continuously provide the worker with detailed instructions, employers did not exercise an overall control over the organisation of work or the activities related to it.[541]

Still, as noted above, a broad legal interpretation is not always the case. In the vast majority of legal systems around the world, the notion of subordination is still perceived through the lenses of direction and control, which still play a key role in the determination of the existence of an employment relationship. On top of that, in some countries, like Slovakia, this notion, as Diggenaro points out, can still be interpreted in a quite inelastic manner that remains solely rooted in the idea of external direction.[542] It can be argued, therefore, that on many occasions, there is a strict interpretation of the courts rather than the legal elements in question per se (as seen, the control test can be also interpreted in broader terms) which can restrict the access of many workers to labour protection. This is something that can be also observed with respect to the case law related to platform work.

536. Benjamin P., *An Accident of History: Who Is (and Who Should Be) an Employee under South African Labour Law*, 25 Industrial Law Journal 787 n. 5 (2004), 787-804.
537. *Supra*, Adams and Deakin (2014), 797.
538. *Ibid.*
539. *Ibid.*, 796.
540. *Supra*, ILO (2016), 264.
541. *Ibid.*, citing the rulings: Corte di Cassazione, 5 May 2004, No. 8569; Corte di Cassazione, 26 February 2002, No. 2842.
542. *Supra*, Digennaro (2020), 15.

3.3.2 Judicial Responses to Platform Work

It comes as no surprise that as in other work-related areas where courts and tribunals have to rule on the existence or not of an employment relationship, their approach regarding platform-mediated work varies significantly, albeit, lately, a more coherent approach can be observed. This is to say that, in several recent cases ruled by national courts, especially within a European context, a 'consistent set of patterns' has emerged, which is more and more applied in order to expose the misclassification of a number of platform workers as independent contractors, by relying on a broad range of factors.[543] Still, as I argue below, this development, although it constitutes a positive sign, should not be perceived as a panacea for all the issues related to the employment status of such workers.

As noted, since the emergence of work offered via digital labour platforms, national courts around the world have demonstrated a considerable divergence with respect to the degree of flexibility afforded to their interpretation when they have to rule on the question of platform workers' employment status. In particular, on several occasions, a rigid reliance on the flexibility of work schedules offered via platform businesses has been proven decisive in classifying platform workers as self-employed. Indeed, either as a primary ground in courts' interpretation or, in other cases, as a complementary justification,[544] continuity in time for the provision of work often remains an insurmountable obstacle for the existence of an employment relationship in a number of countries.[545] This is something that is mainly observed in cases concerning on-demand workers, such as those in delivery and transport services. For instance, in Brazil, in a case brought against Uber, both the *Superior Tribunal de Justiça* and the *Tribunal Superior do Trabalho* were of the opinion that drivers' flexibility regarding their work schedule was enough in order to deny these workers their reclassification as employees.[546]

Furthermore, in Italy, in 2018, a Tribunal in Turin, in a case brought against Foodora, an online delivery platform, rejected the claim of six delivery workers to be reclassified as employees of the platform.[547] The court heavily relied on the fact that these workers '*were allegedly free to decide when to work and to disregard previously agreed shifts*'.[548] In September 2018, a similar line of thought was also adopted by the Milan Tribunal, this time in a case against Glovo; the workers' freedom to choose whether to accept or reject a task and when, was enough for them to be classified as

543. Aloisi, A., *Demystifying Flexibility, Exposing the Algorithmic Boss: A Note on the First Italian Case Classifying a (Food-Delivery) Platform Worker as an Employee*, Comparative Labor Law & Policy Journal, Dispatches (2021).
544. For instance, *see* Fair Work Commission 21 December 2017, Case No. [2017] FWC 6610, *Mr Michail Kaseris v. Rasier Pacific V.O.F* (U2017/9452), §54.
545. *Supra* De Stefano, V., Durri, I., Stylogiannis, C., and Wouters, M. (2021).
546. Superior Tribunal de Justiça, 28 de agosto de 2019, Case No. 164.544 – MG (2019/0079952-0); Tribunal Superior do Trabalho, 5 de fevereiro de 2020, Case No. TST-RR-1000123-89.2017. 5.02.0038.
547. Tribunale Ordinario di Torino 7 maggio 2018, Case No. 778/2018.
548. *Supra*, De Stefano (2018).

self-employed.[549] Instances of such reasoning can also be observed in other cases in countries like France,[550] as well as in the US.[551]

In addition to the flexibility of working time, the element of control can also be particularly challenging in terms of labour protection for those engaged in platform work. The problems indeed arise when such an element is interpreted by courts in a rather narrow manner and without taking into account the impact that new technological tools, such as algorithms and rating systems, have over the direction of platform workers. A court in the US, for instance, in a case against Uber, denied the employee status to a taxi driver, as the company's level of control was incompatible with the control to which a traditional employee is subject.[552] The court went on to point out that it was up to the passengers to direct and assess the performance of the driver via a rate and review system.[553] Moreover, in a recent case deriving from the jurisdiction of New Zealand, the Employment Court in Auckland ruled that the direction and control exerted by Uber were not adequate enough, '*beyond some matters that might be expected given* [the driver] *was operating using the Uber "brand"*'.[554] Consequently, an employment relationship could not be established. The absence of direct control has also been used by other courts around the world as a decisive factor in rejecting the reclassification of several platform workers as employees of the platform in question.[555] It should be mentioned though that, in some cases, this element, or more precisely the lack of this element, was not the sole justification used by courts in denying the role of certain digital platforms, like Uber, as employers pursuant to national legal standards; as it usually happens other work-related aspects were taken into account.[556] This, however, does not negate the fact that a strict interpretation of the existence of 'control' over workers can contribute to the exclusion of workers from the enjoyment of basic labour rights.

Having said that, and fortunately for workers in the platform economy, a number of recent developments reveal that some courts are now ready to expand their interpretation, for instance, by recognising, how technology can enable platforms to enhance their overall control over workers' activities. Illustrative in this regard is the acknowledgement by courts in Brazil and France that algorithmic technology can

549. Tribunale di Milano 10 settembre 2018, Case No. 1853/2018; *see also* Kilhoffer, Z., De Groen, W. P., Lenaerts, K., Smits, I., Hauben, H., Waeyaert, W., Giaumacatos, E., Lhernould, J.-P., Robin-Olivier, S. (2019), *Study to gather evidence on the working conditions of platform workers*, Luxembourg, Publications Office of the European Union.
550. Cour d'appel de Paris du 9 novembre 2017, Case No. 16/12875. This court seems to change its rhetoric in subsequent cases (*see* below).
551. United States District Court E.D. Pennsylvania 11 April 2018, Case No. CV 16-573, *Ali Razak et al. v. Uber Technologies*.
552. U.S.A., District Court of Appeal of Florida 1 February 2017, Case No. 3D15-2758, *McGillis v. Dept. of Economic Opportunity, et al.*, p. 14, available at: https://law.justia.com/cases/florida/third-district-court-of-appeal/2017/3d15-2758.html (accessed 10 September 2020).
553. *Ibid.*, 5.
554. Employment Court of New Zealand Auckland 17 December 2020, Case No. [2020] NZEmpC 230, *Arachchige v. Rasier New Zealand Ltd & Uber BV*.
555. *Supra*, DE STEFANO, et al. (2021), 50-51; For instance, *see Mr Michail Kaseris v. Rasier Pacific V.O.F*, para. 56, in Australia.
556. *Ibid.*, 51-52.

indeed permit platforms to improve their control over workers, in a manner that can be equally effective to the control exercised by a devoted manager.[557] Characteristic in relation to the role of new technologies in modern workplaces are the words of the Brazilian judge who indicates that:

> within the 'brave new world'[558] in which the human acts of exteriorization of directive and supervisory power are no longer necessary and are replaced by algorithmic combinations, thus demanding new theoretical dimensions and updates of labour law, so that this important and civilizing area of law does not let the total form of subordination and control built within a form of flexibilization go unnoticed.[559]

In a similar vein, in October 2020, for the first time, a labour court in Chile ruled that a platform worker is an employee. The ruling was heavily based on the fact that various aspects of the contractual relationship, such as the ranking scores and the ability of the platform to deactivate the worker's account, were indicative of dependence and subordination.[560] Furthermore, in late 2020, the Palermo Tribunal reclassified a rider of Glovo, by rejecting its 'fictional' autonomy, *inter alia,* on the grounds that the platform, via its algorithm, is capable of organising the execution of the work performed, as well as discipline noncompliance through rigid instructions.[561] The ability of algorithms to direct and control the overall performance of platform workers and supervise their activities in a manner that equates to the powers typical of an employer has also been recognised by several other rulings around the world.[562]

Another important development in this context is the fact that several courts have now acknowledged that the feature of flexibility in the working schedules of many platform workers does not by itself preclude the existence of an employment relationship. To this extent, in a seminal case against Glovo, the Spanish *Tribunal Supremo* confirmed that albeit the couriers in question had certain flexibility with regards to their working hours, such elasticity was limited due to the existence of a 'scoring system' utilised by the platform.[563] According to the court, through this system, Glovo, among other things, can get informed about the ratings that customers give to couriers and the performance of services during peak hours. If workers cannot perform a task during peak hours, then their scores drop, and as a result, it gets more difficult for them

557. France, Cour de cassation du 4 mars 2020, Case No. ECLI:FR:CCAS:2020:SO00374, available at: https://www.courdecassation.fr/jurisprudence_2/chambre_sociale_576/374_4_44522.html (accessed 10 September 2020); Brazil, 33ª Vara do Trabalho de Belo Horizonte 13 de fevereiro de 2017, Case No. 0011359-34.2016.5.03.0112, available at: https://www.conjur.com.br/dl/juiz-reconhece-vinculo-emprego-uber.pdf (accessed 10 September 2020).
558. The expression refers to the effects that the advancement of science has on human beings and it is based on the science-fiction novel written by Aldous Huxley, in 1932.
559. *Supra* (Case No. *0011359-34.2016.5.03.0112*), 25.
560. Chile, Juzgado de Letras del Trabajo de Concepción 5 de octubre de 2020, Case No. M-724-2020, available at: https://oficinajudicialvirtual.pjud.cl/indexN.php (accessed 10 September 2020).
561. Tribunale di Palermo 20 novembre 2020, Case No. 3570/2020; *Supra* ALOISI, (2021).
562. *Supra*, De Stefano, et al. (2021); For instance, *see* Tribunal de Apelaciones de Trabajo de Montevideo de 1° Turno, 3 de junio de 2020, Case No. 0002-003894/2019, in Uruguay.
563. Tribunal Supremo 25 septiembre 2020, Case No. ECLI: ES:TS:2020:2924.

to access the time slots with the highest customer demand.[564] Therefore, the 'alleged' flexibility of these workers did not prevent the court from finding that they are actually hooked on an employment relationship. Other courts in Spain have espoused the same reasoning.[565]

In France, moreover, the *Cour d'appel de Paris* highlighted that Uber drivers' sovereignty over their working hours did not necessarily mean that they were not employees of the company. The court went on to argue that they were indeed subject to the control and supervision of Uber, which could also discipline the workers if their performance was not in compliance with the company's instructions.[566] In this way, the court appeared to change its rhetoric from a previous judgment where it had ruled that the freedom of Deliveroo couriers to decide upon their shifts was detrimental to establishing an employment relationship with the digital labour platform in question.[567] In a similar manner, in Germany, the Federal Court, the *Bundesarbeitsgericht*, overruled a decision taken by a labour court in Munich,[568] which, at first, by heavily relying on workers' flexibility of working time had denied that they were actually employed by the platform. The *Bundesarbeitsgericht*, however, was of the opinion that such alleged flexibility was curtailed by an 'incentive system' that was pushing workers to accept specific shifts.[569] On top of that, the platform was directing the performance of tasks. Thus, the court ruled in favour of the workers.

Arguably, this general realisation by national courts as to how platform businesses can, in fact, control, supervise and sanction a great portion of their workers, for instance, via the use of algorithmic technologies, is profoundly expressed by the 2021 ruling of the Supreme Court in the UK, in *Uber v. Aslam*.[570] The long-awaited decision was celebrated by many advocates of labour rights. De Stefano, in this respect, pointed out that the court's analysis '*perfectly captures both the gist of the case at hand and the substance of the whole global debate on platform work*'.[571] Indeed, the Supreme Court, by touching upon a broad range of factors and ruled that 25 Uber drivers should be classified as 'workers',[572] entitled to certain statutory rights, such as a minimum wage and paid holidays. Among other things, it was ruled that Uber retained a sufficient amount of control over its workers, in a manner that was indicative of a classic form of

564. *Supra*, De Stefano, et al. (2021).
565. For instance, *see* Tribunal Superior de Justícia de Catalunya 21 de febrer de 2020, Case No. 1034/2020.
566. Cour d'appel de Paris 10 janvier 2019, Case No. 18/08357.
567. *Supra*, Case No. 16/12875.
568. Landesarbeitsgericht München 4. Dezember 2019, Case No. 8 Sa 146/19, specially para. 35. For a further analysis, *see Supra*, De Stefano, et al. (2021).
569. Bundesarbeitsgericht 1. December 2020, Case No. 9 AZR 102/20.
570. The Supreme Court 19 February 2021, Case No. [2021] UKSC 5, *Uber BV and others v. Aslam and others*.
571. De Stefano, (2021), 'Regulation is not an À la Carte menu: insights from the Uber judgment', 2 March 2021, *UK Labour Law Blog*, available at: https://uklabourlawblog.com/2021/03/02/regulation-is-not-an-a-la-carte-menu-insights-from-the-uber-judgment-by-valerio-de-stefano/ (accessed 29 March 2021).
572. As noted limb-b workers constitutes an intermediate category through they are entitled to certain labour protections.

subordination.[573] Furthermore, the court made it clear that flexibility of work schedules '*does not preclude a finding that the individual is a worker, or indeed an employee*'.[574] After all, as it was argued, such an alleged flexibility was constrained by Uber via its rating system.

3.3.3 Some Observations in Relation to the Case Law in the Context of Platform Work

Undoubtedly, besides any legal complexities, recent developments show that platform work can be embedded within contemporary legal tests for the determination of the employment relationship; thus, it can be argued that platform work is indeed reconcilable with the employee status, and the latter should not be denied to workers in the name of modern business models. Furthermore, some of the recent courts' decisions have caused a sequence of events that have sparked a further sense of optimism. Illustrative is the fact that after the Supreme Court's ruling in the UK, Uber has decided to guarantee its thousands of UK drivers a minimum hourly wage and holiday pay, and they will be automatically enrolled in a company pension plan with contributions from the company alongside their own.[575] It is not yet clear, nonetheless, as to whether Uber will pay its drivers for its past failure to compensate for their working activities. In addition, drivers will be eligible for a minimum wage and holiday payment from the moment that a ride is accepted to when passengers arrive at their final destination and not the whole time drivers are logging on to its application.[576] According to some trade unionists, this can result in a situation where drivers will lose up to 50 per cent of potential earnings.[577] Still, such a development can put further pressure on other platform businesses in the country to adopt a similar stance, by at least offering some minimum labour protections to their workers.

Along the lines of what is happening in the UK after the Supreme Court's ruling, in Spain, the government and the social partners reached an agreement for the introduction of a 'riders law',[578] which enshrines a rebuttable presumption of an employment relationship for food-delivery riders. Importantly, it has been argued that

573. The Supreme Court specifically indicated: '*the ratings are used by Uber purely as an internal tool for managing performance and as a basis for making termination decisions where customer feedback shows that drivers are not meeting the performance levels set by Uber. This is a classic form of subordination that is characteristic of employment relationships*', *supra*, Case No. [2021] UKSC 5, para. 99.
574. *Ibid.*, 91.
575. Butler, S. (2021), 'Uber to pay UK drivers minimum wage, holiday pay and pension', 16 March 2021, *The Guardian*, available at: https://www.theguardian.com/technology/2021/mar/16/uber-to-pay-uk-drivers-minimum-wage-holiday-pay-and-pension (accessed 30 March 2021).
576. Brown, J. (2021), 'Uber's rollout of living wage will put 'further pressure' on other gig economy firms to follow suit, experts warn', 17 March 2021, *People Management*, available at: https://www.peoplemanagement.co.uk/news/articles/ubers-rollout-living-wage-will-put-further-pressure-on-other-gig-economy-firms?fbclid=IwAR0jngPs-ZHwO5G-BlrVmOjCTArLLPGCAXwwukzAGg9NKZrWfHi1IBpjFAw (accessed 30 March 2021).
577. *Supra*, Brown (2021).
578. The agreement available at: https://www.ugt.es/sites/default/files/comunicado_mites_aass_logo_1.pdf (accessed 30 March 2021).

this agreement does nothing more than to transpose into a law '*what has already been recognised by several national courts and the Spanish Supreme Court itself: "riders" ought to be considered workers*'.[579] Such a presumption is implemented into Spanish law through the amendment of the existing Worker's Statute. As a consequence, platform-mediated delivery workers will be able to enjoy the whole range of labour rights and social protection benefits.

Having said that, as noted at the beginning of this section, these recent positive developments, albeit extremely important, should not be expected by themselves to solve all the issues related to platform workers' employment status. First of all, as Dukes and Streeck emphasise, their access to fundamental labour rights and protections '*must not be dependent on the willingness and ability of individual workers to bring claims to the courts*'.[580] On top of that, proceedings before courts can last for a long period of time and be very costly, discouraging this way many workers from vindicating their rights. Second, the determination of the existence of an employment relationship by national courts occurs on a case-by-case basis. Therefore, the aforementioned rulings apply directly solely to those platform workers who brought the claims. Of course, as in the case of *Uber v. Aslam*, in the UK, some court decisions can affect others employed on identical contractual terms.[581] Still, these cases are limited and a great portion of workers engaged in work of a similar nature remains unprotected.

Third, platforms, such as Uber, can unilaterally determine the terms and conditions of their engagement with clients and workers. As a result, for those who will be employed under different contracts, new decisions by courts will be necessary in order to clarify their employment status; until these new rulings will be available, many platform workers can be excluded from labour protections. Fourth, as seen from the above analysis, and partly due to the 'types of contracts' offered through platforms, there has been a number of contradictory rulings that have classified platform workers in different ways when working in the same country, on the same platform. Thus, the determination of employment relationships in the platform economy remains complex and far from settled.[582] This argument can be further supported by some recent decisions made by two lower instance courts in France[583] and Belgium.[584] The courts at issue, by taking a rather restrictive approach towards the interpretation of crucial

579. Aranguiz, A. (2021), 'Spain's platform workers win algorithm transparency', 18 March 2021, *Social Europe*, available at: https://www.socialeurope.eu/spains-platform-workers-win-algorithm-transparency?fbclid=IwAR3cZoGEWJNveKMRScwpkUNnQUMHFAa9htj5-J5IxVxjPE2HsxqEL8SAhOc (accessed 30 March 2021); The new law contains other important provisions, such as the regulation of algorithmic transparency that will be discussed below.
580. Dukes, R. Streeck, W. (2021), 'Putting the brakes on the spread of indecent work', 10 March 2021, *Social Europe*, available at: https://www.socialeurope.eu/putting-the-brakes-on-the-spread-of-indecent-work (accessed 30 March 2021).
581. *Ibid.*
582. *Supra*, De Stefano, et al. (2021).
583. Cour d'appel de Lyon du 15 janvier 2021, Case No. *9/08056*.
584. Tribunal du travail francophone de Bruxelles du 8 Décembre, Case No. *2021/014148*, available at: https://www.tribunaux-rechtbanken.be/sites/default/files/tt_bruxelles/news_files/20211208-ttfb-deliveroo.pdf (accessed 30 March 2021).

elements for the establishment of an employment relationship, such as those in relation to control by technology, ruled against the reclassification of platform workers in two cases against Uber and Deliveroo, respectively. More in particular, the *Cour d'appel de Lyon*, in France, by deciding on Uber's ability to control its drivers, expressed the view that:

> It is the customers who have the possibility of assigning marks at the end of each trip, within the framework of a system of appreciation of the quality of the service rendered. This is a classic practice in this type of digital platform, and it is not Uber itself which assigns the mark, excluding any idea of disciplinary power.[585]

The 'alleged' lack of control, therefore, constituted an insuperable obstacle for the Court in Lyon in finding the existence of an employment relationship. It can be stressed that this is a considerably different position from the one that the *Cour de cassation* adopted in a similar case against the same platform company just a few months before the judgment in question.

Moreover, in my view, equally striking and not necessarily for good reasons was the reasoning from a Belgian court in a case brought by a number of Deliveroo drivers. In this case, the court, by rejecting the latter's reclassification as employees,[586] also focused on the absence of control, which governs the relationship between the platform and its workers. What was particularly interesting and problematic, though, was the analysis of the court in certain parts of the judgment. For example, there is a specific paragraph where the judge reasoned that Deliveroo's delivery drivers are being tracked (by the company's monitoring tools), not for the sake of the platform exerting control, but for the customers to be able to track their order and for Deliveroo to facilitate the delivery in case bikers face an unexpected problem (e.g., they run a flat tyre).[587] Thus, the court proceeded with a narrative that the control exercised by an algorithm, 'it is only the customer' or, it is 'to help out the customers', instead off to control the workers.

Lastly, and moving on with our analysis, it is observed that most of the cases brought in front of national courts are mainly against well-known digital labour platforms, like Uber, Deliveroo, and Glovo, which mainly operate in the delivery and transportation sectors. Considering the broad range of services offered via platforms, as well as the total number of these types of businesses, it seems extremely difficult that the totality of problems regarding platform workers' employment status can be resolved solely through the interpretation of the courts.

Overall, as Supiot observes, despite the fact that national courts have '*identified in management by algorithm all the features of wage subordination*', platform workers continue to be often '*retained in an inferior employment status by political leaders who*

585. *Supra*, Case No. *9/08056*. The analysis was found in *supra* De Stefano et al. (2021), 36.
586. Workers' reclassification was first put forward by the Belgian administrative commission (Commission Administrative de règlement de la relation de travail du 23 février 2018, *Case No. 116 – FR – 20180209*). This decision, however, was later on declared null and void on procedural grounds.
587. *Supra*, Case No. *2021/014148*, pp. 83 and 84 of the judgment.

are subject to intense lobbying by platforms'.[588] As an immediate result, these workers are usually prevented from accessing their fundamental collective rights, also recognised as human rights. Thus, the threat of a chilling effect on the enjoyment of such rights remains imminent. As it is argued below (Chapter 5) a more far-reaching approach is indeed necessary in order for such workers and other workers in NSFE to be able to enjoy important labour protections, including the effective exercise of their fundamental collective labour rights.

3.4 RESPONSES FROM A COMPETITION LAW PERSPECTIVE

The restrictions competition law(s) can impose on the enjoyment of the right to collective bargaining constitutes an issue that for quite some has attracted the attention of lawmakers around the world, at both national and supranational level. According to research conducted by the OECD, some countries have attempted to resolve these issues via a variety of regulatory measures.[589] For instance, a number of domestic legal orders have made the right to bargain collectively available for workers falling in an intermediate status between employment and self-employment, where national legislations provide for the latter classification. As previously mentioned, this is, for example, the case in countries, such as Italy with the so-called category of *lavolatori parasubordinati* (parasubordinate workers), or the UK with the category of limb-b workers.[590] In a similar vein, in Canada, Part I of the Industrial Relations Code enshrines that 'dependent contractors' should be treated as employees with respect to their right to collective bargaining, despite the fact that their employment relationship does not resemble a traditional employer-employee relationship.[591] In doing so, the legislative act in question gives an expansive definition of who can be qualified as an 'employee'.[592] The origins of such an approach derive from the early work of Professor Harry Arthurs, who was of the opinion that self-employed persons have more in common with precarious employees than with genuine entrepreneurs; thus, collective bargaining should not be restricted on the basis of the existence of a traditional employment relationship.[593] That said, the presence of an intermediate status in

588. Supiot, A., *Labour Is Not a Commodity: The Content and Meaning of Work in the Twenty-first Century*, 160 International Labour Review n. 1 (2021), 4.
589. OECD, (2019), *Negotiating our way up: Collective bargaining in a changing world of work*, Paris, OECD.
590. *Ibid.*, 239.
591. *Canada Labour Code*, R.S., c. L-1, section 1; The British Columbia Labour Relations Code enshrines a pretty similar provision (For an analysis *see*: McCrystal, S., *Collective Bargaining Beyond the Boundaries of Employment: A Comparative Analysis*, 37 Melbourne University Law Review 662 n. 3 (2014), 662-698.
592. According to Part I of the Canadian Labour Code: '*employee means any person employed by an employer and includes a dependent contractor and a private constable, but does not include a person who performs management functions or is employed in a confidential capacity in matters relating to industrial relation*'.
593. Secretariat to the Expert Panel on Modern Federal Labour Standards, (2019) *Federal Labour Standards Protections for Workers in NonStandard Work*, Issue Paper, 4, available at: https://www.canada.ca/content/dam/esdc-edsc/documents/services/reports/SPAWID-SPLR-Issue Paper-Non-StandardWork-FINAL-EN.pdf (accessed 8 October 2021).

Canada, as well as in other jurisdictions, should not be seen as a panacea for the exercise of the right to collective bargaining. Intermediate categories mainly include those workers who most closely resemble employment ('employee-like' workers). For instance, their income, or a considerable part of it, should derive from a single employer. As pointed out, within modern workplaces, many of these workers might find it difficult to satisfy some of the current criteria for the existence of dependent self-employment. Along these lines, McCrystal argues that such criteria may be strictly interpreted by courts or labour tribunals, thus '*perpetuate the "employee or contractor" problem, shifting it to a question of "dependent or independent contractor"*'.[594]

Moreover, there are some governments that have decided to alter their competition national laws with the purpose of excluding certain categories of genuine self-employed workers, finding themselves in a power asymmetry in relation to their customer/employer, from the scope of antitrust laws. An illustrative example can be found in Ireland, where the domestic law was recently amended to include some specific categories of workers beyond employees, that may be allowed to conclude a collective agreement.[595] Particularly, the amendment identifies two types of self-employed persons capable of being exempted from antitrust laws, namely, 'false self-employed' and 'fully dependent self-employed' workers. The criteria that need to be identified in order for someone to fall into the former category closely are similar to the ones used by the CJEU in the *FNV Knusten* case. This is to say that a worker should perform '*the same activity or service as an employee of the other person*'.[596] After having established this prerequisite, then further elements need to be satisfied, including whether the worker in question is an integral part of the undertaking and whether she or he works under the direction of another person within a subordinate relationship.[597] In relation to the category of 'fully dependent self-employed', an individual can fall under this definition in cases in which she or he:

> (a) performs services for another person (whether or not the person for whom the service is being performed is also an employer of employees) under a contract [...], and (b) whose main income in respect of the performance of such services under contract is derived from not more than 2 persons.[598]

Having said that, trade unions, which represent the interests of one of these two categories of self-employed workers, may conclude a collective agreement on their behalf. In doing so, the union at issue will have to prove that the collective agreement '*will have no or minimal economic effect on the market in which the class of self-employed worker concerned operates*'.[599] It will also have to show that the agreement will not constitute a significant financial burden for the State and the requirements of the national and EU competition laws will not be contravened.[600] On top of that, the

594. *Supra*, McCrystal (2014), 695.
595. Competition (Amendment) Act 2017.
596. *Ibid.*, section 15 D.
597. *Ibid.*
598. *Ibid.*
599. *Ibid.*, section 15 F.
600. *Ibid.*

Irish Parliament via the 2017 law amendment has also introduced an automatic exemption to the cartel prohibition for certain professions such as freelance journalists and actors.[601] Legal exemptions for specific professions can be also found in other legal systems around the world.[602]

The developments in Ireland have not escaped criticism from different sides. For example, as De Stefano and Countouris have pointed out the explicit reference of the Act to an income derived from not more than two principals can be tricky, particularly as far as platform workers are concerned, as they often work for more than two platforms.[603] In a similar vein, Giorgio Monti in his analysis has expressed his concerns regarding the complex criteria that a trade union has to satisfy in order to conclude a valid collective agreement for the self-employed workers it represents.[604] He argues that after all, if the agreement in question is found to distort EU competition law and its strict requirements, then the latter will eventually fail to be exempted from the domestic antitrust authorities. The 2017 amendment has also been criticised by some Irish employers as they are concerned about the low levels of clarity with respect to the criteria applied to identify 'fully dependent' and 'false' self-employed workers.[605]

Going back to other legal developments, in the Netherlands, the Authority for Competition and Markets (ACM) has recently issued some guidelines that outline the situations in which price arrangements between self-employed persons are to be allowed.[606] Such guidelines, to a certain extent attempt to codify the decision of the CJEU in the *FNV Knusten* case; hence, among other things, they provide that within the meaning of the Dutch Competition Act, self-employed workers will not be treated as undertakings if they work side-by-side with employees, and the kind of work they are performing cannot be distinguished when compared to the work undertaken by these employees.[607] Notably, this comparison can take place not solely with employees working for the same business, but also with employees who perform work of a similar nature elsewhere.[608] Of course, this exercise will require substantive evidence from the side of the parties who have entered the collective agreement that their situation is indeed similar to their alleged counterparts.

Finally, the guidelines as they currently stand, enshrine that a collective agreement concluded by self-employed workers will not be sanctioned by the ACM, if it can

601. According to Schedule 4 of the new Irish Act, these occupations consist of: '*(1) [a]ctors engaged as voice-over actors; (2) [m]usicians engaged as session musicians; (3) [j]ournalists engaged as freelance journalists*'.
602. According to an OECD report such exemptions can be, *inter alia*, traced in countries such as, the US and Australia: *see supra*, OECD (2019), 240.
603. Countouris, N., De Stefano, V. (2019), *New trade union strategies for new forms of employment. ETUC. Brussels*, 50.
604. Monti, G., *Collective Labour Agreements and EU Competition Law: Five Reconfigurations*, 17 European Competition Journal 714 n. 3 (2021), 714-744.
605. *Supra*, OECD (2019), 240.
606. ACM, Guidelines: Price Arrangements Between Self-Employed Workers (updated June 2020) para. 3, available at: https://www.acm.nl/sites/default/files/documents/2020-07/guidelines-on-price-arrangements-between-self-employed-workers.pdf (accessed 21 October 2021).
607. *Ibid.*
608. *Supra*, Monti (2021), 723.

be proved the agreement aims at '*safeguard*[ing] *their subsistence level*'.[609] Albeit, this wording seems promising for self-employed workers in a precarious situation, things are less straightforward than they may look from a first reading. Indeed as Monti explains, the complex part with this provision lies in the fact that in case these kinds of agreements are discovered, then they would be automatically deemed invalid, except if the parties involved are able to amend them in order to comply with competition law.[610] Still, it is not very clear how the agreements in question can be modified so as to escape the antitrust authorities.

The aforementioned examples constitute only some of the regulatory approaches taken around the world in order to resolve some of the issues stemming from the conflict between labour law and competition law. Arguably, workers falling in the grey zone between traditional employment and self-employment can be benefited from such policies. As explained, strict legal tests and labyrinthine conditions, which in many instances are necessary for workers to escape antitrust authorities, continue to impose severe obstacles on the exercise of the right to collective bargaining. These restrictions are present despite the fact that many of these workers do not have many characteristics in common with genuine self-employed persons.

As noted, such limitations have become particularly apparent within the context of the platform economy. In a number of instances, strict antitrust laws have prevented platform workers from entering into collective agreements which aim at improving their working conditions. This is, for example, the case in Seattle, in the US. More specifically, in 2015, the local authorities passed an ordinance that permitted rideshare drivers to collectively negotiate terms and conditions of their relationship with digital labour platforms, like Uber and Lyft.[611] The collective negotiations attempted to increase the wages and improve the working conditions of such workers. However, after a lengthy legal battle initiated by the platforms in question, the ordinance was found to violate the domestic antitrust laws; thereby, it was nullified.[612] Furthermore, the threat of competition laws towards platform workers' collective negotiations with their platforms can be also traced in other countries, such as Denmark, where the national competition authorities have recently 'shown their teeth' against a collective agreement signed between the trade union 3F and the Hilfr platform. Part of the agreement was materially undermined as it was considered price-fixing between undertakings, a decision that has attracted heavy criticism from some scholars.[613]

609. ACM, Guidelines: Price Arrangements Between Self-Employed Workers (updated June 2020) section 7.
610. *Supra*, Monti (2021), 723.
611. Garden, C., *The Seattle Solution: Collective Bargaining by For-Hire Drivers and Prospects for ProLabor Federalism*, 12 Harvard Law and Policy Review Online 1 (2017), 1-22.
612. Groover, H. (2020), 'Lengthy legal fight over Seattle's Uber unionization law comes to an end', 13 April 2020 (updated 14 April 2020), *The Seattle Times*, available at: https://www.seattletimes.com/seattle-news/transportation/lengthy-legal-fight-over-seattles-uber-unionization-law-comes-to-an-end/ (accessed 29 December 2021).
613. For instance, *see* Countouris, N. and De Stefano, V. (2020), 'Collective-bargaining rights for platform workers'. *Social Europe*, 6 October 2020, available at: https://www.socialeurope.eu/collective-bargaining-rights-for-platform-workers. (accessed: 24 October 2020). The conclusion of the agreement at issue as well as the rationale of the antitrust authorities will be further elaborated in Chapter 4, subsection 4.4.1.

That said, some legal systems, especially in Europe, via legislative initiatives, have allowed trade unions representing certain types of self-employed platform workers to negotiate the working conditions of their members; by doing so, they have de facto restricted the intervention from national antitrust authorities on certain occasions.[614] Such examples can be found in countries like Italy.[615] To this extent, some specialists indicate that for quite some time, Italian antitrust authorities have been accepting agreements setting wages for genuine self-employed workers.[616] Still, as research conducted for the OECD points out a '*risk associated with this route is that it potentially creates uncertainty since it could be reversed without any legislative reform*'.[617]

The precarious conditions of many workers in the context of platform work, along with the adverse effects of competition law, have attracted much of the attention of supranational bodies in the EU. To this extent, on 24 October 2019, the EU's competition commissioner, Margrethe Vestager, said: '*platform workers should be able to team up, to defend their rights... and the fact that their employers label those workers as "self-employed" doesn't make those collective agreements into cartels*'.[618] Almost two years after that statement, on 16 September 2021, the European Parliament (EP) released a resolution in which, among other things, it highlights the different types of problems that platform workers are facing and it proceeds with a series of possible solutions for tackling such issues.[619] It was observed that many of such issues are concentrated around both the legal and practical[620] difficulties of platform workers to effectively exercise their collective labour rights, despite the fact that the latter are often finding themselves in '*imbalanced and asymmetrical relationships* [compared to digital labour platforms] ... [and they] *often lack the individual bargaining power to negotiate fair terms and conditions*'.[621] Furthermore, the recommendations at issue were made in light of the proposed EU Commission's Directive on improving working conditions in platform work. In this regard, the EP called the Commission to: '*ensure that collective bargaining frameworks* [for platform workers] *function properly and efficiently*'.[622] In turn, it was emphasised that:

614. Lane, M. (2020), *Regulating platform work in the digital age*, Going Digital Toolkit Policy Note, No. 1, 9, available at: https://goingdigital.oecd.org/toolkitnotes (accessed 29 December 2021).
615. *Ibid.*
616. For instance, *see* Aloisi, A., Gramano, E., *A Solution in Search of a Problem? Collective Rights and the Antitrust Labour Exemption in Italy* (Shae McCrystal, Ewan McGaughey and Sanjukta Paul eds, *The Cambridge Handbook of Labor in Competition Law*, Cambridge University Press 2022), 223-238.
617. *Supra*, Lane (2020), 9.
618. Espinoza, J. (2019), *Vestager says gig economy workers should 'team up' on wages*, available at: https://www.ft.com/content/0cafd442-f673-11e9-9ef3-eca8fc8f2d65 (accessed 21 December 2021).
619. European Parliament resolution of 16 September 2021 on fair working conditions, rights and social protection for platform workers – new forms of employment linked to digital development (2019/2186(INI)).
620. It is mentioned that the practical difficulties include: '[the] *lack of common means of communication and opportunities to meet online or in person, which can prevent collective representation in practice*'.
621. *Ibid.*
622. *Ibid.*

> freedom of association and the right to collective bargaining are fundamental rights for all workers ... [and] calls on the Commission to address such impediments in its proposal; stresses the need for platform workers and platforms to be properly organised and represented in order to facilitate social dialogue and collective bargaining.[623]

A few months after the EP's resolution was released, the EU Commission made available to the public its proposed Directive on platform work. As mentioned, the latter does not directly touch upon the protection of the right to collective bargaining. It solely recognises the difficulties platform workers are facing with respect to their communication with their counterparts and representatives. As such, it calls platform operators to implement policies that will enable workers to contact each other; in doing so, any form of monitoring of these interactions should be absent.[624]

Together with the Directive though, the Commission also published its draft Guidelines on the application of EU competition law to collective agreements with respect to the working conditions of solo self-employed persons, including platform workers.[625] The Guidelines were officially approved on 29 September 2022.[626] As they stand, they have competition law as their starting point, by specifying the situations in which EU competition law will not interfere with the conclusion of collective agreements signed by such workers. Thus, the Commission aims at correcting some of the rigidities identified with respect to the well-established jurisprudence of the CJEU under Article 101 TFEU. According to its public announcement, moreover, such a development illustrates, at least in theory, the EU's commitment to delivering on the European Pillar of Social Rights, something that can also be traced in the wording of both the draft, as well as adopted Guidelines of the Commission.[627]

The issued Guidelines stipulate that they cover three categories of solo self-employed persons; hence, the agreements concluded by those persons would fall outside the ambit of Article 101 TFEU. These categories include: (a) those who are economically dependent, meaning that they have to receive at least 50 per cent of their total annual income from a single principal; (b) those who work 'side-by-side'[628] with

---

623. *Ibid.*
624. Article 15 of the Proposed Directive.
625. European Commission, (2021), 'Approval of the content of a draft for a Communication from the Commission – Guidelines on the Application of EU competition law to collective agreements regarding the working conditions of solo self-employed persons', COM(2021) 8838 final', available at: https://ec.europa.eu/commission/presscorner/detail/en/ip_21_6620 (accessed 18 January 2022).
626. European Commission, (2022), 'Communication from the commission Guidelines on the application of Union competition law to collective agreements regarding the working conditions of solo self-employed persons 2022/C 374/02', available at: https://eur-lex.europa.eu/legal-content/EN/TXT/?uri=CELEX%3A52022XC0930%2802%29 (accessed 14 October 2022).
627. *Supra*, EU Commission's Draft Guidelines (2021), para. 3; para. 4 of the EU Commission's issued Guidelines.
628. *Supra*, EU Commission's issued Guidelines (2022); for the purposes of the official Guidelines, someone is considered to work 'side-by-side' with workers when: '*they provide their services under the direction of their counterparty and do not bear the commercial risks of the counterparty's activity or enjoy any independence as regards the performance of the economic activity concerned*'. (para. 26).

workers working for the same principal; and (c) those who provide their services via the use of digital labour platforms.[629] The latter's definition is compatible with the one used for the purposes of the proposed EU Directive on platform work.[630]

It comes as no surprise that the Guidelines, since their initial draft form, have attracted much of the attention of different parties, such as trade unions and scholars. Thus far, there is a common narrative that perceives the Commission's initiative as a step towards the right direction. In this regard, it has been argued that a positive element derives from the fact the Guidelines, already since their draft format, have a broad scope of application, as they do not solely cover vulnerable platform workers offering their services as self-employed, but they are rather applicable to all sectors and industries. This approach, which is broader compared to what existed in the past, is based on criteria of an economic and practical nature that are capable of mitigating the restrictions stemming from EU competition law to collective bargaining of self-employed workers. For instance, consideration will be given to important elements, like the imbalance in the negotiating position of solo self-employed persons vis-à-vis their counterparty(ies).[631] Moreover, the Guidelines have adopted a 'personal work' approach to competition law and collective bargaining that has been put forward by some academics as possible a way to circumvent the clash between labour law and competition law.[632]

The positive features identified within the text of the recently issued Guidelines, by no means, imply that this very development can go without criticism. This is to claim that as the Guidelines were formulated, it may be still difficult to sufficiently guarantee that collective bargaining protection will cover all vulnerable solo self-employed workers, including platform workers. Particularly, the first set of concerns is related to the provision that such workers will have to receive 50 per cent of their total annual income from a single principal. Such a threshold can be problematic for certain workers who engage in a number of short-term contracts. In the case of domestic workers, for example, it is not uncommon that some of them provide their services to more than one household; hence, due to this provision, they can be still excluded from exercising their right to collective bargaining. Of course, the existence of this threshold can be also challenging for other workers in different sectors, who often do not receive 50 per cent of their annual income from one and only counterparty. A lower bar, therefore, may be necessary in order to capture the working reality of some precarious workers. In this regard, some countries in the EU, such as Germany, have indeed adopted a considerably lower threshold for certain categories of workers in vulnerable situations, like artists who frequently work intermittently and may even work outside the sector at times.[633]

629. *Ibid.*, chapter 3.
630. *Ibid.*, para. 2(d).
631. *Supra*, EU Commission's issued Guidelines (2022), para. 9.
632. For a discussion, see *supra*, Lianos, Countouris and De Stefano, (2019), 332-333; *supra*, Countouris and De Stefano, V. (2019), 33-36; Freedland, M. and Countouris, N., *The Legal Construction of Personal Work Relations* (Oxford University Press 2011).
633. In Germany the threshold is 33%; Section 12a of the Collective Agreements Act in the version published on 25 August 1969 (Federal Law Gazette I, 1323). The information was found in *supra*, EU Commission's Draft Guidelines (2021), footnote 24, 8.

What is more, another problematic aspect is related to the provision(s) which stipulate that solo self-employed persons, in order to be captured by the adopted EU Guidelines, have to work side-by-side with workers employed by the same counter-party and provide the same or similar tasks. Such a requirement, can generate problems for certain types of workers, who are at the moment misclassified as self-employed, such as domestic workers, and they often do not work side-by-side with other workers; thus, it is complex for them to identify a comparable counterpart. This task can be further complicated in situations where employers opt to modify their business model so as to make sure that the employees and self-employed workers engaged by their company do not share the same or similar working conditions.[634] That said, a broader comparative approach, which is not necessarily confined to a particular business, would be advisable. A paradigm as such can be found in the aforementioned Dutch Guidelines (Chapter 2). There, it is enshrined that a comparison of working conditions can take place not only with employees working for the same business but also with employees who perform work of a similar nature elsewhere. Similar reasoning has also been expressed by the Advocate General in the seminal ruling of the CJEU in the case of *Lawrence*,[635] where it was pointed out that '*the argument that a comparison with employees outside a specific undertaking can never be made is untenable*'.[636]

An additional set of concerns may arise regarding the third category of workers the Guidelines aim at covering, namely, persons who provide their services through digital labour platforms. The main problem here can be traced in the definition the Guidelines give to the term 'digital labour platform', which is defined in the very same way as in the Commission's proposal for a Directive on platform work. The issued Guidelines define a 'digital labour platform' as:

> any natural or legal person providing a commercial service which meets all of the following requirements: (i) it is provided, at least in part, at a distance through electronic means, such as a website or a mobile application; (ii) it is provided at the request of a recipient of the service; (iii) it involves, as a necessary and essential component, the organisation of work performed by individuals, irrespective of whether that work is performed online or in a certain location.[637]

634. Georgiou, D. (2022), 'An assessment of the EU's draft guidelines on the application of eu competition law to collective agreements of the "solo self-employed"', *Competition Policy International*, 7, available at: https://www.competitionpolicyinternational.com/wp-content/uploads/2022/07/3-AN-ASSESSMENT-OF-THE-EUS-DRAFT-GUIDELINES-ON-THE-APPLICATION-OF-EU-COMPETITION-LAW-TO-COLLECTIVE-AGREEMENTS-OF-THE-SOLO-SELF-EMPLOYED-Despoina.pdf (accessed 16 November 2022).
635. Case C-320/00 *Lawrence and Others v. Regent Office Care Ltd, Commercial Catering Group and Mitie Secure Services Ltd.* [2002] ECR I-7325.
636. Opinion of Advocate General Geelhoed delivered on 14 March 2002 – *A. G. Lawrence and Others v. Regent Office Care Ltd, Commercial Catering Group and Mitie Secure Services Ltd.* – Reference for a preliminary ruling: Court of Appeal (England & Wales) (Civil Division) – United Kingdom – Principle of equal pay for men and women – Direct effect – Comparison of the work performed for different employers – Case C-320/00, para. 48.
637. *Supra*, EU Commission's issued Guidelines (2022), para. 2(d).

Although the Guidelines, compared to the proposed Directive, elaborate more in detail on what the organisation of work implies, the organisation of work by the platforms remains necessary and essential.[638] The importance attached to such an element may prevent certain crowdworkers, who often organise their work individually, to be benefited from the Guidelines. As the latter stipulates, the definition of digital labour platforms may be subjected to certain alterations in case the adopted version of the Platform Work Directive differs materially from the one currently enshrined in the Guidelines.[639]

Furthermore, albeit the issued Guidelines recognised the important role of social dialogue and collective bargaining for '*a highly competitive social market economy, aiming at full employment and social progress*',[640] they do so by paying lip service to the nature of the right to collective bargaining as a fundamental right. As noted, and it will be further analysed throughout this research, such a right has also been recognised as a human right and constitutes a part of the constitutional order in a number of countries. This omission, moreover, can be problematic considering the nature of the right to collective bargaining as a fundamental right, under the ILO's standards. This is also supported by the text of Conventions Nos. 87 and 98, which explicitly mention that both the rights to freedom of association and collective bargaining should apply to all workers, with only limited exceptions to apply.[641] All EU Member States have ratified these Conventions. Moreover, the Guidelines also refrain from having any reference to the right to strike and its recognised position, under international labour standards as well as to the fact that it constitutes an indispensable component of collective bargaining. The only reference is made in the Draft Guidelines. The latter, however, do not even mention the word 'strike', and they only stipulate that '*a coordinated refusal to supply labour* ... for the negotiation or conclusion of the collective agreement' needs to be '*necessary and proportionate*'.[642] This formulation that, in a certain way, brings to mind the much-discussed *Viking* and *Laval* saga,[643] seems to be at odds with ILO principles in the matter, which point out that '*the right to strike to be one of the principal means by which workers and their associations may legitimately promote and defend their economic and social interests*'.[644]

638. *Ibid.*, para. 30: A digital labour platform must organise the services provided by platform workers '*at a minimum,* [or play] *a significant role in matching the demand for the service with the supply of labour by an individual who has a contractual relationship with the digital labour platform and who is available to perform a specific task*'.
639. *Ibid.*
640. *Ibid.*, para. 4.
641. These are the armed forces and the police, with regard to freedom of association, and also public servants engaged in the administration of the State, with regard to the right to collective bargaining.
642. *Supra*, EU Commission's Draft Guidelines (2021), para. 16.
643. In both cases, the CJEU acknowledged that the right to strike is a 'fundamental right which forms an integral part of the general principles of community law'. It was, however, held that such a right could and needed to be balanced against the commercial principles of EU law; *Case C-438/05, International Transport Workers' Federation v. Viking Line ABP*, 2007 ECR I-10779 and *Case C-341/05, Laval un Partneri Ltd v. Svenska Byggnadsarbetareforbundet*, 2007 ECR I-11767.
644. Gernigon, B., Odero, A., Guido, H., *ILO Principles Concerning the Right to Strike*, 137 International Labour Review 441 n. 4 (1998), 11. The authors refer to: ILO, (1996), *Freedom of*

Overall, without any doubt, the recently adopted Guidelines constitute a positive development. Nonetheless, as other initiatives at a domestic level, they fail to guarantee that the right to collective bargaining will be guaranteed to all those workers who are in need of protection, something that, as noted goes against a number of international standards. Of course, at the time of writing the document remains open to changes as its text is still open to public consultation from the related stakeholders. It remains to be seen whether any important changes will eventually occur. That said, as the last chapter of this research points out, even if the Guidelines were drafted from a labour law perspective, also in line with the requirements of international law (*see* Chapter 5 below), that would not automatically imply that the right to collective bargaining for solo self-employed, can effectively take place in practice. As it will be elaborated, this is due to the present complexions within national systems of industrial relations.

3.5 INTERMEDIATE CONCLUSIONS

Platform-mediated work has raised a number of issues with respect to the labour protection of workers engaged in it. Despite the existence of any challenges, the demand for such workers is expected to become even higher in the near future. It makes no surprise, therefore, that these types of work arrangements have attracted much attention from lawmakers and courts around the world. In that sense, the 'answers' given to the specific challenges stemming from platform work arrangements can, to a certain degree, shape the future of labour relations.[645] Undeniably, as Chapter 3 demonstrated, some of the aforementioned legislative and judicial developments, constitute a step forward in the right direction. The recently proposed Directive of the EU Commissions on improving the conditions of platform work, despite its shortcomings and early stage, stands out from these efforts and as De Stefano and Aloisi contend, '*it takes the lead in regulating platform work*'.[646] The recently adopted EU Guidelines on the application of Union competition law to collective agreements regarding the working conditions of solo self-employed persons constitute another positive initiative in this regard.

As noted, though, none of the developments explored in this chapter can be seen as a panacea for the variety of problems encountered by workers in the platform economy. This is to say that notwithstanding any realisation on behalf of both the lawmakers and courts regarding the often adverse effects of platform work, a large number of workers remain excluded from employment and labour regulations and protections (including their collective labour rights), due to the 'obscure' employment status. Of course, someone may argue that such an assertion does not automatically apply to the whole span of employment rights. There are instances, like in the case of

association: Digest of decisions and principles of the Freedom of Association Committee of the Governing Body of the ILO. Fourth (revised) edition. Geneva, paras 473-475.

645. For a discussion, *see* Hendrickx, F. and De Stefano, V. eds, *Game Changers in Labour Law: Shaping the Future of Work* (Wolters Kluwer 2018).
646. *Supra*, De Stefano and Aloisi (2021).

discrimination rights, where specific protections are considered to be applicable regardless of whether a worker is falling outside of the realm of an employment relationship. Still, even in these cases, the existing protections might not be adequate enough. It has been argued, for instance, that within the EU's legal framework, the adoption of several instruments against discrimination of self-employed persons is still far from guaranteeing the application of the full range of anti-discriminatory measures to self-employed workers.[647] As seen, despite the existence of any positive developments explored in this chapter, similar concerns also arise with respect to the effective exercise of fundamental collective labour rights. Such concerns can be better understood via the analysis of Chapter 4, whereby an evaluation is being made regarding the exercise of platform workers' fundamental collective rights in practice.

647. For instance, *see* Barnard, C., *Discrimination Law, Self-Employment and the Liberal Professions*, 12 European Anti-discrimination Law Review 21 (2011), 21-31; Garben, S. (2017), *Protecting Workers in the Online Platform Economy: An Overview of Regulatory and Policy Developments in the EU*, European Risk Observatory Discussion Paper, Luxembourg, Publications Office of the European Union, available at: https://osha.europa.eu/sites/default/files/publications/documents/Protecting_Workers_in_Online_Platform Economy.pdf (accessed 26 February 2019).

CHAPTER 4

The Exercise of Platform Workers' Fundamental Collective Rights in Practice

4.1 INTRODUCTION

The previous three chapters illustrated that within modern workplaces, forms of work have become more heterogeneous and self-employment, especially in the platform work economy, is on the rise. It was also illustrated that many of these self-employed (platform) workers are dependent upon their principals, and they are actually situated in a comparable predicament to that of employees. As a result, challenges with respect to the scope of labour protection are surfacing to an even greater extent. As noted, this observation is inextricably linked to the present limitations of the labour law framework, where labour protection, including the exercise of fundamental collective labour rights, still, largely, remains concentrated within 'subordinate' wage employment, particularly of a full-time and open-ended nature. On top of that, such rights can also be restricted, in instances where (self-employed) platform workers' working activities come into clash with competition law. A strict application of competition rules has already excluded a considerable number of platform workers from the coverage of collective agreements. It can be claimed, therefore, that the extensive reliance of businesses on freelance jobs entails the risk of excluding a great portion of the workforce from the protection of fundamental collective labour rights, also recognised as human rights.

As noted in Chapter 2, in addition to legal obstacles, platform workers are also facing practical hurdles upon attempting to exercise their collective rights, even if they are considered employees.[648] As other workers in NSFE, among other things, often have to deal with frequent turnovers and a limited attachment to a single workplace.

648. Aloisi, A., *Negotiating the Digital Transformation of Work: Non-standard Workers' Voice, Collective Rights and Mobilisation Practices in the Platform Economy*, EUI Working Paper No. 3 (2019). San Domenico di Fiesole, European University Institute.

Furthermore, many traditional trade unions, at least up until recently, have been hesitant to engage such workers in their actions.[649] Due to the common challenges, therefore, Chapter 4 engages in a broader discussion on the problems that atypical workers are facing with respect to their collective labour rights, as well as on the attempts made by trade unions to engage such workers in their activities. In light of this, more general findings with respect to atypical workers' collective mobilisation, can be important when it comes to platform workers' exercise of their collective labour rights. Before engaging in this discussion, however, let us first refer to the importance of collective labour rights and particularly the significance of the right to collective bargaining, where most of the limitations in the context of platform work, are observed. Such an analysis will assist this research in Chapter 5, in its endeavour to argue about the importance of a HRBA towards the protection of fundamental collective labour rights.

4.2 THE IMPORTANT ROLE OF COLLECTIVE BARGAINING IN FACING CURRENT AND FUTURE CHALLENGES

In light of the wording of the supranational bodies,[650] collective bargaining, as an essential element of the freedom of association, due to its functions and purpose, has been described as a *'"cornerstone" institution for democracy'*.[651] Such a 'weighty' opinion stems from the fact that the employment relationship is characterised by the inequality of bargaining power between the parties involved in it. This is to say that an individual employee is usually subject to the detailed instructions of the employer as to how the work has to be performed. Employers can, in addition, use their superior bargaining power in order to dictate various features of employment, such as the setting of wages to specific levels. Furthermore, an individual employee is to a greater extent dependent upon her or his employer than the other way around; the costs of switching jobs, including the possibility of not finding a new occupation, are in most circumstances, much higher than the costs sustained by an employer in his or her effort in finding a substitute worker.[652] That said, employment regulations can also grant employers excessive authority over their workers.[653] Consequently, as Davidov has argued, the inequality of bargaining power, along with the often 'incomplete nature'[654]

649. Heery, E., *Unions and the Organizing Turn: Reflections after 20 Years of Organising Works*, 26 The Economic and Labour Relations Review 545 n. 4 (2015), 545-560; Gumbrell-McCormick, R., *European Trade Unions and 'Atypical' Workers*, 42 Industrial Relations Journal 293 n. 3 (2011), 293-310.
650. *See* analysis in Chapter 5.2.1.
651. Hayter, S., Fashoyin, T., Kochan, T.A., *Collective Bargaining for the 21st Century*, 53 Journal of Industrial Relations 225 n. 2 (2011), 225.
652. Davidov, G., *Collective Bargaining Laws: Purpose and Scope*, 1 International Journal of Comparative Labour Law and Industrial Relations 81 (2004), 83.
653. De Stefano, V., Aloisi, A., *Fundamental Labour Rights, Platform Work and Human Rights Protection of Non-standard Workers* (Janice R. Bellace and Beryl ter Haar eds, *Research Handbook on Labour, Business and Human Rights Law*, Elgar Publishing 2019), 369.
654. According to the words of Kate Cartier: '*The contract of employment is inherently incomplete because it is impossible for the bilateral arrangement between employer and employee fully to*

of employment contracts can restrict the ability of employees to be a part of decisions that immediately affect their daily lives. Thus, according to him, a democratic deficit is observed. This is exactly where one of the main functions of collective bargaining comes into play, namely, the correction of such deficit. To this extent, as Aloisi rightly points out by reflecting on the work of others, collective bargaining constitutes the '*most effective way to achieve a countervailing power to the employer and re-establish a balance of forces in the employment relationship*'.[655]

According to Davidov, the exercise of this right contains two separate traits which can be perceived as democratic: first, its 'civilising' effect on the employment relationship and second, its ability to pave the way for the participation of workers in the 'self-government of the workplace', though their collective voice.[656] In relation to the first attribute, the author explains that collective agreements, which constitute a product of collective bargaining, can set up a 'rule of law' that in turn prescribes the way that workers should be treated within workplaces; employers need to conform with this set of rules, and as a result, their complete control together with their arbitrariness in decision-making are restricted. In case the collective agreement is not respected by the employer in question, trade unions can challenge this behaviour according to the existing laws and regulations. With respect to the second democratic feature of collective bargaining, Davidov contends that the workers' collective voice permits them to freely raise their concerns and demands at workplaces and in a way enables them to actively participate in the organisation of their activities.[657] On the other end of the spectrum, it would be extremely difficult for an individual worker to have his or her voice taken under serious consideration, and, of course, the risks of such worker being dismissed would be much higher on this occasion. Overall, using the author's words:

> The ability to bargain collectively is thus not merely instrumental; it is rather an important component of, as well as a mean towards human freedom [and] [t]his explains why the right to bargain collectively is [...] considered a basic human right.[658]

Indeed, by effectively using this right, trade unions and other workers' associations have played a vital role in generating better jobs, increasing wages, and improving working conditions, more generally, in various aspects of working life. A recent OECD report confirms, for instance, that the existence of direct forms of workers' voice is correlated with a higher quality of the working environment, in areas, such as health and safety and working time.[659] It is also observed, mainly in Europe, that a strong degree of organisation of social partners within workplaces is associated

---

specify what work is to be done and how', Cartier, K., *The Transaction Costs and Benefits of the Incomplete Contract of Employment*, 18 *Cambridge Journal of Economics* 181 (1994), 182.

655. *Supra*, Aloisi, A. (2019), 6; *see also* Kelly, J., *Rethinking Industrial Relations: Mobilization, Collectivism and Long Waves* (Routledge 1998).
656. *Supra*, Davidov (2004), 4-6.
657. *Ibid.*
658. *Ibid.*, 5-6.
659. OECD, (2019), *Negotiating Our Way Up: Collective Bargaining in a Changing World of Work*, OECD Publishing, Paris; *see also* Addison, J.T., Siebert, S., Wagner J., Xiangdong W., *Worker*

with a lower incidence of various forms of intimidation and discrimination.[660] In many instances, as empirical evidence also suggests, workers' unionisation can be also linked to greater levels of productivity for businesses, albeit this suggestion has been highly contested in literature.[661] Deakin, in this respect, argues that laws which support the voice of workers and promote collective barraging, at both company and sectoral levels, can boost productivity via their impact on workers' motivation and commitment.[662] Collective bargaining, therefore, can be extremely beneficial for workers' remuneration[663] and other non-monetary aspects of job quality and productivity.

Furthermore, collective bargaining and other forms of workers' voices have a key role to play in modern workplaces and the introduction of new technologies.[664] Today's workplace surveillance system is often described as a 'digital panopticon' that does not only keep track of workers' e-mail accounts and phones but also extends to the monitoring of web-browsing patterns, text messages, screenshots, keystrokes, social media posts and private messaging apps like WhatsApp.[665] Furthermore, as De Stefano, among others, observes, employers on many occasions are able to give detailed instructions and direct the work through the use of digital applications, which rely on artificial intelligence and a number of other technological tools; this is not to say that workers' control and surveillance are new elements.[666] There has always been inherent in traditional employment relationships. What has changed, though, is the manner that these features are taking place.

Platform-mediated work constitutes a prominent example of this unprecedented technological progress, which alters modern workplaces in terms of control and supervision of work. As mentioned, artificial intelligence, along with digital surveillance and reputation systems, have been employed in digital business models, in order to ensure productivity and the performance of their workers. In this regard, digital reputation systems have substituted the old-style command and control methods in deciding the selection of platform workers, as well as the quality of their job. Work-related tasks are assigned by algorithms, which in turn assess them based on the

Participation and Firm Performance: Evidence from Germany and Britain, 38 British Journal of Industrial Relations 7 n. 1 (2000), 7-48.

660. *Ibid.*
661. For a discussion, *see*: *supra*, Davidov (2004), 10-13, referring to the empirical studies from: Clark, K. B. (1980), *The Impact of Unionization on Productivity: A Case Study*, Industrial and Labor Relations Review, 33, 451; Galgóczi, B., Glassner, V. (2009), 'Plant-Level Responses to the Economic Crisis in Europe', European Trade Union Institute, Brussel.
662. Deakin, S. (2016), *The Contribution of Labour Law to Economic Development and Growth*, Centre for Business Research, Working Paper No. 478. Cambridge, University of Cambridge, 17.
663. According to Davidov the ability of collective bargaining to often increase worker's wages underlines what he calls the 'distributive function' of such right: *supra* Davidov (2004), 6-10.
664. *Ibid.*
665. Solon, O. (2017), 'Big Brother isn't just watching: workplace surveillance can track your every move, *The Guardian*, 6 November 2017, available at: https://www.theguardian.com/world/2017/nov/06/workplace-surveillance-big-brother-technology (accessed 11 March 2021).
666. De Stefano, V. (2018), *'Negotiating the Algorithm': Automation, Artificial Intelligence and Labour Protection*, 41 n. 1, *ILO Employment Working Paper N. 246.*

reviews of the customers and other factors, like how fast the work is performed.[667] As such, it is often left up to such algorithms to decide whether the tasks are completed according to the requirements set by the platform at issue. Workers who are constantly getting bad ratings are running the risk of being excluded from the service. Rating systems, therefore, have become, as Stanford puts it: '*a powerful and inexpensive weapon in employers' labour extraction arsenal*'.[668]

These developments can be particularly problematic in many respects. Empirical studies, for instance, reveal that rating systems are not to be trusted regarding their main function of distinguishing high-quality, or trustworthy offerings from lower-quality or untrustworthy offerings.[669] Recent research also indicates a growing concern in relation to incidences of discrimination that are linked to such algorithmic decisions,[670] or the severe implications that such developments can have in terms of workers' privacy rights and the collection of big data.[671] As Moore, also, contends the misuse of these new technological tools can impose serious physical and psychological risks, not solely within the realm of NSFE, but also in relation to the workforce as a whole.[672]

In light of these phenomena, a number of trade unions around the world have attempted to mitigate the risks stemming from new technologies. For example, such steps, *inter alia*, have taken the form of collective agreements[673] or the form of information and consultation procedures between social partners in order to assess and regulate the impacts of technology in modern workplaces.[674] More specifically, some of these collective agreements aimed at regulating the use and impact of technology, not only in terms of monitoring workers' activities but also in directing and controlling their work.[675] For instance, Moore et al., refer to the 2002 National Collective Agreement on the protection of employees' private lives in relation to controls on electronic online communications data (No. 81), in Belgium, as a prominent example of trade unions' role in safeguarding workers' personal data.[676] Similar collective

667. Prassl J. (2018), *Collective Voice in the Platform Economy: Challenges, Opportunities, Solutions*, ETUC Report, 12.
668. Stanford, J., *The Resurgence of Gig Work: Historical and Theoretical Perspectives*, 28 The Economic and Labour Relations Review 382 n. 3 (2017), 394.
669. *Ibid.*, citing SLEE, T., *What's Yours Is Mine – Against the Sharing Economy* (O/R Books 2015).
670. For instance, *see* Kullmann, M., *Platform Work, Algorithmic Decision-Making, and EU Gender Equality Law*, 34 International Journal of Comparative Labour Law and Industrial Relations 1 n. 1 (2018), 1-22; Blackham, A., *We Are All Entrepreneurs Now': Options and New Approaches for Adapting Equality Law for the 'Gig Economy'*, 34 International Journal of Comparative Labour Law and Industrial Relations 413 n. 4 (2018), 413-434.
671. *Supra* De Stefano (2018), 9-16.
672. Moore, P.V., *The Threat of Physical and Psychosocial Violence and Harassment in Digitalized Work*, ILO, Geneva (2018).
673. *Supra* OECD (2019), 231-232; Dagino, E., Armaroli, I., A Seat at the Table: Negotiating Data Processing in the Workplace. A National Case Study and Comparative Insights, 41 Comparative Labor Law & Policy Journal 173 (2019), 173-193.
674. For instance, *see* the recent developments in Germany in: Eichhorst, W., Schroeder, W., *The German Employment Model, the Trade Unions and 'Working 4.0'*, Friedrich-Ebert-Stiftung, Bratislava.
675. *Supra*, OECD (2019), 231-232.
676. Moore, P.V. and Upchurch, M., U, M. eds, *Humans and Machines at Work: Monitoring, Surveillance and Automation in Contemporary Capitalism* (Spinger 2018), 33.

agreements can be traced in other countries, such as Italy and Germany,[677] as well as at the international level.[678] As seen below, some alike initiatives have also taken place in the context of platform work.

There are, and there will be instances where an individual worker cannot be expected to possess the knowledge needed or have access to essential information, as to identify all the risks associated with the aforementioned technological developments in modern workplaces. Of course, such an assertion does not apply to all workers. At the same time, trade unions and other workers' associations have the benefits of collective experience, a comparative wealth of resources, and also access to experts, in order to be better positioned to tackle these kinds of issues. Again, this does not mean that trade unions cannot face considerable difficulties in combating risks associated with technological developments. Finally, collective bargaining can assist employers and unions find mutually beneficial solutions and create a level-playing field for all businesses and workers. That said, albeit a key weapon in the hands of workers, the exercise of the right in question, does not constitute the only way through which unions have attempted to tackle challenges within modern workplaces, especially when it comes to the representation of atypical workers, including platform workers. Such a claim becomes apparent as this chapter unfolds.

4.3 TRADE UNIONS' APPROACH TOWARDS WORKERS IN NSFE AND THE PARTICULARITY OF PLATFORM WORKERS

By now, it is well-established that platform-mediated work constitutes part of the overall phenomenon of NSFE, including workers (dependent) self-employed workers. As such, a broader discussion on the approach of trade unions towards atypical workers will assist this thesis in coming up with key observations regarding the mobilisation of platform workers and especially those who fall out of the realm of an employment relationship.

That said, as observed elsewhere, atypical work arrangements have been used long before their platform-based instantiations came to be, with the purpose of, *inter alia*, reducing labour costs, increasing productivity and, more recently, avoiding regulations stemming from labour regulations and collective agreements.[679] Moreover, workers engaged in NSFE used to experience and continue facing serious practical and legal impediments towards the enjoyment of their rights to freedom of association and collective bargaining. One major issue is related to their difficulty to unionise in order to promote their rights and interests. This is also confirmed by the publication of several national statistics on the overall unionisation rates and collective bargaining coverage of non-standard workers. For example, on average, across the 37 members of the OECD, they have 50 per cent lower chances to be unionised compared to standard workers, albeit substantial differences exist between various countries.[680]

677. *Supra*, Dagnino and Armaroli (2019).
678. *Supra*, Moore et al. (2018), 34.
679. *Supra*, Prassl (2018), 73-84; *supra*, Freedland (2019), 180-181.
680. OECD, *Employment outlook 2019: The Future of Work*, Paris, OECD, 2019, 20.

The stance of trade unions regarding these types of precarious work has not been uncontroversial. As Gumbrell-McCormick contents, they have '*naturally opposed the deterioration of job security, pay rates and terms and conditions of work that have accompanied the introduction of more precarious forms of work*'.[681] On many occasions, they have also attempted to obstruct different initiatives deriving from employers or national authorities aimed at the expansion of contingent forms of work.[682] As the same author argues, for quite some time, at least within the European context, a considerable number of trade unions' members assumed that workers preferred full-time occupations, which they perceived as intrinsically superior to other forms of work; flexibility in this sense was generally associated with precariousness.[683] Therefore, as Keune observes, traditional trade unions have been often accused of excluding the so-called outsiders, namely, workers with insecure, precarious, low-paid jobs.[684] Some authors have even interpreted or 'likened' this exclusion to a form of discrimination towards contingent workers, capable of contributing to a further '*inequality between their well-protected core members and the growing marginal workforce*'.[685]

It can be suggested that this phenomenon can, among other reasons, be attributed to the fact that industrial relations systems were, in general, created and expanded under the Fordist model of production, which had as prominent characteristics the rise of mass industry and a relatively homogeneous group of potential members, comprised of workers, mainly male, working in full-time, in relatively secure occupations.[686] Consequently, the characteristics of these industrial systems, as well as the strategies of trade unions, were all shaped according to the particular needs of workers in standard employment relationships. Such issues will be further elaborated in the last chapter of this research. In addition, many of the workers engaged in atypical jobs have felt that their interests cannot be fully represented through the structures of traditional unions.[687] On top of that, according to some authors, the existence of a fragmented workforce can have as a consequence the presence of a variety of different interests and goals, which in turn can trigger further conflicts between workers.[688]

681. *Supra*, Gumbrell-McCormick (2011), 300.
682. *Ibid.*; it should be mentioned, however, that there are also some instances in which trade unions have promoted a further flexibilisation of working arrangements, for example, via the conclusion of collective agreements. *See*, for instance, the role of some trade unions in the Netherlands in: Boonstra, K., Keune, M., VER, E. (2011), *Trade union responses to precarious employment in The Netherlands*, Amsterdam Institute for Advanced Labour Studies, available at: http://www.uvaaias.net/uploaded_files/regular/BARSORIReportTheNetherlands.pdf (accessed 9 March 2021).
683. *Supra*, Gumbrell-McCormick (2011), 298.
684. Keune, M., *Trade Union Responses to Precarious Work in Seven European Countries*, 5 International Journal of Labour Research 59 n. 1 (2013), 66.
685. Benassi, C., Vlandas, T., *Union Inclusiveness and Temporary Agency Workers: The Role of Power Resources and Union Ideology*, 22 European Journal of Industrial Relations 5 n. 1 (2016), 5.
686. *Supra*, Gumbrell-McCormick (2011), 297; *see also*: Hyman, R., *Changing Trade Union Identities and Strategies* (Richard Hyman and Anthony Ferner eds, *New Frontiers in European Industrial Relations*, Blackwell 1994), 108-139.
687. *Supra*, Vandaele (2018), 8-10.
688. Ebisui, M., *Non-Standard Workers: Good Practices of Social Dialogue and Collective Bargaining*, 1 E-Journal of International and Comparative Labour Studies 211, n. 3-4 (2012), 218.

Still, unions have progressively come to realise that the increase in NSFE would weaken their own capacity to act if they are not successful in including such workers in their membership.[689] As Heery points out, this realisation also reflects the fact that unions have a broader societal function that moves further than the protection of their own members.[690] He moves on to explain that one of the historical functions of trade unions is to regulate workplaces in a way that restrains the authority which is present there, as well as ameliorates the conditions of working people in a broader sense.[691] In a similar vein, Ewing argues that the regulatory function of trade unions touches upon the '*process of rule-making that extends beyond their members or their immediate colleagues of their members*'.[692] According to the author, such a function can be materialised in two ways. First, either via multi-employer collective bargaining, which includes the conclusion of collective agreements that cover non-union members and enterprises, where the union may not be recognised and therefore may not be eligible for any rights of collective representation. Second, through the involvement of trade unions in the adoption of regulatory legislation related to workers' rights in general.[693]

The history of labour movement and literature reveal many instances where trade unions have developed a range of initiatives in order to engage with workers in NSFE, including self-employed persons. As noted, these types of initiatives constitute a valuable guide with respect to the current collective mobilisation of platform workers. One of the most traditional approaches in this context constitutes the exercise of collective bargaining that, in many cases, has resulted in the conclusion of collective agreements. Ebiusi and Hayter argue that such an exercise has occurred at different levels and has the purpose of negotiating parity for atypical and precarious workers.[694] In a nutshell, it aims at:

> (a) addressing employment insecurity by either limiting recourse to nonstandard contracts to specific contingencies or facilitating the transition to regular employment; (b) providing equal pay for work of equal value or narrowing the gap between workers with different employment statuses; (c) providing for equal treatment in respect of benefits such as training and social security.[695]

To this extent, collective bargaining has taken place beyond workplaces as well as with multiple employers so as to include workers in NSFE.[696] There is also a number of cases where existing collective agreements, which were signed between single employers or their associations and trade unions, have been extended to certain types of atypical workers who are not unionised.[697] Examples can be traced around the world

689. *Supra*, Gumbrell-McCormick (2011), 300.
690. *Supra*, Heery (2015), 558.
691. *Ibid.*
692. Ewing, K.D., *The Function of Trade Unions*, 34 Industrial Law Journal 1 n. 1 22 (2005), 4; The regulatory function is one of five trade unions' functions that the author identifies.
693. *Ibid.*
694. Hayter, S., Ebisui, M., *Negotiating Parity for Precarious Workers*, 5 International Journal of Labour Research 79 n. 1 (2013), 79-96.
695. *Ibid.*, 85.
696. *Supra*, Ebisui (2012), 219-224; *see also* Lodovici, M. (2018), *Independent Workers and Industrial Relations in Europe, The Role of Trade Unions*, Istituto per la Ricerca Sociale.
697. *Ibid.*, Ebisui (2012), 224.

and within many different industrial systems. It can be, thus, argued that such developments confirm the description given by Ewing in relation to the regulatory function of trade unions.

Importantly, in addition to collective bargaining unions have also espoused other strategies in order to engage with atypical workers. These, among other things, are the influence of national policies and legislation through social dialogue and campaigning, litigation in court, the organisation of precarious workers and the provision of services and the promotion of campaigns to influence public opinion.[698] As is seen below in relation to platform workers, unions have also deployed less traditional means in order to approach these types of workers. Illustrative in this regard is the launching of online forums, which can be used as a meeting point for workers in organising their collective actions.

As mentioned, notable examples where unions have attempted to incorporate these categories of workers within their policies can be found around the world. In Germany, the country's largest union, IG Metall, recently modified its statutes in order to allow self-employed workers to join. The same stance has also been adopted by *Unionen*, a Swedish trade union, since 1998, whilst in the Netherlands, the Dutch Trade Union Federation - FNV, the largest trade union confederation in the country, represents non-standard workers in sectors where workers face particular risks, like the domestic aid and cleaning sectors. In Slovenia, since 2016, *Sindikat prekarcev*, which is part of the main union confederation (ZSSS - Association of Free Trade Unions of Slovenia), has been seeking to organise workers engaged in atypical employment.[699] Similar examples can be traced to other European countries, such as Spain and Italy. In the US, some unions, like the Service Employees International Union (SEIU), have also attempted to advance the working conditions of low-paid precarious workers in non-standard work arrangements, with some success stories to be reported thus far.[700] Furthermore, research indicates that alike 'initiatives of engagement' have also taken place in other parts of the world. In Japan, for instance, some community-based unions aim at organising workers irrespective of their contractual status, including independent contractors and unemployed workers,[701] while in Argentina, the Argentine Street Vendors Union includes in its activities workers from the private and public sector and its actions by the conclusion of several collective agreements have been crucial in order '*to overcome the dispersion across the self-employed*'.[702]

It is true that workers in NSFE continue to be under-represented by trade unions. This is also a trend that takes place within a general decline in unionism around the

698. *Supra*, Keune (2013), 65-66; ITUC, (2019), *Organising and Collective Bargaining in Non-Standard Forms of Work*, Policy Brief 17 October 2019, available at: https://www.ituc-csi.org/Organising-CollectiveBargaining-in-NonStandard-Work (accessed 10 February 2021).
699. OECD, (2019), *Negotiating our way up: Collective bargaining in a changing world of work*, Paris, OECD, 243.
700. For instance, the 'Justice for Janitors' campaigns organized by SEIU and in some instances led to the increase of wages of certain types of atypical workers. *See supra*, Ebisui (2012), 222-223.
701. *Supra*, Ebisui (2012), 221.
702. *Supra*, ITUC (2019).

world. What is also true, however, is a gradual tendency on the part of the unions in opening up to new members that, in many instances, have different characteristics and needs than those of standard workers. This is a phenomenon that someone can observe in relation to unionism in platform economy.

That said, the question which arises is whether the representation of platform workers by traditional unions bears any specific particularities when compared to other workers in NSFE. In this respect, it has been claimed that organising workers in the context of the platform economy is 'uniquely' difficult.[703] This is not to say that all the challenges such workers face are completely new for trade unions. Take, for instance, their often unclear employment status along with the existence of strict antitrust laws, or their regular turnover from one job to another, and therefore their difficulty in finding a single collective identity. These, arguably, are some issues that have also impeded the unionisation of workers in other forms of atypical jobs.[704] What is particularly challenging in the context of platform work, however, is the fact that many of these issues can be exacerbated.

Specifically, platform businesses, via the use of new technologies, have the unprecedented ability to access a wide pool of workers, both high-skilled and low-skilled, who share many different occupational and even class identities (including many migrant and young workers), and have very different incentives when engaging with a specific platform.[705] Even though, as literature confirms, the heterogeneity of the workforce in the context of atypical work arrangements is not a novel feature,[706] new digital tools can enable labour platforms to reach out to an even greater number of workers with distinct characteristics and needs.[707]

Moreover, in general, when compared to a regular firm, digital labour platforms have particularly low entry barriers,[708] which also entails that workers on a platform have a more diverse range of reasons to engage in this type of work.[709] As noted in previous sections, this model might benefit certain workers, such as workers with physical impairments. In relation to worker's organisation, however, it can further complicate the creation of a common collective identity and cooperation in order to

703. Lenaerts, K., Kilhoffer, Zachary, Z., Akgüç, M., *Traditional and New forms of Organisation and Representation in the Platform Economy*, 12 Work Organisation, Labour & Globalisation 60 n. 2 (2018), 72.
704. *Supra*, Ituc (2019).
705. Newlands, G., Lutz, C., Fieseler, C., *Collective Action and Provider Classification in the Sharing Economy*, 33 New Technology, Work and Employment 250 n. 3 (2018), 250-267; Vandaele, K., *Collective Resistance and Organizational Creativity Amongst Europe's Platform Workers: A New Power in the Labour Movement?* (Julieta Haider and Maarten Keune, eds, *Work and Labour Relations in Platform Capitalism*, Cheltenham, Edward Elgard 2021), 206-235.
706. *Supra*, Hyman (1994), 108-139.
707. To this extent *see* the analysis from: Hua, J., Ray, K., *Beyond the Precariat: Race, Gender, and Labor in the Taxi and Uber Economy*, 24 Social Identities 271 n. 2 (2018), 271-289.
708. Drahokoupil, J., Piasna, A., *Work in the Platform Economy: Beyond Lower Transaction Costs*, 52 Intereconomics 335 n. 6 (2017), 336; Engels, S., Sherwood, M. (2019), *What If We All Worked Gigs in the Cloud? The Economic Relevance of Digital Labour Platforms*, European Economy Discussion Paper, No. 099, 14.
709. For instance, *see* Schor, J. B., *After the Gig: How the Sharing Economy got Hijacked and How to Win It Back* (University of California Press 2020), 272.

address workplace-related problems. It has been observed, for instance, that, on some occasions, workers who are not relying on the platforms as their main source of income are less eager to organise.[710] Some platforms, like Uber, seem to be very well aware of this diversity and dynamic among their workforce, ranging from recreational to full-time drivers; consequently, the company's business model tends to rely on the '*least invested drivers*', who have less chances to unionise.[711] This phenomenon, as Lehdonvirta argues, can, in turn, undercut the interests of heavily invested platform workers who might wish to mobilise in order to ameliorate their working conditions.[712] On top of that, many platforms do not expedite the communication between workers who find difficulties in sharing their experiences.[713] This is something that can also occur due to the fact that many platform businesses are under no obligation to provide information on the number of workers who are using their app, or any other detail in relation to who is actually working from them.[714] On a number of occasions, they also have to deal with a '*heightened sense of anonymity*' and isolation, especially where the performance of work occurs online.[715]

It can be argued that the lack of human-to-human communication enabled via new technologies, like the introduction of algorithms, and the spatial fragmentation of the workforce, constitute elements that can prevent worker's mobilisation. Within the context of the platform economy, such features can be intensified along with the advancement of technology.[716] Last but not least, as Heinland and Brinkmann observe, platform workers' organisation compared to other workers in NSFE can be exceptionally challenging as a result of the 'novelty' and 'ever-changing' nature of these types of work; hence, they are still in the process of learning how to deal with these new aspects in an area in which certain structural forms of industrial relations are not yet established.[717]

As stated, despite all these problems, some unions have shown a noteworthy interest in organising platform workers. What is also of interest is the proliferation of workers' associations that do not necessarily fit the traditional model of trade unions.

710. *Ibid.*, Newlands et al. (2018), 264; *supra*, Vandaele (2018), 11.
711. Rosenblat, A., *Uberland: How Algorithms are Rewriting the Rules of Work* (University of California Press 2018), 53-55 and 72; *see also* Schor, J.B., Attwood-Charles, W., Cansoy, M., Ladegaard, I., and Wengronowitz, R., *Dependence and Precarity in the Platform Economy*, 49 Theory and Society 833 n. 5-6 (2020), 855.
712. Lehdonvirta, V., *Algorithms that Divide and Unite: Delocalisation, Identity and Collective Action in 'Microwork'* (Jörg Flecker, ed., *Space, Place and Global Digital Work*, London, Palgrave Macmillan 2016), 76.
713. *Supra*, Newlands et al. (2018), 263; *supra*, Prassl (2018), 14-15.
714. Heiland, H. (2020), *Workers' Voice in platform labour: An Overview*, WSI Study No. 21, Hans-Böckler-Stiftung, Wirtschafts- und Sozialwissenschaftliches Institut (WSI), Düsseldorf, available at: https://www.boeckler.de/de/faust-detail.htm?sync_id=9041 (accessed 15 March 2021).
715. Johnston H., *Labour Geographies of the Platform Economy: Understanding Collective Organizing Strategies in the Context of Digitally Mediated Work*, 159 International Labour Review 25 n. 1 (2020), 29.
716. *Supra*, Vandaele (2018), 27.
717. Heiland, H., Brinkmann, U., *Liefern am Limit: Wie die Plattformökonomie die Arbeitsbeziehungen verändert*, 27 Industrielle Beziehungen 120 n. 2 (2020), 120-140.

4.4 PLATFORM WORKERS' COLLECTIVE INITIATIVE(S)

Recent developments indicate that some traditional trade unions around the world have shown a particular interest in incorporating platform workers in their strategies.[718] As research moreover points out, these initiatives have taken various forms that range from typical recourses of organisation, such as through the conclusion of collective agreements, to less traditional approaches, like the creation of online forums where workers can discuss and get informed regarding many of the issues stemming from such work arrangements.[719] Having said that, the mobilisation of workers presents considerable differences which depend upon the nature of platform work per se. For instance, as seen below, collective representation for on-demand, place-based workers can be achieved in a rather easier way compared to online workers (crowdworkers). Specifically, workers falling in the former category, due to the fact that work activities are performed on a more local basis, find fewer obstacles in coordinating their actions, identifying common interests, and cultivating solidarity.[720]

In addition, as Johnston argues, they find themselves in the same national regulatory framework, where '*the legal provisions for collective bargaining frequently have clear geographic bounds, with legislation providing for the possibility of representation at the level of the worksite, the firm, or the industry*'.[721] Conversely, crowdworkers, as platforms generally operate internationally, have to operate in labour markets beyond the local level; hence, spatial constraints, in many instances, can be considered detrimental to their collective organisation. Still, as noted, unions have attempted to challenge these issues. What is also striking is that in cases where institutional unions have not been as proactive, or the representation of such workers is considered impractical for the reasons outlined above, there is an increased number of alternative organisations that represent workers' collective interests.

4.4.1 Collective Agreements in the Platform Economy: The Case of On-Demand Workers

The conclusion of collective agreements constitutes one of the main ways through which trade unions have attempted to challenge the issues related to platform-mediated work. In this regard, a number of agreements have emerged within the context of on-demand, place-based workers. More specifically, in the UK, in 2019, the GMB union signed a collective agreement with Hermes, a courier platform company. Hermes' self-employed couriers now have the option to acquire a 'self-employed plus' status that provides them with important benefits, such as holiday payments and

718. *Ibid.*, Vandaele (2018); Johnston H., Land-Kazlaukas, C., *Organizing On-demand: Representation, Voice, and Collective Bargaining in the Gig Economy*, Geneva, ILO (2019).
719. *Supra*, Aloisi (2019).
720. For example, *see* Marrone, M, and Finotto, V., *Challenging Goliath. Informal Unionism and Digital Platforms in the Food Delivery Sector. The Case of Riders Union Bologna*, 12 PACO 691 n. 3 (2019), 691-716.
721. *Supra* Johnston H. (2020), 25-45.

guaranteed earnings.[722] Innovative in its own way, the agreement further attempts to challenge the isolation of platform workers by permitting the GMB union with the company's assistance to hold recruitment days eight times a year. The development at issue was celebrated by both the trade union and the team management of the company, as a groundbreaking agreement that is capable of paving the way for more initiatives of this kind in the UK. It was the first and the sole instance that a digital platform has permitted its alleged self-employed workers to be represented by a trade union.[723] That said, as Katsabian observes, it is highly contested whether the new agreement really allows the 'self-employed plus' to enjoy their collective labour rights, as it solely refers to '*the individual right of each courier to negotiate her pay separately from the other workers*'; hence, the right to collective representation appears to be purposely missing from this agreement at issue.[724]

In Australia, moreover, in 2017, Unions New South Wales (NSW), a peak body union, concluded an agreement with Airtasker, a platform that facilitates the matching of home-based tasks created by customers with workers who are willing to accept and, in turn, perform the job. Through the agreement, the platform company agreed to post on its site recommended pay rates based on legal minima. On top of that, workers are provided with minimum labour standards of protection, including, among other things, the existence of injury insurance and other safety guidelines, in compliance with national health and safety regulations.[725] Even though an important development, the agreement at issue was concluded outside the formal system of employment regulation and therefore is not enforceable.[726] Its non-binding status can be particularly problematic considering Airtasker's organisational model.[727] The latter relies on a 'bidding' for work system, a model that in reality opposes the creation of a minimum wage.[728] Still, as Forsyth claims, it offers an example for other unions as to how to adopt more effective forms of organising within the hostile context of the platform economy.[729]

722. GMB Union. 2019. 'Hermes and GMB in groundbreaking gig economy deal', 4 February 2019. https://www.gmb.org.uk/news/hermes-gmb-groundbreaking-gig-economy-deal. (accessed: 24 October 2020).
723. Katsabian, T. (2021), *Collective Action in the Digital Reality: the Case of Platform-Based Workers, The Modern Law Review*, 84 n. 5, 1005.
724. *Ibid.*, 1006.
725. Minter, K., *Negotiating Labour Standards in the Gig Economy: Airtasker and Unions New South Wales*, 28 The Economic and Labour Relations Review 438 n. 3 (2017), 449.
726. Under the Fair Work Act (FWA) 2009, collective agreements in Australia can only take place between an employer and its employees; *See* FORSYTH, A., *The Future of Unions and Worker Representation: The Digital Picket Line* (Hart Publishing 2022), 184.
727. Kaine, S. (2017), 'All care and no responsibility: why Airtasker can't guarantee a minimum wage', *The Conversation* (online source), 2 May 2017, available at: https://theconversation.com/all-care-and-no-responsibility-why-airtasker-cant-guarantee-a-minimum-wage-76943 (accessed 20 September 2020).
728. The lowest bid is possible to take the job. This model can lead to an unfair competition between workers who are competing against each other in a reverse auction. For more information *see* the following footnote.
729. Forsyth, A., *Collectivising the Gig Economy in Australia*, 27 Journal of the International Centre for Trade Union Rights 28 n. 3 (2020), 19.

A similar observation according to the author, can also be made in relation to Transport Union Workers (TWU) and its efforts to collectively represent platform workers and, more specifically, a group of Deliveroo workers. Following the death of four delivery riders in the course of their work, Deliveroo workers supported by the TWU, requested the company to initiate the formation of work groups and election of health and safety representatives.[730] Under the relevant national law(s), such representatives can be elected upon the request of 'workers' in one or more 'work groups'.[731] For the purposes of the law at issue, the definition of who is a worker makes no distinction between an independent contractor and an employee.[732] Deliveroo, which had previously appointed its own 'rider panel', comprised of workers selected by the company itself, opposed the idea brought forward by the union. Its denial led the TWU to bring a claim before the work health and safety regulatory agency. Importantly, the latter provided Deliveroo with a notice obliging it to comply with the national legislation and permit the election of workers' representatives.[733] Albeit that was not a typical scenario of collective bargaining, the agreement between Deliveroo and TWU represents an alternative method by which unions have attempted to safeguard workers' rights via specialised legislation with a broad scope of application.

That said, a number of (typical) collective agreements are observed as far as Scandinavian countries are concerned, a region in which a long history of collective bargaining exists. Particularly, in Sweden, the Swedish Transport Workers Union, concluded a company-level collective agreement with the transportation start-up Bzzt, a company using electronic taxis based on the model of Uber.[734] Due to this development workers are now having access to the same standards as traditional taxi drivers. It is worth mentioning that in contrast to many other platform businesses, Bzzt's drivers are offered marginal part-time contracts.[735] In a similar vein, in Norway, Foodora has also accepted that its couriers can be hired on a marginal part-time basis (10 hours per week). As some national experts indicate, Foodora's acceptance of using employees was the result of important pressure from trade unions, labour inspectorates as well as from the general regulation in the Norwegian labour market.[736] As a result, in September 2019, by taking advantage of the courier's employee status, Fellesforbundet, the Transport Workers Union (*Norsk Transportarbeiderforbund* (NTF)), succeed in concluding a collective agreement with the digital labour platform in question. The latter, *inter alia*, provides for a salary increase, a supplement for seniority, a pre-delivery bicycle equipment allowance and an extra payment during wintertime.[737]

730. *Supra*, Forsyth (2022), 185.
731. *See* Work Health and Safety Act 2011 (NSW) (WHS Act), section 50.
732. WHS Act, section 7.
733. *Supra*, Forsyth (2022), 185.
734. *Supra*, Johnston and Land-Kazlauskas (2019), 30.
735. Digital Platform Observatory, available at: https://digitalplatformobservatory.org/initiative/agreement-between-bzzt-and-the-swedish-transport-workers-union/ (accessed 20 September 2020).
736. Ilsoe, A., Jesnes, K. (2020), *Collective Agreements for Platforms and Workers – Two Cases from the Nordic Countries*, Nordic Council of Ministers, Copenhagen, 57-67.
737. *Ibid.*

These achievements, nonetheless, are threatened by the fact that other platform businesses in the country, such as Wolt, are taking up the competition with Foodora by chiefly relying on couriers that are hired as independent contractors. It remains to be seen as to whether Foodora will continue to constitute the exception within the country's online food-delivery market, or it will follow the example of other businesses in the sector which prefer more flexible work arrangements that entail reduced labour costs and, in many occasions, poor working conditions.[738]

Arguably, the most interesting example within the context of the Nordic countries can be traced to Denmark, where, in 2018, a company-level collective agreement was signed between the trade union 3F and Hilfr.dk, a platform offering cleaning services.[739] It was the first agreement in the platform economy that attempted to regulate the effects that new technologies can have on workers. More specifically, it enshrines that consent needs to be given in a form for:

> [the] publication of personal data on the platform [...] that contains voluntary, specific, informed and unambiguous consent from the registered person, including consent to the use and posting of his/her personal' and 'the employee may, at any time, request the removal of any derogatory, false and offensive content from the app.[740]

On top of that, a decision was reached that together with the existing freelance contracts (Freelancehilfrs), a 'new category' of worker, with employee status, is to be introduced.[741] Unless they decide otherwise, workers who have completed 100 hours of work are eligible to fall into this employee category, labelled as 'SuperHilfr(s)'. They could apply for this employment status even if they have not met the aforementioned criterion. In this case, it is up to the platform to decide whether to accept or reject their application.[742] The agreement stipulates that SuperHilfrs are entitled to labour protections, such as minimum hourly wages, holiday benefits, and sick leave payments. Concomitantly, it also provides for minimum fees to be established for the freelancers of the platform. This development did not go unnoticed by the national competition and consumer authority (DCAA). The latter, took action against the agreement as it considers both SuperHilfrs and Freelancehilfrs to be undertakings and, therefore, cannot proceed to the fixing of prices.[743]

738. *Ibid.*
739. Collective agreement Between Hilfr ApS. CBR. no.: 37297267 and 3F Private Service, Hotel and Restaurant, available at: https://www2.3f.dk/~/media/files/mainsite/forside/fagforening/privat%20service/overenskomster/hilfr%20collective%20agreement%202018.pdf (accessed 20 December 2020).
740. *Ibid.*
741. The agreement in relation to the Super Hilfr is available at: https://blog.hilfr.dk/en/historic-agreement-first-ever-collective-agreement-platform-economy-signed-denmark/ (accessed 20 December 2020).
742. *Supra*, Vandaele (2021).
743. Opinion of the Danish Competition and Consumer Authority is available at: https://www.en.kfst.dk/nyheder/kfst/english/decisions/20200826-commitment-decision-on-the-use-of-a-minimum-hourly-fee-hilfr/ (accessed 20 December 2020).

As a consequence of the aforementioned developments, Hilfr has now offered to meet the concerns of the DCCA, by removing the minimum hourly fee for Freelance-hilfrs from the platform and by ensuring that there is legal subordination between Hilfr and Superhilfrs. As such,'[the platform] *will bear the financial risk for Superhilfr's cleaning work through the platform'*.[744] These commitments appear to be binding for Hilfr for an indefinite period of time. As Countouris and De Stefano contend, the Hilfr agreement demonstrates how antitrust legislation can impede the fundamental rights of workers to freely associate and bargain collectively.[745] For instance, the *a priori* conclusion of the DCCA that all the workers of the platform are undertakings, without the reliance on empirical evidence, or the absence of any consideration of the existence of disguised employment relationships, is indicative of what the authors describe. The DCCA's verdict also had an adverse impact on other collective agreements concluded for self-employed platform workers in the country, namely, the agreement between the digital platform Voocali and the trade union of HK. The latter decided to finally step back from the agreement in question due to the DCCA's 'hostile behaviour' towards the Hilfr collective agreement.[746]

Moving on to other examples from Denmark, the trade union 3F and the Danish Chamber of Commerce, reached a nationwide agreement for delivery riders valid from 2021 to 2023.[747] Importantly, it is the first sectoral collective agreement which is concluded specifically for platform workers.[748] In addition to other benefits, riders will be receiving a base hourly wage. Platforms will also be obliged to provide workers with a vehicle and safety equipment. The agreement was initially signed only by the company of Just Eat, but it is now open to other platform businesses.[749]

Moving to other examples, in Austria the transport and services union, namely *Vida*, established a works council for Foodora cyclists, with the ultimate target of negotiating a collective agreement for all bicycle delivery services.[750] The agreement does not include any provisions related to the legal classification of bike couriers; it

744. *Ibid.*
745. Countouris, N. and De Stefano, V. 'Collective-bargaining rights for platform workers'. *Social Europe*, 6 October 2020, available at: https://www.socialeurope.eu/collective-bargaining-rights-for-platform-workers. (accessed 24 October 2020).
746. Hadwiger, F., *Realizing the Opportunities of the Platform Economy Through Freedom of Association and Collective Bargaining*, ILO Working Paper 80, Geneva, ILO, (2022) 65.
747. European Transport Workers' Federation (2021), '3F secures ground-breaking national sectoral agreement for delivery riders', 4 February 2021, available at: https://www.etf-europe.org/3f-secures-ground-breaking-national-sectoral-agreement-for-delivery-riders/ (accessed 29 August 2022).
748. Boto, M.J.M., *Collective Bargaining and the Gig Economy: Reality and Possibilities* (José M. Boto and Elisabeth Brameshuber eds, *Collective Bargaining and the Gig Economy A Traditional Tool for New Business Models*, Hart Publishing, 2022), 13. As it is explained below in Italy and Spain there are also sectoral collective agreements that cover platform workers. However, those agreements already existed and they just expanded their scope so as to cover such workers. As noted, the Danish agreement constitutes the first ever sectoral agreement, signed solely for platform workers.
749. *Ibid.*
750. Vida, Works council for foodora bicycle delivery service (translation), available at: www.vida.at/cms/S03/S03_0.a/1342577497037/home/artikel/betriebsrat-fuer-fahrradzustelldienst-foodora (accessed 24 October 2020).

does provide, nonetheless, a number of statutory rights, such as a minimum wage and holiday allowances, for those workers who are qualified as employees.[751] In Spain, furthermore, in 2019, the General Union of Workers (UGT) and the Workers' Commissions (*Comisiones Obreras*), agreed on expanding the scope of the collective agreement in the hospitality and catering sector with the purpose of including platform workers, who enjoy the employee status, within it.[752] Sectoral unions and employers' organisations, more specifically, decided that this extension was essential, both in reducing the risks of unfair competition in this area due to the proliferation of platform businesses, as well as preserving the working conditions already established in the sector.[753] Despite this development, however, it has been argued that the majority of platform workers engaged in this particular sector remain unaffected because of their status as self-employed workers.[754]

In February 2019, moreover, again at sectoral level, a new collective agreement was signed in Switzerland between Syndicom, the Swiss media and communication union, and Swissmessengerlogistics, which is the courier employers' association. The agreement enshrines minimum standards, like regulation of working hours and sick-related benefits, for bike couriers and city courier services.[755] According to national experts, the problem with this agreement lies in the fact that important platform businesses, like UberEats, are excluded from the collective agreement; hence, only a small number of platform workers is covered at the moment of writing.[756] The general lack of willingness of digital labour platforms to participate in the conclusion of collective agreements can also be observed in Germany. In 2017, one of the largest unions in the country, namely, IG BAU (*Industrielle Gewerkschaft Bauen-AgrarUmwelt*, Trade Union of Construction, Agriculture, and Environment) signed a sectoral agreement that affects 600,000 cleaners who enjoy the employee status.[757] As a consequence, some digital cleaning platforms, such as BOOK A TIGER and Helping, which are hiring their cleaners as employees, must comply with the provisions of the agreement. Still, there is no evidence that the platforms in question ever wanted or actually did participate in the negotiations with the trade union.[758] There is also no evidence with respect to the exact number of platform workers who are generally covered by the agreement and the effects of it.

---

751. Widner, J. 'Gig economy un-gigged: collective bargaining agreement for bike couriers', *Lexology* (website), 18 December 2019, available at: https://www.lexology.com/library/detail.aspx?g=0771b65a-6105-4128-a8a1-f384982f474d (accessed 24 October 2020).
752. Agreement available at: https://www.boe.es/boe/dias/2019/03/29/pdfs/BOE-A-2019-4645.pdf (accessed: 24 October 2020).
753. Hermoso, M., *Spain. Case Study Report*, Don't Gig Up Project, 2019, 9-10, available at: http://www.dontgigup.eu/wp-content/uploads/2020/05/Casestudy_ES.pdf (accessed: 24 October 2020).
754. *Ibid.*, 10.
755. Dunand, J.P., Mahon, P. (2019), *Switzerland* (Dauareilh, I., Degryse, C., Pochet, P. eds *The Platform Economy and Social Law: Key Issues in Comparative Perspective, ETUI Working Paper)*, Brussels, 111.
756. *Ibid.*
757. *Supra* Heiland (2020), 36.
758. *Ibid.*

In Italy, in 2017, again at the sectoral level, some of the country's largest trade unions, such as the Italian Federation of Transport Workers (Filt-Cgil), signed a collective agreement in the area of logistics that contains a number of significant labour protections.[759] Importantly, since 2018 and its amendment in order to address the emerging challenges stemming from digital platforms, the agreement covers food-delivery riders in its contractual provisions, regardless of their employment status.[760] Assodelivery, the employer's association, which includes big digital platforms, like Deliveroo and Glovo, never accepted the collective agreement; instead, they signed an agreement with a far-right-affiliated Italian Unione Generale del Lavoro (UGL), with the purpose to maintain the status of workers as self-employed and in exchange providing them with a minimum wage and bonuses.[761] This development appears to come as a response to the 2019 law amendment in Italy,[762] which, as noted in a previous section, aims at extending the scope of employment protection beyond the employment relationship to all workers providing work organised by another party, including through a platform. In this regard, employment and labour protection would apply to these platform workers, except in situations where a collective agreement stipulates otherwise.[763] It makes no surprise that the country's most representative unions characterised UGL's agreement as a 'fake improvement' that attempts to grant to workers fewer rights than the ones the new law aims at giving them.[764] Also, the Italian Ministry of Labour has recently expressed the opinion, albeit not binding, that the agreement is not valid, on the grounds that it is not in accordance with the recent national legislation and UGL does not sufficiently represent delivery workers in Italy.[765] This example reveals, therefore, how far, some platform businesses, are ready to go in order to pursue their policies, by finding ways to circumvent existing legislation. It also shows there are instances that some collective agreements will attempt to further flexibilise employment regulations in order to promote political and other interests.

Last but not least, let us refer to two of the most recent collective agreements (at least at the time of writing this part) concluded in Europe. More precisely, as of January 2022, platform workers of Just Eat in Spain and Deliveroo in the Netherlands will now be covered by collective agreements.[766] The latter are the result of a long process and enshrine beneficial provisions for these workers. The Just Eat collective agreement took place in the aftermath of the adoption of the Riders' Law, and it was signed

759. *Supra*, Vandaele (2021).
760. *Ibid.*
761. Heikkla, M., Tamma, P. (2020), 'Delivery companies unveil labor deal with Italian far-right union'. *Politico*, 16 September 2020, available at: https://www.politico.eu/article/delivery-companies-unveil-labor-deal-with-italian-far-right-union/ (accessed 10 February 2021).
762. Decreto-Legge 3 settembre 2019, n. 101 disposizioni urgenti per la tutela del lavoro e per la risoluzione di crisi aziendali.
763. Aloisi, A., De Stefano, V. 'Delivering employment rights to platform workers'. *il Mulino*, 31 January 2020.
764. *Supra*, Heikkla and Tamma (2020).
765. *Ibid.*
766. UNI Global Union, (2022), 'Historic victories for Just Eat and Deliveroo workers in Europe', 5 January 2022, available at: https://uniglobalunion.org/news/historic-victories-just-eat-and-deliveroo-workerseurope?fbclid=IwAR3x3BJeUIuhBsICKGZCElYF3yeAYiT739oOAP2ZnKc4eyzC2ibv4JFF93s (accessed 6 January 2022).

between the unions of CCOO and UGT and the platform in question. As noted above, the new law in Spain, via the inclusion of a rebuttable presumption, provides for the classification of food-delivery couriers as employees. Under the agreement, delivery workers can now be the beneficiaries of a number of rights, including health and safety protections and an annual leave of 30 days.[767] Notably, they also have the right to disconnect and, at the same time, enjoy more protections with respect to their privacy rights. In a similar vein, in the Netherlands, the FNV union signed a collective agreement with Deliveroo. This development occurred right after the platform at issue lost a 'legal battle' in front of the Court of Appeal in Amsterdam, where it was ruled that Deliveroo's riders should enjoy employee status.[768] Such a verdict, which according to the Court applies retroactively to all delivery couriers who currently work for the company means that these workers are to be covered under FNV's collective agreement for the transport of goods. The latter, *inter alia*, includes benefits related to annual leave entitlements, payments during waiting time, and compensation in case a worker gets sick.[769]

4.4.2 Platform Workers' Collective Agreements: Some Main Observations to Keep in Mind

Arguably, the recent proliferation of collective agreements within the platform economy constitutes a positive sign. As it has been argued: '*traditional trade unions have been the main actors, following traditional rules*'.[770] Minimum remuneration, health, and safety guarantees, and training are just some of the benefits reaped by many platform workers. In this respect, the content of collective bargaining in the platform economy does not really differ from traditional collective negotiations in other sectors of the labour market. That said, there are a few exceptions, such as the Hermes' collective agreement and the recent Danish agreement of the trade union 3F, which also attempt to capture some of the particularities of platform work, including the loneliness often faced by these workers. It remains to be seen whether future agreements will also include provisions of a similar nature.

At this point, though, some problematic aspects can be observed. First, the fact that a big number of platform workers are considered self-employed, excludes them from the coverage of existing collective agreements. This, as noted, occurs despite the fact that, in a number of instances, they share many of the characteristics traced in a typical employment relationship. That said, even if some collective agreements for self-employed platform workers already exist, it is, however, observed that those have not necessarily followed the typical scenario of collective bargaining. This is to say that they have adopted a more 'diluted' version of collective bargaining, like in the case of

767. *Ibid.*; *see also* Rodríguez, R. (2022), 'First collective agreement for platform workers in Spain', *Social Europe*, 13 January 2022, available at: https://socialeurope.eu/first-agreement-for-platform-workers-in-spain?fbclid=IwAR0UoNfpKG3V8nqbVQUfiB5EvASfKieH45EnBp2TXV9un1WnQprxnyBYenw (accessed 13 January 2022).
768. Gerechtshof Amsterdam 16 februari 2021, Case No. *ECLI:NL:GHAMS:2021:392*.
769. *Supra*, UNI Global Union (2022).
770. *Supra*, Boto (2022), 14.

the Hermes collective agreement in the UK. The latter, albeit an important step in the right direction, is omitting to secure the collective representation of the couriers involved in the agreement. The last chapter of this research will further assess these types of agreements, and it will also discuss what their conclusion may entail for the exercise of the right to collective bargaining.

Second, a considerable number of the first collective agreements signed for platform workers have taken place at the company level, even in countries like Denmark, where collective agreements are mostly negotiated at the industry level.[771] This development, arguably, follows general trends in many countries towards the decentralisation of collective bargaining procedures in favour of individual agreements, a phenomenon that in some cases can lead to less advantageous agreements for the workers and therefore limited protection.[772] Moreover, at least to a certain extent, the focus at the enterprise level may also indicate that digital labour platforms are not affiliated with national employers' organisations or other sectoral organisations.[773] It can be observed, however, that some of the most recent collective agreements, like in the case of Italy and Spain, have been concluded at branch level. Those agreements actually enlarged their personal scope so as to include platform workers in their system. Albeit a very important development, as Boto observes, a simple extension of already existing agreements entails the risk of failing to adequately address the specialties of the platform economy.[774] The same cannot be argued with respect to the new collective agreement in Denmark, which as noted was specifically designed for platform delivery riders.

Finally, an issue that has not been sufficiently covered in the literature thus far is the existence of some problematic aspects within the already existing agreements touching upon platform work. Such challenges can be attributed to different reasons.[775] This is to say that some agreements may contain provisions, which in practice, can be problematic for workers covered by them. In addition, they may have failed to incorporate some important insights which can be considered necessary in addressing a number of critical issues, such as challenges related to the use of new technologies. Moreover, there may be the absence of additional tools which will enable those collective agreements to be fully functional for workers. Illustrative in this respect is the collective agreement signed between Hilfr and 3F. More specifically, a year after its conclusion, the latter was re-evaluated and some research was made on the dynamics between the platform, the customers and the workers. It was soon realised by the union that the original collective agreement has had some serious flows and therefore more regulations are needed in order to create some basic regulatory standards for the future. To this extent, since 2019, the renegotiation of the Hilfr agreement is still in progress.

771. *Supra*, Johnston (2020), 36.
772. Baccaro, L., Howell, C., *A Common Neoliberal Trajectory: The Transformation of Industrial Relations in Advanced Capitalism*, 39 Politics & Society 521 n. 4 (2011), 521-563.
773. *Supra*, Hadwiger (2022), 56.
774. *Supra*, Boto (2022), 12.
775. The discussion is based on the observations of Thorkild Holmboe-Hay, expressed in a webinar organised by CGIL on the gig economy and workers' involvement. The seminar took place online on 17 December 2020.

This time, however, the discussions are not taking place only with the platform in question, but also with the Confederation of the Danish Industry (DI). This means that if the parties agree on a new collective agreement, then the latter will be applicable at a sectoral level, and it will also cover a variety of platforms that are members of the DI.

Going back to the first agreement, three fundamental problems have been recognised until now. The first issue is related to the organisation of workers, meaning that it is difficult for the union to find out who are the workers of the platform, where they are working from, and when they are actually performing their tasks. Up to this point, there is an agreement with the DI that in the future, digital labour platforms must have a link on their website, which will lead platform workers to a virtual union, where they will have the chance to have discussions and get informed on their rights, as well as elect new trade union representatives. There will also be the opportunity for the creation of online forums, where new agreements can be discussed. According to the 3F union's representatives, the association of employers has already agreed on this development.

The second main problem lies in the fact that the initial agreement has failed to address some crucial issues stemming from the organisational structure of platform businesses. Specifically, according to the 3F's analysis, the business model of such companies is so diverse that it makes it impossible to agree on a collective agreement capable of covering all platforms. Thus, a suggestion has been made for a paragraph to be added to the new agreement with the purpose of either conforming the platforms' organisational framework with the specificities of the collective agreement itself or adjusting the latter in a way that covers the particularities of the organisational structure of the platform in question. Arguably, this proposal seems complicated, also considering the amount of digital platforms in the country. There are still ongoing discussions as to how this provision can actually materialise.

Third, when negotiating the Hilfr agreement, 3F was apparently unaware of how workers' remuneration which is currently calculated on the basis of an hourly minimum wage, can lead to some serious problems regarding the actual hours of the work performed. This is due to the fact that the remuneration of workers is calculated by an algorithm that converts hourly wages to job wages. Similar kinds of algorithms are also used by other platforms. In relation to Hilfr, a platform that offers cleaning services, the procedure goes as follows: each time customers connect to the app in order to find a worker to clean their place, the app requires them to type in the square meters that need to be cleaned. After inserting this variable, the platform offers a price. This calculation, however, presupposes that the algorithm knows how many hours a worker needs to clean a certain number of square meters.[776] The same algorithm can, later on, decide that for the same place to be cleaned, a less amount of time is necessary. Such an approach can be highly problematic as neither the union nor the workers really know how the algorithm functions and what criteria are used in determining the actual working hours. The calculation, therefore, can be arbitrary, by failing to take under consideration other important work aspects, such as the age of the

776. This can also be the case for riders (in km rather than sq m). It is the algorithm that determines the real wage that is paid to such workers.

worker in question as well as the differences between various places (e.g., the structure of the building), even if the square meters that need to be cleaned are the same. This method of calculation is not only capable of amplifying work intensity, but it can also lead to (indirect) discriminatory practices. 3F union wants to address these very issues as part of the agreement's revision. It remains to be seen if these concerns will be addressed in the near future.

Overall, it can be argued that the aforementioned example reveals that the dialogue for the conclusion of collective agreements within the context of the platform economy can be particularly complicated and constitute a learning exercise for trade unions. The different organisational structures of platform businesses, along with the extensive use of algorithms, render such discussions particularly demanding. In this respect, it is very important for unions to learn from previous mistakes and reach new agreements that touch upon modern aspects of work, such as proceeding to negotiate the manner in which algorithms should function.

4.4.3 Other Strategies

Besides the conclusion of collective agreements, unions, have also diversified their strategies in order to extend their reach to platform workers. Such initiatives have taken various forms which can also be observed in relation to the organisation of other workers in NSFE.

First of all, some traditional unions have participated in collective actions against digital labour platforms, including strikes and protests. For instance, in Norway, the conclusion of the aforementioned collective agreement between the NTF Union and Foodora, took place after the union at issue went on a strike action that lasted for several weeks.[777] As noted, the agreement now contains a number of beneficial for workers provisions. In Italy, moreover, the CGIL union has supported strike actions, which have been initiated by independent movements of delivery workers in different cities of the country.[778] In a similar vein, in the Netherlands, back in 2018, the FNV union supported strikes organised by Riders' Union Netherlands, a grassroots union comprised of Deliveroo riders, against workers' forced self-employment.[779] Moreover, in Spain, traditional unions, such as the UGT and the Workers Commission (*Confederación sindicale Comisiones Obreras*, CCOO) have also assisted groups of striking riders in their demand for better working conditions.[780] At this point, it should be mentioned that despite the existence of some examples in which traditional trade unions have been involved in strikes, such instances are limited. That said, the sole

777. *Supra*, Vandaele, K. (2021), 19.
778. Haipeter, T., Owczarek, D., Faioli, M., Iudicone, F. (2020), *Don't Gig Up*, Final Report, 24, available at: http://www.dontgigup.eu/wp-content/uploads/2020/04/Final-Report-3.pdf (accessed 9 February 2021).
779. Eurofound, (2021), 'Riders' Union Netherlands', 19 May 2021, available at: https://www.eurofound.europa.eu/data/platform-economy/initiatives/riders-union-netherlands (accessed 9 June 2021).
780. Eurofound, (2021), 'Deliveroo strike Spain', 9 April 2021, available at: https://www.eurofound.europa.eu/data/platform-economy/initiatives/deliveroo-strike-spain (accessed 9 June 2021).

example that a traditional union actually organised a strike action can be traced to Norway, where Foodora drivers were already considered employees. The rest of the developments are mainly concentrated around support initiatives towards strikes organised by grassroots unions. Indeed, as seen below grassroots unions seem to have prioritised these types of actions as they are the ones that have organised the vast majority of protests and strikes in different countries around the world.[781] The reason(s) as to why this might be the case will be also discussed below.

In addition to their support towards collective actions, some traditional unions have cooperated with labour inspectorates in order to ensure that existing labour regulations are indeed respected. For example, in Slovenia, drivers working for GoOpti, a platform offering transportation services, with the assistance of the trade union ZSSS (*Zveza svobodnih sindikatov Slovenije*, Association of Free Trade Unions of Slovenia), reported to the labour inspectorate that the company misclassifies its workers and therefore violates many of their rights.[782] As a consequence, GoOpti, in 2015, changed its business model by starting to subcontract the tasks to other transport companies instead of 'enlisting' the drivers themselves. In Poland, in 2019, the NSZZ *Solidarność* trade union requested the national labour inspectorate to audit Uber. By focusing mostly on health and safety problems as well as some issues related to irregularities in payments, the labour inspectorate concluded that the current national legislation is inadequate to address the majority of practices adopted by Uber and other businesses with a similar business model.[783] In Spain, moreover, *Unión General de Trabajadores*, UGT, filed a complaint with the Madrid labour inspectorate against the Amazon Flex platform, claiming that the company has been relying on bogus self-employed workers.[784] It should be noted that in Spain, claims on workers' classification are dealt with by the social courts of first instance, as well as by the labour inspectorate (though an administrative decision).[785] In the case in question, the latter ruled that Amazon has to pay over EUR 6 million in unpaid social security contributions and it remains to be seen as to whether the company will appeal this decision.

Having said that, a number of trade unions around the world have assisted the claims of platform workers in front of national courts. In Spain, for instance, the union *Intersindical* Valenciana, assisted a Deliveroo rider to be reclassified as an employee, rather than an independent contractor; this was the first court victory for food couriers in Europe.[786] In the UK, GMB, the union for professional drivers, has supported cases

---

781. *Supra*, Heiland (2020), 33.
782. Eurofound, (2021), 'GoOpti worker protest', 22 January 2021, available at: https://www.eurofound.europa.eu/data/platform-economy/initiatives/goopti-worker-protest (accessed 9 February 2021).
783. *Supra*, Haipeter, et al. (2020), 23.
784. Eurofound, (2021), 'Registration of Amazon Flex deliverers', 22 January 2021, Available at: https://www.eurofound.europa.eu/data/platform-economy/initiatives/registration-of-amazon-flex-deliverers (accessed 9 February 2021).
785. Barrio, A., *Contradictory Decisions on the Employment Status of Platform Workers in Spain*, Comparative Labor Law & Policy Journal Dispatches no. 20 (2020).
786. ITUC, (2019), *Organising and Collective Bargaining in Non-Standard Forms of Work*, Policy Brief, 17 October 2019, 14, available at: https://www.ituc-csi.org/Organising-Collective Bargaining-in-NonStandard-Work (accessed 9 February 2021).

brought by drivers and riders against a number of platform businesses, claiming for the reclassification of workers who were considered self-employed.[787] With the union's assistance, approximately 30,000 drivers in the UK, managed to acquire the 'worker' status; hence, they are eligible to access important employment protections, such as minimum wage and holiday benefits. In Australia, the Transport Workers Union has also assisted platform workers' reclassification against companies, like Foodora and Deliveroo.[788] In the Netherlands, furthermore, the FNV union, bought two lawsuits in front of a court of first instance in Amsterdam, against Deliveroo, arguing that the couriers in question were not self-employed workers and should be reclassified as employees of the platform. Such claim, among other reasons, was based on the fact that Deliveroo was able to exert a considerable control over its workers, by directing the various elements of their work performance.[789] At first, the court rejected the union's claims, mainly, due to the alleged flexibility of work schedules the workers enjoyed. Still, in late 2019 and following an appeal of the initial decision, another court of first instance issued a ruling in favour of the trade union and the couriers. As a result, the latter were found to be covered by an employment contract, despite the significant amount of freedom enjoyed.[790]

Moreover, in Italy, in December 2019, a group of Deliveroo drivers backed by the Italian General Confederation of Labour (CGIL), decided to bring charges against Deliveroo at Bologna's courthouse. It was claimed that the platform's algorithm discriminates against workers who participated in strikes and took sick leave by gradually reducing their shifts, sometimes even leading to the termination of the contract. In January 2020, the court ruled that the algorithm used by Deliveroo to allegedly assess the 'reliability' of riders was indeed discriminatory, *inter alia*, because it unfairly penalised workers who had a legitimate reason for not working. The decision was characterised by members of the CGIL as '*an epochal turning point in the conquest of workers*'.[791] This example, arguably, demonstrates the crucial role that trade unions can play in relation to challenges stemming from the inappropriate use of new technological tools.

In addition to 'court battles', institutional trade unions, on some occasions, have also used their political influence, resources and power in order to influence public authorities in taking measures to address and regulate the adverse impacts of platform work. For instance, in Australia, the Report of the Inquiry into the Victorian On-Demand Workforce was released.[792] It is the first extended national inquiry, which attempts to tackle some of the main problems that many workers in the platform

787. *Supra*, Aloisi (2019), 19.
788. *Supra*, Forsyth (2020), 19.
789. Rechtbank Amsterdam 23 juli 2018, Case No. ECLI:NL:RBAMS:2018.
790. Rechtbank Amsterdam 15 juli 2019, Case No. *ECLI:NL:RBAMS:2019*.
791. Pulignano, V., Mara, C. (2021), 'Food-delivery riders, algorithms and autonomy'. *Social Europe*, 21 January 2021, available at: https://www.socialeurope.eu/food-delivery-riders-algorithms-and-autonomy (accessed 10 February 2021).
792. The Inquiry into the Victorian On-Demand Workforce can be found here: https://engage.vic.gov.au/inquiry-ondemand-workforce (accessed 15 November 2022).

economy are facing, such as their employment status and accordingly their access to protective legislation.[793] The Inquiry aims at bringing more certainty and fairness in the realm of platform work, by reforming parts of the Victorian and federal laws. One of the most important suggestions in this regard was to codify work status' through a new statutory definition in the Fair Work Act, instead of relying on the present 'vague' common law tests.[794] As Forsyth argues, the decision of the Victorian government to issue the Inquiry was highly influenced by the lobbying and efforts of the TWU and other unions in the country. TWU, together with Victorian Trades Hall Council's Young Workers Centre, have been also providing the state government with data deriving from a survey on platform workers' views and experiences. These data have been also used to inform the On-Demand Food Delivery Rider's Charter of Rights, which constitutes part of the so-called campaign, Rights for Riders, and was published in 2019. The Charter, among other things, demands minimum rates and the right to freely bargain for better working conditions.[795]

The Australian developments are not the only example where unions have used their powers to influence public policies. In the US, for instance, the Transport Workers Union of America (AFL-CIO), the largest federation of unions in the US, strongly supported the enactment of the AB5 law, by spending financial resources in lobbying for its adoption. This is something that will also be discussed below in this chapter. The impact of trade unions' powers can be further observed in other initiatives that are not necessarily linked to public regulations, however, they can considerably impact some of the functions of national labour markets. Illustrative is the case of the Slovenian trade union *Mladi Plus*, which, *inter alia*, is committed to protecting the rights of young students and self-employed workers. *Mladi Plus* with the assistance of other unions in the county, such as the one of taxi drivers, managed to be one of the chief actors that prevented Uber from accessing the Slovenian labour market, by arguing that the national legislation cannot be altered in favour of a single company.[796] Of course, such an 'achievement' has not prevented other platform companies that have entered the county, like Wolt, from attempting to circumvent national laws by heavily relying on self-employed workers. To this extent, the union in question has been largely focusing on the recognition of couriers as employees in situations when it is believed that a platform such as Wolt does not comply with national legislation on the classification of workers.[797]

4.4.4 Innovative Strategies

Institutional unions have adopted other ways of promoting platform workers' interests; ways, that as Aloisi argues may differ from the classical resources of organisation, like

793. *Supra*, Forsyth (2020), 18.
794. *Ibid.*
795. The Charter can be found here: https://www.twu.com.au/wage-theft/food-delivery-riders-survey/ (accessed 15 November 2022).
796. Eurofound, (2021), 'Mladi Plus', 22 January 2021, available at: https://www.eurofound.europa.eu/data/platform-economy/initiatives/mladi-plus (accessed 10 February 2021).
797. *Ibid.*

collective bargaining.[798] As noted, one of the main difficulties trade unions face in relation to the representation of platform workers lies in the fact that isolation and anonymity of such workers need to be surmounted. In this respect, the largest industrial trade union in Europe, the German *IG Metall*, together with the Austrian Chamber of Labour, the Swedish Union, Unionen, trade unions representatives from Denmark and the US, as well as a group of international experts of industrial relations, have launched a cross-border initiative with the creation of the website that contains information, as well as advice to platform workers and in particular produces a rating system of working conditions on various platforms based on workers' reviews.[799] On top of that, in 2017, *IG Metall* with the assistance of the German Crowdsourcing Association and several digital platforms, established an Ombudsman's Office, with the intention of addressing complaints and resolving conflicts between workers, clients, and platforms.[800]

In Italy, moreover, the CGIL union, with the involvement of experts on the digitalisation of work and managers who cooperate with the union, have developed *Idea Diffusa*, an online collaborative platform.[801] Through this tool, the parties involved are provided with the sharing of knowledge and best practices, with the purpose of facilitating collective bargaining within digital workplaces. It further aims at placing trade unionism at the centre of discussions as to how new technological tools should be incorporated at work. In order to achieve this, among other things, there is a shared agenda and a public forum for debate, as well as a public magazine. These examples, indeed, reveal that unions around the world, aside from traditional collective bargaining, are in many instances, ready to adopt different strategies, and with the assistance of specialists develop new expertise in order to accommodate the peculiarities of platform worker's representation. Furthermore, in Spain, in 2017, UGT launched its online portal, with the name '*Your Union Response Now*', where workers can be informed about the union's activities, discuss their problems, as well as organise their future actions against platforms if necessary.[802] In a similar vein, in France, the French Democratic Confederation of Labour (CFDT), since 2016, has its own online platform that permits self-employed, including platform workers, to access a number of services, such as the provision of legal advice and complementary health insurance.[803]

798. *Supra*, Aloisi (2019), 17.
799. *Supra*, Vandaele (2018), 22.
800. IG Metall, Ombudsstelle für Crowdworking Plattformen vereinbart, available at: https://www.igmetall.de/download/2017_11_8_Presseinformation_OmbudsstelleCrowdworking_ef5ebcd3b52f834a38b64ec80377aee518d11009.pdf (accessed 4 January 2022).
801. Idea Diffusa, available at: http://www.cgil.it/cose-la-piattaforma-idea-diffusa/ (accessed 4 January 2022).
802. Royo M.R.P., *Spain* (Daugareilh, I., Degryse, C., Pochet, P. eds, *The Platform Economy and Social Law: Key Issues in Comparative Perspective*, European Trade Union Institute Working Paper 2019), Brussels, 103.
803. *Supra*, Heiland (2020), 39, citing: IRES, (2019), *Don't gig up!*, State of the Art Report. Institut de Recherches Économiques et Sociales, 31.

4.4.5 'Alternative' Unions

What is striking regarding workers' mobilisation in the platform economy constitutes the fact that in cases where traditional unions have not been as proactive, or the representation of such workers is considered impractical for the reasons outlined above, there is an increased number of alternative organisations that represent platform workers' collective interests. Examples of grassroots unions can be observed worldwide. In order to avoid any misunderstandings, it should be pointed out that the evolution of these unions, which some authors (mainly within literature coming from the US) refer to as 'alt-labour', is by no means correlated to the emergence of platform work.[804] These types of unions existed in the past, mostly in cases where low-wage, non-unionised workers felt that their interests could not be fully represented by traditional and well-established unions.[805] Still, the often poor working conditions along with the obscure employment status of a great portion of workers in the platform economy, are factors that appear to increase the presence of this kind of labour movement.

As research indicates, in numerous cases, alternative unions have been pivotal in addressing platform workers' specific concerns. Such representation has been manifested and facilitated through the use of new technologies, like online forums and social media, that workers use as labour campaigning tools.[806] As this section unfolds, it becomes clear that grassroots unions have adopted several strategies in their attempt to address problems related to platform work. In this regard, one of the most common ways in which they have managed to challenge platform businesses is through strike actions. As already noted, the majority of strikes around the world have been initiated by grassroots unions, in most situations, without the involvement of traditional unions. As Tassinari and Maccarrone observe, such a phenomenon is not due to the fact that grassroots unions are against traditional unionism; it is rather because platform workers, such as riders, as a result of their legal fragmentation, have limited or no access at all to representation rights and, thus, have to adopt approaches similar to the ones of informal workers.[807] That said, from Barcelona to Berlin and from Buenos Aires to Mexico City, grassroots unions have initiated a plethora of protests and strike actions against platform businesses. This is particularly the case within the sectors of transportation and food delivery. Notably, some of the collective actions that have taken place thus far have also extended to include other precarious workers; another illustration is that platform work shares many of the issues faced by other workers in non-standard work arrangements.[808]

804. For instance, *see* Duff, M.C., *ALT-Labor, Secondary Boycotts, and Toward a Labor Organization Bargain*, 63 Catholic University Law Review 843 n. 4 (2014), 843-878.
805. For grassroots labour movements in the past, for instance, *see* Scolnik, F., *Grassroots Labor Organizations in Metropolitan Buenos Aires, 2003-2007*, 42 Latin America Perspectives 30 n. 2 (2015), 30-41.
806. *Supra*, Aloisi (2019), 13.
807. Tassinari, A., Maccarrone, V., *Riders on the Storm: Workplace Solidarity Among Gig Economy Couriers in Italy and the UK. Work*, 165 Employment and Society 35 n. 3 (2019), 9.
808. *Supra*, Heiland (2020).

To begin with, in the UK, the Independent Workers Union of Great Britain (IWGB) which mainly consists of precarious workers, although not affiliated with the Trade Union Confederation, has facilitated wildcat strikes and negotiations with several platforms, and it has gained an increased media attention.[809] Probably, the most well-documented series of events took place in August 2016, when the food-delivery platform company of Deliveroo announced its willingness to switch from hourly wage to payment by the task.[810] The IWGB union supported a seminal strike that lasted for six days, during which a considerable number of riders of the platform decided to disrupt the labour process by logging off from their accounts; they also protested in front of the company's main offices in London. As a consequence, Deliveroo was obliged to announce that the change with respect to payments will not become mandatory, and will just be carried out on a voluntary basis.[811] Similar kinds of strikes occurred in 2017 and 2018 in other cities in the UK, such as Leeds and Brighton. IWGB has also collaborated with various media outlets in order to make Deliveroo's abuses of labour rights known to the public; such revelations have had a negative impact on the company's reputation as recent developments indicate. For example, a top UK fund, in early 2021, refused to invest in Deliveroo amid concerns over riders' rights.[812]

Furthermore, in Germany, in 2018, the Freie Arbeiterinnen-und Arbeiter-Union in Berlin, founded the International Labour Confederation, together with other unions around the world.[813] These unions have engaged in mobilisation campaigns and strikes in many European countries, like the Netherlands, Spain and Belgium.[814] Many of these actions have offered better working conditions for platform workers, even though the resistance from the side of the platforms remains strong. In Italy, furthermore, grassroots unions have been really active in engaging with platform workers and organising several protests and strike actions. Some of these collective actions have also attracted broad media coverage.[815] This is especially the case with respect to a protest campaign against the delivery platform of Foodora, that followed by multiple

809. *Ibid.*, 20.
810. Cant, C. (2017), 'Precarious couriers are leading the struggle against platform capitalism', *Political Critique*, 3 August 2017, available at: http://politicalcritique.org/world/2017/precarious-couriers-are-leading-the-struggle-against-platform-capitalism/ (accessed 4 January 2022); For a more in depth analysis, *see also* Cant, C., *Riding for Deliveroo: Resistance in the New Economy* (Polity Express 2019).
811. *Ibid.*
812. Jolly, J., Partridge, J. (2021), 'Top UK fund refuses to invest in Deliveroo amid City concern over riders' rights', *The Guardian*, 24 March 2021, available at: https://www.theguardian.com/uk-news/2021/mar/24/top-uk-fund-refuses-to-invest-in-deliveroo-amid-concern-over-riders-rights?fbclid=IwAR3ydNIWF7fWvckmLR0T-ugF14pgYLlvVIljDAVVhpwNKR0oPV8-StxXpD0 (accessed 4 January 2021).
813. Staunton, B. (2018), 'Grassroots action prominent in the platform economy'. *Open Democracy*, 16 December 2018, available at: https://www.opendemocracy.net/en/can-europe-make-it/grassroots-action-prominent-in-platform-economy/ (accessed 11 March 2021).
814. *Supra*, Vandaele (2018), 18-23.
815. *Supra*, Heiland (2020), 31.

strikes in a number of Italian cities, such as Rome and Milan.[816] Albeit workers' mobilisation led to a minimal improvement in payments, Foodora, nonetheless, proceeded with the dismissal of 15 riders who were particularly active during the strike actions.[817] In addition to Foodora, other digital platform businesses have also shown 'punitive behaviour' towards workers' exercise of collective action. For instance, some platforms have offered extra bonuses during strike times and other additional adjustments, which on some occasions have limited the effectiveness of strikes, or they have even resulted in the prevention of such actions in general.[818]

Another development that attracted broad media coverage, at least at a local level, is related to a wildcat strike action organised by delivery couriers working for the food platform of Efood, the largest courier business in the country. The strike, which is considered the largest ever in the sector in Greece, took place soon after Efood's announcement that a considerable number of its workers hired in 3-month contracts will be turned into freelancers. Such a decision was taken despite the fact that the company's profits soared during the pandemic.[819] Efood, moreover, made it clear via an e-mail that those who are not willing to accept their status as freelancers, will not have the chance to renew their existing contracts. In response to this development, thousands of riders went on 4 hours work stoppage, followed by a 24-hour strike the day after. Efood couriers were also supported by riders of another platform, as well as several unions involved in tourism and food-delivery sectors.[820] The e-mail(s) sent by Efood also went viral on social media and thousands of consumers by using the *#cancel_efood*, castigated the company's hostile policy. Customers also downgraded the app's performance from 4.5 to 1 star, and many others deleted the app from their phones.[821] Worker's actions, together with customers' outcry, forced the platform company to make a U-turn by offering an unlimited number of contracts to its riders, while self-employed status will remain an option, rather than an obligation. Undeniably, the recent events in Greece reveal the potential stemming from the close cooperation between workers and customers against platform businesses' exploitative practices.

Furthermore, important developments in relation to strikes and other collective actions, including boycotts, can also be traced in other parts of the planet. To this extent, what is happening in different countries of Latin America is indicative. Indeed, a few months after the coronavirus outbreak, platform workers in many different

816. *Ibid.*; *see also* Zamponi, L. (2018), 'Bargaining With the Algorithm', *Jacobin Magazine*, 6 September 2018, available at: https://www.jacobinmag.com/2018/06/deliveroo-riders-strike-italy-labor-organizing (accessed 4 January 2022).
817. *Ibid.*, Heiland (2020).
818. *Supra*, Marrone and Finotto, V. (2019), 691-716.
819. Doherty, I. (2021), 'How Greek Delivery Riders Are Fighting the Gig Economy', *TRIBUNE* (magazine), 12 October 2021, available at: https://tribunemag.co.uk/2021/10/how-greek-delivery-riders-are-fighting-the-gig-economy#:~:text=Riders%20conducted%20a%20four%2Dhour,from%204.5%20stars%20to%20one. (accessed 21 January 2022).
820. *Ibid.*
821. The Gig Economy Project, (2021), 'Gig Economy Project – Riders set to strike across Greece after viral #Cancel_EFoodcampaign', *Brave New Europe* (blog), 18 September 2021, available at: https://braveneweurope.com/gig-economy-project-riders-set-to-strike-across-greece-after-viral-cancel_efood-campaign (accessed 21 January 2022).

countries, including Brazil, Argentina, Ecuador, Chile, and Mexico, began to strike as a result of the precarious working conditions and low payments during the pandemic.[822] These strikes have been characterised as a historical event. According to some researchers, this is because such actions '*represent the first real example of an international, sector-wide, strike movement in the gig economy*'.[823] Social media organisations played a big role in bringing workers together. For example, via the hashtag *#BrequeDosApps*, or *#StopTheApps*, striking platform workers in Brazil called consumers to show solidarity towards their demands by stopping the use of platforms' apps during the actions.[824] Alike initiatives have also been taken in other countries, like Chile. Consequently, across the region, some of the collective actions have secured some victories, including, *inter alia*, the raise of salaries and the introduction of compensation schemes for riders who were infected with COVID-19 and were unable to work.[825] Additional successful initiatives of platform workers' mobilisation in the context of the pandemic, will be further analysed below. Multiple strike initiatives have also been undertaken in other parts of the so-called 'Global South', in countries, like India and Kenya.[826]

As noted at the beginning of this section, grassroots unions in addition to strike actions, have also adopted further strategies in order to address some of the adverse effects of platform-mediated work. Recent developments deriving from the US are illustrative of this claim. To be more specific, the New York Taxi Workers Alliance (NYTWA), which is affiliated with the AFL-CIO, has also adopted a model of organisation, which focuses on the representation of workers in NSFE. NYTWA, though registered as non-profit, strongly identifies as a union and has as a primary goal the improvement of working conditions for taxi drivers in New York city.[827] One of the biggest achievements of the union was to bring a successful claim on unemployment benefits against Uber, but it did not stop there. In August 2019, NYTWA won a

822. *See* Castro, BV., Partenio, F., Cordero, K. H. (2020), 'Pandemic Meets Precarity: The Case of Platform Delivery Work in Latin America', *DAWN (online article)*, 6 July 2020, available at: https://dawnnet.org/wp-content/uploads/2020/10/CASTRO-PARTENIO-CORDERO_Pandemic-Meets-Precarity-The-Case-of-Platform-Delivery-Work-in-Latin-America.pdf (accessed 4 January 2021).
823. Howson, K., Ustek-Spilda, F., Grohmann, R., Salem, N., Carelli, R., Abs, D., Salvagni, J., Graham, M., Balbornoz, M.B., Chavez, H., Arriagada, A., Bonhomme, M., *'Just Because You Don't See Your Boss, Doesn't Mean You Don't Have a Boss': Covid-19 and Gig Worker Strikes Across Latin America'*, 27 Journal of the International Centre for Trade Union Rights 20 n. 3 20 (2020), 20.
824. Pskowski, M., Vilela, R. (2020), '"They Aren't Anything Without Us": Gig Workers Are Striking Throughout Latin America', *Vice (website)*, 12 August 2020, available at: https://www.vice.com/en/article/jgxazk/they-arent-anything-without-us-gig-workers-are-striking-throughout-latin-america (accessed 4 January 2020).
825. Nugent, C. (2021), 'Migrants in Latin America Have Turned to Delivery Gigs During the Pandemic. But Drivers Say They're Facing Hostility and Mistreatment', *Time (website)*, 10 April 2021, available at: https://time.com/5953683/delivery-drivers-latin-america-migrants/ (accessed 16 November 2021).
826. Rani, U., Gobel, N., Rishabh K.D., *Is Flexibility and Autonomy a Myth or Reality on Taxi Platforms? Comparison Between Traditional and App-Based Taxi Drivers in Developing Countries* (Valerio De Stefano, Ilda Durri, Charalampos Stylogiannis and Mathias Wouters eds, *A Research Agenda for the Gig-Economy and Society*, Edward Elgar Publishing 2022), 187.
827. *Supra*, Johnston and Land-Kazlauskas (2019), 11-12.

landmark case against Uber and Lyft that brought up the country's first cap on ride-sharing company vehicles, forcing them in this way to pay their drivers a minimum wage.[828]

It is furthermore observed that militant unions, like the NYTWA, have used their political resources to lobby for several pieces of legislation and proposals that are designed to ameliorate the working conditions of platform workers. NYTWA, for instance, has pushed public authorities, such as the New York Taxi and Limousine Commission (TLC), in accepting higher wage rates, lowered lease rates for its drivers, and other regulatory reforms.[829] In addition, the Rideshare Drivers United-Los Angeles (RDU-LA), a democratic and independent association of US rideshare drivers, mostly relying on social media advertising has managed to build a strong organisational base of 3,000 members.[830] RDU-LA has been instrumental in elevating the conditions of platform workers in the rideshare industry to a major political issue, mainly through strikes in May 2019 that spread to over 10 cities in the US. What is noteworthy is the fact that RDU-LA has deployed an app that allows the organisers to communicate with the drivers in a much easier and faster way than via social media and other forums; simultaneously, it is simpler for workers to be engaged in RDU-LA's activities.[831] In other words, the app in question constitutes a way to '*organize a work force that doesn't come to an office*'.[832] The union's role was also significant in lobbying for the adoption of the AB5 law, as its members have met with state legislators to push forward this bill.[833] To this extent, the support, such as financial aid, of the Transport Workers Union was important, indicative of solidarity unionism. An example that can also be found in the territorial collective agreement concluded in Bologna, through the establishment of the 'Charter of fundamental digital workers' rights within an urban setting'.[834] The latter was signed by institutional trade unions, workers' autonomous collectives, the city council and the local food-delivery platform Sgnam eMyMenu.[835] The Charter, though applicable on a voluntary basis, contains minimum standards on working aspects, like remuneration and working time. It also has a broad scope of application as it is applicable to all platform workers operating in the city of Bologna, irrespective of their employment status.[836] Furthermore, in the UK, the cooperation between IWGB and GMB unions compelled the delivery platform Just Eat to offer to

828. Brooks, C., 'Meet the Militant Taxi Drivers Union That Just Defeated Uber and Lyft'. *INTHESETIMES*, 5 August 2018, available at: http://216.243.143.31/working/entry/21386/militant_taxi_drivers_union_uber_lyft_alliance_new_york_city (accessed 11 March 2021).
829. *Supra*, Johnston and Land-Kazlauskas (2019), 11-12.
830. Dolber, B., *Building Solidarity Among Gig Workers through Digital Organizing*, Media, Inequality, and Change Center Report, University of Pennsylvania, 10 (2019).
831. Scheiber, N., Conger, K., 'Uber and Lyft Drivers Gain Labor Clout, With Help From an App', *The New York Times*, 14 July 2020, available at: https://www.nytimes.com/2019/09/20/business/uber-lyft-drivers.html (accessed 11 March 2021).
832. *Ibid.*, The words belong to Debra Cleaver, an organizer and the founder of a digital voter-registration service, Vote.org.
833. *Supra*, Dolber (2019), 10.
834. The Charter is available at: http://www.comune.bologna.it/sites/default/files/documenti/CartaDiritti3105_web.pdf (accessed 16 November 2022).
835. *Supra*, Aloisi (2019), 2.
836. Article 1.2 of the Bologna Charter.

1,000 new couriers certain labour protections that, among other benefits, include sick pay and pension contributions.[837]

Let us conclude this part by referring to a recent and maybe one of the most encouraging developments regarding platform workers' mobilisation related to grassroots movements. In the US, The NDWA Gig Worker Advocates, an independent entity affiliated with the National Domestic Workers Organisation, recently reached a new pilot agreement with the cleaning platform of Handy.[838] Although the agreement's structure does not amount to full collective bargaining, it does contain significant provisions, including minimum wage coverage, health insurance in case of occupational accidents and the creation of an online forum where work-related issues can be addressed.[839] To this extent, it attempts to cover domestic workers who have been previously excluded from labour coverage due to their employment status as independent contractors. Albeit '*the pilot falls short of extending full organizing and bargaining rights to these workers*',[840] it, however, constitutes a big achievement and its results remain to be seen in practice.

4.4.6 COVID-19 and Trade Unions' Responses in the Platform Economy

As highlighted in Chapter 2, the COVID-19 pandemic has had a tremendous negative impact on the world of work. A considerable number of workers have lost their jobs, or they have seen their income shrinking, while millions of them have been infected by the virus. Arguably, these adverse effects can be even harsher for workers in NSFE, including many workers in the platform economy. Indeed, as seen, they are particularly vulnerable to the loss of income or jobs, and their coverage by existing social protection schemes is limited.[841] Moreover, on many occasions, the pandemic has magnified the risks that are associated with occupational health and safety. For instance, on a daily basis, many platform workers who are working as couriers find themselves at great risk of contracting the virus.[842] This threat comes to be added in other hazards they face, such as the ever-present risks of road accidents. In this respect, some digital labour platforms have unilaterally adopted measures in order to protect workers. Exceptional protective policies have also been adopted by national actors. This, for instance, has been achieved by relaxing some of the already existing criteria that enable workers in atypical arrangements to access important labour protections.

837. Bradshaw, T., 'Just Eat offers hourly wages in UK gig economy shake-up'. *Financial Times*, 9 December 2020, available at: https://www.ft.com/content/352e3c09-7ce3-466a-b941-921f0d3906c7 (accessed 11 March 2021).
838. Andrias, K., Sachs, B. (2021), 'NDWA-Handy Pilot: Major Gains for Workers Long Excluded from Labor Law's Protections', *OnLabor* (blog), 17 June 2021, available at: https://onlabor.org/ndwa-handy-pilot-major-gains-for-workers-long-excluded-from-labor-laws-protections/ (accessed 21 February 2022); The agreement will be applicable in three US states: Florida, Kentucky, and Indiana.
839. *Ibid.*
840. *Ibid.*
841. OECD, (2020). *Employment Outlook 2020: Worker Security and the COVID-19 Crisis*, OECD Publishing, Paris.
842. *Supra*, Fairwork (2020), 16.

Still, these developments, as research indicates, have not prevented the deterioration of working conditions within the context of the platform economy.

That said, since the beginning of the outbreak of the virus, many trade unions around the world have warned national authorities about the effects the health crisis can have vis-à-vis a great portion of platform workers. It can be observed that such concerns are mostly related to health and safety (OSH) issues, as well as the provision of payments. In Spain, for example, the union of UGT has pointed out that certain platform companies, mostly in the delivery sector, have failed to comply with OSH regulations.[843] The Special Directorate of Labor Inspection, which falls under the Ministry of Labour, has verified the lack of certain standards of protection. The union, however, urged the labour inspectorate to move beyond monitoring and proceed with sanctions when necessary.[844] In a similar vein, the General Confederation of Labour – Workers' Force (FO) in France – voiced its concerns that bicycle delivery workers working for digital platforms have not solely 'left behind' with respect to financial emergency measures, but also regarding health security policies.[845] The inclusion of these workers in the solidarity fund for independent contractors, where they can obtain capped and tax-free aid, has not been considered enough by FO.[846]

As a result of these types of problems, several actions have been employed, by both institutional trade unions and other worker's associations, in order to improve the working environment within the framework of platform-mediated work. Once more, these initiatives have taken various forms, extending from 'court battles' to strike actions. As noted, health and safety-related problems appear to be at the centre of workers' mobilisation. To begin with, a really important development derives from the UK. More specifically, on 21 October 2020, the IWGB Union brought a judicial review[847] case before the High Court against the UK government.[848] The legal action was based on the fact that public authorities had failed to grant workers in the platform economy, such as taxi drivers and couriers, the rights are entitled to in accordance with the EU Health and Safety law. According to the IWGB, such a failure was particularly significant during the COVID-19 pandemic. Less than a month later, the court ruled in favour of the union by arguing that the government was indeed unsuccessful in transposing essential EU health and safety protections into UK law, and thus it needed to take the appropriate steps in order to correct its failure. This groundbreaking decision means that many precarious workers, including platform workers, are now

843. UGT, (2018), 'The Labor Inspectorate should sanction digital platforms that threaten health (translation)', 18 May 2018, available at: https://www.ugt.es/la-inspeccion-de-trabajo-deberia-sancionar-las-plataformas-digitales-que-atentan-contra-la-salud (17 February 2021).
844. *Ibid.*
845. Hiesse, E. (2020), 'FO fully mobilized for bicycle deliverers working for the platforms (translation)', *FO's Coronavirus / Covid19 File*, 10 May 2020, available at: https://www.force-ouvriere.fr/fo-pleinement-mobilisee-pour-les-livreurs-a-velo-travaillant?lang=fr (accessed 15 February 2021).
846. *Ibid.*
847. For more information on what a judicial review is, look at: https://publiclawproject.org.uk/wp-content/uploads/data/resources/6/PLP_Short_Guide_3_1305.pdf (accessed 15 February 2021).
848. High Court of Justice 13 November 2020, Case No. [2020] EWHC 3050.

eligible to have the same access to health and safety rights, such as the provision of personal protective equipment, as regular employees. In addition, workers who were dismissed for refusing to work in dangerous conditions potentially have the right to take legal action against the platforms which terminated or suspended their contracts. Finally, important was also the fact the union's claim was supported by a public crowdfunding initiative that received more than a hundred donations.[849]

In Italy, moreover, *Nuove Identità di Lavoro* NIdiL which constitutes CGIL's section for the representation of atypical workers, has initiated multiple campaigns, which aim at raising the awareness of both the government and private businesses in relation to the threats of COVID-19 on platform workers. For example, a nationwide campaign was launched, the so-called *#dimenticatidaconte* action, through which the union has called out the Italian government to adopt special measures in order to protect riders in the platform economy. NIdiL CGIL has further supported a strike action taken by Amazon workers in Piedmont, as a result of the inadequate measures the company has taken to protect its workers from the deadly virus.[850]

CGIL, together with other unions, such as the Italian Confederation of Workers' Trade Unions, as well as other actors, have also been involved in the 'Safety Delivery Initiative' that took place in Bologna, in 2020. The initiative was promoted by the parties who signed the Bologna Charter and aimed at improving the working conditions related to the occupational health and safety of riders. According to Eurofound, digital platforms, like Just Eat and Ethical Delivery, have supported this development and have already informed their riders about it.[851] Importantly, on 11 December 2020, as a result of the 'Safety Delivery Initiative', the Municipality of Bologna offered to approximately 500 riders from all delivery platforms operating in the city, a free-of-charge anti-COVID-test, which was carried out by the local health authorities.[852] This procedure is expected to take place on a regular basis. Similar initiatives are likely to be extended to the entire logistics sector and other production sectors.

Some important developments are also observed beyond Europe. In Australia, for example, in 2020, TWU and the American platform business, DoorDash, entered an agreement with the purpose of protecting food-delivery workers during the pandemic, including financial aid to those who have been affected the most. In this respect, the

849. IWGB, (2020), 'IWGB wins groundbreaking health and safety legal challenge against the Government', 13 November 2020, available at: https://iwgb.org.uk/post/iwgb-wins-ground breaking-health-and-safety-legal-challenge-against-the-government#: ~ :text = IWGB % 20wins % 20groundbreaking % 20health % 20and % 20safety % 20legal % 20challenge % 20against % 20the % 20Government,-13 % 20November % 202020&text = The % 20High % 20Court % 20ruling % 20 means,gig % 20economy' % 20and % 20precarious % 20workers (accessed 15 February 2021).
850. Eurofound, (2021), 'NIdiL and CGIL', 22 January 2021, available at: https://www.eurofound.europa.eu/de/data/platform-economy/initiatives/nidil-and-cgil (accessed 15 February 2021).
851. Eurofound, (2021), 'Safety Delivery Initiative', 1 February 2021, available at: https://www.eurofound.europa.eu/data/platform-economy/initiatives/safety-delivery-initiative (accessed 15 February 2021).
852. Bertossi, E. (2020), 'Riders in fila per il tampone rapido: "Torno a casa per Natale. Meglio perdere il lavoro che infettare qualcuno"', 11 December 2020, available at: https://www.bolognatoday.it/cronaca/tampone-rapido-covid-riders-autostazione-bologna.html (accessed 15 February 2021).

agreement includes five main provisions.[853] Specifically, these include financial support for those who have tested positive for the virus, have been instructed by a medical expert to self-isolate, are at high risk if they contract the virus, or have a housemate who fulfils at least one of these criteria. On top of this, through the agreement in question, workers should also be provided with personal safety equipment, such as disinfectants and protective masks. TWU has also entered into two additional agreements with two supermarket companies, namely, Woolworths and Coles, which rely on digital platform labour to deliver their products. Such agreements feature practices that attempt to enhance safety regulations in the platform economy, like the provision of specific standards in the road transport supply chain.[854]

Finally, in the US, in March 2020, workers of Instacart, a grocery delivery platform, with the support of the US labour movement and the Gig Workers Collective, went on nationwide strike following, as it was maintained, the constant refusal of the company to undertake proper safety precautions against the pandemic.[855] Earlier the same month, Instacart had announced new health and safety guidelines, resources, and investments to further support its workers.[856] These measures, nonetheless, were considered inadequate by them, who among other things asked for safety protections at no costs and the introduction of hazard payment, which would include an extra USD 5 per order and defaulting the in-app tip amount to at least 10 per cent of the order total.[857] A few days after the strike took place, Instacart started to provide its workers with safety kits that contain a reusable cloth face mask, hand sanitiser and a thermometer.[858] The company has also announced that it created a COVID-19 resource centre, which includes information for shoppers and customers. No further developments have been reported so far.

To conclude, it would be difficult for someone to deny that since the outbreak of the virus, many platform workers have contributed to the continuation of essential services during lockdowns by performing frontline duties. In this regard, within various national contexts, some of them were declared as part of the 'emergency services' in the fight against the virus.[859] For example, delivery and transportation platform workers have played a central role in providing essential products to

853. Masige, S. (2020), 'DoorDash and the Transport Workers Union have entered an agreement to support drivers during the pandemic, including financial help if they contract the virus', *Business Insider Australia*, 28 July 2020, available at: https://www.businessinsider.com.au/doordash-transport-workers-union-agreement-delivery-drivers-2020-7 (accessed 17 February 2021).
854. *Ibid.*
855. Taylor, D.B. (2020), 'Instacart Shoppers Plan to Strike Over Coronavirus Protections', *The New York Times*, 28 March 2020, available at: https://www.nytimes.com/2020/03/28/business/coronavirus-instacart-strike.html (accessed 17 February 2021).
856. The new measures by Instacart can be found here: https://medium.com/shopper-news/shopper-health-safety-update-ec518ad3841c (accessed 17 February 2021).
857. *Supra*, Taylor (2020).
858. Bursztynsky, J. (2020), 'Instacart to provide workers with safety kits following strike over coronavirus protections', *CNBC*, 2 April 2020, available at: https://www.cnbc.com/2020/03/27/instacart-updates-pay-safety-guidelines-as-workers-plan-monday-strike.html (accessed 17 February 2021).
859. Rani, U., Dhir, K.R., *Platform Work and the COVID-19 Pandemic*, 63 The Indian Journal of Labour Economics 163 n. 1 (2020), 163-171.

customers, such as food, groceries, goods and even medical equipment. These types of services have become increasingly important for those in quarantine, as well as for persons particularly vulnerable in the case of contracting the virus. Moreover, as Rani and Dhir observe, many of these workers have assisted '*in connecting consumers with enterprises, including Small and Medium Enterprises and contributed towards meeting demands and ensuring business continuity*'.[860] The performance of these tasks, however, has come at a price. This is to say that a great portion of them are immediately exposed to the virus, while, on many occasions, their access to health and safety provisions is limited. On top of that, a number of platform businesses around the world have used the pandemic as an alibi for reducing payments. As some authors highlight, for instance, some digital platforms in Latin America, such as Glovo and Rappi, based on social solidarity rhetoric, have reduced delivery commissions for their riders; a justification that, in turn, has led to the occurrence of extensive strikes in countries, like Ecuador.[861]

As seen from the aforementioned examples, institutional unions and other worker's associations have adopted various strategies which aim at assisting platform workers in these extreme situations. Arguably, this development is not only important for platform workers per se but can have a positive impact on society at large, as the virus does not make any distinction whatsoever based on the profession of people. To put it otherwise, the more certain types of workers are exposed to the virus, the greater the chances for a bigger portion of the population to be contaminated. Through some of these practices, a number of protections have been attributed to such workers. It is also worth mentioning that, many of such developments have been achieved due to the preexisting efforts of unions within the context of platform work. For instance, in Australia, the agreement between DoorDash and TWU came right after the release of the Report of the Inquiry into the Victorian On-Demand Workforce. This report, as was explained in a previous section, was considerably influenced by TWU's lobbying and actions. In a similar vein, in Italy the presence of the Bologna Charter and the previous efforts made by unions, such as the CIGL, have led authorities of Bologna, to be the first city in the country to offer *gratis* anti-COVID-tests. Arguably, this chain of events can be characterised as a positive sign for further advances in the protection of platform workers, not solely against the virus, but also against other work-related risks in general. Such developments also illustrate the vital role that workers' organised activities can play in emergency situations.

4.5 INTERMEDIATE CONCLUSIONS

Recent developments indicate some positive signs in relation to platform workers' mobilisation and resistance. Against this background, Johnston and Land-Kazlauskas observe that there is a substantial overlap between the emergence of grassroots unions and revitalisation efforts of institutional unions towards an inclusive labour movement

860. *Ibid.*, 164.
861. *Supra*, Howson et al. (2020), 20-22.

that needs to be able to face current and future challenges.[862] As seen, many of these types of collective initiatives have already been proven beneficial for a number of platform workers. For example, some of them have already been reclassified as employees, whereas others are now enjoying certain labour protections, irrespective of their employment status. Of course, such protections are much more apparent for workers already enjoying the employee status. As discussed, workers' mobilisation has also brought about a number of protective measures against COVID-19, especially for workers, like riders, who run a high risk of contracting the virus.

Workers, moreover, through their representatives have pushed for the enactment of protective regulations and laws. Some of these policies aim at resolving issues around the (mis)-classification of platform workers, while others provide for minimum protection standards. For instance, in Spain, trade unions and other workers' associations played a vital role in the adoption of the so-called Riders law.[863] The same can also be argued for the enactment of the AB5 law in California.[864]

Remarkable victories are also documented in different occasions in which platform workers decided to resort to various forms of industrial action(s), including wildcat strikes, walkouts, and protests. As noted, such initiatives were mostly organised by platform workers' associations that do not necessarily fit the traditional model of trade unions. These unions are often comprised of workers who have limited or no access at all to representation rights, as the absence of an employment relationship makes them fall through the cracks of employment and labour legislation. Ironically enough, as Bogg and Buendia observe, albeit highly problematic, it is indeed the very obscure employment status of these workers, which, in certain instances, has facilitated their actions.[865] To prove their point, the authors focus on some recent strike activities undertaken by platform workers in the UK. At common law, in the UK, a strike action can be potentially unlawful, under one or more of the 'economic torts', like conspiracy or inducement to breach a contract, which exist in the country.[866] Consequently, an industrial action might be restricted by an injunction brought by the employer, who may also be able to claim compensation for damages. Thus, the legality of strikes is based on a statutory 'immunity' for the person(s) responsible for the organisation of the strike. In the context of casual work arrangements, such as those in the platform economy, '*where there is no legal obligation to undertake work, the scope for the tort of inducing breach of contract is diminished*'.[867] At the same time, if a

862. *Supra*, Johnston and Land-Kazlauskas (2019), 10.
863. Eurofound, (2021), 'Riders' law', 20 August 2021, available at: https://www.eurofound.europa.eu/nl/data/platform-economy/initiatives/riders-law (accessed 21 January 2022).
864. Dubal, V. (2019), 'AB5: Regulating the Gig Economy Is Good for Workers and Democracy', *LPEProject* (blog), 3 October 2019, available at: https://lpeblog.org/2019/10/03/ab5-regulating-the-gig-economy-is-good-for-workers-and-democracy/ (accessed 22 February 2022).
865. Bogg, A., Buendia, R., *The Law and Workers Voice in the Gig Economy* (Valerio De Stefano, Ilda Durri, Charalampos Stylogiannis and Mathias Wouters eds, *A Research Agenda for the Gig-Economy and Society*, Edward Elgar Publishing 2022), 86.
866. In the UK there has never existed any positive right to strike or other similar actions; *See* Smith, I. and Baker, A., *Smith & Wood's Employment* Law (11th ed. Oxford University Press 2013), 687.
867. Bogg, A., *Taken for a Ride: Workers in the Gig Economy*, 135 Law Quarterly Review 219 (2019), 224.

platform asks to be awarded a strike injunction is like admitting the existence of a contractual obligation to offer work. Paradoxically, therefore, '*the contractual vulnerability* [of platform workers] *can be flipped into a potent weapon of resistance*'.[868]

Moreover, when someone considers workforce diversity within the platform economy, such developments can constitute a novel source of membership for institutional unions.[869] This is, of course, not to argue that many of the practical issues that these workers face with respect to the exercise of their collective labour rights have totally disappeared. For instance, albeit encouraging messages have started to emerge regarding workers' cooperation and communication, as well as unionisation (especially because of the existence of online forums and actions via social media), the often turnovers from one job (or, platform) to another and thus their difficulty to unionise, is still present. Also, a number of digital platform operators continue to implement a business model that '*anonymises and atomises the workforce*'.[870] Concomitantly, some platform giants, such as Amazon, continue to do their best to keep unions out of their ranks, even if this involves tactics that are potentially unlawful.[871]

Having said that and based on the analysis so far, what undoubtedly still constitutes a reality is the existence of legal obstacles which deny a considerable number of platform workers access to the enjoyment of their collective labour rights, such as their right to bargain collectively. Indeed, as noted, due to their status as self-employed, many of them continue to, *inter alia*, be excluded from the protective framework of collective agreements. This exclusion, as is also illustrated in the case of the Hilfr collective agreement, is also inextricably linked to the presence of strict antitrust regulations.

Furthermore, most of the initiatives which have taken place until now, especially with respect to trade unions' court battles', have a rather narrow scope of application. Indeed, these developments mostly concern the protection of workers in the transport and delivery sectors. Concomitantly, legal proceedings targeted at the protection of platform workers in other occupations, like domestic services, are much less prevalent.[872] In any case, as it was earlier pointed out, workers' access to their fundamental labour rights and protections should not be dependent upon the ability of individual workers and their representatives to bring their claims in front of courts and administrative bodies. On top of that, proceedings before courts can last for a long period of time and be very costly, discouraging this way many workers from vindicating their rights. It is also observed that even in situations where the collective mobilisation of workers contributed to the adoption of legislation, which could potentially benefit certain platform workers, such as in the case of the AB5 law in California, then the

868. *Supra* Bogg and Buendia (2022), 86.
869. *See also* discussion in Chapter 6 below.
870. *Supra* Bogg and Buendia (2022), 84.
871. Palmer, A. 'How Amazon keeps a close eye on employee activism to head off unions', *CNBC*, 24 October 2020, available at: https://www.cnbc.com/2020/10/24/how-amazon-prevents-unions-by-surveilling-employee-activism.html (accessed 22 February 2022).
872. *See also* Sedacca, N., *Domestic Work and the Gig Economy* (Valerio De Stefano, Ilda Durri, Charalampos Stylogiannis and Mathias Wouters eds, *A Research Agenda for the Gig-Economy and Society*, Edward Elgar Publishing 2022), 140-166.

platform operators' resistance and economic power have resulted in keeping their workforce outside the scope of legal implications.[873] Finally, one prominent characteristic of platform work is the ease with which digital labour platforms tweak their terms and conditions to escape or undermine legal challenges. Oftentimes, '*the corresponding transformation is also factual, materially altering the working conditions of platform workers; at other times, the changes are merely cosmetical*'.[874]

Reflecting on the aforementioned realities, it can be contented that, at a fact-based level, a considerable number of platform workers, by exercising their collective labour rights have managed to illustrate the importance that such rights can have in practice. What the practice of these rights also reveals, however, is that, as noted, legal obstacles persist; hence, excluding a considerable number of precarious workers from the protection of fundamental collective labour rights, like the rights to freely associate and bargain collectively, which as the next section shows are also recognised as human rights. As a matter of law, therefore, the question which arises is how the rights at issue can be adequately protected.

This research argues that a possible way forward towards the better protection of workers' collective labour rights can derive from a HRBA in labour policy, whereby workers can enjoy such rights, regardless of their employment status. This approach has been also advanced by the trade union movement, such as by the ETUC which, among other things, recognises the clear need to safeguard collective bargaining as a fundamental right of all workers no matter their status.[875] A point of caution should be added here. For the purposes of this research, a HRBA does not intend to force the requalification of workers who find themselves in a 'grey' zone between employment and self-employment, including many platform workers. It rather seeks to provide a protection floor to all workers who, by exercising their rights to freedom of association and collective bargaining will be able to ameliorate their working conditions and produce adequate labour standards that will not depend on their employment status.

873. De Stefano, V., Durri, I., Stylogiannis, C., Wouters, M., *Platform Work and the Employment Relationship*, ILO Working Paper, Geneva, ILO (2021), 25.
874. De Stefano, V., Durri, I., Stylogiannis, C., Wouters, M., *Introduction* (Valerio De Stefano, Ilda Durri, Charalampos Stylogiannis and Mathias Wouters eds, *A Research Agenda for the Gig-Economy and Society*, Edward Elgar Publishing 2022), 2.
875. ETUC, (2020), *Feedback on the Commission Inception Impact Assessment on Competition Law and Collective Bargaining for Self-employed*, Background Paper, 3 February 2020, available at: https://ec.europa.eu/info/law/better-regulation/have-your-say/initiatives/12483- Collective-bargaining-agreements-for-self-employed-scope-of-application-EUcompetition-rules/F156764 3_en (4 January 2022).

CHAPTER 5
The Implications of a HRBA Towards Fundamental Collective Labour Rights

5.1 INTRODUCTION

This chapter aims to explore the particular features and implications of a HRBA towards fundamental collective labour rights. As noted at the beginning of this research, a HRBA identifies workers, regardless of their employment status, as rights-holders entitled to rights derived from international human rights and labour rights treaties. This approach is very relevant for self-employed workers, like those in the platform economy who find themselves in a comparable predicament to that of employees, where their weak negotiating position and economic dependency towards their principals often make for a precarious situation. That said, as it will be further elaborated, fundamental collective labour rights fall into the catalogue, or a list of human rights. Against this background, this chapter first delves into the legal basis of a HRBA in labour policy, by particularly focusing on the rights to freely associate, bargain collectively and the right to industrial action. It, then, examines some of the positive consequences of a HRBA towards fundamental collective labour rights in relation to the labour protection of platform workers and other workers in NSFE.

5.2 A LEGAL BASIS FOR A HRBA IN LABOUR POLICY MORE IN GENERAL

Discussions on the relationship between labour rights and human rights have preoccupied multiple scholars and courts around the world for quite some time now. Thus far, there is extended literature that acknowledges the categorisation of labour rights as human rights.[876] Usually, these views are supported by the inclusion of fundamental labour rights within international instruments and human rights treaties, as well as by the rulings of international and national supreme courts.[877] Often enough, they are also reinforced by a normative analysis that indeed recognises the convergence and interdependence between the two legal fields.[878] Labour issues have, thus, increasingly been examined from the standpoint of human rights law.

The EU Commission, for example, recently presented its much-anticipated proposed Directive on Corporate Sustainability Due Diligence, which, among other aims, provides for a number of human rights objectives.[879] Under the new draft Directive, EU Member States are responsible for ensuring that businesses introduce due diligence mechanisms in relation to the effects of their operation(s), including its subsidiaries, suppliers and contractors. On top of that, businesses will be obliged to detect, prevent, end or alleviate actual or potential violations of human rights standards.[880] The UN Guiding Principles on Business and Human Rights (UNGP) and the vast ongoing discussion over corporate social responsibility for human rights constitute another illustration of the enlarged convergence between human rights and labour rights and of the contentious permeability of human rights in the private sphere.[881] The

876. For instance, *see* Hepple, B., *Rights at Work* in Ghai, D. (ed.), *Decent Work: Objectives and Strategies*, 33-73, Geneva: ILO (2006), International Institute for Labour Studies; Fenwick, C. & Novitz, T. eds, *Human Rights at Work, Perspectives on Law and Regulation* (Hart Publishing 2010); Gearty, C. and Mantouvalou, V. eds, *Debating Social Rights* (Hart Publishing 2011); Mantouvalou, V., *Labour Law and Human Rights*, 41 New Zealand Journal of Employment Relations 3 n. 2 (2016), 3-20; Bellace, J. and ter Haar, B. eds, *Research Handbook on Labour, Business and Human Rights Law* (Elgar Publishing 2019); Dawkins, C., *Disciplining the Notion of 'Labour Rights as Human Rights'*, 13 Global Labour Journal 1 n. 1 (2022), 1-18. For views that put in question the relationship between human rights and labour rights, *see*: Koblen, K., *Labor Rights as Human Rights?*, 50 Virginia Journal of International Law 450 n. 2 (2009), 450-484; Collins, H., *Theories of Rights as Justifications for Labour Law* (Guy Davidov and Brian Langille eds, *The Idea of Labour Law*, Oxford University Press 2011), 137-153; Youngdahl, J., *Solidarity First: Labor Rights Are Not the Same as Human Rights*, 18 New Labor Forum 31 n. 1 (2009), 31-37; Stammers, N., *Social Movements and the Social Construction of Human Rights*, 21 Human Rights Quarterly 980 n. 4 (1999), 980-1008.

877. For instance, since 2009 within the EU's legal system, the CFREU has the same primary EU law value as the Treaties. The CFREU includes a number of fundamental workers' rights in its provisions.

878. For instance, *see* Mantouvalou, V., *Are Labour Rights Human Rights?*, 3 European Labour Law Journal 151 n. 2 (2012), 151-173. Atkinson, J., *Human Rights as Foundations for Labour Law* (Hugh Collins, Gillian Lester and Virginia Mantouvalou eds, *Philosophical Foundations of Labour Law*, Oxford University Press 2018).

879. European Commission, Proposal for a Directive of the European Parliament and of the Council on Corporate Sustainability Due Diligence and amending Directive (EU) 2019/1937 COM(2022) 71 final.

880. *See* the critical analysis from: Potocka-Sionek, N., *Crowdwork and Global Supply Chains: Regulating Digital Piecework* (Valerio De Stefano, Ilda Durri, Charalampos Stylogiannis and Mathias Wouters eds, *A Research Agenda for the Gig-Economy and Society*, Edward Elgar Publishing 2022), 215-233; Sjåfjell, B., Jukka M. (2022), 'Corporate Purpose and the EU Corporate Sustain-ability Due Diligence Proposal', *Oxford Business Law* (blog), 25 February 2022, available at: https://www.law.ox.ac.uk/business-law-blog/blog/2022/02/corporate-purpose-and-eu-corporate-sustainability-due-diligence (accessed 1 March 2022).

881. UN Guiding Principles on Business and Human Rights: https://www.ohchr.org/documents/publications/GuidingprinciplesBusinesshr_eN.pdf.

UNGP explicitly recognise the rights enshrined in the ILO's 1998 Declaration, as human rights.

Therefore, a considerable number of trade unionists and labour lawyers are now gradually using the rhetoric of human rights to enhance their claims. For instance, the International Trade Union Confederation (ITUC), an international coalition of trade unions, places the protection of both human rights and labour rights under its remit.[882] At domestic level, similar observations can be made. In Canada, for example, as Judy Fudge discusses, several unions have gone in front of the courts, by arguing that their rights to freedom of association and collective bargaining should be interpreted and protected in accordance with international human rights standards, especially in compliance with International Labour Conventions.[883] In addition to human rights litigation, as an avenue to justify their claims, some trade unions have also employed the '*ethical lingua-franca*'[884] of human rights in a different manner. In the US, AFL-CIO, which as noted, constitutes the largest federation of unions in the country, has launched a wide-ranging 'Voice@Work' project. The latter, *inter alia*, aims at assisting workers' rights to form unions and improve their working conditions; in this regard, a human rights rhetoric is used during rights awareness-raising campaigns organised around the country.[885] Vice versa, numerous human rights organisations are now actively engaging in the protection of labour rights.[886] A prominent example can be found in the language used by a number of reports published by Human Rights Watch, in which poor working conditions are framed as possible human rights violations.[887]

That said, the realisation that labour cannot be seen as something isolated from overall protection afforded to individuals is not novel.[888] It goes back to the ILO's 1944 Declaration of Philadelphia that predated the Universal Declaration on Human Rights (UDHR), the seminal document of the modern human rights regime, which also enshrined several labour provisions. Indeed, there are the very principles enshrined in

882. ITUC, Human and Trade Union Rights: https://www.ituc-csi.org/human-and-trade-union-rights#: ~ :text = The%20ITUC%20defends%20trade%20unionists,where%20these%20affect %20working%20people.
883. Fudge, J., *Constitutionalizing Labour Rights in Canada and Europe: Freedom of Association, Collective Bargaining, and Strikes*, 68 Current Legal Problems 267 (2015), 267-305; Similar claims by trade unions have been also made in other parts of the word, at both national and international level. For instance, *see supra*, Mantouvalou (2016), 3-20.
884. Baldissone, R., *Human rights: a lingua franca for the multiverse*, 14 The International Journal of Human Rights 1117 n. 7 (2010), 1117-1137.
885. Compa, L., Gross, J.A., *Introduction* (Lance Compa and James A. Gross eds, *Human Rights in Labor and Employment Relations: International and Domestic Perspectives*, IL: Labor and Employment Relations Association Series 2009), 3.
886. Evans, M., *Trade Unions as Human Rights Organizations*, 7 Journal of Human Rights Practice 466 n. 3 (2015), 466-483; For more examples of trade unions using the language of human rights in the US, *see also*: Comp Compa, L., *Trade Unions, NGOs, and Corporate Codes of Conduct*, 14 Development in Practice 210 n. 1-2 (2004), 210-215.
887. *See*, for instance, Human Rights Watch, (2010), *A Strange Case*, Report, New York, Human Rights Watch.
888. Bellace, J., Haar, B., *Perspectives on Labour and Human Rights* (Janice R. Bellace and Beryl ter Haar eds, *Research Handbook on Labour, Business and Human Rights Law*, Elgar Publishing 2019), 6.

the ILO's Declaration that led Supiot to argue that this is the oldest human rights instrument, even if there is no explicit mention of human rights.[889] As explained in the second chapter, the most fundamental of these principles is that labour is not a commodity; hence, labour should not be exchanged in the markets for the lowest price, as workers are human beings with dignity and rights. It is, therefore, the reference to human dignity that indicates the interconnection and common roots of human rights and labour rights and the notion that human rights should not be positioned outside the realm of work. The majority, if not all, of human rights documents adopted under the auspices of the United Nations, as well as within the framework of regional systems, such as the CoE, make an explicit remark to this principle. Moreover, as Lee Swepston observes, important labour rights were included in the text of relevant United Nations (UN) instruments, '*based very closely on the ILO standards already adopted*'.[890] In a similar vein, the ILO Committee of Experts on the Application of Conventions and Recommendations (CEARCR) has emphasised that the ILO's standards and practical activities on human rights can be considered inextricably linked to the values enshrined within the UDHR.[891] As will also be explained below, all these developments set the foundations for the adoption of the 1998 Declaration on Fundamental Principles and Rights at Work, that due to its universal application, it is also considered by many authors as a '*non-binding declaration on human rights*', even though the document in question makes no explicit reference to human rights per se.[892]

As noted, from a positive law perspective, the interrelationship and interdependence between labour rights and human rights have been acknowledged both by the inclusion of fundamental labour rights within supranational human rights instruments and by the verdict of their supervisory bodies. For example, the ECtHR, through an 'integrated approach'[893] has shown a considerable willingness to protect certain workers' rights as human rights and, it has, as Dorssemont highlights, rejected the notion that the enjoyment of human rights protection should evaporate at workplaces.[894] The Inter-American Court of Human Rights (IACtHR) has also embraced a

889. Supiot, A., *L' esprit of Philadelphie* (Seuil 2010), 9. In a similar vein Lee Swepston also contends that the Declaration of Philadelphia enshrined the very first and clear statement of a commitment to human rights ever espoused by a multilateral organization; in the document it is indicated that: '*all human beings, irrespective of race, creed or sex, have the right to pursue both their material well-being and their spiritual development in conditions of freedom and dignity, of economic security and equal opportunity*'. (Swepston, L., *How the ILO Embraced Human Rights* (Janice R. Bellace and Beryl ter Haar eds, *Research Handbook on Labour, Business and Human Rights Law*, Elgar Publishing 2019), 300).
890. *Ibid*., 301.
891. Norman, K., *ILO Freedom of Association Principles as Basic Canadian Human Rights: Promises to Keep*, 67 Saskatchewan Law Review 591 n. 2 (2004), 592.
892. *Supra*, Swepston (2019), 307. *See also* Maupain, F., *Revitalization Not Retreat: The Real Potential of the 1998 ILO Declaration for the Universal Protection of Workers' Rights*, 16 The European Journal of International Law 439 n. 3 (2005), 439-465.
893. *Supra* Mantouvalou (2013), 536-541.
894. Dorssemont, F., *The European Convention on Human Rights as a Fountain of Labour Rights* (Janice R. Bellace and Beryl ter Haar eds, *Research Handbook on Labour, Business and Human Rights Law*, Elgar Publishing 2019), 314-316.

method that treats a list of workers' rights as human rights with universal application, in a way that reaffirms their peremptory nature.[895]

5.2.1 The Human Rights to Freedom of Association and Collective Bargaining Through the Lenses of International Instruments

In light of the aforementioned conversation and due to broad international support, the rights to freedom of association and the right to collective bargaining are included in the 'universal list' of human rights.[896] According to the early observation of Otto Kahn-Freund, the inclusion of rights in a catalogue, or a list of human rights can be an admirable source of justice and such a development should not be overlooked.[897] More particularly, the right to freely associate is contained in a number of human rights instruments around the world.[898] For instance, the UDHR, perhaps the most seminal document of the modern human rights regime, recognises that '*everyone has the right to freedom of peaceful assembly and association*', including the '*the right to form and to join trade unions for the protection of his interests*'.[899] By relying on this very formulation, Compa and Gross observe that the UDHR was not addressed to individuals as isolated and distinct persons, but rather as members of the human society; an acknowledgement that the Declaration's full realisation can be solely achieved within a '*community of persons interacting with each other in a society characterized by cooperation and co-responsibility that respects the personal dignity and equality of its members*'.[900] The right to freedom of association is also enshrined in both the International Covenant on Civil and Political Rights (ICCPR) and the International Covenant on Economic, Social and Cultural Rights (ICESCR).[901]

895. Canessa Montejo, M., *Labor Human Rights and the Jurisprudence of the Inter-American Court of Human Rights* (Janice R. Bellace and Beryl ter Haar eds, *Research Handbook on Labour, Business and Human Rights Law*, Elgar Publishing 2019), 334-357.
896. The author is aware that in some legal jurisdictions, these rights are not considered fundamental rights, or human rights (e.g., in China). This is the reason that the word 'support' is used, instead of 'consensus'. Similar concerns were also raised during the adoption of the 1998 Declaration. Some countries opposed the idea of universal standards, as they mostly represent Western values. As such, the enforcement of a set of minimum rights that had to be respected by all ILO Member States could be used to impose restrictions on international trade; a situation that would benefit the developed countries (*Supra*, Swepston (2019), 309). As a response the ILO included Article 5 in the Declaration that reads as follows: '*Stresses that labour standards should not be used for protectionist trade purposes, and that nothing in this Declaration and its follow-up shall be invoked or otherwise used for such purposes; in addition, the comparative advantage of any country should in no way be called into question by this Declaration and its follow-up.*'
897. Kahn-Freund, O., *The Impact of Constitutions on Labour Law*, 35 Cambridge Law Journal 240 n. 2 (1976), 270-271.
898. For instance, *see* ECHR, Article 11; ACHR, Article 16; Additional Protocol to the ACHR in the Area of Economic, Social and Cultural Rights, OAS Treaty, Series No. 69, 1988, Article 8; CFREU, Article 12; African Charter on Human and Peoples' Rights, Article 10; European Social Charter (Revised), Article 5.
899. UDHR, Articles 20(1) and 23(4), respectively.
900. *Supra*, Compa and Gross (2009), 21.
901. ICCPR, Article 22; ICESC, Article 8.

As earlier mentioned, furthermore, since 1998, the right at issue has been enshrined in the ILO Declaration on Fundamental Principles and Rights at Work, which although not a human rights instrument, stipulates that those rights are universal and should be applicable to all workers in all Member States, by the very fact of their membership and irrespective of ratification of the relevant conventions.[902] Besides being a right per se, the right to freedom of association constitutes an '*enabling right*' whose effective protection can be crucial for the actual exercise of other human rights and labour standards, something that has also been pointed out by the ILO Committee of Experts.[903] Such a right, in addition, can be extended from the workplace into the public sphere, including, *inter alia*, the formation, and support for political parties and public institutions. The interconnection between civil liberties and the right to freedom of association has also been highlighted by the ILO CFA, with special reference to be made to core UN instruments on human rights.[904]

Having said that, an essential element in the exercise of the right to freedom of association, as the CFA has multiple times indicated, is the right to collective bargaining.[905] It is also enshrined as a fundamental human right in several human rights instruments,[906] as well as in the 1998 ILO Declaration which, as noted, has universal applicability.[907] Furthermore, even if the right to collective bargaining itself is not clearly mentioned in the UDHR, some scholars, such as Adams, observed that the drafters intended to include such a right as a prime facet of freedom of association.[908] This idea has been emphatically confirmed by the jurisprudence and pronouncements of bodies supervising the implementation of human rights treaties. The ECtHR, for example, in the landmark case of *Demir and Baykara*,[909] for the first time explicitly recognised that the right to bargain collectively is an inherent feature of Article 11 of the ECHR on freedom of assembly and association. In doing so, as Lörcher contents, '*it*

902. ILO, Convention No. 87.
903. ILO Committee of Experts on the Application of Conventions and Recommendations, (2012), *Giving globalization a human face: General survey on the fundamental conventions concerning rights at work in light of the ILO Declaration on Social Justice for a Fair Globalization*, Geneva, ILO.
904. '*On many occasions, the Committee has emphasized the importance of the principle affirmed in 1970 by the International Labour Conference in its resolution concerning trade union rights and their relation to civil liberties, which recognizes that "the rights conferred upon workers' and employers' organizations must be based on respect for those civil liberties which have been enunciated in particular in the Universal Declaration of Human Rights and in the International Covenant on Civil and Political Rights, and that the absence of these civil liberties removes all meaning from the concept of trade union rights"*', ILO CFA, 'Freedom of Association: Digest of decisions and principles of the Freedom of Association Committee of the Governing Body of the ILO', Geneva, ILO (2006), para. 31.
905. ILO CFA (2018), *Freedom of Association. Compilation of decisions of the Committee on Freedom of Association. Geneva*, ILO, para. 1232.
906. ECHR, Article 11; CFREU, Article 28; ESC, Article 6; Additional Protocol to the ACHR in the Area of Economic, Social and Cultural Rights, OAS Treaty, Series No. 69, 1988, Article 8.
907. ILO, Convention 98.
908. Adams, R.J., *From Statutory Right to Human Right: The Evolution and Current Status of Collective Bargaining*, 12 Just Labour 48 (2008), 49.
909. *Demir and Baykara v. Turkey*, App. no. 34503/97 [2008].

opened up the whole Convention to a more socially oriented interpretation'.[910] The Strasbourg Court espoused, though not for the first time,[911] a 'living instrument' approach construing rights in a way that renders them 'practical and effective, not theoretical and illusory'.[912]What was novel in the Court's methodological approach, nonetheless, was its systematic reliance on external instruments. It has been observed that never before had the Grand Chamber dedicated so much time and space in the course of acknowledging the specific role played by instruments, such as ILO Conventions, the European Social Charter, the CFREU and the ICESCR, in an overall '*internationally friendly interpretation*'.[913] In this regard, Ewing and Hendy contend that the ESC and ILO fora were no longer processes for reporting grievances and causing some gentle diplomatic embarrassment for domestic authorities; they rather constitute authoritative tools that the Court takes under consideration regarding the interpretation of Article 11 ECHR.[914] The Grand Chamber, moreover, relied on common practices among the Member States of the CoE; as noted in the second chapter, the right to collective bargaining finds itself within the constitutional order of many of these countries.

In a similar vein, the IACtHR has also referred in its case law to international standards and principles, such as Convention No. 87 on Freedom of Association and Protection of the Right to Organise, 1948 and Convention No. 98 on the Right to Organise and Collective Bargaining, 1949, as well as to the ILO Committee of Experts.[915] According to Duhaime and Décoste the frequent use of ILO standards by the IACtHR in justifying the interpretation of certain provisions of the American Convention on Human Rights (ACHR), '*contributes to making universal the interpretation of provisions issued by the ILO; it* [thus] *creates a greater regulatory convergence at global, regional and national level*'.[916] In 2019, the Inter-American Commission on Human Rights, the other supervisory body of the ACHR, in a request for an advisory opinion

910. Lörcher, K., *The New Social Dimension in the Jurisprudence of the European Court on Human Rights (ECHR): The Demir and Baykara Judgment, Its Methodology and Follow-up* (Filip Dorssemont, Klaus Lörcher and Isabelle Schömann eds, *The European Convention on Human Rights and the Employment Relation*, Oxford and Oregon, Hart Publishing 2013), 4.
911. It is recalled that in the case of *Schmidt and Dahlström v. Sweden* the verdict was reached by reference to ILO standards and the requirements of the European Social Charter.
912. *Supra, Lörcher* (2013), 10.
913. *Ibid.*
914. Ewing, K., Hendy, J., *The Dramatic Implications of Demir and Baykara,* 39 Industrial Law Journal 1 n. 1 (2010), 6; It should be also argued that the ECHR is not always consistent in referring to ILO standards. For a critical analysis on this issue see: Teklè, T., *The Contribution of the ILO's International Labour Standards System to the European Court of Human Rights' Jurisprudence in the Field of Non-Discrimination,* 49 International Labour Review 86 n. 1 (2019), 86-112.
915. For instance, *see Baena-Ricardo et al. v. Panama. Merits,* Reparations and Costs, judgment of 2 February 2001, Series C No. 72, para. 171; Cantoral-Huamaní and García-Santa Cruz v. Peru. Preliminary Objection, Merits, Reparations and Costs. Judgment of 10 July 2007. Series C No. 167, para. 146.
916. Duhaime, B., Décoste, E., *From Geneva to San José: The ILO Standards and the Inter-American System for the Protection of Human Rights,* 159 International Labour Review 525 n. 4 (2020), 541.

submitted to the IACtHR pointed out that: '*trade union freedom or the rights of trade union are fundamental human rights*'[917] and therefore '*collective bargaining, as a component of trade union freedom, has a direct impact on the rights of workers as a democratic means of establishing* [fair] *working conditions*'.[918] The verdict of the IACtHR will be discussed below, when reference is made to the personal scope of fundamental collective labour rights.

All in all, under international and regional human rights law, there is broad support that the rights to freedom of association and to bargain collectively are human rights with a binding and universal nature; the latter view has also been espoused by the ILO. In the context of the ECHR, for instance, any restriction on their application should be justified under the law, and it should be considered necessary in a democratic society. On top of that, according to the case law of the ECtHR, Member States may, in addition, undertake positive obligations to secure these rights.[919] Still, as seen despite any sort of recognition, a considerable number of workers in NSFE, including many platform workers, due to their status as self-employed persons, continue to be denied from accessing their collective labour rights, also acknowledged as human rights. It will be discussed below that, as a matter of law, many of these restrictions are at odds with international standards deriving from human rights bodies and the ILO.

5.2.2 The Human Right to Industrial Action

When considering the human rights to freely associate and bargain collectively, one cannot avoid also mentioning the right to industrial action, including the right to strike. As Ewing and Hendy have nicely put it: '*in the absence of the right to strike, the right to collective bargain*, [as an indispensable right of the right to freedom of association] *is no more than a right to collective begging*'.[920] The inextricably interwoven nature of these rights has also been pointed out by maybe one of the most influential dissent opinions in the history of the Supreme Court of Canada regarding the notion of the right to freedom of association. The famous opinion belongs to Chief Justice Dickson in the so-called *Alberta Reference* case.[921] Through a 'purposive' analysis of the right to freely associate, CJ Dickson referred to the vital function of the right to collective bargaining

917. I/A Court H.R., Request for an Advisory Opinion submitted by the Inter-American Commission on Human Rights before the IACtHR of 31 July 2019, para. 2, available at: https://www.corteidh.or.cr/docs/solicitudoc/soc_3_2019_ing.pdf (accessed 3 March 2022).
918. *Ibid.*, para. 36.
919. *Demir and Baykara*, para. 110.
920. *Supra* Ewing and Hendy (2010), 10.
921. *Reference re Public Service Employee Relations Act (Alta)* [1987] 1 SCR 313. This case constituted part of the so-called Trilogy of cases ruled by the Canadian Supreme Court in the late 1980s (together with the cases of *PSAC v. Canada* [1987] 1 SCR 424; *RWDSU v. Saskatchewan* [1987] 1 SCR 460), where it was held that section 2(d) of the Canadian Charter did not include neither a right to collective bargaining nor a right to strike. For a summary of the 'Alberta Reference' ruling *see*: Bogg, A., *Subsidiarity or Freedom of Association? A Perspective from Labor Law*, 61 The American Journal of Jurisprudence 143 n. 1 (2016), 143-174.

for workers' collective interests by adding that '*effective constitutional protection of the associational interests of employees in the collective bargaining process requires concomitant protection of their freedom to withdraw collectively their services*'.[922] His influential approach was subsequently used by the Canadian Supreme Court in more recent cases, where in contrast to previous jurisprudence, it was established that the Canadian Charter of Rights and Freedoms enshrines both the right to collective bargaining and the right to strike.[923]

Despite the fact that restrictions on the right to strike may vary from one legal order to another, there is a broad acknowledgement the right exists, and any constraints must be reasonable. In 2016, Maina Kiai, the UN Special Rapporteur on the rights to freedom of peaceful assembly and of association, explained that the right to strike had been recognised under international law for a long time in global and regional instruments, and it is also included in the constitutional order of at least 90 countries around the world.[924] Such recognition has led some authors to now perceive the right in question as part of customary international law.[925] It is indeed enshrined in a number of regional human rights instruments around the world, such as the Arab Charter on Human Rights,[926] the Charter of the Organization of American States[927] and the CFREU.[928] The ESC also contains an explicit reference to the right to strike in its Article 6(4). As it has been argued, the latter's formulation is significant because it calls Member States to '"recognise" *the right to strike in contrast to more diluted formulations in relation to other Charter rights*'.[929] This is also why the European Committee of Social Rights (ECSR) has made it clear that such a right '*represents an essential basis for the fulfillment of other fundamental rights guaranteed by the Charter*'.[930]

922. *Alberta Reference* case, para. 97. For a recent analysis of his approach, *see* Arabadjieva, K., *Worker Empowerment, Collective Labour Rights and Article 11 of the European Convention on Human Rights*', Human Rights Law Review 1 (2021), 1-30.
923. *See* for instance, *Dunmore v. Ontario (Attorney General)* [2001] SCC 94, 3 SCR 1016; *Health Services and Support – Facilities Subsector Bargaining Assn v. British Columbia* [2007] 2 SCR 39; *Saskatchewan Federation of Labour v. Saskatchewan* [2015] 1 SCR 245. It was in the latter case where the Supreme Court recognised that the right to strike is safeguarded by the Canadian Charter of Rights and Freedoms. For more information on the protection of the right to strike in Canada *see* Fudge, J., Jensen, H., *The Right to Strike: The Supreme Court of Canada, the Charter of Rights and Freedoms and the Arc of Workplace Justice*, 27 King's Law Journal 89 n. 1 (2016), 89-109.
924. UN General Assembly, (2016), 'Report of the Special Rapporteur on the Rights to Freedom of Peaceful Assembly and of Association', A/71/385, 14 September 2016, para. 56, available at: www.undocs.org/A/71/385 (accessed 24 March 2022). The reference was found in Vogt, J., Bellace, J., Compa, L., Ewing, KD., Hendy, J., Lörcher, K., Novitz, T., *The Right to Strike Is Recognised as Customary International Law* (Jeffrey Vogt et al., *The Right to Strike in International Law*, Oxford, Hart Publishing 2020), 169.
925. Brudney, J.J., *The Right to Strike as Customary International Law*, 46 The Yale Journal of International Law 1 n.1 (2021), 1-56; *supra* Jeffrey et al. (2020).
926. Article 35(3) of the Arab Charter on Human Rights.
927. Article 45(c) of the Charter of the Organization of American States.
928. Article 28 of the Charter of Fundamental Rights of the European Union.
929. *Supra* Jeffrey et al. (2020), 100-106; *see also* Kovacs, E., *The Right to Strike in the European Social Charter*, 26 Comparative Labor Law & Policy Journal 445 n. 4 (2005), 445-476.
930. *LO and TCO v. Sweden*, Complaint No 85/2012, ECSR Decision (3 July 2013), para. 109.

Furthermore, since 1999, albeit it is not explicitly included in the wording of the ICCPR, the Covenant's supervisory body, namely the Human Rights Committee (HRC), has accepted the right to strike as an integral feature of the instrument. More specifically, in its Concluding Comment on Chile's periodic report on compliance with the ICCPR, the HRC communicated its '*serious concerns*' over the country's general prohibition on '*the right of civil servants to organize a trade union and bargain collectively, as well as their right to strike* [...] *under article 22 of the Covenant*'.[931]

Contrary to the ICCPR, the right to strike is clearly incorporated in Article 8(1)(d) of the ICESCR. It is enshrined that '[t]*he States Parties to the present Covenant undertake to ensure* [...] *the right to strike, provided that it is exercised in conformity with the laws of the particular country*'.[932] Moreover, Article 8(3) makes it explicit that nothing in its ambit should allow ILO's Member States that have ratified Convention No. 87 to '*take legislative measures which would prejudice, or apply the law in such a manner as would prejudice, the guarantees provided for in that Convention*'.[933] As Ewing observes, the language used in the ICESCR suggests in a powerful manner that the right to strike is protected under ILO standards and particularly Convention No. 87.[934]

Having said that, the status of the right to strike in the ILO has not always been uncontroversial. This situation is inextricably linked to the position of the Employers Group of the ILO, which has repeatedly challenged that the right at issue is at the heart of ILO standards, as there is no specific reference enshrined in Convention No. 87, nor in the ILO Constitution or in the Declaration of Philadelphia.[935] Still, despite any objections, throughout the history of the ILO, there has been a broad consensus that the right to strike constitutes a fundamental aspect of freedom of association; thereby, it has been considered an integral part of Convention No. 87. As the literature indicates, both the CFA and CEACR, as well as ILO constituents, have repeatedly embraced such right as an inevitable corollary of the right to freedom of association.[936] In this regard, in the 2012 General Survey, the CFA found that: '[a]*lthough the exercise of the right to strike is in most countries fairly commonly subject to certain conditions or restrictions,*

931. *CCPR/C/79*/Add.104. (30-03-1999), para. 25. The reference of the decision was found in: Macklem, P., *The Right to Bargain Collectively in International Law: Workers' Right, Human Right, International Right?* (Philip Alston ed., *Labour Rights as Human Rights*, Oxford University Press 2005), 72-73.
932. Article 8(1) ICESCR.
933. Article 8(3) ICESCR.
934. Ewing, K., *Myth and Reality of the Right to Strike as a 'Fundamental Labour Right'*, 2 International Journal of Comparative Labour Law 145 (2013), 146.
935. *Supra*, Jeffrey et. al. (2020); also *see* the discussion from Velyvyte, V., *The Right to Strike in the European Union after Accession to the European Convention on Human Rights: Identifying Conflict and Achieving Coherence*, 15 Human Rights Law Review 71 n. 1 (2015), 80-81.
936. *See* for instance, Gernigon, B., Odero, A., Guido, H., *ILO Principles Concerning the Right to Strike*, 137 International Labour Review 441 n. 4 (1998), 441-482; Bellace, J., *The ILO and the Right to Strike*, 153 International Labour Review 29 n. 1 (2014), 29-70; Garcia, J.A.L., *The Right to Strike as a Fundamental Human Right: Recognition and Limitations in International Law*, 44 Revista Chilena de Derecho 781 (2017), 781-804.

the principle of this right as a means of action of workers' organizations is almost universally accepted'.[937]

Such recognition can also be traced in the language of the ECtHR. This is to say that a few weeks after its landmark decision on the *Demir* and *Baykara* case and the recognition of the right to collective bargaining under Article 11 ECHR, the Court went on to also acknowledge the right to strike. In the case of *Enerji Yapi-Yol Sen v. Turkey*, the Second Section of the Court, by relying on the methodological framework adopted in *Demir*, contented that *'strike action, which permits a trade union to express their concerns, is an essential feature in the protection of trade unions' members interests'*.[938] Also, it referred to the protection that the right to strike enjoys under other international instruments, like ILO Convention 87.[939] Consequently, the Court moved away from s previous line of jurisprudence and reluctance to accept that the right to strike should be protected under the Convention.[940] This development took place despite the fact the Strasbourg Court left the question as to whether the right to strike constitutes an 'essential' or an 'important' facet of Article 11 open for interpretation. This semantic difference has been proven detrimental to the protection of the right to strike under ECHR in some subsequent cases, such as the so-called *RMT* case, where a wide margin of appreciation was given to o the respondent State as to how trade union freedom may be secured.[941] Still, these issues have been extensively analysed elsewhere and for the purposes of this research, no further engagement is necessary.[942] It is important to keep that under the Convention, the right to strike is perceived as a human right, something that has also been confirmed in a number of other cases.[943] Thus, any restriction on this right, therefore, has to be proportionate and necessary in a democratic society. As Fabbrini suggests, it is now confirmed that the right to collective bargaining and the right to collective action, including the right to strike, constitute 'two sides of the same coin'; trade unions are awarded actual bargaining power only in circumstances where they are able to have the choice to strike action in order to bolster their assertions; to this extent, the protection of the right to bargain collectively should automatically imply the preservation of the right to collective action.[944]

937. *Supra*, ILO CEACR, 50.
938. *Enerji Yapi-Yol Sen v. Turkey*, App no. 68959/01 [2009], para. 24.
939. *Ibid.*
940. *See National Union of Belgian Police v. Belgium*, App. No. 4464/70 [1975]; *Schmidt and Dahlström v. Sweden*, App. No. 5589/72, [1976].
941. *National Union of Rail, Maritime and Transport Workers v. United Kingdom*, App. No. 31045/10 [2014].
942. For a critical analysis, *see* Bogg, A., Ewing, K., *The Implications of the RMT Case*, 43 Industrial Law Journal 221 n. 3 (2014), 221-252; Barrow, C., *RMT v. United Kingdom [2014]: The European Court of Human Rights Intimidated into Timidity or Merely Consistent in Its Inconsistency?*, 3 European Human Rights Law Review 277 (2015), 277-285; Stylogiannis, C., *The Protection of the Right to Strike under the European Convention on Human Rights*, 6 UCL Journal of Law and Jurisprudence 142 n. 1 (2017), 142-167.
943. *See Saime Özcan v. Turkey*, App. No. 22943/04 [2009]; *Kaya and Seyhan v. Turkey*, App. No. 30946/04 [2009]; *Hrvatski Lijecnicki Sindikat v. Croatia*, App. No. 36701/09 [2014]; *Ognevenko v. Russia* App. No. 44873/09 [2018].
944. Fabbrini, F., *Fundamental Rights in Europe* (Oxford University Press 2014), 142.

5.3 THE BENEFITS OF A HRBA

The previous section, predominantly through a positive law perspective, established the nature of fundamental collective rights (rights to freely associate, the right to bargain collectively, and the right to industrial action) as human rights. The next sections aim at exploring some of the positive implications that a HRBA towards fundamental collective labour rights can bring about in relation to the labour protection of (self-employed platform) workers and other workers in NSFE, including dependent self-employed workers. First, as it was already examined, an approach as such can help modern labour law systems to start moving away from a strict binary distinction between employment and self-employment. Such a proposition will be further elaborated based on the shortcomings identified in this research regarding the existing responses from both lawmakers and the courts with respect to the labour protection of platform workers. Of course, the very reference to the proposed 'retreat' from a strict binary divide between waged employment and self-employment does not mean that certain restrictions cannot still be valid. Fundamental collective labour rights, such as the right to collective bargaining, also recognised as human rights, do not constitute absolute rights, and they can be subject to limitations. Still, such restrictions, as a number of human rights treaties clearly suggest, need to be proportionate and be justified in a democratic society; something that as it is also discussed can be attributed to the normative weight of human rights. Having said that, a HRBA towards collective labour rights can also have significant implications for competition law and the existence of strict antitrust laws, which consider self-employed workers (including many workers in the 'grey zone') as undertakings.

Furthermore, a HRBA becomes particularly prominent when considering the phenomenon of managerial prerogatives. As discussed, in multiple instances, platform businesses, even though they have managed to escape the liabilities associated with a formal employer, nonetheless contractually possess managerial powers and share many of the features of a typical employment relationship. As it will be further discussed, due to a variety of reasons, those powers can be further magnified within NSFE, including platform workers.

Third, a HRBA towards collective labour rights can be seen as a 'preventative measure' in relation to the violation of other human rights, which can also touch upon civil and political entitlements. As seen, for instance, workplaces with high coverage of collective bargaining are less likely to suffer from incidents of discrimination.

Finally, and not in purely legal terms, the benefits of such an approach can also be relevant in circumventing some of the practical issues that platform workers, and other workers in NSFE, are facing. For instance, a human rights oratory can act as a common language for workers with different occupational and even class characteristics, thus, bridging some of the gaps in their social background and attracting the attention and support of non-traditional partners.

5.3.1 No Legal Basis under Human Rights Law for a Divergent Treatment Between Employment and Self-Employment

While under international law, there is a strong legal basis and a broad consensus that both the rights to freedom of association and collective bargaining are human rights with universal application, there is no justification that they should only be enjoyed within the realm of an employment relationship. To put it otherwise, many of these restrictions are indeed incompatible with the wording and principles of human rights and international labour rights instruments.

To begin with, ILO Convention No. 87 is clear on the scope of the application of such rights. Its Article 2 enshrines that: '[w]*orkers and employers, without distinction whatsoever, shall have the right to establish and, subject only to the rules of the organisation concerned, to join organisations of their own choosing without previous authorisation*'.[945] As Dorssemont argues, the phrase '*without distinction whatsoever*', does not solely constitute a warning against the recognition of the right to freedom of association in a discriminatory manner, which would, for example, exclude some workers on the basis of their sex or religious belief, but it also seems to accord to the word '*worker*', the broadest possible denotation.[946]

Furthermore, both the CFA and the CEACR have repeatedly pointed out that Conventions Nos. 87 and 98, should apply to all workers, regardless of the existence of an employment relationship that is often non-existent.[947] Only limited categories of workers can fall outside the scope of application of the principles and rights enshrined in these Conventions.[948] For instance, the CFA has requested the government of the Dominican Republic to:

> (i) to ensure that 'self-employed' workers fully enjoy freedom of association rights, in particular the right to join the organizations of their own choosing; (ii) to hold consultations to this end with all the parties involved with the aim of finding a mutually acceptable solution so as to ensure that workers who are self-employed could fully enjoy trade union rights for the purpose of furthering and defending their interest, including by the means of collective bargaining; and (iii) in consultation with the social partners concerned, to identify the particularities of self-employed workers that have a bearing on collective bargaining so as to develop specific collective bargaining mechanisms relevant to self-employed workers, if appropriate.[949]

945. ILO Convention No. 87, Article 2.
946. Dorssemont, F., *Les travailleurs de plateforme face au droit des relations collectives du travail. Les droits fondamentaux des travailleurs, one porte d'entrée?*, Journal of Social Law 111 n. 1 (2019), 120.
947. Freedom of Association. Compilation of decisions of the CFA, *International Labour Office* – Geneva: ILO, 6th edition, 2018.
948. These are the armed forces and the police, with regard to freedom of association, and also public servants engaged in the administration of the State, with regard to the right to collective bargaining.
949. ILO CFA, (2010) Report No. 363, Case No 2786, para. 349.

Similar wording has also been used by the CFA in a more request towards the Korean government.[950] In an alike manner, the CEACR has also made clear that:

> the right to organise should be guaranteed to all workers without distinction or discrimination of any kind, including to workers without an employment contract, domestic workers, agricultural workers, workers in the informal economy and self-employed workers.[951]

Much of the literature instantly associates the broad scope of application regarding the rights to freedom of association and bargain collectively with ILO Conventions 87 and 98 and the verdict of ILO's supervisory bodies on these very instruments. This is something that, of course, makes sense due to the inclusion of these Conventions in the 1998 ILO Declaration on Fundamental Principles and Rights at Work and, thereby, their universal nature. Something that is often overlooked though is that the ILO has also attempted to secure a wide application of these rights in other instances. Very early in its existence, the ILO acknowledged the special challenges faced by vulnerable workers in the agricultural sector and, in particular, issues related to their freedom to associate. As such, in 1921, the Right of Association (Agriculture) Convention No. 11 was adopted. The latter in its Article 1 enshrines that:

> [e]ach Member of the International Labour Organisation which ratifies this Convention undertakes to secure to all those engaged in agriculture the same rights of association and combination as to industrial workers, and to repeal any statutory or other provisions restricting such rights in the case of those engaged in agriculture.[952]

The ILO made further efforts to secure freedom of association for self-employed rural workers. In 1975, the Rural Workers' Organisations Convention, No. 141 was adopted. The instrument, besides reiterating the importance of rural worker's right to organise regardless of their employment status, also calls for the Member States which have ratified the Convention to:

> play their role in economic and social development, and adopt and carry out a policy of active encouragement to rural workers organisations [...] and to 'ensure that national laws or regulations do not, given the special circumstances of the rural sector, inhibit the establishment and growth of rural workers' organisations.[953]

It is, moreover, worth mentioning that Convention No. 141 defines rural workers as ' *any person engaged in agriculture, handicrafts or a related occupation in a rural area, whether as a wage earner or, subject to the provisions of paragraph 2 of this Article,*

950. ILO CFA, (2012) Report No. 363, Case No. 2602, para. 461.
951. ILO CEACR, (2021), Observation – Bosnia and Herzegovina, published 109th ILC session. *See also* ILO CEACR, (2021), Direct Request – Central African Republic, published 109th ILC session; ILO CEACR, (2021), Direct Request – Uzbekistan, published 109th ILC session; ILO CEACR (2016), Observation – Ireland, published 105th ILC session.
952. Right of Association (Agriculture) Convention, 1921 (No. 11), Article 1.
953. Rural Workers' Organisations Convention, 1975 (No. 141), Article 5(1) and (2).

as a self-employed person such as a tenant, sharecropper or small owner-occupier'.[954] As Dorssemont explains, what is interesting with respect to this definition is that the instrument does not address the question of whether an agricultural worker managing a business has an economic 'autonomy'; thereby, the right of agricultural workers to establish, or to join a trade union must be assessed independently.[955] In a nutshell, according to the Convention's provisions, as long as a rural worker is not an employer, then she or he should be able to enjoy the right to freely associate. After all, as the same author points out, from a historical perspective, trade unions were established and acquired a legal status before the invention of the employment contract based on a subordination relationship.

The broad personal scope of application in relation to the rights to freedom of association and bargaining collectively can also be traced in the language embraced in the Report of the ILO's Global Commission on the Future of Work.[956] Importantly, the document does not reflect the views of the ILO, but rather those of its members.[957] The Report, particularly, suggests the establishment of a Universal Labour Guarantee that provides a labour protection floor for all workers, including fundamental workers' rights, an 'adequate living wage', limits on hours of work and safe and healthy workplaces.[958] In this regard, not only the Report reminds us that the eight Fundamental Conventions of the ILO should be applied irrespective of any contractual arrangement, but it also advocates for the elevation of three other sets of rights to the status of fundamental labour rights. It can be argued, therefore, that the Global Commission on the Future of Work adopts a 'universalistic' approach that it can equally be found in human rights law.

In a similar vein, the supervisory bodies within the CoE, have explicitly confirmed the wide scope of the application of collective labour rights. In *Sindicatul Pastoral Cel Bun v. Romania*,[959] for instance, the ECtHR had to consider whether members of the clergy of the Romanian Orthodox Church could invoke freedom of association in the face of their bishopric. Romania contested this applicability by refusing that popes were bound by an employment contract. This exercise presupposed an interpretation of the concept of the worker that can invoke freedom of association under Article 11 ECHR. The Court, nonetheless, seemed to insist only on the question

954. *Ibid.*, Article 2(1); The provisions of Article 2(2) read as follows: '*This Convention applies only to those tenants, sharecroppers or small owner-occupiers who derive their main income from agriculture, who work the land themselves, with the help only of their family or with the help of occasional outside labour and who do not – (a) permanently employ workers; or (b) employ a substantial number of seasonal workers; or (c) have any land cultivated by sharecroppers or tenants.*'
955. *Supra*, Dorssemont (2019), 120-121.
956. Global Commission on the Future of Work, (2019), *Work for a brighter future*, Geneva, ILO.
957. The Global Commission was formatted in order to undertake an in-depth examination of the future of work that can provide the analytical basis for the delivery of social justice in the 21st century. The independent Report is the outcome of research and consultation with the Governments and social partners of the ILO Members States and the work of the 28 members of the Global Commission.
958. *Supra*, Global Commission on the Future of Work (2019), 38.
959. *Sindicatul Pastorul cel Bun v. Romania*, App. no. 2330/09 [2014].

of subordination, work and financial compensation. Neither the origin of this relationship (a civil law contract or a vow of a sacred nature) nor the source of funding (the Church or the State) was relevant. The Court explained that the only relevant question, in this case, was as to whether the duties performed by the members of the clergy, '*notwithstanding any special features they may entail, amount to an employment relationship rendering applicable the right to form a trade union within the meaning of Article 11*'.[960] In addressing this question, the Grand Chamber made an explicit reference to the 'primacy of facts' principle contained in the ILO Recommendation No. 198 concerning the employment relationship, as well as to the ILO Convention No. 87, which enshrines that '*workers and employers, without distinction whatsoever*' have the right to establish organisations of their own choosing.[961] Against this background, as the Court has also established in a number of other rulings, the permissible exceptions to the right to freedom of association must be narrowly construed, so as to offer practical and effective protection to the freedom in question.[962]

Scholars like Dorssemont,[963] or Countouris and De Stefano,[964] are using, among other examples, the approach taken by the ECtHR in the *Sindicatul Pastorul cel Bun* case in order to further prove their thesis on the applicability of the right to freedom of association irrespective of the contractual relationship. Bogg, however, does not seem that convinced by the Grand Chamber's position. He argues that in this case, the applicants were eligible to invoke freedom of association under Article 11, as the Court considered that their duties were indeed performed within the context of an employment relationship.[965] This is also the reason why the direct reference was made to ILO Recommendation No. 198. Moreover, in paragraph 148 of the judgment the Court mentions that '*notwithstanding their special circumstances, members of the clergy fulfil their mission in the context of an employment relationship*';[966] hence, they fall within the ambit of Article 11.[967] That said, in my opinion, albeit the Court explicitly refers to

960. *Ibid.*, para. 141.
961. *Ibid.*
962. *See*, for instance, *Demir and Baykara v. Turkey*, para. 146; *Sidiropoulos and Others v. Greece*, App. no. 26695/95 [1998], para. 38; *Norwegian Confederation of Trade Unions (LO) and Norwegian Transport Workers' Union (NTF) v. Norway, App. no. 45487/17 [2021]*, para. 96.
963. Dorssemont, F., *Collective Workers' Rights for Workers in the Gig Economy* (Maria T. Carinci and Filip Dorssemont eds, *Platform Work in Europe: Towards Harmonisation?*, Intersentia 2021), 212.
964. Countouris, N., De Stefano, V. (2019), *New Trade Union Strategies for New Forms of Employment. ETUC. Brussels*, 38.
965. Bogg, A., *Economic Coordination as Freedom of Association* (Shae McCrystal, Ewan McGaughey and Sanjukta Paul eds, *The Cambridge Handbook of Labor in Competition Law*, Cambridge University Press 2022), 36-37.
966. *Supra*, *Sindicatul Pastorul cel Bun v. Romania*, para. 148.
967. One might argue that what Alan Bogg claims can be further reinforced by a recent decision taken by the ECtHR in the case of *Yakut Republican Trade-Union Federation v. Russia, App. no. 29582/09 [2021]*. In this ruling, the Court accorded a wide margin of appreciation to the respondent state in restricting the right of working prisoners to freely join a trade union. As such, a statutory ban on the unionisation of prisoners was found to be proportionate and therefore necessary in a democratic society. It was held that '*prison work differs from the work performed by ordinary employees in many aspects* (para. 44)'. Therefore, the right to freedom of association was strongly related to persons in an employment relationship. The decision was criticised by a joint dissenting decision of two judges, who pointed out that: '[g]*iven their*

the working conditions of the members of the clergy and the latter's similarities to employees, there is no point in the ruling, where the Grand Chamber highlighted that only employees should enjoy their right to freedom of association. In other words, it is different for the Court to say that in this case the applicants indeed resemble employees and employees do deserve protection under Article 11, from saying that such a right should be only reserved for persons in an employment relationship.

The aforementioned ruling does not constitute the only instance where the ECtHR has indeed opinioned that the distinction between employment and self-employment is not relevant for the purposes of Article 11 ECHR. In the case of *Sigurdur Sigurjónsson v. Iceland*, it was pointed out that '*the right to form and join trade unions in that provision* [i.e., Article 11] *is an aspect of the wider right to freedom of association, rather than a separate right*'.[968] In this regard, it is important to reiterate that according to Article 11, '*everyone has the right to freedom of peaceful assembly and to freedom of association with others*'.[969] It would be at least problematic for the word '*everyone*' to refer to every person, excluding only those who find themselves outside the realm of an employment relationship. This can also be confirmed by the stance taken by the ECtHR in the case *Vördur Ólafsson v. Iceland*, in which a self-employed craftsman was eligible for protection under Article 11.[970]

The openness towards the right to freedom of association and collective bargaining is also apparent when it comes to the other supervisory body within the CoE, namely, the ECSR.[971] The latter, based on Article 6§2 of the ESC, has recently clarified that all workers should have the right to bargain collectively, including self-employed workers.[972] More specifically, the case concerned the pre-2017 ban on collective bargaining for freelance journalists, voiceover actors, and session musicians, in Ireland. As explained in Chapter 4, the domestic law was recently amended to include some specific categories of workers beyond employees that may be allowed to conclude a collective agreement.[973] The case was brought in front of the ECSR by the Irish Congress of Trade Unions (ICTU), back in 2016. It was claimed that the blanket ban towards all agreements between self-employed workers and organizations of self-employed workers[974] was at odds with the country's obligations to protect the rights of workers as those enshrined under Article 6 ESC. Despite the 2017 amendments, which as previously developed are now exempting certain categories of self-employed workers from antitrust laws, the ICTU insisted that restriction on the right to bargain collectively still remained.

The ECSR hold that the blanket ban in Ireland prior to the 2017 amendments was indeed in breach of Article 6 of the Charter. It seized the opportunity to point out that

vulnerable position, prisoners may even have a strong interest in securing respect for their right to join an association that defends their individual and collective rights' (para. 7, dissenting opinion).

968. *Sigurdur Sigurjónsson v. Iceland* (1993) 16 EHRR 462.
969. Article 11(1) ECHR.
970. *Vördur Ólafsson v. Iceland* (2013) 56 EHRR 21.
971. The ECSR monitors compliance with the European Social Charter.
972. *Irish Congress of Trade Unions v. Ireland*, Complaint No. 123/2016.
973. Competition (Amendment) Act 2017.
974. Such agreements were seen as a restriction to competition rules in the county.

the purpose of competition law is not to restrict the rights to freedom of association and collective bargaining for those workers who may need it the most; in this particular case self-employed workers, such as voiceover actors, freelance journalists, and musicians. It went on to mention that:

> an outright ban on collective bargaining of all self-employed workers would be excessive as it would run counter to the object and purpose of this provision' and, therefore, it was 'not necessary in a democratic society in that the categories of persons included in the notion of 'undertaking' were over-inclusive.[975]

Throughout its ruling, the ECSR made an extensive reference to international labour standards and especially to the universal applicability of the ILO Conventions 87 and 98. That said, in 2015, the CEACR also called the Irish authorities together with the social partners to identify groups of self-employed workers that can potentially be covered by collective bargaining agreements.[976] In relation to the ICTU's position on the 2017 statutory amendments, the majority of ECSR's members found no violation of Article 6(2). The claim was considered to be '*speculative*', as there was still not enough evidence as to how the new law will be applied in practice by the relevant authorities.[977]

Such a conclusion was criticised by a joint dissenting opinion, comprised of two Committee Members, namely, Petros Stangos and Barbara Kresal.[978] They expressed the fear that, in practice, the amended legislation continues to adopt a rather restrictive approach as there are high chances that '*other category of self-employed workers with the same or similar characteristics as the three categories of workers explicitly exempted from the prohibition*' will not enjoy equal protection with respect to their fundamental right to bargain collectively.[979] In this regard, they argue that Articles 15E and 15F, as those are enshrined in the 2017 Act, offer to all other categories of self-employed workers a 'quasi-exemption', which cannot be considered of equal value as the one enjoyed by voiceover actors, freelance journalists, and musicians. They also argued that the legislation, as it stands, accords a considerably wide margin of appreciation to the executive. The latter can impose restrictions on collective bargaining in relation to all other categories of self-employed workers, while at the same time, the 2017 Act (specifically Article 15F) fails to adopt any detailed objectives or coherent criteria.

As Pecinovsky points out, the lack of any clear criteria can indeed pave the way for the executive to espouse a strict interpretation in practice when assessing the conditions necessary in order to allow a relevant category of self-employed workers to

975. *Ibid.*, paras 40 and 98.
976. *Supra* Countouris and De Stefano (2019), 51. The authors refer to: ILO, Third item on the agenda: Information and reports on the application of Conventions and Recommendations. Report of the Committee on the Application of Standards (2016) International Labour Conference 105th Session, Geneva, Provisional Record, May-June 2016 16(Rev) Part 2.
977. *Irish Congress of Trade Unions v. Ireland*, para. 89; A minority of the Committee's members disagreed with this conclusion in a dissenting opinion. For an analysis of the opinion *see*: Doherty, M., Franca, V., *Solving the 'Gig-saw'? Collective Rights and Platform Work*, 49 Industrial Law Journal 353 n. 3 (2020), 352-376.
978. ECSR, *ICTU v. Ireland*, Joint dissenting opinion of Petros Stangos and Barbara Kresal.
979. *Ibid.*

bargain collectively and conclude a collective agreement.[980] Such a view can be supported by the fact that the Irish statutory definition of false self-employment still requires a 'relationship of subordination' as a necessary condition for someone to be exempted from the ambit of competition law.[981] Furthermore, no independence as regards the determination of the time schedule constitutes another pre-condition in this respect.[982] As discussed throughout this research, provisions of this kind can be proven an insurmountable obstacle for many casual workers in NSFE, especially platform workers. Of course, all these observations remain to be seen in the near future. It can be presumed, however, that the narrow statutory definition contained in the 2017 amended Act in relation to false self-employment, it may be found to go against Article 6 ESC in a future legal dispute.

In a critical analysis of the case, Bogg describes the methodology adopted by the Committee as *integrated, contextual* and *substantive*.[983] According to the author, the integrated method stems from the inclination of the Committee to engage with sources of international law, like the ILO and the ECHR. This is something that the other supervisory body of the CoE, namely the ECtHR, has done on several occasions, as discussed above. Those sources are indeed acknowledging collective bargaining as an essential element for the effective exercise of the right to freely associate. Moreover, the contextual method applied in this case can be traced in the ESC's realisation that within modern workplaces, there are multiple occasions in which contractual agreements are specially designed to escape from formal regulation and save labour costs. The present-day proliferation of casual work arrangements, like those within platform work, constitutes an illustration of the problem. Consequently, a great number of workers who are enjoying limited bargaining power, are now falling outside the definition of a dependent employee and its associated benefits. The analysis of the Committee seems to adequately grasp such challenges. Finally, as Bogg explains, the ESC's substantive method can be found in paragraph 38 of its decision. In particular, it is pointed out that:

> [i]n establishing the type of collective bargaining that is protected by the Charter, it is not sufficient to rely on distinctions between worker and self-employed, the decisive criterion is rather whether there is an imbalance of power between the providers and engagers of labour. Where providers of labour have no substantial influence on the content of contractual conditions, they must be given the possibility of improving the power imbalance through collective bargaining.[984]

Reflecting on the analysis of the Committee, therefore, it can be argued that as far as the enjoyment of fundamental collective labour rights is concerned, the Committee

980. Pecinovsky, P., *The Right to Collective Bargaining for Economically Dependent Workers with a Self-Employed-Status* (Barry Cofler ed., *European Trade Unions in the 21st Century: The Future of Solidarity and Workplace Democracy*, St Antony's Series (e-book), Palgrave Macmillan 2018), 39.
981. Competition (Amendment) Act 2017, Article 15D.
982. *Ibid.*
983. *Supra*, Bogg (2022), 45.
984. *Irish Congress of Trade Unions v. Ireland*, para. 38.

not only moves away from a formalistic distinction between employment and self-employment, but it also moves a step further by generating a normative framework for the application of the right to collective bargaining. In relation to the first point, the ESC's majority appears to embrace a notion of a 'worker', which is different and, or 'autonomous' from the notion of a 'worker' that is usually used by labour courts in determining whether someone can fall within an employment relationship *sensu stricto*. In other words, the Committee does not qualify what types of workers should enjoy the right to collective bargaining; based on the majority, every worker should be entitled to the right in question and thereby, any restriction should be justified under Article G of the ESC.[985]

Moreover, as far as the development of a normative framework for the application of the right to collective bargaining is concerned, this can be traced in the combination of the ESC's contextual and substantive approaches, as those identified by Bogg above. The majority of the Committee by espousing a wide personal scope on the application of the right at issue. In doing so, it recognised that the world of work is changing and the lines between employment and self-employment have become particularly blurry; in this context, a considerable number of people who are truly in need of protection are now falling outside the protective realm of an employment relationship. Not only this, but they are usually neither able to unionise nor engage in collective bargaining (contextual approach). To this extent, it is the comparably weak position of workers in a given situation (e.g., the power to influence the terms and conditions of a contractual agreement) that justifies the enjoyment of the right to collective bargaining as an essential element of the right to freely associate (substantive approach).[986] The key question that ought to be asked therefore is 'to whom should this right apply', rather than 'is that person an employee or a self-employed'? According to Bogg, such consideration is based on the notion of substantive equality: if employees are eligible to enjoy the right to collective bargaining due to the inequality of power compared to their employers, then such right should '*extend to those self-employed workers who display similar relevant features of subordination and dependence*'.[987] This is crucial to understanding why collective bargaining as an 'indispensable' element of the right to freedom of association, should not be reserved as a right solely available to employees. Importantly, all these considerations are supported by the recognition that the right to bargain collectively enjoys under international law, where a wide consensus exists in relation to the latter's nature as a fundamental labour right is also recognised as a human right (integrated approach).

985. Article G, ESC: '1. *The rights and principles set forth in Part I when effectively realised, and their effective exercise as provided for in Part II, shall not be subject to any restrictions or limitations not specified in those parts, except such as are prescribed by law and are necessary in a democratic society for the protection of the rights and freedoms of others or for the protection of public interest, national security, public health, or morals. 2. The restrictions permitted under this Charter to the rights and obligations set forth herein shall not be applied for any purpose other than that for which they have been prescribed.*'
986. *Supra*, Bogg (2022), 45-46.
987. *Ibid.*, 45.

Having said that, if a broad personal scope of application in relation to the rights to freedom of association and collective bargaining can be justified under the aforementioned sources of international and regional instruments, then it is also reasonable to apply the same rationale for the right to strike. As noted, there has been a wide consensus that the right to strike constitutes an integral part of ILO Convention No. 87. Over the years, this position has been also confirmed multiple times by both the CFA and CEACR. In the context of the ILO, freedom of association, including the right to collective bargaining, should have universal applicability to all workers without a distinction whatsoever. If the right to strike is an essential part of the right to freely associate, then it should be also enjoyed by self-employed persons, or at least by those who experience an imbalance of bargaining power. In 2012, the CFA, in a detailed examination of the scope of the right to strike and its permissible limitations under Convention No. 87 explained that:

> The right to strike is not absolute and may be restricted in exceptional circumstances, or even prohibited. Over and above the armed forces and the police, the members of which may be excluded from the scope of the Convention in general, other restrictions on the right to strike may relate to: (i) certain categories of public servants; (ii) essential services in the strict sense of the term; and (iii) situations of acute national or local crisis, although only for a limited period and solely to the extent necessary to meet the requirements of the situation. In these cases, compensatory guarantees should be provided for the workers who are thus deprived of the right to strike.[988]

Nowhere in the CFA's analysis, can someone come across an explicit prohibition concerning the right of self-employed workers to go on a strike. The same can be also argued in relation to the language embraced by other international supervisory bodies that are not related to the ILO.

In 2001, the CESCR in its Concluding Comment on South Korea regarding the application of Article 8 of the Covenant found that the provisions of the article in question: '*guarantee for all persons the right to freely form and join trade unions, the right to engage in collective bargaining through trade unions for the promotion and protection of their economic and social interests, as well as the right to strike*'.[989] The reference of the Committee to '*all persons*' can be seen as an acknowledgement or rather a suggestion that the right to strike can also expand to workers who may not find themselves in an employment relationship.

Furthermore, within the context of the CoE, a broad personal scope on the right to strike can also be justified to a great extent. As discussed, in multiple cases, the ECtHR has not perceived the existence of an employment contract as a prerequisite for the protections afforded under Article 11 ECHR. To this extent, as Dorssemont observes, in the case of *Hrvatski liječnički sindikat v. Croatia*,[990] where a violation was found in relation to the right of a doctors' and dentists' trade unions to strike, there was

988. *Supra*, ILO CEACR, 50.
989. E/C.12/1/Add.59 (09-05-2001), para. 39, available at: https://www.refworld.org/pdfid/45c30b330.pdf (accessed 16 November 2022).
990. *Hrvatski liječnički sindikat v. Croatia*, App no 36701/09.

no indication that the respondent unions were only organising professionals with an employment contract.[991] At the same time though he admits that it would be presumptuous for someone to consider that the ruling at issue *'definitively and explicitly settles the question of the ownership of the right to strike in favour of self-employed workers'*.[992] Still, the absence of any explicit reference by the Court to the existence of an employment relationship as a prerequisite for the exercise of the right to strike constitutes at least another indication of the latter's wide personal scope of application.

In a similar vein, considering the decision of the ECSR in the case of *ICTU v. Ireland* and the confirmation that the right to collective bargaining should extend to self-employed workers, it can be claimed that the right to strike must equally extend to such workers, especially to those finding themselves in a situation where they share similar characteristics of subordination and dependence with employees. More specifically, as mentioned above, the Committee substantiated its decision to adopt a broad personal scope regarding the exercise of the right to bargain collectively by relying on a normative justification based upon the context of unequal power relations within the modern world of work. Considering the nature of the right to strike, it can be presumed that the very same justification(s) can also be applicable towards such a right. This is to say that it enjoys a wide international consensus as a fundamental labour right, also acknowledged as a human right (integrated approach). Moreover, within contemporary labour relations, where the boundaries between employment and self-employment have become less apparent (contextual approach), many workers find themselves in a situation where there is an imbalance of power between the providers and engagers of labour. A broad personal scope of the right to strike can be therefore justified on the grounds that it can provide workers, as in the case of the right to collective bargaining, with the bargaining power to drive fair and meaningful negotiations, offsetting this way the inherent inequalities of bargaining power in their given situation (substantive approach). As explained in Chapter 4, many platform workers with 'obscure' employment status, by using this right, have managed to improve their working conditions, at least to a certain extent. After all, as Barbara Kresal points out, there can be no effective right to collective bargaining without the right to strike, or collective action in general.[993] Collective bargaining, as contained in Article 6 ESC, represents a core right,[994] as it is considered to be essential for the enjoyment of other fundamental rights guaranteed by the Charter.[995] A different approach towards the right to strike, therefore, would automatically undermine the substance of Article 6, and could also endanger the very essence of the Chapter as a whole.

991. *Supra*, Dorssemont (2021), 220-221.
992. *Ibid.*, 221.
993. Kresal, B., *Collective Bargaining for Platform Workers and the European Social Charter* (José M. Boto and Elisabeth Brameshuber eds, *Collective Bargaining and the Gig Economy a Traditional Tool for New Business Models*, Hart Publishing, 2022), 61-62.
994. The ESC establishes an 'à la carte system' of ratification (Article 20 ESC). Contracting states have to accept a minimum of six among the nine of Part II, referred to as constituting its 'hard core provisions'. Article 6 ESC constitutes one of the core rights.
995. For instance, among others, the right to just conditions of work (Article 2, ESC), to safe and healthy working conditions (Article 3, ESC).

Overall, it can be claimed that the protection of fundamental human rights and human dignity is not something that should be confined only to the realm of an employment relationship. In a seminal case related to undocumented workers' rights, including fair working conditions and freedom of association, the IACtHR in its Advisory Opinion stated that '*the safeguard of these rights for migrants has great importance based on the principle of the inalienable nature of such rights, which all workers possess, irrespective of their migratory status, and also the fundamental principle of human dignity embodied in Article 1 of the Universal Declaration*'.[996]

In 2021, moreover, the IACtHR issued another important Advisory Opinion on the application of collective labour rights and their personal scope, including the rights to freely associate, bargain collectively and strike.[997] As noted in a previous section, the request for an Advisory Opinion was made by the Inter-American Commission back in 2019. The importance of the IACtHR's decision lies in the fact that the request was drafted in the context of the tremendous influence new technologies have on the labour market. To this extent, the Commission wanted to clarify the personal scope of human rights, in the context of modern workplaces. The intentions of the Committee became even more apparent during the hearings called by the IACtHR, where the latter was called to establish standards in order to assist the signatory states to comply with their obligations under the ACHR.[998]

Similarly, some of the participants in the procedures, like the Human Rights Commission of Mexico City and the Public Labour Prosecutor's Office in Brazil, highlighted the need to protect workers whose main income is based on digital labour platforms.[999] The IACtHR went on to reiterate the fundamental nature of the rights in question as human rights, by also espousing a purposive approach. For instance, it highlighted the importance of the rights to collective bargaining and the right to strike as essential tools in the hands of workers in improving their living and working conditions and compensating for the imbalance of powers that exist between workers and employers. In this regard, it was pointed out that signatory states should maximise their efforts to preserve trade union rights for all workers. Nowhere in the decision, was a reference made that such rights should apply solely to employees. The broad personal scope of application of collective labour rights was also supported by the reference made by the IACtHR to the ILO Conventions Nos. 87 and 98.

All in all, it is indeed the inalienable nature of these rights and a broad international consensus in relation to their broad personal scope that generates a strong legal basis for platform workers, as well as other workers engaged in NSFE, to be able to enjoy their human rights, such as the rights to freedom of association and collective

996. Juridical Condition and Rights of the Undocumented Migrants, Advisory Opinion OC-18/03, 17 September 2003, Inter-ACtHR (Ser A) No. 18 (2003).
997. Advisory Opinion OC-27/21 of 5 May 2021, requested by the Inter-American Commission on Human Rights.
998. DRIMMER, J. (2021), 'The Inter-American Court of Human Rights and the Gig Economy', Lexology, 11 February 2021, available at: https://www.lexology.com/library/detail.aspx?g=e88aa8ad-447d-42d9-9f4a-650f3f1944ad (accessed 8 April 2022).
999. *Ibid.*

bargaining. Importantly, these rights should not be seen as privileges stemming from employment status, but rather as rights applicable to all workers. As a consequence, this very position should also be reflected in existing and future legal instruments that touch upon fundamental collective labour rights. That said, in connection with the recent developments at the EU level (as those explained in Chapter 3), this is not the case, as far as the new proposed EU Directive on improving the working conditions in platform work is concerned. Arguably, the latter falls short of supranational law's mandate of acknowledging the fundamental status of collective bargaining rights for all workers, regardless of their status. Ironically enough, the draft Directive does not adopt a similar stance when it comes to other fundamental human rights that are also included in the CFREU, such as the right to protection of personal data (Article 9 CFREU) in the context of algorithmic management. The provisions of the draft instrument are clear on that. For instance, Articles 6 and 7 should be applicable to all platform workers, including those finding themselves outside an employment relationship. This is justified by the recognition that automated decision-making systems can negatively impact workers, regardless of their status. Still, as it will be argued below, limited protection towards the exercise of fundamental collective labour rights can negatively affect the enjoyment of other individual human rights; thus negating, at least to a certain extent, the 'all-encompassing approach' that the new proposed Directive chose to adopt in relation to certain rights.

5.3.2 Fundamental Human Rights as the 'Rule': Possible Ramifications

Thus far, in the context of this research and via a positive law angle, the nature of fundamental collective labour rights as human rights has been established. As seen, they also constitute part of the constitutional order of a significantly high number of countries, particularly within Europe. Against this background, any restrictions upon such rights should be proportionate and be considered necessary in a democratic society. As Countouris and De Stefano put it: '*if a right* [such as the right to collective bargaining] *is held to be a fundamental or a constitutional, then it is typically approached as being the rule*'.[1000] It can be argued, therefore, that a positive implication which stems from a HRBA lies in the normative weight and significance fundamental human rights possess. In this sense, they should depart from a position of superiority due to their constitutional status and the supra-legislative status as transnational human rights. In turn, their superiority and status, at least at a theoretical level, should be capable of generating a hierarchy of norms, where workers' fundamental collective rights enjoy a higher legal status when, for instance, compared to other legal sources that do not share the same legal value. Of course, on multiple occasions, the normative weight of fundamental collective rights has not prevented the latter's subjection to economic considerations that can even derive from soft law international obligations towards states; a situation that has often caused what Katsaroumpas calls the

1000. *Supra*, Countouris and De Stefano (2021), 5.

'de-constitutionalisation of collective labour rights'.[1001] Still, this subjection should not obstruct us from re-iterating the normative weight of the rights in question and asking for their effective application.

Jacques Ziller describes the notion of the hierarchy of norms in the following terms. He first mentions that such hierarchy occurs due to the existing relationship between two different legal sources '*according to which the legitimacy of norm B is conditioned by its conformity with another norm A*'.[1002] In the 'balancing exercise', a reason that situates norm A in a superior position compared to norm B may be attributed to the former's inclusion within a legal instrument that is formally superior, such as a constitution, or a human rights treaty (formal hierarchy).[1003] Another reason may be traced to the important content of norm A, which expresses fundamental values, like the protection of human dignity.[1004] Those reasons, according to the author, can complement each other. Therefore, considering Ziller's analysis, it can be argued that fundamental collective labour rights satisfy both reasons that should position them into a superior hierarchical superior position compared to other legal sources.

A good illustration of the interplay between different legal sources can be found in a recent decision delivered by the ECtHR, in the so-called *Holship* case.[1005] The ruling at issue concerned the interpretation of Article 11 ECHR and particularly the right to industrial action. The facts involved the Supreme Court of Norway's judgment, which declared that a proposed boycott, organised by the Norwegian Transport Workers' Union (NTF), was unlawful, as it was in breach of the fundamental freedom of establishment that is secured under the European Economic Area (EEA) law.[1006] The unlawfulness of the boycott had also been confirmed by the Court of Justice of the European Free Trade Association (EFTA) States (after an advisory opinion was requested by the Supreme Court), which ruled that under the proportionality test, the planned boycott had indeed to be considered as a restriction on the right of establishment. In justifying its conclusions, it referred to the case law of the (CJEU) and specifically to the reasoning followed in the 'infamous' cases of *Viking* and *Laval*.[1007]

1001. Katsaroumpas, I., *De-Constitutionalising Collective Labour Rights: The Case of Greece*, 47 Industrial Law Journal 465 n. 4 (2017), 465-503.

1002. Ziller, J., *Hierarchy of Norms: Hierarchy of Sources and General Principles* (Ulrich Becker, Armon Hatje, Michael Potacs and Nina Wunderlich eds, *European Union Law' Verfassung und Verwaltung in Europa Festschrift für Jürgen Schwarze zum*, Nomos Verlagsgesellschaft 2014), 336.

1003. *Ibid.*

1004. *Ibid.*, 336-337.

1005. *Norwegian Confederation of Trade Unions (LO) and Norwegian Transport Workers' Union (NTF) v. Norway*, App. no. 45487/17 [2021] [hereinafter Holship case]. For an analysis *see*: Stylogiannis, C. (2021), *The 'Back and Forth' in the Protection of (Collective) Labor Rights under the ECHR Continues: The Holship Case*, Comparative Labor Law & Policy Dispatch No. 36, Champaign: University of Illinois College of Law.

1006. The Agreement on the EEA, 1 January 1994, 1994 O.J. (No. L 1) 3, [hereinafter EEA], brings together the EU Member States and the three EEA EFTA States – Iceland, Liechtenstein, and Norway – in a single market, known as the 'Internal Market', available at: https://www.efta.int/eea/eea-agreement (accessed 29 May 2022).

1007. In both cases, the CJEU acknowledged that the right to strike is a 'fundamental right which forms an integral part of the general principles of community law'. It was, however, held that

As a result, the NTF brought the case in front of the ECtHR. Among other things, the Strasbourg Court had to first assess whether the right to boycott is protected under Article 11 ECHR and then engage in a balancing exercise between economic freedoms on the one hand (i.e., the freedom of establishment) and fundamental human rights on the other (i.e., the right to industrial action in the form of a boycott). In relation to the first point, albeit previously uncertain as to whether Article 11 also includes a 'right to boycott' as a form of industrial action that can be used as a tool in labour conflicts, the Court found that: '*the exercise of a blockade by an applicant trade union can also give rise to the applicability of Article 11 of the Convention [...] [as] a boycott may be the only means available to a trade union to put pressure on an employer in defense of workers' rights*'.[1008] Accordingly, as in the cases of *Demir* and *Enerji* mentioned above, the Court was ready to once again give a broad interpretation to Article 11, by also referring to relevant sources of international law.

Furthermore, with respect to the aforementioned balancing exercise, the Court pointed out that the freedom of establishment constitutes an important factor in assessing whether interference with the freedom of association is proportionate. It was stressed, however, that the freedom in question does not share the same legal value as human rights, which are protected under the Convention, including the right to industrial action. In the exact words of the Court: '*from the perspective of Article 11 of the Convention, EEA freedom of establishment is not a counterbalancing fundamental right to freedom of association but rather one element, albeit an important one, to be taken into consideration in the assessment of proportionality under Article 11(2)*'.[1009] To this extent, it was also argued that '*the degree to which a collective action risks having economic consequences cannot* [...] *in and of itself be a decisive consideration in the analysis of proportionality under Article 11, paragraph 2 of the Convention*'.[1010]

A counterclaim raised by the respondent state was that even though Norway is not a Member State of the EU, it is, nevertheless, part of the EEA Agreement that enshrines the incorporation of EU legislation covering the four freedoms – the free movement of goods, services, persons and capital – throughout all EEA States. According to Norway, therefore, the latter '*provides for the protection of human rights which* [is] *similar to the protection provided for by the Convention, and that there [is] a presumption of compliance with the Convention which* [is] *the same as or similar to that set out in Bosphorus Hava Yolları Turizm ve Ticaret Anonim Şirketi v. Ireland*'.[1011] That said, ever since 2005 and the seminal 'Bosphorus' ruling, it has been established that the Strasbourg Court will not rule on issues related to EU law and decisions touching upon CJEU's jurisdiction. Particularly, the so-called Bosphorus doctrine provides for a presumption that generally perceives EU law as offering a level of protection of

such a right could and needed to be balanced against the commercial principles of EU law; Case *C-438/05, International Transport Workers' Federation v. Viking Line ABP*, 2007 ECR I-10779 and Case C-341/05, *Laval un Partneri Ltd v. Svenska Byggnadsarbetareforbundet*, 2007 ECR I-11767.

1008. *Supra, Holship case*, para. 80.
1009. *Ibid.*, para. 118.
1010. *Ibid.*
1011. *Ibid.*, para. 79.

fundamental rights which is equivalent to that offered under the Convention. To this extent, cases arriving in front of the ECtHR and concerning the implementation of EU law are to be considered inadmissible. Still, despite Norway's' claims on the similarities between EU law and EEA law, the majority of the Fifth Section of the ECtHR ruled that for the purposes of this case, the Bosphorus presumption does not apply to EEA law by leaving it open to reassessing the subject matter in future case law.[1012] Importantly, it was, moreover, pointed out that: '[...]*when implementing their obligations under EU or EEA law,* [...] *contracting Parties should ensure that restrictions imposed on Article 11 rights do not affect the essential elements of trade union freedom, without which that freedom would become devoid of substance*'.[1013] Arguably, such a statement can bring about possible implications not only in relation to the legal relationship between EEA law and the Convention but also with respect to the latter's interplay with EU law. As it has been already argued, it is indeed difficult to speak with certainty that through these very words, the Bosphorus presumption is formally called into question; still, it can be claimed that the door remains open for such a development and future case law is expected to make things clearer.[1014]

By reading the analysis produced by the Court, someone would expect that in a balancing exercise between 'important factors versus fundamental human rights', the latter would take precedence over the former. This, nonetheless, was not the case in the Holship ruling, as a wide margin of appreciation was given to the respondent state. As I have argued elsewhere, the final verdict of the Court is open to a variety of criticisms, such as the level of protection that the right to industrial action, including the right to strike, enjoys under the ECHR.[1015] Still, for the purposes of this research, it can be contented that the words used by the Court can have some significant implications for fundamental collective labour rights, which also constitute part of the 'universal list' of human rights. Through its judgment, the Court made a step forward towards a fairer balance in favour of labour rights, recognised as human rights, when compared to the economic freedoms and interests of businesses. Indeed, such an interpretation creates, at least at a theoretical level, a hierarchy of rights where workers' rights enjoy a higher legal status than economic freedoms, a statement that can also be seen as a belated response to the 'infamous' decisions of the CJEU in *Viking* and *Laval* cases. Importantly, such a hierarchy can also be traced in the language of the other supervisory body within the CoE, namely, the ECSR.

As the previous section examined, the ECSR, in the case against Ireland, also appeared ready to interpret the right to collective bargaining as 'the rule', where every restriction or limitation on this 'rule' should be necessary in a democratic society. That being said, Bogg argues that the Committee seems to adopt a much more robust

1012. By taking this stance, the ECtHR seemed to accept the arguments which brought forward by the applicant trade union, namely, NTF. The latter pointed out that the EEA law in itself has no direct effect and no supremacy, in addition to the lack of a binding legal effect of advisory opinions from the EFTA Court. In doing so, the NTF relied on the words of the ECtHR in an earlier judgment. *See Konkurrenten.no AS v. Norway*, App. No. 47341/15 [2019], para. 42.
1013. *Supra*, *Holship case*, para. 118.
1014. *Supra*, Stylogiannis (2021), 7.
1015. *Ibid.*

approach towards the protection of the fundamental collective rights, in that case regarding the right to collective bargaining, compared to the one espoused by the ECHR. This is because the Committee, by identifying the right to bargain collectively as the fundamental rule (through an integrated, contextual and substantive interpretation), then assessed the situation both before and after the entry into force of the 2017 statutory amendments in light of Article G of the Charter. As Bogg observes, it did not follow from this assessment that national authorities were obliged to balance the right to collective bargaining against the requirements of competition law by using a proportionality test based on a decision-by-decision basis. As seen, certain exclusions were adopted that provide for immunities or exclusions from liabilities stemming from competition law, such as in the case of certain occupations (e.g., musicians and actors) or 'false self-employed' workers. Thus, according to the same author, Article G's limitation clause '*represents an approach that gives focal position to legislation in the specification of the right to bargain collectively in national legal orders*'.[1016] The fact that such legislation was formed around specific exemptions from antitrust laws did not distract the Committee from predominantly putting its emphasis '*on the substance of the legal protection rather than its form*'.[1017] Of course, as the previous section argued, fears still exist that the amended legislation persists in adopting a rather restrictive approach to the application of collective bargaining, something that remains to be seen in the future. That is why the Committee avoided finding a violation of Article 6(2) ESC.

All in all, regardless of their shortcomings, the aforementioned developments indeed confirm that fundamental collective labour rights, due to their nature as human rights, should enjoy an elevated status when compared to other legal sources which do not share the same status. Of course, such rights do not constitute absolute rights and can be indeed restricted. These restrictions, nonetheless, have to be necessary in a democratic society.

5.3.3 So What About Competition Law?

Despite the fact that this research does not initiate from a competition law perspective, it would be difficult for someone to deny that the aforementioned discussion regarding the status of collective labour rights as fundamental human rights can also be related to the coexistence between collective bargaining and competition law. As Chapter 2 examined, competition laws around the world continue to impose limits on the scope of collective labour law, as it prevents self-employed workers, including many platform workers, from collective bargaining. Such a phenomenon occurs even though such workers share many of the features typical of an employment relationship. As also discussed in Chapter 1, a big portion of them is also characterised by an increased precariousness, which is often accompanied by poor working conditions capable of interfering with workers' dignity as human beings. Therefore, as Countouris and Rainone point out, '*disenfranchising self-employed workers from the right to collective*

1016. *Supra* Bogg (2022), 47.
1017. *Ibid.*

bargaining means accepting that their precarious negotiating position will almost invariably result in degrading working conditions'.[1018]

Broadly speaking, competition law systems are principally concerned with the concentration of market power and its possible (negative) effects on the market mechanism; this also explains the reason why, among other things, anti-competitive agreements are strictly prohibited and why businesses' monopolistic, or oligopolistic powers are generally regarded undesirable, at least at a theoretical level.[1019] There is a strong consensus that in conditions of unfair competition, consumers' welfare and the economic liberty of individuals to choose between different products and services can be seriously damaged.[1020] To this extent, the protection of consumers can also have broader ramifications. It has been argued, for instance, that individual freedom and fair competition are essential, not only for prosperity but also for the realisation of political freedom; a situation that as Deutscher and Makris point out, is perceived by many as '*desirable both on egalitarian grounds and on a certain notion of democracy*'.[1021]

Taking a bird's eye view on the evolution of competition law, one can observe that over the years, the role and values of competition law regimes have certainly not been static.[1022] This remark equally applies to the methods through which competition law has attempted to achieve its goals. That said, it is a common observation within the literature that the 'modernised' version of competition law has progressively espoused the notion that neoclassical economics should inform the quiescence of competition law norms; hence, as Lianos explains, economics has become the absolute guide in competition law's implementation.[1023] The primary concern of neoclassical price theory lies in '*allocative and productive efficiency, reduced prices and increased output*' and a rationale that individual freedom(s) can be best guaranteed through a competitive market.[1024] In this context, efficiency is exclusively perceived as '*a market*

1018. Countouris, N., Rainone, S. (2021), *Collective Bargaining and Self-Employed Workers: The Need for a Paradigm Shift*, ETUI Policy Brief, 3.
1019. *See* for instance: Hamner, K. J., *The Globalization of Law: International Merger Control and Competition Law in the United States, the European Union, Latin America and China*, 11 Journal of Transnational Law & Policy 385 n. 2 (2002), 385-406; Patel, K. and Schweitzer, H. eds, *The Historical Foundations of EU Competition Law* (Oxford Scholarship Online 2013), available at: https://oxford.universitypressscholarship.com/view/10.1093/acprof:oso/9780199665358.001.0001/acprof-9780199665358 (accessed 29 June 2022); Gerbrandy, A., *Rethinking Competition Law within the European Economic Constitution*, 57 Journal of Common Law Studies 127 n. 1 (2019), 127-142.
1020. *Supra*, Davidov (2004), 15; *see also* Fox, E.M., *The Modernization of Antitrust: A New Equilibrium*, 66 Cornell Law Review 1140 n. 6 (1981), 1140-1192.
1021. Deutscher, E., Makris, S., *Exploring the Ordoliberal Paradigm: The Competition-Democracy Nexus*, 181 Competition Law Review 807 (2016), 807-859; Gerber, D. J., *Constitutionalizing the Economy: German Neo-liberalism, Competition Law and the 'New' Europe*, 42 The American Journal of Comparative Law 83 n. 1 (1994), 25-83; Waller, S.W., *Antitrust and Democracy*, 46 Florida State University Law Review 807 n. 4 (2019), 807-860.
1022. *See*, for instance, Bostoen, F. (2021), 'Abuse of Platform Power: Leveraging Conduct in Digital Markets under EU Competition Law and Beyond'. PhD, available at: https://lirias.kuleuven.be/3439114?limo=0 (accessed 7 August 2022).
1023. Lianos, I., *Polycentric Competition Law*, 71 Current Legal Problems 161 n. 1 (2018), 162.
1024. Amber, D. 'Competition Law and Human Rights: A Complex Relationship', *Wirtschaft und Wettbewerb* Online Article (2021), 1, available at SSRN: https://ssrn.com/abstract=3915662 (accessed 7 August 2022).

mechanism in which the price manifests itself where supply meets demand'.[1025] Against this background, competition law, *inter alia*, is understood as a means to decrease inequality by, for example, combating anti-competitive behaviour stemming from business practices, capable of harming the most vulnerable consumers.[1026] Thus, it mostly operates to protect individuals as consumers and at the same time, it aims at securing fair competition in the markets. Presumably, such a 'formula' will result in the best possible allocation of resources, the highest quality of products, and reduced prices. Innovation can also be highly benefited via this process.[1027] Still, questions in relation to non-price related aspects of competition law, seem to either be ignored or at least have a marginal role to play.[1028]

The dominant focus on economics for the purposes of competition law constitutes a phenomenon that has become apparent worldwide. For example, Cengiz, among others, observes that in the US, since the 1970s and the prominence of neoliberal theories, there is an agreement within the mainstream competition law and economics scholarship that economic efficiency and consumer welfare are and should continue to be the chief objectives of competition law.[1029] In this regard, consumer welfare can solely derive from lower prices. Albeit not identical in many respects,[1030] a similar dimension appears to be also present with respect to EU competition law, which this section will mostly touch upon. The motto of a 'more economic approach' put forward by the European Commission since the early 1990s, following the reform of competition laws, seems to be still present, with only some exceptions to be recently observed.[1031] It has been argued that such a trajectory has gradually departed from 'older' theories on competition law, where the countering of economic power was traced both in its impact on economic freedoms, as well as to the fact that unfair competition practices can possibly lead to unfair societal outcomes.[1032] A more 'holistic' approach, therefore, used to be embraced, which also included broader non-price-related considerations. This is also confirmed by the CJEU, which as Ezrachi mentions, has not entirely directed its focus on considerations related to consumer

1025. *Supra*, Cengiz (2020), 2; The author refers to the work of: Buch-Hansen, H., Wigger, A., *Revisiting 50 Years of Market-Making: The Neoliberal Transformation of European Competition Policy*, 17 Review of International Political Economy 20 (2010), 20.
1026. *Supra*, Davidov (2004), 13-16.
1027. Encaoua, D., Hollander, A., *Competition Policy and Innovation*, 18 Oxford Review of Economic Policy 63 n. 1 (2002), 63-79.
1028. *Supra*, Lianos (2018), 161-165.
1029. *Supra*, Cengiz (2020), 3.
1030. For instance, unlike the US, EU competition law has been developed with the purpose of, *inter alia*, assuring market integration among the different EU countries. For a comparison between EU and US competition laws, *see*: Fox, E., *US and EU Competition Law: A Comparison* (Edward M. Graham and David Richardson eds, *Global Competition Policy*, Institute for International Economics 1997); K Kolasky, W. J., *What Is Competition? A Comparison of US and European Perspectives*, 49 The Antitrust Bulletin 29 n. 1-2 (2004), 29-53.
1031. *See*, for instance, discussion in: *Supra*, Gerbrandy, (2019), 127-128; Schmidtchen, D., *Introduction* (Dieter Schmidtchen, Max Albert and Stefan Voigt eds, *The More Economic Approach to European Competition Law*, Mohr Siebeck 2007), 1-6.
1032. *Ibid.*; *see also* the seminal work of Müller-Armack, A., *The Principles of the Social Market Economy* (Peter Kolsowski ed., *The Social Market Economy: Theory and Ethics of the Economic Order*, Springer 1998).

welfare and economic efficiencies.[1033] For example, the Luxemburg Court has emphasised the importance of turning away '*competition from being distorted to the detriment of the public interest, individual undertakings and consumers, thereby ensuring the well-being of the European Union*'.[1034]

As also explained in Chapter 2, restrictions on the right of weak self-employed workers, dependent upon their principals, including platform workers, to bargain collectively, constitute an illustrative example of the monocentric approach (i.e., price-related), adopted by mainstream competition laws. The vulnerability of many of these workers, the inequality of their bargaining power, as well as their weak economic position within the labour market, are all considerations that to a great extent seem to be neglected in the debate on why these workers should be able to exercise the right in question. Therefore, it can be claimed that a monocentric dimension appears to turn a blind eye to what actually happens during the labour and production processes before consumers meet the products and services in question.[1035] Furthermore, as Cengiz points out, competition laws fail to notice that '*consumers and workers are essentially the same group of people and one's welfare cannot be increased or decreased without affecting the others*'.[1036] Some authors also indicate that competition law's focus on predominantly price-centric considerations neglects to address rights-based considerations founded on procedural fairness and social justice.[1037]

Of course, some might argue that at the EU level, the recent Guidelines on competition rules and collective bargaining proposed by the Commission, as described above,[1038] are somehow deviating from a single-centred approach that exclusively focuses on consumer welfare and efficiency.[1039]

The issued Guidelines, at least to a certain extent, seem to accept the significance of collective bargaining for a number of solo self-employed workers in ameliorating their working conditions by correcting the imbalance in their bargaining power in relation to their counterparts. Thus, a rationale is advanced, which besides the protection of consumers' economic freedom(s), also attempts to address issues stemming from the weak bargaining position of certain types of workers. They enshrine, for instance, that '*in some cases, solo self-employed persons who are not in a situation comparable to that of workers may nevertheless have difficulties in influencing their working conditions because they are in a weak negotiating position vis-à-vis their*

1033. Ezrachi, A. (2018), *The Goals of EU Competition Law and the Digital Economy*, Oxford Legal Studies Research Paper No. 17/2018, Oxford, 5-8.
1034. *Case C-209/10 Post Danmark A/S v. Konkurrencerådet* [2012] ECLI, para. 22.
1035. *Supra*, Cengiz (2020), 2.
1036. *Ibid.*
1037. Jedličková, B., *Beyond the Economic Approach: Why Pluralism Is Important in Competition Law*, 37 U. Queensland LJ 41 n. 1 (2018), 42, the author refers to the work of Guttuso, L. (2016), 'In Pursuit of Cartels – a Critical Analysis of the Dynamics Between Public and Private Enforcement' (Confirmation of PhD Candidature Document, The University of Queensland).
1038. *See* Chapter 3.
1039. *See* Rainone, S., *Labour Rights Beyond Employment Status: Insights from the Competition Law Guidelines on Collective Bargaining* (Tindara Addabbo, Edoardo Ales, Ylenia Curzi, Tomasso Fabri, Olga Rymkevich, Iacapo Senatori eds, *Defining and Protecting Autonomous Work*, Palgrave 2022), 167-199.

counterparty/-ies'.[1040] Thereby, '*collective agreements can be a legitimate means to correct the imbalance in bargaining power between the two sides*'.[1041] In such situations, the Commission will not intervene against the conclusion of these types of agreements.[1042] These provisions indeed seem to move away from an exclusive focus on price-related considerations. This shows that competition policy can also pursue its efficiency goals while considering socially embedded concerns.

At the same time, from a historical perspective, a discussion on collective bargaining should be not seen in isolation from deliberations around efficiency rather than the opposite. Indeed, besides other functions one might observe (e.g., correcting the democratic deficit in employment relationships), collective bargaining laws were indeed designed and promoted in order to limit industrial conflicts, which were apparently perceived as having a detrimental effect on efficiency.[1043] To this extent, the fields of collective bargaining and competition law are not to be conceived per se in opposite terms.

It is quite soon to argue with confidence that EU competition law has completely abandoned its monocentric approach, an observation that can be highly relevant for the effective protection of collective bargaining as a human right. It has been already discussed that the adopted Commission Guidelines, initiating from a competition law perspective by dictating the occasions in which EU competition law, will not interfere with the conclusion of collective agreements signed by such workers. However, as noted, some of the prescribed conditions traced in the Commission's Guidelines will still make it difficult for some solo-self-employed persons, including a number of platform workers, to be covered by collective bargaining schemes.[1044] The Guidelines, moreover, appear to pay lip service to the nature of the right to collective bargaining as a fundamental human right. Arguably, as far as the EU legal order is concerned, such a discussion, namely the ability of EU competition law to pursue social progress, is extremely relevant to the values and objectives set out by the EU 'constitutional' apparatus.[1045]

In particular, Article 2 of the Treaty on European Union (TEU) enshrines that: '[t]*he EU's founding values are "human dignity, freedom, democracy, equality, the rule of law and respect for human rights, including the rights of persons belonging to minorities"*'.[1046] In turn, Article 3 TEU sets out the objectives of the Union, where there is a direct link to the social aspects the latter aims at promoting. Indeed, Article 3(3) makes an explicit reference to the pursuit of a highly competitive social market

1040. *Supra*, EU Commission's issued Guidelines (2022), para. 32.
1041. *Ibid.*, para. 33.
1042. *Ibid.*, para. 32.
1043. *Supra*, Davidov (2004), 10-16; Schiek, D., Gideon, A., *Outsmarting the Gig-Economy Through Collective Bargaining – EU Competition Law as a Barrier to Smart Cities?*, 32 International Review of Law, Computers & Technology 275 n. 2-3 (2018), 283.
1044. In theory the Guidelines should cover all platform workers, but the ambiguous definition given to platform work can raise issues. *See* analysis in Chapter 3.
1045. Holmes, S., *Climate Change, Sustainability and Competition Law*, 8 Journal of Antitrust Enforcement 354 n. 2 (2020), 354-405.
1046. TEU, Article 2.

economy and social progress as core EU objectives.[1047] To this extent, economic and social objectives should coexist in order to protect the values underpinning the EU. Article 7 TEU is clear on that via its imperative wording: '[t]*he Union shall ensure consistency between its policies and activities taking all of its objectives into account*'.[1048] That said, EU competition law is one of the multiple tools used to promote and safeguard the values and goals enshrined within the wider EU constitutional order. Since 2009, part of the latter is also considered to be the CFREU, which enshrines both the rights to freedom of association and collective bargaining (Articles 12 and 28 respectively). Importantly, as Lianos, Countouris and De Stefano have observed,[1049] the Charter in its Article 52(3) mentions that:

> In so far as this Charter contains rights which correspond to rights guaranteed by the Convention for the Protection of Human Rights and Fundamental Freedoms, the meaning and scope of those rights shall be the same as those laid down by the said Convention.[1050]

As previously discussed, the ECtHR has interpreted Article 11 ECHR as having a broad personal scope of application. Thus far, the distinction between employment and self-employment has not been relevant for the purposes of the Article at issue. But even if the Strasbourg Court had openly opposed the right of self-employed persons to bargain collectively, this would not necessarily prevent the Union from allowing the enjoyment of this right to self-employed workers. The last sentence of Article 52(3) enshrines that: '*this provision shall not prevent Union law providing more extensive protection*'.[1051] In other words, as Bogg explains, protections afforded under the ECHR should be seen as the 'floor', rather than the 'ceiling'.[1052] Such an observation brings us to another important provision included in the CFREU. More specifically, its Preamble reaffirms that:

> '[...] *the rights as they result, in particular, from the constitutional traditions and international obligations common to the Member States, the European Convention for the Protection of Human Rights and Fundamental Freedoms, the Social Charters adopted by the Union and by the Council of Europe* [...]'. In this regard, '*the Charter will be interpreted by the courts of the Union and the Member States with due regard to the explanations prepared under the authority of the Praesidium of the Convention which drafted the Charter and updated under the responsibility of the Praesidium of the European Convention*'.[1053] The Explanations relating to the CFREU make an explicit reference to Article 6 ESC. In other words, Article 28 CFREU is based on Article 6 ESC and the interpretation given to it by the supervisory body of the ESC. As previously explained, the ECSR in *ICTU v. Ireland*, via a contextual and substantive interpretation (as those identified by Bogg), has espoused a broad personal scope in relation to the application of Article 6, by pointing out that the right to collective bargaining should be available to self-employed workers. This

1047. TEU, Article 3.
1048. TEU, Article 7.
1049. *Supra*, Lianos, Countouris and De Stefano (2019), 308.
1050. CFREU, Article 52(3).
1051. *Ibid.*
1052. *Supra*, Bogg (2022), 49.
1053. CFREU, Preamble.

> approach is considered necessary in order to address the vulnerability of many of these workers, as well as to redress the imbalance of powers towards their counterparts.[1054] On top of that, such an understanding is also consistent with the Preamble's reference to '*international obligations common to the Member States*'. All EU countries are members of the ILO; hence they should fulfil their obligations under Conventions Nos. 87 and 90. As noted, the ILO's supervisory bodies have multiple times highlighted that self-employed workers should also be able to bargain collectively.

All in all, it has been pointed out that '*competition law cannot be exclusively conceived through a price-centric approach*' [and] '*it should also be oriented to pursuing the social objectives of the Union*',[1055] as those are enshrined in its constitutional order. A HRBA can be important in this respect, as it can inform the actions of policymakers in adopting a social exemption protecting self-employed workers from strict antitrust laws, in line with different sources of supranational and international law, such as the ILO and the ESC. In a similar vein, a HRBA can also guide the actions of the courts and competition authorities in espousing a different hermeneutic approach when dealing with the question of who should be allowed to bargain collectively.

Having said that, a HRBA towards the right to collective bargaining should not be seen as conflicting with the broader objectives of competition law. Davidov, for instance, explains that the protection of democratic values constitutes a concern for both competition law policies and collective bargaining.[1056] Furthermore, as noted, efficiency is a key objective for competition law, but it can also be seen as a goal for collective bargaining. It has been observed that the concertation of power and resources in the hands of few not only worsens inequality between workers and poor working conditions within specific segments of the labour market, but it also has negative macroeconomic effects. It indeed leads to lower levels of employment and, thereby, an overall lower economic growth.[1057] Arguably, such an observation is illustrative as to why economic justifications and social concerns should be equally addressed, even when the discussion takes place through the lenses of competition law.

Without a doubt, the aforementioned discussion cannot be detached from the actual realities within the platform economy. As it is discussed in different parts of this research, platform giants have assumed the de facto role of powerful monopolies, which can preclude new entrants from coming into the labour market.[1058] Therefore, platform work, on top of problems related to its often poor working conditions, can also induce a negative spiral of competition, a situation which as Schiek and Gideon point

1054. LOI, P., *The Boundaries between Collective Agreements and Statutory Legislation* (José M. Boto and Elisabeth Brameshuber eds, *Collective Bargaining and the Gig Economy A Traditional Tool for New Business Models*, Hart Publishing, 2022), 35.
1055. *Supra*, Rainone and Countouris (2021), 5.
1056. The author argues that democracy is a primary concern of collective bargaining, but it can also be seen as one of the objectives of competition law (*Supra*, Davidov (2004), 16).
1057. Posner, E.A., *How Antitrust Failed Workers* (Oxford University Press 2021), 2-3.
1058. Choudary, S.P. (2017), 'The Dangers of Platform Monopolies', *Knowledge* (online source), 8 May 2017, available at: https://knowledge.insead.edu/entrepreneurship/dangers-platform-monopolies (accessed 18 August 2022).

out, '*collective bargaining was designed to interrupt, and indeed to convert*'.[1059] Offering the right to collective bargaining to those who need it the most not only can profit workers per se, but it can also be beneficial from a competition law perspective. Effective protection of collective bargaining rights can level the plain field between companies by ensuring respect for minimum labour standards and, concomitantly, increasing the productivity of businesses.[1060] Take, for instance, the Hilfr, or Hermes collective agreements, discussed above.[1061] They constitute clear examples where agreements between undertakings and just some freelancers (cleaners and riders respectively) can hardly be perceived as distorting competition.[1062] In fact, both Hilfr's and Hermes' CEOs have expressed their confidence that their business model offers '*innovative ways of working to meet peoples' differing needs*',[1063] both in relation to consumers and workers.[1064]

5.3.4 The Implications of a HRBA on the Limitation of Managerial Prerogatives

As it has been argued elsewhere,[1065] a HRBA becomes even more relevant considering the phenomenon of managerial prerogatives, along with the consequences they can have on workers. Indeed, '*the employment relationship is by definition based on the social and legal power of one contractual party vis-à-vis the other*'.[1066] Employers, notably, are able to use their superior bargaining power, stemming, among other things, from contract law and employment regulation, in order to dictate various

1059. *Supra*, Schiek and Gideon (2018), 285; *see also* OECD, *Employment outlook 2019: The Future of Work*, Paris, OECD, 2019, 204.
1060. Albeit not concerning platform workers, but other types of vulnerable self-employed workers, the ESCR in *ICTU v. Ireland*, made a similar observation: '[...], *the Committee does not consider that permitting the self-employed workers in question to bargain collectively and conclude collective agreements, including in respect of remuneration, would have an impact on competition in trade that would be significantly different from the impact on such competition of collective agreements concluded solely in respect of dependent workers (employees)*'. (para. 100). Moreover, '[w]*here providers of labour have no substantial influence on the content of contractual conditions, they must be given the possibility of improving the power imbalance through collective bargaining*'. (para. 38).
1061. *See* Chapter 4.
1062. *Supra*, Monti (2021), 18.
1063. Muller-Heyndyk, R. (2019), 'Hermes to offer drivers "self-employed-plus" status', *Hrmagazine* (online magazine), 4 February 2019, available at: https://www.hrmagazine.co.uk/content/news/hermes-to-offer-drivers-self-employed-plus-status (accessed 18 August 2022).
1064. As explained, the Hilfr collective agreement was materially undermined by the Danish competition authorities, which also relied on rules established under EU competition law (*see* Chapter 4). Things in relation to the future of the GMB agreement are less clear, especially due to the fact that the UK, since 'Brexit' has left the jurisdiction of the CJEU: *see* Boto, M.J.M., *Collective Bargaining and the Gig Economy: Reality and Possibilities* (José M. Boto and Elisabeth Brameshuber eds, *Collective Bargaining and the Gig Economy a Traditional Tool for New Business Models*, Hart Publishing, 2022), 14.
1065. De Stefano, V. (2017), *Non-Standard Work and Limits on Freedom of Association: a Human Rights- Based Approach*, International Law Journal, 46 n. 2, 185-207.
1066. De Stefano, V., Aloisi, A., *Fundamental Labour Rights, Platform Work and Human Rights Protection of Non-standard Workers* (Janice R. Bellace and Beryl ter Haar eds, *Research Handbook on Labour, Business and Human Rights Law*, Elgar Publishing 2019), 369.

features of employment, such as the setting of wages to specific levels, or the manner in which the work has to be performed. To put it another way, employers have the discretion to make all work-related decisions, unless contractual agreements, statutes or court decisions say otherwise.[1067] For these reasons, it has been claimed that managerial prerogatives are not merely the outcome of economic and social phenomena, like the inequality of bargaining power and who possesses the means of production. As De Stefano and Aloisi argue, they can also be found in contract law and employment regulation, granting employers excessive authority over their workers.[1068] The often exorbitant concentration of powers in the hands of employers, as expressed through the contract of employment,[1069] have made some authors liken this type of authority to that of a government in an undemocratic regime. For instance, Racabi, by contemplating the workplace sovereignty of employers in the US, likens the latter's powers to those possessed by kings.[1070] Elisabeth Anderson, furthermore, describes workplaces as authoritarian private governments, where the phenomenon of managerial prerogatives can extend far beyond the State and public powers.[1071] Against this background, according to the same author, workers are to a certain degree 'unfree'; this is due to the fact that the excessive powers held by employers permit them to dictate workers' lives not solely within workplaces in a strict sense, but also as far as their private sphere is concerned.[1072] In the context of the new world of work, such powers can be further exacerbated. As explained, the use of new technologies, such as algorithmic management, has enabled employers to screen the work pace and intensity of work via the use of pervasive monitoring systems.[1073] Not only this but as De Stefano points out, workers can now '*face a 360-degree monitoring of their behaviour, that extends control over their bodies and minds and their most private sphere, once again to an extent unheard of in the past*'.[1074]

Thus, as Hugh Collins observes, the authoritarian structure often embedded within employment relationships seems to be '*at odds with the commitment in liberal societies to values such as liberty, equal respect, and respect for privacy*'.[1075] Having said

1067. Racabi, G., *Abolish the Employer Prerogative, Unleash Work Law*, 43 Berkeley Journal of Employment and Labor Law 79 n. 1 (2022), 79; *see also* Collins, H., *Is the Contract of Employment Illiberal?* (Hugh Collins, Gillian Lester and Virginia Mantouvalou eds, *Philosophical Foundations of Labour Law*, Oxford University Press 2018), 49-51.
1068. *Ibid.*
1069. As noted, in the entirety of legal systems, the contract of employment constitutes the principal regulatory tool for a allocating rights and obligations between an employee and an employer.
1070. *Supra*, Racabi (2022), 79.
1071. Anderson, E., *Private Government: How Employers Rule Our Lives and Why We Don't Talk about It* (Princeton University Press 2017).
1072. *Ibid.*; *see also* Estlund, C., *Rethinking Autocracy at Work*, 131 Harvard Law Review 795 n. 3 (2018), 795-826.
1073. Pervasive monitoring systems and surveillance constitute phenomena that expand much beyond workplaces. For an analysis on these very issues *see* (Srnicek, N., *Platform Capitalism* (Polity Press 2017)).
1074. De Stefano, V., *'Masters and Servers': Collective Labour Rights and Private Government in the Contemporary World of Work*, 36 International Journal of Comparative Labour Law and Industrial Relations 425 n. 4 (2020), 436; *see also* Ajunwa I., Crawford K., Schultz J., *Limitless Worker Surveillance*, 105 California Law Review 735 n. 3 (2017), 735-776.
1075. *Supra*, Collins (2018), 48.

that, although many platform workers are not hooked on an employment contract and platforms are, thus, not legally bound by labour law to enforce such managerial prerogatives; platforms do contractually vest themselves with managerial powers and they share many of the characteristics of a typical employment relationship. As noted, platform operators can, *inter alia*, determine the remuneration of workers, supervise their work and have the ability to delete workers' accounts from their apps when they consider that the work is not performed according to the agreed terms and conditions of the contract at issue.

Moreover, as De Stefano argues, the situation for platform workers and other types of NSFE can be even more complex compared to typical employees, as within atypical forms of work such managerial prerogatives can be further magnified.[1076] Workers in NSFE, including platform workers, find themselves in a weaker position compared to workers in standard employment relationships. This can occur for a number of reasons. For example, as noted, workers in temporary contracts, irrespective of their employment status, can be exposed to an 'implicit-threat mechanism', a notion that underlines their hesitation to properly exercise their contractual and labour rights due to a fear that their contract will not be renewed, or lengthened.[1077] This equally applies to casual work arrangements, like those in the platform economy, where platforms are able to punish 'unwanted activism' by simply erasing the profile of workers from their database, without any justification. Whereas employees can be protected from unfair dismissal laws in instances where their dismissal was not properly justified by the employer, in most cases this is not true in relation to workers who find themselves outside an employment relationship.

In addition, workers in NSFE have a lower probability to unionise because of further practical reasons, *inter alia*, such as frequent turnovers and a limited attachment to a single workplace and fissured workplaces. Furthermore, as earlier developed, many traditional trade unions, up until recently, were also hesitant to engage such workers in their actions.[1078] This situation can result in less bargaining power in negotiations for payments and a subsequent wage gap and, more generally, it can lead to inferior working conditions. Finally, as already illustrated, workers in the 'grey zone' between dependent employment and self-employment, on top of practical obstacles, also face severe legal restrictions in instances where their activities clash with other areas of law, like competition law. As a result of these challenges, the collective power of such workers is considerably limited and often non-existent compared to employees. In a situation as such, extensive prerogatives can indeed interfere with workers' dignity as human beings, especially within the modern world of work, an issue that as explained throughout this research, is also pertinent from a human rights point of view.

Considering all the above, a HRBA towards collective labour rights can play an essential role in constraining managerial prerogatives and correcting part of the

1076. *Supra*, De Stefano (2017), 191-198.
1077. *Ibid.*
1078. Heery, E., *Unions and the Organizing Turn: Reflections after 20 Years of Organising Works*, 26 The Economic and Labour Relations Review 545 n. 4 (2015), 545-560; Gumbrell-McCormick, R. (2011), *European Trade Unions and 'Atypical' Workers*, Industrial Relations Journal, 42 n. 3, 293-310.

democratic deficit that is observed within employment relationships. As Weiler has highlighted, unionisation and the exercise of collective labour rights can introduce a form of political democracy into the workplace, subjecting the parties involved in an employment relationship alike to the rule of law.[1079] Similarly, Gramano and Aloisi observe that collective labour rights have been of paramount importance in limiting managerial prerogatives, including the monitoring of workers.[1080] Indeed, it is reiterated that collective bargaining, as an essential element of the freedom of association, constitutes the most effective means through which workers can achieve a countervailing power to the employer.[1081] According to Davidov, '*this does not imply that both parties to the negotiations* [will] *possess equal bargaining power* [...]; [still] *the imbalance of power can be expected to be much less dramatic under a regime of collective bargaining*'.[1082] Indeed, as discussed, by effectively using this right, trade unions and other workers' associations have managed to raise their concerns and demands at work, as well as to actively participate in the organisation of the workplace. Moreover, its exercise has played a vital role in generating better jobs, increasing wages, and improving working conditions more generally, in various aspects of working life.[1083] Similar observations can also be made for the right to strike, which has also been acknowledged as a crucial component of workplace democracy.[1084] It constitutes the sole way through which workers can exert pressure on employers to improve labour conditions; hence, as in the case of collective bargaining, the re-establishment of the imbalance of powers between the negotiating parties occurs. To this extent, as previously noted, the right to strike is not perceived '*as a breakdown of collective bargaining; it is* [rather] *the indispensable cornerstone of that process*'.[1085]

All in all, it has long been claimed that one of the chief goals of labour law is '*to be a countervailing force to counteract the inequality of bargaining power, which is inherent and must be inherent in the employment relationship*'.[1086] Such a goal, as it was argued at the end of Chapter 2, is inextricably linked to the idea that labour is not a commodity. In order for this notion to be still applicable in a modern context, a HRBA towards collective labour rights is essential, considering the function of these rights as discussed above.

1079. Weiler, P., *Reconcilable Differences: New Directions in Canadian Labour Law* (Carswell 1980), 31-32.
1080. Aloisi, A., Gramano, E., *Workers Without Workplaces and Unions Without Unity: Non-Standard Forms of Employment, Platform Work and Collective Bargaining* (Valeria Pulignano and Frank Hendrickx eds, *Employment Relations in the 21st Century: Challenge for Theory and Research in a Changing World of Work*, Kluwer Law International 2020), 43-44.
1081. Aloisi, A. (2019), *Negotiating the Digital Transformation of Work: Non-Standard Workers' Voice, Collective Rights and Mobilisation Practices in the Platform Economy*, EUI Working Paper No. 3. San Domenico di Fiesole, European University Institute, 6.
1082. *Supra*, Davidov (2004), 4.
1083. OECD 2019; *see also* ILO, *Social Dialogue Report*, ILO, Geneva (2022).
1084. Nkabinde, B., *The Right to Strike, an Essential Component of Workplace Democracy: Its Scope and Global Economy*, 24 Maryland Journal of International Law 270 n. 1 (2009), 270-282.
1085. These words belong to: Paul Clark, U.S. Labour Historian, 1989.
1086. Davies, P. and Freedland, M., *Kahn-Freund's Labour and the Law*, (Stevens & Sons 1983), 18.

5.3.5 The Implications of a HRBA Towards Collective Labour Rights on Other Human Rights at Work

The previous section highlighted the importance of a HRBA towards collective labour rights in restricting the excessive managerial prerogatives often held by employers. In turn, it can be argued that a HRBA can also result in enhanced protection with respect to other human rights at work, a proposition that underlines the indivisibility, interdependence, and interrelation of human rights.[1087]

Undeniably, the threats identified within modern workplaces are not solely limited to the enjoyment of collective labour rights. For instance, as already noted, algorithmic management, if not properly regulated, can result in various instances of discrimination, both direct and indirect. Due to the frequent lack of transparency on how they are actually programmed and function, algorithms can be the carriers of human discriminatory biases.[1088] Not only this but according to De Stefano and Taes, there are also occasions that their '*decision-making systems are too rigid and unable to differentiate between situations that would warrant different decision outcomes*'.[1089] What the authors describe is supported by the recent ruling of the Bologna Tribunal, in Italy. The latter ruled that the algorithm used by Deliveroo indirectly discriminated against workers (e.g., by deleting them from the app) who after having booked a certain working slot via the company's algorithm, later decided to cancel their shifts for legitimate reasons.[1090] Such reasons could be related to an urgent medical condition, or workers' constitutionally protected right to take collective action.

In addition to violations of the right to not be discriminated against, contemporary workplaces can put into question the enjoyment of other human rights, such as workers' right to privacy. As noted, through the use of AI systems, employers have the unprecedented ability to gain access to intimate information on workers' private worlds.[1091] Furthermore, intense monitoring practices can have an adverse impact on workers' occupational health and safety, with high levels of stress being just one of the immediate consequences, which increases workers' psychosocial risks.[1092]

1087. As a matter of law, the 1993 Vienna Declaration and Programme of Action is clear on this, by emphasising the thesis on indivisibility, interdependence and interrelation of human rights. Furthermore, since 1979 and the case of *Airey v. Ireland*, the ECtHR has recognised that along with civil and political rights, national authorities should take positive steps to safeguard socioeconomic norms as well (*Airey v. Ireland*, App. No. 6289/73 [1979]).

1088. *See* European Economic and Social Committee (2017), *Opinion of the European Economic and Social Committee on 'Artificial intelligence – The consequences of artificial intelligence on the (digital) single market, production, consumption, employment and society' (own-initiative opinion)*, Official Journal of the European Union, C 288, 31 August 2017.

1089. De Stefano, V., Taes, S. (2021), *Algorithmic Management and Collective Bargaining*, ETUI Research Paper, Brussels, 7.

1090. For an analysis, *see* Gramano, E., Kullmann, M., *Algorithmic Discrimination, the Role of GPS, and the Limited Scope of EU Non-discrimination Law* (Valerio De Stefano, Ilda Durri, Charalampos Stylogiannis and Mathias Wouters eds, *A Research Agenda for the Gig-Economy and Society*, Edward Elgar Publishing 2022), 55-57.

1091. *See* Chapter 1.

1092. TUC, (2021) *Dignity at work and the AI revolution: a TUC manifesto*, London, Trade Union Congress, available at: https://www.tuc.org.uk/sites/default/files/2021-03/The_AI_ Revolu tion_20121_Manifesto_AW.pdf (accessed 21 June 2022).

Even though this research does not intend to analyse these issues in much more detail, it should be, nonetheless, stressed that workers' restrictions on their fundamental collective labour rights can also impact the enjoyment of individual human rights. To put it otherwise, an effective application of collective labour rights via a HRBA can mitigate the risks towards individual human rights. For example, literature observes that the right to strike has multiple times been brought to the fore as the means of giving effect to the enjoyment of civil and political rights at work.[1093] Furthermore, as was previously mentioned, workplaces with high coverage of collective bargaining are more insulated from instances of discrimination.[1094] In a similar vein, research also highlights the importance of collective agreements in relation to the processing of personal data rights and the overall function of algorithmic decision-making.[1095] In the context of the platform economy, illustrative is the Hilfr collective agreement that as noted, enshrines provisions which explicitly stipulate that the publication of personal should, *inter alia*, contain voluntary and informed consent from workers using the platform in question. As a matter of law, the essential role of collective bargaining regarding data protection and the right to privacy has also been identified in the text of Article 88 of the EU GDPR.[1096]

In this respect, what is also important is the 'preventive' nature of the right to bargain collectively. While traditional human rights redress mechanisms usually apply after a related violation has taken place, collective labour rights and specifically collective bargaining, can offer an *ex ante* protection towards workers' rights. According to De Stefano and Taes, this function is particularly significant within modern workplaces, considering the transformative use of new technologies; thereby, collective agreements can reduce the risks that AI-enabled surveillance based on algorithms can pose on workers' fundamental human rights.[1097] What the authors describe also appears to be accepted by recent initiatives which have been taken at the domestic level. For instance, in the Green Paper on the Future of Work in Portugal, it is suggested to:

> encourage, in particular, the regulation of the use of algorithms in the context of collective bargaining, involving the social partners and ensuring the treatment of the matter at the level of collective agreements, in order to ensure adequate use of AI and to reflect the needs specific to each sector.[1098]

1093. *See* for instance, Ewing, K., *Laws Against Strikes Revisited* (Catherine Bernard, Simon Deakin and Gillian S. Morris eds, *The Future of Labour Law*, Liber Amocorum Bob Hepple QC, Hart Publishing 2004), 50-51.
1094. *See* Chapter 4.2.
1095. *Supra*, De Stefano and Taes (2021); Todolí-Signes, A., *Algorithms, Artificial Intelligence and Automated Decisions Concerning Workers and the Risks of Discrimination: The Necessary Collective Governance of Data Protection*, 25 Transfer: European Review of Labour and Research 465 n. 4 (2019), 465-481.
1096. *Supra*, De Stefano (2020), 441.
1097. *Supra*, De Stefano and Taes (2021), 9-10.
1098. Green Paper on the Future of Work, 2021, available at: https://www.portugal.gov.pt/pt/gc23 (accessed 11 July 2022). Legal initiatives that highlight the importance of collective bargaining and social partners' involvement in the shaping of new technologies at work, can be equally observed in other countries, such as Germany (e.g., Platform Industrie 4.0). For an analysis *see*: Schroeder, W. (2016), *Germany's Industry 4.0 strategy*, Friedrich-Ebert-Stiftung Report.

All in all, as Miranda Boto explains in a recent publication, the regulation of AI through the conclusion of collective agreements can indeed, *inter alia*, reinforce principles that ensure the protection of privacy and personal data rights, non-discrimination entitlements, as well as guarantee transparency and the explicability of systems that rely on algorithms.[1099]

5.3.6 Other (Non-Legal) Benefits of a HRBA: Attracting the Support of External Actors

As seen, the rapid expansion of platform businesses and their associated power within modern labour markets can be attributed to a variety of reasons. As a matter of law, platform operators have profited from the existing limitations of protective labour laws around the world, let alone social security systems. As such, they have managed to avoid tremendous costs related to employment and labour protections, by leaving a considerable number of their workforce outside the realm of an employment relationship and its related benefits. Of course, as examined, their success would not be possible without the contribution, both intentional and unintentional, of a number of different actors, such as consumers. For instance, it is observed that consumers can play a multifold role, capable of boosting the powerful position of platforms.[1100] Their important role is not solely confined to considerations related to how much people make use of platform apps, or reasons related to consumption in general. This is to say that, on many occasions, platform businesses have crow-sourced workers' quality control in the hands of consumers through the use of rating systems. It is then up to the algorithms to decide whether the tasks are completed in a successful manner according to the terms and conditions of the contract at issue. In this context, consumers' evaluation(s) are used to reward and, or punish workers.[1101] Not only this but the very same evaluations are also used by platforms in order to '*improve their management algorithms with a view to maximise revenues*'.[1102]

Furthermore, as it was highlighted above, there are instances where consumers have stood as an obstacle towards protective regulations that can indeed threaten the tactics of platforms to exclude workers from their inclusion into an employment relationship. The recent Proposition 22 Referendum in California, as explained above, constitutes a good illustration of this phenomenon. In my view, considering the aforementioned discussion, a human rights discourse, besides any possible (purely) legal ramifications, can also assist platform workers and their unions in building partnerships capable of challenging the manner in which platform businesses are operating. As Kevin Koblen has pointed out:

1099. *Supra*, Boto, 17.
1100. For instance, *see* Culpepper, P.D., Thelen, K., *Are We All Amazon Primed? Consumers and the Politics of Platform Power*, 53 Comparative Political Studies 288 n. 2 (2020), 288-318.
1101. Muldoon, J., Raekstad, P., *Algorithmic Domination in the Gig Economy*, European Journal of Political Theory 1 (2022), 13, available at: https://doi.org/10.1177/14748851221082078 (accessed 30 May 2022).
1102. Engels, S., Sherwood, M. (2019), *What If We All Worked Gigs in the Cloud? The Economic Relevance of Digital Labour Platforms*, European Economy Discussion Paper, No. 099, 14.

> framing labor rights as human rights [...] shifts the labor discourse from economics and special interest politics to ethics and morality [...] [as such] activists [...] seek to harness the hegemonic status of human rights discourse in order to gain public support for a number of legal, political, and strategic objectives.[1103]

In a similar vein, Compa claims that workers can be empowered when they persuade themselves and also convince the public, that they are defending their fundamental human rights and not solely looking for a wage increase or other job-related benefits.[1104] In other words, the authors observe that a human rights rhetoric can benefit the workers themselves in the sense of pursuing a common goal and at the same time this very strategy can attract the attention of external actors, such as mainstream human rights movement(s) and traditional human rights non-governmental organisations (NGOs). To this extent, it has been observed that the latter have the ability to gain a high media profile, a factor that can be particularly helpful in order to bring unfair labour practices of businesses to the fore.[1105] Of course, as mentioned earlier and also confirmed by further literature, trade unions have been pivotal in articulating and promoting human rights claims.[1106] This is why, among their other functions, trade unions have also been characterised as another type of 'human rights organisations'.[1107] On many occasions, they have done so, by being part of wider social movements with other actors, like civil society organisations.

Some authors suggest that 'coalition partners' not only can offer additional legitimacy to trade unions' action(s), but they can also provide the latter with expertise and mobilising capacity to their campaigns.[1108] Importantly, they can '*act as a channel through which unions can contact hitherto unorganized workers*'.[1109] Such cooperation can, moreover, inform the general public, including consumers, about the adverse impacts that certain businesses may have on the enjoyment of fundamental human rights. In this regard, there is an extended literature which indicates that on a number of occasions, consumers have demonstrated their willingness to pay considerable attention to standards and practices used by companies in the production process and they may even boycott products that are produced, or offered in violation of human rights standards.[1110] Apart from consumers, human rights considerations can also be

1103. *Supra* Koblen (2009), 462.
1104. Compa, L., *Trade Unions and Human Rights* (Cynthia Soohoo, Catherine Albisa, Martha F. Davis eds, *Bringing Human Rights Home: A History of Human Rights in the United States*, Praeger Publishing 2008), 246.
1105. Spooner, D., *Trade Unions and NGOs: The Need for Cooperation*, 14 Development in Practice 19 n. 1-2 (2004), 28.
1106. Stammers, N., *Human Rights and Social Movements* (Pluto Press 2009).
1107. *Supra* Evans (2015), 466-483.
1108. Frege, C., Heery, E. Turner, L., *The New Solidarity? Trade Union Coalition-Building in Five Countries* (Carola M. Frege and John Kelly eds, *Varieties of Unionism*, Oxford, Oxford University Press 2004), 137-158; Tattersall, A., *There Is Power in Coalition: A Framework for Analysing How and When Union-Community Coalitions Are Effective and Enhance Union Power*, 16 Labour and Industry 97 n. 2 (2005), 97-112.
1109. Heery, E., Williams, S., Abbott, B., *Civil Society Organizations and Trade Unions: Cooperation, Conflict, Indifference*, 26 Work, Employment and Society 145 n. 1 (2012), 147.
1110. Weissbrodt, D., Kruger, M., *Norms on the Responsibilities of Transnational Corporations and Other Business Enterprises with Regard to Human Rights*, 97 American Journal of International Law 901 n. 4 (2003), 902.

important for other actors within labour markets. For example, there is evidence that some shareholders are seeking to purchase shares in socially responsible companies.[1111] That said, in the past, shareholder and consumer dissatisfaction and labour concerns regarding human rights violations have also led to policy changes within businesses.[1112] Thus, as Dawkins observes by also referring to the work of others, a human rights rhetoric retains an elevated public status due to its emotive urgency, capable of casting the labour rights agenda in a different light.[1113]

As examined in Chapter 4, in some instances, platform workers' mobilisation against platform businesses has already gained increased media attention. Such attention has, at least to a certain extent, exposed some of the unfair labour practices which often take place in the context of the platform economy. This is, for example, the case in relation to the wildcat strikes organised by IWGB in the UK against Deliveroo. The union's actions and the broad media coverage forced the company in question to take back its questionable proposal to switch the way of remuneration from hourly wage to payment by the task. As noted, despite this withdrawal, Deliveroo's reported abuses of labour rights and general concerns regarding the company's reputation over riders' rights, have already made a top UK fund to refuse in investing in the company. Furthermore, sometimes workers' mobilisation has also enjoyed the support of consumers. As seen above, in Greece, thousands of consumers by using the #cancel_efood, contemned Efood's hostile policy to reclassify a considerable amount of its workers to freelancers. The delivery company was forced to stand back.

Undeniably, the aforementioned and other recent developments illustrate that workers' collective actions have managed to draw the attention of a number of actors, such as consumers and shareholders. It is argued that a human rights oratory can further contribute to workers' efforts to build coalition partners which, in turn, will be able to support platform workers' demands for the enjoyment of their fundamental collective labour rights, also recognised as human rights. Against this background, platform work represents another occasion through which trade unions and other workers' associations can be recognised as human rights defenders within modern workplaces. Human rights can also be used as a source to attract workers that up until now did not wish to get involved in the union's actions. In particular, considering the diverse occupational and class features of platform workers, a human rights discourse can play the role of a common language for such workers, where some of the gaps in their social background can be bridged.

1111. *Ibid.*
1112. Frey, B.A., *The Legal and Ethical Responsibilities of Transnational Corporations in the Protection of International Human Rights*, 29 Minnesota Journal of International Law 153 (1997), 159; *see also* Wouters, J., Chanet, L., *Corporate Human Rights Responsibility: European Perspective*, 6 Northwestern University Journal of International Human Rights 262 n. 2 (2008), 262-303.
1113. *Supra*, Dawkins (2022), 7. The author also refers to the work of: Powers, M., *The Structural Organization of NGO Publicity Work: Explaining Divergent Publicity Strategies at Humanitarian and Human Rights Organizations*, 8 International Journal of Communication 90 n. 8 (2014), 90-107.

5.4 INTERMEDIATE CONCLUSIONS

This chapter, from a positive law perspective set out the legal basis for a HRBA towards the enjoyment of collective labour rights. The language used by several international labour and human rights instruments, as well as the findings and wording of their respective supervisory bodies, illustrate that such rights should enjoy a broad personal scope of application, irrespective of workers' employment status. In light of this, any limitations should take into consideration the fundamental nature of such rights. The language used by both the ILO's and the ESC's supervisory is clear on that. All workers should be eligible to exercise their right to freedom of association and collective bargaining. A similar observation can also be made for the right to collective action, including the right to strike. At the same time, one might argue that things are less straightforward with respect to the ECtHR. Still, the latter has never explicitly opinioned that only employees should enjoy the rights in question. Equally, the Court has not hesitated to find violations under Article 11 ECHR in cases that were brought by workers without an employment relationship.

This chapter, in turn, discussed some of the positive outcomes of a HRBA approach. For instance, as it was argued, the latter can be used in re-establishing the relationship between labour law and competition law. The nature of collective labour rights as human rights should guide this interplay. As noted, moreover, among other things, a HRBA towards collective labour rights can function as a shield of protection for the enjoyment of other rights at work, like discrimination-related entitlements. Human rights arguments can also assist workers in dealing with some of the practical challenges they are currently facing, such as the lack of a common identity.

That said, it would be difficult for someone to deny that the application of this approach, as well as the overall discussion of this research on the collective experiences of platform workers and other atypical workers, does not bring up considerations, which are inextricably related to the future of industrial relations. For example, albeit with limitations, the fact that platform workers and other workers in NSFE are already exercising their collective labour rights in practice entails certain implications for union movement as a whole. Arguably, furthermore, making collective labour rights, such as the right to collective bargaining, available to all workers can possibly benefit the labour movement in re-establishing its position within modern workplaces. Concomitantly though, as the next chapter discusses by using platform work as a point of reference, a mere permission for the exercise of those rights does not automatically guarantee their effective application in practice within existing national systems of industrial relations. The reasons are explained below.

CHAPTER 6

The Future of Industrial Relations and the Difficulties for the Effective Application of a HRBA

6.1 INTRODUCTION

As mentioned, the final Chapter aims to discuss the future of industrial relations based on both the findings of this research so far and by bringing to the table some additional considerations. What can the developments in the context of platform work tell us about the future of industrial relations? Why should unions see the inclusion of platform workers, and other workers in atypical work arrangements, as a chance to re-establish their power within the new world of work? That said, can existing structures of collective bargaining accommodate the needs of these types of workers, or would it be necessary to consider a different (maybe softer) form of a regulatory model of collective bargaining? After all, are industrial systems ready to allow solo-self-employed workers to exercise their fundamental right to collective bargaining, despite any restrictions stemming from competition law(s)? In light of this, can a HRBA towards collective labour rights be applied in practice, considering both the legal and practical obstacles platform workers and other weak self-employed persons are currently experiencing? These are some of the questions that this final Chapter discusses.

Bearing in mind the diversity of industrial systems around the world, it would be excessive for this research to forward specific recommendations and suggestions on how national industrial systems should solve some of their existing pathogenies, especially regarding the effective application of collective labour rights in line with international and regional (human rights) standards. The hazards of a 'one-size-fits-all solution', which can derive from a comparative analysis of industrial relations systems, have long been identified by the seminal work of Otto Kahn-Freund.[1114] In each country, collective labour relations are, *inter alia*, strongly influenced by varied political and cultural traditions, the degree and level of workers' participation, as well as the role, played by workers and employers' organisations *'as political pressure groups promoting legislation, and as rule making agencies through the procedures of collective bargaining'*.[1115] At the same time though, such a diverse landscape should not be seen as an impediment in proceeding with some crucial observations, which can shape future discussions on the field of industrial labour relations and its connection to fundamental human rights.

6.2 'THE LABOUR MOVEMENT IS DEAD, LONG LIVE THE LABOUR MOVEMENT': LESSONS TO BE LEARNED FROM PLATFORM WORKERS' RESISTANCE

Throughout the journey of this research, many of the challenges related to the contemporary world of work have been identified. Just to mention some: the use of new technologies, such as algorithmic decision-making, along with its associated risks, is now well-embedded within modern workplaces; outsourcing of activities and fragmented workplaces continue to rapidly grow, with new technological developments to indisputably facilitate these phenomena; private companies, like platform businesses, have taken advantage of various legal gaps and have emerged as powerful actors in labour markets, often enough to the detriment of their workforce; simultaneously, many of the available work-related opportunities are precarious with short-term contracts and bogus self-employment to be prevalent in this regard. Thus, as Hyman points out, *'what was once considered 'atypical' employment is now increasingly typical'*.[1116] Unsurprisingly, such developments have contributed to a plethora of discussions in relation to the future of trade unions and their undergoing transition in order to face new challenges and search for solutions for the future of workers' representation in general.[1117] Certainly, it is not the first time that someone can hear, or read about 'trade unions in transition'.[1118] Unions have a long history of adjusting to

1114. Kahn-Freund, O.O., *On Uses and Misuses of Comparative Law*, 37 Modern Law Review 27 n. 1 (1974), 1-27.

1115. *Ibid.*, 20; *see also* Weiss, M., *Challenges for Workers' Participation* (Tindara Addabbo, Edoardo Ales, Ylenia Curzi, Tomasso Fabri, Olga Rymkevich, Iacapo Senatori eds, *The Collective Dimensions of Employment Relations: Interdisciplinary Perspectives on Workers' Voices and Changing Workplace Patterns*, Palgrave Macmillan (eBook) 2021, available at: https://doi.org/10.1007/978-3-030-75532-4 (accessed 18 July 2022).

1116. Hyman, R., *What Future for Industrial Relations in Europe?*, 40 Employee Relations 569 n. 4 (2018), 571.

1117. *See* for instance, Forsyth, A., *The Future of Trade Unions and Worker Representation: The Digital Picket Line*, (Hart Publishing, 2022); Fairbrother, P., *Rethinking Trade Unionism: Union Renewal as Transition*, 26 The Economic and Labour Relations Review 561 n. 4 (2015), 561-576; Daniels, G. and McIlroy, J. eds, *Trade Unions in a Neoliberal World* (Taylor & Francis 2009).

1118. *See* for instance, Lipset, S.M. ed., *Unions in Transition: Entering the Second Century* (ICS Press 1986); Herod, A., *Theorising Unions in Transition* (John Pickles and Adrian Smith eds,

new labour and industrial transformations, and to a great extent, their actual survival depends on this adaptation.

Importantly, in order to cope with new challenges, trade unions need to look afresh. Solutions that were valid some years ago might not be valid or at least equally valid today. The differences that have developed over the years are both quantitative and qualitative. Unions' adaptation to new realities takes place within an environment where worldwide, there is a significant drop in union membership or density,[1119] albeit such an observation can considerably vary across countries and among different indicators of unionisation.[1120] Moreover, as Visser among others indicates, one of the most 'warning signs' pointing towards a further membership decline is the ageing of trade union membership; such a phenomenon is observed in the majority of developed countries.[1121] Concomitantly, the unionisation rates among young people are considerably less than what they used to be some decades ago.[1122] It has been contended that the low engagement of young workers with trade unions can be expected to have long-term consequences, as workers usually join unions at a relatively young age, shortly after they enter the labour market.[1123]

Furthermore, as noted in previous chapters, the profile of the workforce composition has undergone major alterations in most countries. For example, workers in atypical arrangements and foreign-born workers have increased in the last decades.[1124] As research indicates, a considerable number of such workers have a lower attachment to the labour force and they are less exposed to trade unions; hence, their chances to unionise are indeed less compared to full-time employees. The particular needs of these workers can be, moreover, different from the ones observed in relation to the classical employees. This is also the reason that, as Chapter 4 explained, many workers in NSFE have felt that their interests cannot be fully addressed by institutional trade unions. To this extent, some atypical workers have also chosen to join grassroots unions and other workers' associations that do not necessarily fit the traditional model of trade unions,

---

Theorising Transition: The Political Economy of Change in Central and Eastern Europe, London, Routledge 1998), 197-217.

1119. The reasons that influence trade unions' membership can be attributed to a variety of factors that have been thoroughly analysed by interdisciplinary studies, including research deriving from sociologists and political scientists. For an analysis *see*: Bryson, A., Ebbinghaus, B., Visser, J., *Introduction: Causes, Consequences and Cures of Union Decline*, 17 European Journal of Industrial Relations 97 n. 2 (2011), 97-105; Schnabel, C., Wagner, J., *Union Density and Determinants of Union Membership in 18 EU Countries: Evidence from Micro Data, 2002/03 1*, 38 Industrial Relations Journal 5 n. 1 (2007), 5-32; Clawson, D., Clawson, M.A., *What Has Happened to the US Labor Movement? Union Decline and Renewal*, 25 Annual Review of Sociology 95 (1999), 95-119.
1120. Schnabel, C., *Union Membership and Collective Bargaining: Trends and Determinants*, Discussion Paper Series (2020), IZA Institute of Labor Economics; The author refers to the comprehensive comparative study conducted by Visser, J., *Trade Unions in the Balance*, ILO ACTRAV Working Paper, Geneva (2019).
1121. Vandaele, K. (2019), *Bleak Prospects: Mapping Trade Union Membership in Europe Since 2000*, ETUI, Brussels.
1122. *Supra*, Schnabel (2020), 14.
1123. *Ibid.*
1124. *Ibid.*, 11; The author also refers to the work of: Kranendonk, M., de Beer, P., *What Explains the Union Membership Gap Between Migrants and Natives?*, 54 British Journal of Industrial Relations 846 (2016), 846-869.

as the former are often considered to be in a better position to address the needs and problems stemming from their specific job-related characteristics. These, along with other challenges, have generated the impression, as Schnabel argues, that '*unions are a vanishing species*'.[1125]

Undoubtedly, many of the issues that trade unionism faces today are not novel. As previously explained, the increasing diversity of the workforce and the difficulties in reaching out to workers in NSFE, including platform workers, are for instance, challenges that have preoccupied unions for quite some time now.[1126] Still, it can be argued that these problems appear to be exacerbated in recent times. The developments in the context of the platform economy are indicative. As seen, technology has given platform businesses the unprecedented ability to engage with a large pool of workers, both high-skilled and low-skilled.[1127] Such workers, including numerous migrant and young workers, share many different occupational and class identities and their motives can considerably vary when they decide to provide their services via a specific platform. As this type of work is characterised by intensified anonymity and isolation, especially for online workers, the obstacles for trade unions to establish communication channels with them are particularly high. Of course, as already described, the contested entrepreneurial nature of platform workers makes the circumvention of such impediments even more challenging. Against this background, at least in theory, the motivation or cohesion to organise can be pretty low, as solidarity, unity and a sense of a common identity are indeed difficult to be achieved. This is important considering that labour movements usually rely on the collective power of a large workforce that has similar shared experiences.[1128]

Having said that, in spite of the aforementioned obstacles, this research explored many instances where trade unions have shown a great interest in organising and defending platform workers, on many occasions irrespectively of their employment status.[1129] In this respect, a number of strategies have been deployed by traditional unions. As it was discussed in Chapter 4, these, *inter alia*, include the conclusion of collective agreements, litigation in front of the courts, and several campaigns so as to influence public opinion regarding the often poor working conditions of such workers. Moreover, on a number of occasions, labour activism has been tailored to the particular features of the platform economy. This is to say that unions have employed new technological tools, like online forums and social media, as a means to bring workers together and organise collective actions, a phenomenon that is often referred to as

1125. *Ibid.*, (2020), 3.
1126. *Supra*, Lipset (1986).
1127. *See* Chapter 4 section 3.
1128. Kominers, S.D., Jin, L. (2021), *A Labor Movement for the Platform Economy*, Harvard Business Review (online magazine), 24 September 2021, available at: https://hbr.org/2021/09/a-labor-movement-for-the-platform-economy (26 July 2022).
1129. As noted in Chapter 4, this is also the case in relation to other types of atypical workers. For an additional analysis also *see*: Doellgast, V., Lillie, N. and Pulignano, V. eds, *Reconstructing Solidarity: Labour Unions, Precarious Work, and the Politics of Institutional Change in Europe* (Oxford University Press 2018).

'*cyber-unionism*'.[1130] As furthermore examined, much of the successes identified thus far with respect to platform workers' over-increasing mobilisation have been achieved through the cooperation of traditional trade unions with grassroots unions, or 'alt-labour' workers' associations, which mainly attract low-wage, non-unionised, or informal workers. Examples of solidarity unionism can be observed in many countries and on different occasions.[1131] Such cooperation can benefit all the actors involved. For example, grassroots unions, which in many instances are comprised of young freelancers, have, due to the nature of their work, '*develop*[ed] *or adopt*[ed] *creative strategies and new digital literacies*' in order to attract new members or contest the unfair practices of digital labour platforms.[1132] These actions can inform and update the methods used by traditional unions in reaching out to workers within fissured and fragmented workplaces. Vice versa, among other things, grassroots unions can profit from the experience that institutional unions have acquired in organising and representing various types of atypical workers, as well as their financial resources and infrastructure.

Arguably, the recent developments in the context of platform work illustrate that trade unions '*are willing to engage into sectors that the odds are against them*'.[1133] This engagement appears to be vital in terms of their revitalisation efforts. The workforce diversity of platform workers can be seen as a novel source of membership. This is particularly true, as in many countries, young workers compose a considerably large amount of the overall 'platform workers population'.[1134] In this way, as Visser puts it: '*trade unions* [can] *regain their vitality and youthfulness, find ways to expand beyond their current membership base and succeed in organizing parts of the 'new unstable workforce' in the digital economy*'.[1135] The synergies between institutional and grassroots unions are also important in this respect. Juravic points out that the formers' support for grassroots movements has to keep growing, not solely due to rationales that touch upon an increase in their membership, but also as a way to combat injustice.[1136] What the author describes is inextricably linked to the broader role of trade unions and more specifically to what Ewing calls their regulatory function, namely, a rule-making process that aims at benefiting the society at large and not only the members of unions themselves.[1137] Along the same lines, Doellgast, Lille and Pulignano observe that

1130. Shostack, A.B., *CyberUnion: Empowering Labor Through Computer Technology* (Ebook, Routledge 2016), available at: https://www.taylorfrancis.com/books/mono/10.4324/9781315292250/cyberunion-empowering-labor-computer-technology-arthur-shostack (accessed 26 July 2022).
1131. *See* Chapter 4.
1132. Sutherland, W., Jarrahi, M.H., Dunn, M., Nelson, S.B., *Work Precarity and Gig Literacies in Online Freelancing*, 34 Work, Employment and Society 457 n. 4 (2020), 472.
1133. *Supra*, Forsyth (2022), 203.
1134. Pesole, A., Brancati, U., Fernández-Macías, E., Biagi, F., Gonzalez Vazquez, I. (2018), *Platform Workers in Europe: Evidence from the COLLEEM Survey*, Luxembourg, Publications Office of the European Union.
1135. *Supra*, Visser (2019), 68.
1136. Juravich, T., *Constituting Challenges in Differing Arenas of Power: Worker Centers, the Fight for $15, and Union Organizing*, 43 Labor Studies Journal 104 n. 2 (2018), 114.
1137. *See* Ewing in chapter 4; *see also* Andrias, K., *The New Labor Law*, 126 Yale Law Journal 1 (2016), 2.

European trade unions have gradually intensified their efforts to represent precarious workers, not only in order to protect their own members from practices of low-cost competition, but also to stay loyal to their wider commitments to equity and social justice.[1138] In turn, an inclusive labour movement based on such commitments can attract and keep a loyal membership that is able to face current and future challenges. As noted in the previous Chapter, a human rights oratory can also assist in this direction.

All in all, it is not the first time that some have rushed to make an announcement on trade unions' obituaries. Still, as this research has illustrated, recent developments reveal a growing mobilisation of platform workers and cooperation between traditional unions and a number of alternative organisations that represent workers' collective interests. This is something that can also be observed in other areas of NSFE, including self-employed persons. Thus, it can be argued that '*the labour movement lives*'[1139] and as long as it remains inclusive and consistent with its broader societal objectives, will become stronger. That said, the effective protection of atypical workers, including platform workers, will also depend on other factors as the next section discusses. This is to say that such workers' collective interests cannot be fully realised if significant obstacles towards the effective exercise of collective bargaining persist.

6.3 ARE INDUSTRIAL SYSTEMS READY FOR A HRBA TOWARDS COLLECTIVE LABOUR RIGHTS? THE CASE OF COLLECTIVE BARGAINING

> When all is going well, there is little need to look around or to look within. But when the present gets shaky and the future threatening, it becomes necessary to ask what is wrong. Easy answers give way to hard questions.[1140]

These words belong to Gus Tyler, an American socialist activist, a labour union official, and an author who, by writing back in 1986, like many authors nowadays, was troubled by the inability of labour law to protect some of the most vulnerable workers. Labour law was partly designed to provide workers with adequate minimum labour standards, including access to collective labour rights. For quite some time, the limitations of labour law's protective framework were well hidden behind a relatively homogeneous workforce, working full-time, in relatively secure occupations, and within a vertically integrated workplace, where a rather strict hierarchical control was clearly present. Therefore, there was no reason, at least an urgent one, to 'look around, or to look within'. Since these times, nonetheless, the situation has dramatically changed. The 'carefree moments' of labour law were terminated soon after the stereotypical model on which the latter was based, started to give way to atypical forms

1138. *Supra*, Doellgast, Lillie and Pulignano (2018), 1.
1139. Compa, L. (2015), 'Labor at a Crossroads: How Unions Can Thrive in the 21st Century', *The American Prospect* (online magazine), 27 January 2015, available at: https://prospect.org/justice/labor-crossroads-unions-can-thrive-21st-century/ (accessed 28 July 2022).
1140. Tyler, G., *Labor at the Crossroads* (Seymour M. Lipset ed., *Unions in Transition: Entering* the Second *Century*, ICS Press 1986), 374.

of work and fissured corporate structures, where many aspects of the production process are subcontracted and outsourced. The purpose has always been almost the same, that is, the reduction of labour costs stemming from employment and labour regulations, as well as collective agreements. Previous chapters illustrated that such phenomena have been intensified within the context of modern workplaces, especially through the use of new technological tools, which have allegedly allowed people to work for themselves as self-employed persons, away from any supervision or control. As noted, however, in many instances, this is far from the reality these workers are facing. A considerable portion of them is actually situated in a comparable predicament to that of employees, where their weak negotiating position and economic dependency towards their principals make for a precarious situation. In the case of (weak) self-employed workers though, the protection afforded to them is traditionally limited to the bare minimum. This is arguably the point where the 'present gets shaky and the future threatening'.

It makes no surprise that systems of industrial relations have also been affected by these developments. The remarkable growth of self-employment that has taken place over the last decades is expected to continue, especially considering that work arrangements, such as those in the platform economy, will carry on by probably attracting even more people. The situation, therefore, makes it even more urgent than in the past to ask the right questions by 'look[ing] around or [and] [by] looking within' the current system(s) of industrial relations. When someone attempts to look around, as previous sections pointed out, one of the main challenges derives from the clash of competition law and collective bargaining.[1141] As has been argued elsewhere, existing approaches to competition law(s) appear too narrow to sufficiently address the changing realities and inequalities within contemporary labour markets.[1142] As suggested moreover, competition law's relationship with labour law ought to be re-established through the prism of the recognition of the right to bargain collectively as a fundamental human right. Of course, the acknowledgement of the human rights status of fundamental collective labour rights, including the right to collective bargaining, has not prevented strict antitrust laws from obstructing the conclusion of collective agreements of self-employed workers as price-fixing agreements, which can possibly hamper competition. Examples of this kind can be traced in the context of the platform economy.

That said, what if competition laws ceased to constitute an indeed serious impediment to the effective exercise of collective bargaining as a human right? In other

1141. This is not to argue that competition law constitutes the sole external challenge for labour law. Political choices promoting deregulation of labour standards, including neoclassical economic theories that perceive labour protections as a threat to competition and efficiency, constitute extremely important factors, which arguably are inextricably linked to current competition policies. That said, it is not within the scope of this research to touch upon these issues in detail; that is why the author, as a matter of law, only refers the issue of competition law and the latter's clash with collective bargaining.

1142. *See* Aloisi, A., Gramano, E., *A Solution in Search of a Problem? Collective Rights and the Antitrust Labour Exemption in Italy* (Shae McCrystal, Ewan McGaughey and Sanjukta Paul eds, *The Cambridge Handbook of Labor in Competition Law*, Cambridge University Press 2022), 223.

words, what if, under competition law, the conclusion of collective agreements for self-employed workers were completely legitimate (or, with only a few restrictions in cases of dominant market power);[1143] thus, in case someone was attempting to 'look around', the situation would not look as challenging as in reality? But then, the question that arises is how the situation looks alike when we wish to 'look within' the current framework of industrial relations. As the next sections discuss, the current legal apparatus for collective bargaining seems, in many cases, out of date and does not match the realities within the new world of work and the increase of self-employed workers dependent upon their principals. Such an observation, in turn, begs the question as to whether is necessary to rethink how industrial systems should work in order to cope with the new existing realities, as well as to comply with the language of international human and labour rights instruments and their supervisory bodies regarding the right to collective bargaining. As noted, due to the diverse landscape within national industrial systems, the purpose of these final sections is to make some important observations and ignite a discussion on the future of industrial relations, considering the nature of collective bargaining as a human right rather than to offer firm solutions that can be universally applicable.

6.4 COLLECTIVE BARGAINING FOR PLATFORM WORKERS AND OTHER SELF-EMPLOYED WORKERS: 'THE ENEMY WITHIN'

In the majority of countries, at least in a European context, there are no legal obstacles for unions in their efforts to recruit and organise self-employed workers, including platform workers. Concomitantly though, as Fulton points out, trade unions find it much more challenging to undertake collective bargaining for these types of workers.[1144] As previously developed,[1145] there are some national models that actually facilitate self-employed workers' access to collective bargaining.[1146] In some countries, for example, it is common to permit self-employed persons in specific occupations and industries, such as journalists, actors, artists, and farmers, to conclude collective agreements.[1147] Moreover, in some legal systems, mainly in Europe, there are provisions in mainstream collective bargaining statutes that authorise workers falling in an intermediate category between employment and self-employment to undertake

1143. In Italy, for instance, as Aloisi and Gramano observe, historical evidence suggests that collective agreements covering genuine self-employed have never constituted the target of the Italian competition authority. Still as the authors contend, for reasons other than strict antitrust laws, collective bargaining for such workers remains unpopular for such workers. The reasons behind this phenomenon, *inter alia*, include trends towards the decentralisation of collective bargaining and difficulties of self-employed workers to access formal structures of representation (*Ibid.*, 223-238).

1144. Fulton L. (2018), *Trade Unions Protecting Self-Employed Workers*, ETUC, Brussels, 11.

1145. Some of the potential challenges with respect to these approaches were discussed in Chapter 3, subsection 4.

1146. Different approaches regarding the facilitation of collective bargaining for self-employed workers are not mutually exclusive and they can coexist (*see supra*, Fulton (2018)).

1147. *See* Chapter 3, subsection 4.

collective bargaining.[1148] Some countries have, furthermore, amended the provisions of other statutes in order to permit certain self-employed persons to have their terms and conditions set by collective agreements, an action that otherwise would be possibly unlawful. This is, for instance, the case in Ireland, where the Competition Act was recently amended so as exempt self-employed workers in certain sectors from the ambit of antitrust laws. All these types of national models are not mutually exclusive.

Importantly, despite its limitations, maybe the most significant recent development at the EU level derives from the publication of the Commission's Guidelines on the application of EU competition law to collective agreements in relation to the working conditions of solo self-employed persons, including platform workers. As seen, according to the recently issued Guidelines, three categories of self-employed workers can be possibly excluded from the scope of EU competition.[1149] Some of the downsides regarding the aforementioned developments were already discussed in Chapter 3.

In the context of the platform work, moreover, this research referred to a few instances where platform workers enjoying the self-employed status have managed to negotiate collective agreements or similar types of settlements. Illustrative in this respect is the conclusion of the Hermes collective agreement in the UK and the conclusion of the Bologna Charter in Italy back in 2020. In Australia, the TWU has also taken advantage of the broad definition of who constitutes 'a worker' for the purposes of health and safety laws in the country in order to force Deliveroo to comply with the election of workers' representatives for occupational health and safety-related issues. Albeit not collective bargaining of a traditional nature, the agreement in question constitutes an important step towards the better protection of workers in transportation services.

That being said, putting the obstacles competition authorities can generate on the side, it can be argued that traditional unions and grassroots unions representing solo self-employed workers, including platform workers, are in many instances allowed to negotiate working conditions for their members, irrespective of their status. This is also confirmed by a series of international studies.[1150] The key question that arises, however, is whether simply permitting solo self-employed persons to bargain collectively is enough. To put it otherwise, does mere permission implies that solo self-employed persons, including platform workers, can fully exercise their right to collective bargaining? Authors like Christina Heißl, appear to be certain about the answer. By basing her reasoning on a comparative analysis between 11 European countries, she contends that '*simply allowing collective bargaining for the self-employed*

1148. This is also the case for Canada, where an intermediate category (dependent contractors) exists.

1149. These are: (i) economically dependent self-employed workers; (ii) self-employed workers 'side-by-side' with employees; and (iii) self-employed workers working via digital labour platforms.

1150. *See*, for instance, OECD, (2019), *Negotiating Our Way Up: Collective Bargaining in a Changing World of Work*, OECD Publishing, Paris.

may not be sufficient to enable significant bargaining activities in reality'.[1151] Such an observation can lead to what Bogg describes as a '*mere "liberty" to bargain collectively, rather than a "right" to bargain collectively*';[1152] a situation that, as explained throughout this research, can be at odds with countries' (positive) obligations, under international labour and human rights law, to facilitate and support social dialogue and collective bargaining for self-employed workers.

Indeed, despite their differences, it can be claimed that existing national systems of collective bargaining appear incapable of accommodating the needs of self-employed workers, even if, in theory, the latter are allowed to bargain collectively. This is because, in most cases, collective bargaining systems are still structured around formal employees and on some occasions, employees working full-time in fixed workplaces. Taking a bird's eye view of the international encyclopaedia for labour law and industrial relations which includes a comparative exercise in a high number of countries around the world, one may observe that the word 'self-employed' is consistently missing, or scarcely showing up in the respective part(s) of national research related to collective labour relations.[1153] This is indeed a preliminary indication that national legislators did not have the self-employed in mind when drafting the provisions in question. Among other things, high representation thresholds for unions' recognition, lack, or decline of multi-employer collective bargaining, and the absence of statutory rights to compel employers to recognise collective agreements for self-employed workers, constitute, so far, insuperable hindrances towards the effective exercise of the right to collective bargaining for such workers. Apart from this, practical difficulties, such as low unionisation rates, limited workplace attachment and individualised work arrangements, should not be overlooked. They can also play a negative role. In some national contexts, such issues have been proven even more serious than, for instance, the intervention of competition authorities and other purely legal obstacles.[1154] Needless to say that depending on the national system in question, impediments can take different forms.

Let us take, for instance, the example of Belgium. On a theoretical basis, especially if we accept that due to the recently issued EU Guidelines, collective bargaining agreements for solo self-employed, including platform workers, will not violate competition law, then a preliminary assumption can be that in the near future, the conclusion of such agreements will not look as challenging. As Pecinovsky,

1151. Heißl, C., *National Approaches to Collective Bargaining for the Self-employed: Common Trends, Innovative Potential and Unresolved Problems* (Bernd Waas and Christina Heißl eds, *Collective Bargaining for Self-employed Workers in Europe: Approaches to Reconcile Competition Law and Labour Rights*, Kluwer Law International 2021), 278.

1152. Bogg, A., *Square Pegs in Round Holes? Collective Bargaining and the Self-Employed*, 42 Comparative Labor Law & Policy Journal 409 n. 2 (2021), 412.

1153. *See*, for instance, Butler, M., *Great Britain* (Frank Hendrickx ed., *International Encyclopaedia of Laws: Labour Law and Industrial Relations*, Kluwer Law International 2017), 241-302; Alvin, L.G., Corrada, L.R., *United States of America* (Frank Hendrickx ed., *International Encyclopaedia of Laws: Labour Law and Industrial Relations*, Kluwer Law International 2018), 225-243; TREU, T., *Italy* (Frank Hendrickx ed., *International Encyclopaedia of Laws: Labour Law and Industrial Relations*, Kluwer Law International 2020), 165-259.

1154. *Supra*, Aloisi and Gramano (2022).

however, among others explains, on a practical level, things are not that straightforward.[1155] The relevant legislation in relation to the right to bargain collectively is included in the Collective Labour Agreement Act of 1968.[1156] The latter prescribes that collective agreements can be '*concluded between one or more employees' organisations on the one hand, and one or more employers' organisations or one or more employers' on the other hand* [...]'.[1157] Against this background, collective agreements, governed by the Act of 1968, are considered binding in nature, whereas those which are falling outside the ambit of the Act, are regarded as 'second-rate' collective bargaining agreements; albeit they come with rights and obligations, they, nonetheless, do not possess the (legal) power to be enforced against many people or offer collective protection.[1158] That said, as Pecinovsky informs us, the major obstacle for solo self-employed persons' access to the Act for the purposes of collective bargaining, constitutes the latter's limited personal scope of application. This is because Article 2 of the law is only applicable to workers in furtherance of an employment contract and to employers.[1159] According to Belgian labour law, an employment contract '*is defined as the agreement whereby an employee undertakes, in return for remuneration, to perform work under the authority of an employer*'.[1160] At first glance, the Act indeed looks as de facto excluding solo self-employed from its scope. Nevertheless, as Franquet and Maisin thoroughly explain, it is by now settled law that the Act's provisions are also applicable to '*all persons who provide work benefits under the authority of another person, whether or not under a contract of employment*'.[1161] The key factor in this case, therefore, is to determine what the concept of authority entails, as the Act stays silent on this. There are different indications or indicia under national law that courts are using to indicate the presence of authority (subordination).[1162] For example, these, *inter alia*, include the power of employers to control and supervise the execution of the work performed, the existence of a work schedule, etc.[1163] To this

1155. Pecinovsky, P. (2022), 'Are national collective bargaining systems ready for solo, self-employed persons?', *Global Workplace Law & Policy (blog)*, Wednesday, 20 April 2022, available at: http://global-workplace-law-and-policy.kluwerlawonline.com/2022/04/20/are-national-collective-bargaining-systems-ready-for-solo-self-employed-persons/ (accessed 25 November 2022).
1156. Collective Labour Agreement Act 1968, Belgian Official Gazette 15 Jan. 1969.
1157. *Ibid.*, Article 5. The translation and analysis of the Act can be found in: Hendrickx, F., *Belgium* (Frank Hendrickx ed., *International Encyclopaedia of Laws: Labour Law and Industrial Relations*, Kluwer Law International 2022), 202.
1158. *Supra*, Pecinovsky (2022).
1159. The Act of 1968 does not contain a definition of who should be considered an employee.
1160. Cf. Articles 2 and 3 of the Employment Contracts Act of 3 Jul. 1978. The translation and analysis of the Act can be found in: *Supra*, Hendrickx (2022), 43.
1161. Draft law on collective bargaining and joint committees, explanatory memorandum, *Doc. Parl. Sen., sess.* 1966-1967, No. 78, 7. The reference found in Franquet, V., Maisin, J.B., *Belgium* (Bernd Waas and Christina Hießl eds, *Collective Bargaining for Self-employed Workers in Europe: Approaches to Reconcile Competition Law and Labour Rights*, Kluwer Law International 2021), 90.
1162. *Supra*, Hendrickx (2022), 43.
1163. In order to assess whether authority exists or not, courts in Belgium examine four (different) general criteria, enshrined in the Labour Relations Act 2006; *see* above in Chapter 3.

extent, Frank Hendrickx points out that the meaning of 'authority' does not unavoidably imply that a person has to give up all autonomy regarding her or his work; a subordinate relationship may, in reality, exist, even in situations where a person '*retains full independence of the work and responsibility for the work*'.[1164] As the same author explains though, it is indeed crucial that the authority remains present in the organisation of the independent work performance; in a different case, a person will most likely fall into the self-employment category.[1165]

According to Franquet and Maisin, a flexible interpretation of the concept of authority can possibly offer a leeway for the application of the Collective Labour Agreement Act to self-employed persons, but as they argue, it will not be sufficient in offering concrete solutions regarding the obstacles such workers are facing with respect to their right to collective bargaining.[1166] It is indeed difficult to imagine, for example, how freelance crowdworkers, who are usually organising and managing their work by themselves, will be covered under the Act. After all, as Pecinovsky contends, to a great extent, a debate around authority, even if the latter can be interpreted in rather a broad manner, brings us back to the conversation about an employer-employee relationship and its complexities,[1167] as those discussed in previous chapters. That said, as Pecinovsky highlights, the challenges for self-employed persons' collective interests do not end here. More specifically, in line with the Act of 1968, the only 'organisations' that can actually act as representatives and negotiate on behalf of self-employed workers are employers' organisations.[1168] Albeit in practice, organisations representing solely self-employed workers, like *Unizo* and the *Union des Classes Moyennes*, have negotiated working conditions for their members, such organisations, are also considered to be part of employers' organisations; this is because '*they both represent their members in the National Labour Council among the quota allocated to employers*'.[1169] Cumulatively, therefore, the Collective Labour Agreement Act of 1968, drafted a long time ago, does not seem to be able to accommodate the complexities of modern work arrangements, with the increase of self-employed workers in need of collective representation. As noted, collective agreements concluded for self-employed and fall outside the Act's scope do not have a binding force. On top of that, unlike collective agreements protected by the Act at issue (based on its Articles 19 and 26), they cannot have universal applicability, meaning that they do not possess the legal force to cover all self-employed workers engaged, for instance, in a specific sector or industry.[1170]

Moving on, the complex legal landscape with respect to self-employed workers' right to bargain collectively can also be found in other countries, with a less 'institutionalised' system of collective bargaining, compared to Belgium. This is, for instance,

1164. *Ibid.*, The author refers to the case of Cass. 27 March 1968, TSR 1968, 110.
1165. *Ibid.*
1166. *Supra*, Franquet and Maisin (2021), 90-91.
1167. *Supra*, Pecinovsky (2022).
1168. *Ibid.*, The authors also explains that according to the Act, an alternative in the representation of solo self-employed workers can derive from the recognition of associations that the National Labour Council, acknowledges as representative in some particular industries. Once again though, employers' organisations are beneficiaries of this option.
1169. *Supra*, Franquet and Maisin (2021), 95.
1170. *Supra*, Pecinovsky (2022).

the case in the UK: a country which 'hosts' one the few occasions where self-employed platform workers have concluded a collective agreement with a digital labour platform, namely Hermes, irrespective of their employment classification. Arguably, albeit an important development, such an example should not automatically lead us to jump to easy conclusions. As several authors have demonstrated, platform workers and other self-employed persons can hardly conform to the list of requirements enshrined in the Trade Union and Labour Relations (Consolidation) Act 1992 (TULRCA).[1171] The latter offers the statutory mechanism for trade union recognition. Solely recognised unions are protected by the Act and have the legal prerogative to negotiate with employers, as well as engage in collective bargaining or action. Once again, as in the case of Belgium developed above, the problem with the Act in question lies in its limited personal scope of application. According to TULRCA a 'trade union' is defined as an organisation that is comprised '*wholly or mainly of workers of one or more descriptions and whose principal purposes include the regulation of relations between workers of that description or those descriptions and employers or employers' associations*'.[1172] Conversely, where an association is not comprised 'wholly or mainly' of 'workers', it cannot constitute a trade union for the purposes of the Act; a status that, as it is explained elsewhere, is essential in order to apply for a certificate of 'independence'.[1173] As Bogg discusses, without the formal recognition and certificate, a workers' association is barred from accessing the legal apparatus (schedule 1 of the Act), which offers legal support for collective bargaining.[1174]

That said, the definition of who actually constitutes a worker is defined broadly enough to include persons falling into the intermediate category of 'limb-b workers'.[1175] At the same time, nonetheless, solo self-employed workers are falling outside the personal scope of application of the Act. That was also recently confirmed by the Central Arbitration Committee (CAC) in a case against Deliveroo, where it was pointed out that section 296 of TULRCA, which sets the personal scope of the instrument, does not apply to workers who are classified as independent contractors.[1176] Such a limitation though does not mean that independent contractors cannot be organised by trade unions. As Chapter 4 illustrated, the IWGB and GMB unions have shown a great interest in representing self-employed workers, like those engaged in the platform economy. Concomitantly though, if these workers wanted to form their own union(s) instead, tailored to their specific particularities and needs, then under the current Act,

1171. For instance, *see* Katsabian, T., *Collective Action in the Digital Reality: the Case of Platform-Based Workers*, 84 The Modern Law Review 1005 n. 5 (2021), 1005-1040; Freedland, M., Dhorajiwala, H., *UK Response to New Trade Union Strategies for New Forms of Employment*, 10 European Labour Law Journal 281 n. 3 (2019), 281-290; *Supra*, Bogg, A. (2021), 409-448.
1172. TULRCA 1992, Schedule 1.
1173. *Supra*, Bogg (2021), 417-418.
1174. *Ibid.*
1175. TULRCA, section 296(1): '*In this Act worker means an individual who works, or normally works or seeks to work – (a)under a contract of employment, or (b)under any other contract whereby he undertakes to do or perform personally any work or services for another party to the contract who is not a professional client of his* [...].'
1176. *Independent Workers' Union of Great Britain v. RooFoods T/A Deliveroo*, TUR1/985 (2016); The CAC acknowledged that except of employees, TULRCA also covers limb-b workers as those are defined in section 230 (3) (b) of the Employment Relations Act 1996.

such an endeavour would not be enough to get a certificate of independence; hence, accessing the statutory rights reserved for certified trade unions, including legal support for collective bargaining. Of course, this restriction does not mean that independent self-employed workers are legally prohibited from engaging in collective bargaining with employers. As Bogg explains, considering the 'voluntarist' roots of industrial relations in the UK,[1177] there is nothing to prevent employers '*from negotiating with any labor association, regardless of whether it is a "trade union" or whether the represented individuals are "self-employed"*'.[1178] The Hermes collective agreement is illustrative of what the author describes. Still, as in the case of Belgium, such agreements can be characterised as 'second-rate collective bargaining'. According to Bogg, among other limitations one may observe, not only is an employer not legally obliged to bargain collectively with the union comprised of self-employed, but it is also very doubtful that a voluntary recognition will occur in the first place unless the union has adequate power to push that employer to accept its claim.[1179] In practice, therefore, solo self-employed workers, as Freedland and Dhorajiwala, put it, '*have no statutory right to compel an employer to recognise them for the purposes of collective bargaining*'.[1180]

The two aforementioned country examples, albeit briefly explained, reveal that simply allowing self-employed workers to bargain collectively at a theoretical level does not necessarily constitute a recipe for success in practice. As previously noted, outdated systems of collective bargaining, together with practical obstacles, can create a 'deadly' amalgam for the effective exercise of the right to collective bargaining. Another example, in my view, a rather straightforward one can also be traced in Poland and the recent labour law amendment that took place back in 2018 and entered into force a year later. Particularly, in order to comply with international standards and the Polish Constitution, national law was amended by extending collective bargaining rights to '*all persons working for money*'.[1181] Consequently, as Mirtus explains, the right to collective bargaining is now vested in self-employed workers who are economically dependent upon a single client and do not employ other people.[1182] As the same author as well as other national experts argue though, it is difficult to imagine that due to this change, collective agreements would start covering non-employees in practice, including platform workers.[1183] So far, negotiations for non-employees are

1177. This concept entails that an employer agrees in negotiating with an association of workers and there is evidence of a sincere desire to do so in good faith (*Supra*, Bogg (2021), 421).
1178. *Ibid.*
1179. *Ibid.*, 421-422.
1180. *Supra*, Freedland and Dhorajiwala (2019), 287.
1181. Journal of Laws 2019, item 263, as amended.
1182. Mirtus, L., *Poland* (Bernd Waas and Christina Hießl eds, *Collective Bargaining for Self-employed Workers in Europe: Approaches to Reconcile Competition Law and Labour Rights*, Kluwer Law International 2021), 213-214.
1183. *Ibid.*; *see also* Czarzasty, J., *Collective Bargaining in Poland: A Near-Death Experience* (Torsten Müller, Kurt Vandaele, and Jeremy Waddington eds, *Collective Bargaining in Europe: Towards an Endgame*, Vol. 2, ETUI, 2019), 465-481.

absent.[1184] Due to trends towards decentralisation, multi-employer collective bargaining, which could possibly benefit solo self-employed workers, is almost non-existent in the country, albeit in theory is permitted.[1185] At the same time, although the number of company-level agreements is larger, these have been mostly negotiated for specific types of establishments; in the private sector, these types of agreements are very few and in small and medium enterprises almost non-existent.[1186] On top of that, as Pisarczyk highlights, the factual challenges are currently magnified by inadequate legislative solutions that further complicate the works of trade unions and the enabling of collective bargaining.[1187] In a similar vein, it has been also contended that the Polish state has done little for the facilitation of social dialogue at a national level.[1188] Thus, once again, a mere permission to bargain collectively for self-employed workers does look enough in bringing about the full realisation of the right at issue.

To sum up, in general terms, as Carinci and Dorssemont nicely put it: '*systems of collective employment relations have been established in an industrial setting that respects the rules of classical theatre*'.[1189] Such rules, though, based on a reality of a different era (e.g., a fixed workplace and a homogeneous workforce, working full-time), do not seem capable of accommodating the need(s) of solo self-employed workers with respect to their collective protection, and specifically their right to collective bargaining; a right, that although not absolute, should be accorded to them in line with international labour and human rights law. The aforementioned obstacles constitute only some of the possible legal impediments which hinder the effective enjoyment of the right in question by self-employed persons, including platform workers. Anthony Forsyth, for example, dedicates a considerable space in his recent book to address the challenges stemming from high representation thresholds for unions' recognition and the validity of collective agreements; a phenomenon that can indeed obstruct self-employed workers' efforts to form trade unions and bargain collectively.[1190] Obstacles of this nature can go against recognised international standards, according to which '*social partners or governments shall install objective procedures for recognising the most representative organisations (in so far as only these may bargain collectively) with reasonable quotas if representative quotas are imposed*'.[1191] Moreover, there is also a plethora of views pointing out that industrial

1184. Kozak-Maśnicka, M. and Pisarczyk, L., *Extending the Personal Scope of Collective Bargaining as a Chance for Gig Workers?: The Polish Case* (José M. Boto and Elisabeth Brameshuber eds, *Collective Bargaining and the Gig Economy a Traditional Tool for New Business Models*, Hart Publishing, 2022), 226.
1185. *Ibid.*, 223-224.
1186. Pisarczyk, L., *The Crisis of the Collective Bargaining System in Poland*, 35 International Journal of Comparative Labour Law and Industrial Relations 58 n. 1 (2019), 63.
1187. *Ibid.*, 66.
1188. *Supra*, Kozak-Maśnicka, M. & Pisarczyk, L., (2022), 224.
1189. Carinci, M. T., Dorssemont, F., *A Comparative Analysis* (Maria T. Carinci and Filip Dorssemont eds, *Platform Work in Europe: Towards Harmonisation?*, Intersentia 2021), 237.
1190. *Supra* Forsyth (2022).
1191. Pecinovsky, P., *EU Economic Governance and the Right to Collective Bargaining. Part 1. Standard and Extreme Governance and the Indicators and Limits of the Right to Collective Bargaining*, 9 European Labour Law Journal 374 n. 4 (2018), 381.

systems, such as the one in the US,[1192] currently structured around collective bargaining procedures in a single worksite, and at most with a single employer, are unable to face the challenges derive from fissured workplaces and the increase in the number of self-employed.[1193] As a consequence, less and less atypical workers are covered by collective agreements. That said, it is beyond the scope of this section to fully address the totality of legal obstacles embedded within national industrial systems, which render the application of a HRBA towards collective labour rights an extremely challenging task. Still, even this small sample of legal complexities illustrates that even if we take for granted that *all* workers, irrespective of their employment status, can enjoy their right to collective bargaining, then the implementation of such an assumption seems practically impossible for many solo-self-employed workers.

6.5 LOOKING AHEAD: 'EASY ANSWERS (OFTENTIMES) GIVE WAY TO HARD QUESTIONS'

Arguably, the findings of the aforementioned section may lead to some straightforward answers. For instance, the response can be rather clear as to whether current industrial systems are well equipped to address the needs of collective representation and protection of solo self-employed, including platform workers, in line with the requirements of international instruments related to labour law and human rights. As it was argued above and further literature also accepts, existing national industrial systems, fall short in enabling the conclusion of collective agreements for self-employed workers, albeit some exceptions are observed.[1194] This is to say that in many instances, a mere freedom in allowing these workers to bargain collectively, has proven nothing more than an 'empty shell'. As a result, they are facing serious limitations in the enjoyment of their fundamental human rights, like the right to collective bargaining, which, as noted constitutes an indispensable element of the right to freedom of association. In turn, though, such an answer gives way to even harder questions for policymakers, trade unions themselves, as well as scholars. These inquiries, in my view, can be subdivided into two parts. The first set of questions can be related to the manner in which national industrial systems can sufficiently ensure the right to collective bargaining for self-employed workers. Should they, for example, attempt to generate new collective bargaining laws in order to accommodate the needs of self-employed, and if so, is this endeavour even possible? Or, should they adjust the already existing ones? Such questions, or ones of a similar nature, have already been

1192. The National Labor Relations Act, the principle statute governing labour relations, is solely providing for collective bargaining negotiations with a single employer. The result is that unions find it difficult to bargain collectively beyond the worksite. *See* Rhinehart, L., McNicholas, C. (2020), 'Collective bargaining beyond the worksite: How workers and their unions build power and set standards for their industries', *Economic Policy Institute (online source)*, 4 May 2020, available at: https://www.epi.org/publication/collective-bargaining-beyond-the-worksite-how-workers-and-their-unions-build-power-and-set-standards-for-their-industries/ (accessed 25 October 2022).

1193. *Ibid.*

1194. *Supra*, Heißl, (2021); *Supra* Bogg, (2021).

posed by some authors.[1195] After all, it is indeed obscene to discuss the ways in which competition law can be amended so as to comply with the nature of collective bargaining, as a fundamental human right applicable to all workers, and not to have a similar kind of conversation regarding collective labour law.

That said, the second set of inquiries can be related to the situation if things remain unchanged or if the progress is rather 'sluggish'. Can we expect the proliferation of 'diluted version(s)' of collective bargaining, meaning the increase of soft models of engagement that do not necessarily resemble strong or binding models of traditional collective bargaining? In the context of platform work, these, for example, can include agreements on a voluntary or non-binding basis, such as the 2020 Bologna Charter, or agreements with a narrow material scope, such as the transport workers' agreement in Australia, for the election of health and safety representatives.

Of course, in order for someone to address these complicated questions may require a new research or even multiple publications. In relation to the first set of questions, the complexity, diversity as well as varied traditions of national systems of industrial relations make such a task extremely challenging. As previously noted, moreover, a 'one-size-fits-all solution' entails several hazards. Even if someone was attempting to address these inquiries by having a single country in mind, the very same exercise could be equally difficult, as a single collective bargaining framework may not be enough to accommodate the needs of self-employed workers. Along these lines, back in 2005, Cranford, Fudge, Tucker and Vosko expressed the view that the '*law must support a variety of collective representation and bargaining schemes because no single mechanism can possibly respond to the diverse needs of the self-employed*'.[1196] Such an observation, nonetheless, along with the diversity of collective labour laws around the world, should not discourage us from seeking to identify some common requirements, capable of facilitating in practice the exercise of collective bargaining for self-employed, including many platform workers. A first requirement, for example, can provide that only for the purposes of unionisation and collective labour laws more broadly, an 'autonomous' notion of worker should be adopted, in harmony with international obligations. As it was observed, both the ILO and the ESC, via the language of their supervisory bodies, have embraced an all-inclusive notion of a 'worker' that is different and, or 'autonomous' from the notion of a 'worker' that employment and labour acts are currently using; or similarly, a notion of a 'worker' that labour courts are typically referring to when ruling whether someone can fall within an employment relationship *sensu stricto*. In line with international obligations, therefore, national labour acts setting out the conditions for unions' recognition and the exercise of collective bargaining should insulate themselves from definitions, traced in other parts of legislation regulating employment and labour relations more in general, as well as labour courts' decisions on the existence of an employment relationship ('insulation approach'). For instance, in the UK, section 296(1) of the TULRCA, which stipulates who is a 'worker' for the purposes of the Act in question, is

1195. *Supra* Pecinovsky (2022), *Supra*, McCrystal, S. (2014).
1196. Cranford, C., Fudge, J., Tucker, E., Vosko, L.F., *Self-Employed Workers Organize: Law, Policy, and Unions* (McGill-Queen's Press 2005), 184.

identical to section 230(3)(b) of the Employment Rights Act 1996.[1197] This 'cross-reference', if I may say, seems incapable of delivering the right to collective bargaining to all self-employed in need of it, let alone its complications with respect to unions' official recognition. A similar observation can also be made with respect to the Collective Bargaining Act in Belgium, which, as mentioned, also covers persons who although they do not have an employment contract, work under the authority of another person. Due to the fact, however, that the notion of authority, is not defined within the very Act, a reference needs to be made to other pieces of legislation, such as the Labour Relations Act 2006. This reference can open the 'Pandora's box' on the classic discussion on the employee-employer relationship.[1198] Having such complexities in mind, collective labour laws should include their own 'autonomous' definition of worker, away from the influence of definitions used for the exercise of other labour-related rights. In this way, an 'insulation approach' can prevent considerations around authority and subordination, to considerably restrict the personal scope of application of unionisation and collective bargaining rights. Moreover, the exercise of such rights will not be dependent upon the eagerness and capacity of individual workers to bring claims in front of the courts.

In line with the ESC's language, among other possible elements, a decisive criterion for the establishment of the 'insulation approach' can be found in the '*imbalance of power between the providers and engagers of labour*'.[1199] When the former '*have no substantial influence on the content of contractual conditions, they must be given the possibility of improving the power imbalance through collective bargaining*'.[1200] Criteria, such as the 'personal work approach' advocated by scholars, like Freedland, Countouris and De Stefano can be also relevant in this respect.[1201] That said, proposals for an 'autonomous' definition of who should be considered a 'worker' for the purposes of unionisation and collective bargaining, but solely in the case of platform workers, have already been advanced in some countries.[1202] For instance, a Sharing Economy Committee, appointed by the Norwegian Government, expressed the view that self-employed platform workers who do not influence the setting of prices should have the right to collective bargaining'.[1203] Tammy Katsabian on her side, contends that only for the purposes of platform workers' unionisation rights, the term 'worker' in the UK can be redefined and expanded under the TULRCA, based on the

1197. Employment Rights Act 1996, 230(3)(b) of the '*In this Act 'worker" (except in the phrases "shop worker" and "betting worker") means an individual who has entered into or works under (or, where the employment has ceased, worked under) – [...] (b) any other contract, whether express or implied and (if it is express) whether oral or in writing, whereby the individual undertakes to do or perform personally any work or services for another party to the contract whose status is not by virtue of the contract that of a client or customer of any profession or business undertaking carried on by the individual.*'
1198. *Supra*, Pecinovsky (2022).
1199. *Irish Congress of Trade Unions v. Ireland*, para. 38.
1200. *Ibid.*
1201. For instance, *see* Freedland, M., Countouris, N., *Some Reflections on the 'Personal Scope' of Collective Labour Law*, 46 Industrial Law Journal 52 n. 1 (2017), 52-71.
1202. *Supra*, Katsabian (2021).
1203. *Ibid.*, 1031. The author refers to OECD, (2019), *Employment outlook 2019: The Future of Work*, Paris, OECD.

criterion of economic dependency.[1204] She also argues that the extension in question can be possibly used for other self-employed workers with similar characteristics.

Arguably, the detachment of collective labour laws from definitions on the notion of 'worker' provided in other legal sources and the adoption of an 'autonomous' definition, albeit a first very important step, will not be enough by itself. Labyrinth requirements for the establishment and official recognition of trade unions can still generate serious impediments towards the collective action of platform workers and other self-employed. Formal processes developed on the existence of a workforce, working full-time on the basis of a stable and continuous employment relationship, need to be (re)adjusted, or redefined in order to capture the realities of self-employed persons. Relaxing the requirements for unionisation enshrined within national collective labour laws is an idea that has already been put forward by some scholars.[1205] Proposals as such, will really depend on the particularities of the national legal system in question. This is why this section prefers to move on with another requirement that the author believes is of paramount importance for self-employed workers' right to collective bargaining, namely, the enabling and facilitation of multi-employer collective bargaining settings.

As seen, the lack or restriction of such procedures can be detrimental to the conclusion of collective agreements for self-employed persons, even in countries, like Poland, which theoretically have opened up the right to bargain collectively to these types of workers. Research indicates that countries with more centralised bargaining systems, enabling multi-employer negotiations, demonstrate considerably higher rates of unionisation and coverage of their workforce from collective agreements.[1206] As Schnabel explains, this phenomenon is potentially linked to the fact that national systems of this nature may limit employers' motives to eliminate unions from their workplaces, as well as reduce transaction costs for both unions and employers.[1207] As a result, unions and especially grassroots unions, like those in the platform economy, with limited financial resources and reduced negotiating powers can benefit from such a system. The same author, moves on to mention that centralised systems also mitigate '*the need for unions to gain recognition and recruit members in small firms*, [a situation that in turn] *helps to solve the latent conflict between capital and labor and can bring macroeconomic benefits so that governments may have an interest in maintaining strong unions*'.[1208] It has been furthermore contented that multi-employer bargaining settings are associated with more inclusive labour protection, as they establish minimum standards for payment and other work-related aspects in a specific sector or

1204. *Supra*, Katsabian (2021), 1026-1032.
1205. *Ibid.*, (2021); *Supra* Forsyth (2022).
1206. *Supra* Visser (2019); *Supra*, Schnabel (2020); *see also* Scruggs, L., Lange, P., *Where Have All the Members Gone? Globalization, Institutions and Union Density*, 64 The Journal of Politics 126 (2002), 126-153; Moreover, as Forsyth indicates by relying on an international study, multi-employer bargaining at sectoral, or national level have collective bargaining coverage rates of between 50% and more than 90 per cent, compared to 11 per cent and 34 per cent in countries which are relying on company-level bargaining (*Ibid.*, Forsyth, 209).
1207. *Ibid.*, Schnabel (2020), 16.
1208. *Ibid.*, 16-17.

industry.[1209] To this extent, the coverage of collective bargaining agreements tends to exceed trade union membership.[1210] The introduction of minimum standards can be beneficial for low-income workers, but also for the exercise of fair competition between firms. Cumulatively, in my view, the effective exercise of the right to collective bargaining for self-employed, including platform workers, is difficult to be implemented without the facilitation and establishment of multi-employer collective bargaining settings. In countries where the latter are either missing or constrained, proposals for legal reforms of this kind already exist.[1211] The implementation of these proposals though, among other things, also requires a political will. Trends towards the erosion of multi-employer collective bargaining systems are, to a great extent, going hand in hand with a 'neoliberal trajectory'.[1212] Whether the enabling of multi-employer collective bargaining systems is feasible within this political environment, albeit an important inquiry, is outside the scope of this section, but undoubtedly this observation should be kept in mind for future interdisciplinary discussions.

Moving on, a final remark regarding the requirements necessary in facilitating and promoting the exercise of collective bargaining for self-employed in practice is related to the difficulties many self-employed workers, and especially platform workers, experience in communicating with each other. As noted, the dispersed character of the work for many workers in these arrangements constitutes a practical obstacle towards their unionisation and collective negotiations. In some cases and at least to a certain extent, such a practical obstacle can be considered as severe as the legal conundrums faced by such workers.[1213] The practical nature of this issue, nonetheless, should not prevent national authorities from ensuring that in the context of industrial relations, employers undertake commitments for the creation of mechanisms through which workers can communicate with each other and via which the organisation of workers by unions can indeed be facilitated. Such obligations on employers' side are extremely important, especially as far as platform work is concerned. This research observed in Chapter 4, for instance, that the significance of the conclusion of the Hilfr collective agreement in Denmark, has been weakened by the inability of the 3F union to trace the workers of the platform at issue and to know where they are working from and when they are actually performing their tasks. The lack of communication channels has been currently addressed by the draft EU Directive on platform work, where in its Article 15 calls Member States to guarantee that digital labour platforms

1209. *See* Visser, J., Hayter, S., Grammarano, R., *Trends in Collective Bargaining Coverage: Stability, Erosion or Decline?, Issue Brief No. 1,* Geneva, ILO (2017).

1210. Hayter, S., *Unions and Collective Bargaining* (Janine Berg ed., *Labour Markets, Institutions and Inequality: Building Just Societies in the 21st Century,* Edward Elgar Publishing 2015), 109.

1211. Baccaro, L., Howell, C., *A Common Neoliberal Trajectory: The Transformation of Industrial Relations in Advanced Capitalism,* 39 Politics & Society 521 n. 4 (2011), 521-563. *See also* Baccaro, L. and Howell, C., *Trajectories of Neoliberal Transformation. European Industrial Relations since the 1970s* (Cambridge University Press 2017).

1212. *See,* for instance, Barenberg, M. (2015), *Widening the Scope of Worker Organizing: Legal Reforms to Facilitate Multi-Employer Organizing, Bargaining, and Striking,* Roosevelt Institute Report, available at: https://rooseveltinstitute.org/wp-content/uploads/2015/10/RI-Widening-Scope-Worker-Organizing-201510-2.pdf (accessed 12 November 2022).

1213. *Supra,* Aloisi and Gramano (2022).

will enable the creation of such mechanisms and will abstain from interfering with workers' communication. The facilitation of communication channels and supervision of their correct implementation can be considered as part of countries' positive international obligations towards collective labour rights.

The aforementioned examples constitute only some of the possible requirements necessary in enabling the exercise of collective bargaining for self-employed in practice and not only on a theoretical basis. Of course, such conditions are just the beginning of a challenging journey, and further research is needed to, for instance, know how national industrial systems can accommodate the extension of collective agreements currently concluded for employees, to self-employed persons. The needs of the latter can considerably differ from the needs of employees and vice versa. Should such agreements be re-drafted, or just special provisions on self-employed persons need to be inserted in the already existing ones? Also, considering the diversity between self-employed, such an exercise can be further complicated. Arguably, these types of questions will, to a great degree preoccupy policymakers and workers' representatives in the course of future discussions related to adaptation(s), or even the re-designing of national systems of collective barraging. The answers to such questions do not only concern the protection of self-employed workers, including workers in the platform economy per se. They are also extremely important for the whole edifice on which labour law is based. Against this background, as Bogg rightly points out: '"*If labor law is to maintain its normative coherence and integrity, the allocation of its fundamental rights must be sensitive to social and economic disadvantages, rather than tied to specific contractual forms like a" contract of service.*'[1214] As such, many self-employed workers must fall within the scope of fundamental collective labour rights, also recognised as human rights, like the right to collective bargaining.

Still, even if some actual changes take place in the future, in accordance with international obligations, these amendments will take time and their success will depend on a variety of factors. But, what this possible delay entails for the right to collective bargaining in current times? This question brings us to the second set of inquiries, identified at the beginning of this last section.

It can be suggested that the recent developments in the context of platform work, such as those developed in this research, can provide a useful guide on this very matter. It was explained that some digital labour platforms and trade unions representing self-employed platform workers have attempted to conclude collective agreements. Some of these agreements were materially undermined or even suspended due to the existence of hostile antitrust laws, such as in the cases of the Voocali and Hilfr collective agreements in Denmark. Of course, as noted, the recently issued EU Guidelines on collective bargaining for solo self-employed may solve these issues at an EU level. Other agreements for self-employed platform workers, moreover, have failed to pass the necessary representativeness thresholds required for their enforcement. As seen, the UGL collective agreement in Italy, albeit highly contested in nature because

1214. *Supra* Bogg (2021), 410.

of its obscure content and the far-right affiliations of the union in question,[1215] failed to be enforced as UGL lacked sufficient representativeness among platform workers.

That being said, the current (aforementioned) legal complexities within national industrial systems have 'forced' self-employed platform workers to proceed with collective negotiations that do not necessarily represent collective bargaining procedures of a traditional nature. As it was observed in Chapter 4, for instance, the Hermes collective agreement in the UK, is lacking a reference to the right of 'self-employed plus' workers to collective representation; in this regard, it only includes a provision which confers to couriers the individual right to negotiate their payment separately from other workers. Thus, although important for certain protections, the Hermes agreement curtails the collective power of self-employed platform workers, a limitation that can be at odds with the purposes of collective bargaining. In Italy, furthermore, a significant development derives from the conclusion of a territorial agreement through the establishment of the so-called Bologna Charter. The latter, as explained, contains several labour protections for all platform workers, including self-employed persons. This agreement does not possess the setting of traditional collective bargaining procedures, as it is applicable only on a voluntary basis. Lastly, this research also referred to the collective negations of self-employed transport workers in Australia, which in turn led to the election of health and safety representatives. In this context, the TWU union took advantage of the broad definition of 'worker', under the health and safety laws in the country. Once again, what can be observed here, is an alternative way through which unions attempted to safeguard their workers' interests.

It can be claimed that such developments reveal a proliferation of either 'soft' or 'diluted version(s)' of collective bargaining that, as noted, do not necessarily resemble strong or binding models of traditional regulatory forms of collective bargaining. Undoubtedly, often due to lack of alternative methods, these forms of collective bargaining, in certain instances, are able to offer temporary solutions or a sense of relief to platform workers. They can also inform the works of trade unions representing self-employed workers, other than platform workers. To this extent, the Australian example illustrates how self-employed workers, in general, can make use of other pieces of legislation in order to better protect themselves in certain areas of their occupation.[1216] One might also argue that such initiatives also expand the notion of collective bargaining and how collective negotiations can be actually exercised. At the same time, though, in my opinion, these soft and diluted models of collective bargaining should not be seen as a panacea. In other words, it is doubtful whether they overall strengthen the right to collective bargaining, as their often limited material scope or legal enforceability can constitute some problematic aspects that should not be overlooked. An observation as such brings us back to the first set of concerns.

Particularly, as long as national collective bargaining systems fall short in securing the effective exercise of the right to collective bargaining for self-employed, including platform workers, the aforementioned models of collective bargaining will proliferate. I do not intend, of course, to argue that unions and other associations

1215. *See* discussion in Chapter 4.
1216. *Supra*, Forsyth (2021).

representing these types of workers should abstain from using any possible armoury they have in their hands, in order to seek better working conditions. By exercising, albeit with limitations, their human rights to freedom of association, collective bargaining and strike have already achieved significant victories against powerful opponents, such as platform giants. In order for those wins, nonetheless, to be multiplied and also achieved by other workers, the effective enablement and application of the right to collective bargaining for self-employed persons, is one important step towards that direction and also in line with the requirements of international labour and human rights instruments. Arguably, until this moment comes, as other authors also argue, among other things, is extremely important to 'free up' the right to strike for such workers.[1217] This research observed many instances where platform workers, irrespective of their contractual status, have managed to achieve remarkable successes by withdrawing their labour. Some of these actions have also led to the conclusion of collective agreements, or other types of agreements, especially during the COVID-19 pandemic, which have benefited their working conditions. As Dorssemont and Carinci put it: '*it is inherent in the dialectics of systems of industrial relations that economic actors offering employment are more inclined to bargain under the threat of some collective pressure that is being exerted against them*'.[1218] In the context of the platform economy, it was explained that such pressure exists, even if (potential) employers, like digital labour platforms, keep refusing that they actually offer any type of employment. As seen from the analysis of Bogg and Buendia in Chapter 4, the often absent employment status of platform workers in the UK has been flipped into a strong weapon in their hands, as there is no need for them to comply with the complex prerequisites related to the legality of strikes in the country. Of course, the situation differs from one country to another, therefore, the creation of frameworks which promote and secure the right to strike for self-employed workers (also in line with international requirements) and when necessary, prevent the latter's contractual liability when refusing to offer their services, is another aspect that needs to be addressed in the future discussions on the functioning of industrial systems and their conformity with international standards.[1219]

All in all, there is still a long way to go in order for someone to speak with certainty that a HRBA towards collective labour rights can be effectively implemented in practice. The legal nature of collective labour rights as human rights with universal applicability can constitute a valuable guide towards that direction. That said, the resistance of workers in the platform economy, constitutes an illustrative example not only regarding the significance those rights have in tackling challenges within modern workplaces but also in relation to the manner that these rights can be exercised despite the existence of current legal and practical complexities.

1217. *Ibid.*, 217-218.
1218. *Supra*, Dorssemont and Carinci (2021), 241.
1219. In this respect and in relation to platform work, Dorssemont and Carinci refer to Article L 7342-5 of the Labour Code in France, as a good practice. The latter, as they explain and as noted in Chapter 4, '*recognises that the concerted refusal* [of platform workers'] *to offer their services cannot give rise to contractual liability, nor does it constitute a reason for stantepede termination of the employment relation, nor a reason for retaliation*'.

6.6 INTERMEDIATE CONCLUSIONS

Chapter 6 delved into the implications of a HRBA on industrial relations. Against this background, platform workers' exercise of their fundamental collective labour rights (discussed in Chapter 4) was used as a point of reference. It was, first, illustrated that the dynamic mobilisation observed with respect to platform workers is important not only for the latter but also for the future of trade unionism in facing novel challenges and searching for solutions. As noted, the synergies within platform work can assist trade unions in their undergoing transition. For instance, the organisation and representation of platform workers appear to be essential in terms of trade unions' revitalisation efforts. In this context, the workforce diversity of platform workers can be perceived as a new source of membership, especially considering that young workers compose a significantly large amount of the overall 'platform workers population'. The cooperation between institutional and grassroots unions is also important in this regard. Moreover, the ever-increasing numbers of weak self-employed workers engaged in the platform economy and their constant efforts to unionise and exercise their collective labour rights (e.g., via the use of new technological tools), can constitute a valuable guide for unions' attempts to face current challenges within modern workplaces. After all, as mentioned, the engagement with such workers, along with the existence of an inclusive labour movement, is also in line with trade unions' broader commitments to equity and social justice.

Still, as Chapter 6, in turn, demonstrated the effective protection of self-employed platform workers, including other workers in a grey zone between employment and self-employment, is also dependent upon another key factor. More specifically, this is the readiness of national systems of industrial relations to effectively allow self-employed workers, including platform workers, to bargain collectively in harmony with the requirements derived from a HRBA. As the Chapter in question pointed out, due to the current structure(s) of systems of industrial relations, the effective application of a HRBA can be considerably challenging, regardless of the existence of problems stemming from competition law. To this extent, simply allowing self-employed workers to bargain collectively may not be sufficient to enable substantial bargaining activities in practice. The examples of Belgium and the UK developed in this part are illustrative of the difficulties in this respect. Among other reasons, the lack or decline of multi-employer collective bargaining systems, together with the absence of statutory rights to compel employers to recognise collective agreements for self-employed workers, are only some of the obstacles self-employed platform workers and other self-employed persons have to deal with when they attempt to exercise their right to collective bargaining.

As explained, furthermore, legal complications with respect to the conclusion of collective agreements have forced self-employed platform workers to resort to collective negotiations that do not necessarily represent collective bargaining procedures of a traditional nature. In this sense, the latter can take the form of 'soft' or 'diluted version(s)' of collective bargaining, like the so-called Bologna Charter in Italy. As argued, it is doubtful whether these types of agreements are capable of enabling an effective application of a HRBA in practice. To this extent, the last chapter went on to

requirements, capable of facilitating in practice the exercise of collective bargaining for self-employed, including many platform workers (e.g., for the purposes of unionisation and collective labour laws more broadly, an 'autonomous' notion of worker should be adopted, in accordance with international obligations).

Summary of Findings and Conclusion(s)

1 THE CENTRAL RESEARCH QUESTION

The world of work is changing. In this context, the lines that divide self-employed and employed persons are becoming less and less discernible. This phenomenon has led to the numerical increase of atypical workers, including dependent self-employed persons who find themselves in a comparable predicament to that of employees, where their weak negotiating position and economic dependency on their principals often make for a precarious situation.

The vast majority of labour and employment protections, including the enjoyment of fundamental collective labour rights, is still concentrated within 'subordinate' wage employment. Conversely, self-employed persons are usually expected to be able to defend their interests on the market; hence, with only a few exceptions, they have generally been excluded from the ambit of protective labour law(s), including the enjoyment of their fundamental collective labour rights. Considering, nonetheless, the often weak bargaining position of many self-employed workers, including, as noted, their dependence upon their principals, such a treatment can be particularly problematic from a labour law perspective; a statement that can also be made for other workers who are situated in the sphere of NSFE. Against this background, the developments which take place in the context of platform work constitute an illustrative example of many of the challenges traced within modern workplaces.

Thus, the central research question of this research was: *Can a HRBA) towards collective labour rights bridge the labour protection gap of self-employed platform workers?*

In response to the main research question, this research was subdivided into six sub-questions, addressed in six respective Chapters.

2 MAIN FINDINGS

2.1 The Key Characteristics of Platform Work and Their Relevance for the Current Challenges in the World of Work

This research, in Chapter 1, set out to discuss the phenomenon of platform work, discover its main features and challenges stemming from it, as well as explore its relevance for the challenges with respect to labour protection within modern workplaces. Particularly, it was initially highlighted that, at least to a certain extent, much of the certainties that labour law was built on, such as the existence of models of production that relied on vertically integrated workplaces and standard employment relationships (e.g., full-time work in fixed workplaces), are no longer the rule. Among other factors, the vertical disintegration of firms, expedited by new technological tools, including digital outsourcing, along with the ever-increasing heterogeneity of the workforce and the proliferation of atypical work arrangements, are all issues that have indeed changed things within labour markets. In light of these ongoing alterations, the distinction between employment and self-employment has become an extremely difficult task. As noted, this situation has raised many problems for labour law, as many workers in the 'grey' zone between employment and self-employment remain without or with limited labour protection.

That said, Chapter 1, in turn, pointed out that platform work constitutes an illustrative example of these phenomena. As mentioned, since the advent of platform economy, businesses running these platforms advocate that people can allegedly work autonomously, away from any supervision or control. Contrary to such claims, this research by relying on interdisciplinary evidence, observed that platform work is nothing more than another type of casualised form of work. Such work arrangements, which predate the developments in the platform economy, have been used for a long time with the purpose of, *inter alia*, reducing labour costs and avoiding labour and employment regulations. In this regard, digital labour platforms tend to classify a considerable number of their workers as self-employed, despite the existence of evidence that may indicate a subordinate relationship, often enough well-hidden behind a 'cloak' of organisational and economic independence. Of course, as explained, the presence of similarities in relation to the organisation of work with other examples of casual work arrangements does not negate the fact that platform-mediated work also contains some particular characteristics, capable of generating some new realities within contemporary labour markets, or exacerbating already existing issues of a legal nature. It was observed, for instance, that platform businesses through the use of new technologies, such as algorithms, have the unprecedented ability to access a wide pool of workers, both high-skilled and low-skilled, who share many different occupational and even class identities. As seen moreover, the use of digital reputation systems, like those someone can come across via the Uber and Deliveroo apps, has substituted the old-style command and control approach adopted by traditional employers.[1220] Such techniques, which, as noted, are more advanced and pervasive than employers' physical methods of the past, have resulted in further corrosion of the subordinate contract of employment and have, at least up until recently, pushed many workers outside the realm of an employment relationship and its associated benefits.

2.2 The Implications of Platform Work on Working Conditions, Including the Exercise of Collective Labour Rights

After having identified the particular characteristics of platform work, then this research, in Chapter 2, focused on the implications of these work arrangements on working conditions, including the exercise of collective labour rights, such as the rights to freely associate and bargain collectively. To this extent, it was stated that work provided through platforms has the potential to offer new and more flexible - mostly in terms of time and location - opportunities to people that are seeking employment. Concomitantly, nonetheless, as explained (based on empirical and socioeconomic studies), such work arrangements can be detrimental to workers' labour protection. As it happens in the case of casual and other forms of atypical work, platform work, regardless of its online or offline nature,[1221] is often associated with problematic employment practices, poor working conditions, including law payments and overall job insecurity. In this context, as this research observed, labour is often perceived as a commodity that can be exchanged in the market like any other article of commerce.

Furthermore, as Chapter 2 pointed out, the extensive reliance of platform businesses on freelance jobs, along with other issues related to labour protection, can also impose serious limitations on the meaningful exercise of fundamental collective labour rights, such as the rights to freedom of association and collective bargaining, which constitute a part of the constitutional order of many countries. At the international level, the rights in question are enshrined in the 1998 ILO Declaration on Fundamental Principles and Rights at Work. The rights and principles contained in the Declaration, are considered to be universal; hence, they should be applicable to all workers, notwithstanding their employment status, in all ILO Member States, by the very fact of their membership and irrespective of ratification of the relevant conventions. Such rights, moreover, are also part of the 'universal list' of human rights, as they have been incorporated in a number of international human rights instruments, such as the ECHR and the ESC. Their nature as human rights has also been confirmed by numerous judgments of international courts and national supreme courts.

As this research illustrated, much of the restrictions platform workers and other atypical workers are facing towards the effective exercise of their collective labour rights can be attributed to the very limitations of labour law's own framework, where rights and obligations are mostly secured via the existence of an employment relationship. Furthermore, there are still some national jurisdictions, which forbid the majority

1220. Chapter 1, subsection 6.3.

1221. As explained platform-based work is usually understood to include two forms of work, namely, crowdwork and work-on-demand through applications. For an analysis, *see* Chapter 1, subsection 1.5.

of self-employed workers to be members of trade unions, or in a similar vein, there is no clear right for them to become members of a union. On top of that, collective labour rights can also be constrained, in occasions where platform workers' collective activities come into clash with competition law. In different instances, competition authorities, by adopting a rather strict 'free competition', have been using their authority to obstruct certain categories of workers, including platform workers, from concluding collective bargaining agreements on the ground that these are price-fixing agreements between undertakings; thus, they are capable of hindering fair competition and consumer's welfare. As noted in Chapter 2 (and also in Chapter 5), for a long time, economic efficiency and consumer welfare are perceived as the chief objectives of competition law. However, as this research explained, what is often discounted in this regard, is the procedure that was followed before consumers meet products and services and the vulnerable position of workers within it. Not only this, but, as noted, strict antitrust laws can be also at odds with sources of international labour and human rights law, which dictate the universal applicability of the right to collective bargaining. Of course, such a right is not an absolute right and certain limitations can be applicable. As explained, though (mainly in Chapter 5), the latter need to be proportionate and justified in a democratic society, at least as far as the CoE is concerned.

In addition to legal obstacles, Chapter 2 illustrated that practical hurdles can also constitute a threat towards platform workers' collective labour rights, even if they are considered employees. Among other reasons, as other workers in atypical jobs, they deal with frequent turnovers and limited attachment to a single workplace. As such, it is difficult for them to be approached by unions, or even to communicate with each other in order to organise their collective actions. Also, many traditional trade unions, at least up until recently, have been hesitant to engage such workers in their actions. Vice versa, workers in NSFE, including platform workers, on some occasions, have felt that their particular interests cannot be fully addressed by unions representing classical employees.

The focus on fundamental collective labour rights does not mean that platform work cannot also put at risk the enjoyment of other human rights at work. As noted, for example, the very nature of platform work has generated a growing concern regarding incidences of discrimination, which are inextricably linked to algorithmic decision-making.[1222] Concerns with respect to privacy rights, as well as health and safety entitlements, are equally observed.[1223] That said, as this research points out, challenges in relation to individual human rights at work can be further magnified in workplaces with low unionisation levels, or when workers are excluded from collective bargaining schemes and other collective initiatives.

As demonstrated, the aforementioned risks on fundamental human rights, along with the overall poor working conditions traced within the platform economy, constitute phenomena that can be especially challenging from both a human rights law angle as well as a labour law perspective. Particularly, it was explained that as far as labour

1222. *See* Chapter 2, subsection 2.3.3.
1223. These fundamental human rights are generally accepted as being applied to self-employed workers, contrary to the collective labour rights this thesis is discussing.

law is concerned, the way in which many platform businesses often treat the labour of their workforce can directly challenge the main, or at least one of the main foundations that labour law was based on, namely, that 'labour is not a commodity'. Labour law's inability to address some of the most vulnerable workers can have deeper foundational implications, as its whole edifice can be put into question.

2.3 Platform Work's Exceptionalism Is Over. Is This Enough Though?

This research arrives at a moment when 'disruptors', as platform businesses are often described, have started to be 'disrupted'. Regulatory initiatives, both at national and international levels, and seminal court decisions have indeed attempted to address the challenges derive from platform work arrangements. Particularly, this research, in its third Chapter, based on a number of legal sources, observed that platform work can be embedded within current legal tests for the determination of the employment relationship.[1224] As seen, a number of courts and other administrative bodies around the world have used a wide variety of indications or indicia in order to expose the misclassification of a number of platform workers as self-employed persons. National Supreme Courts, like in the UK and Spain, have pointed out that algorithmic technology can indeed permit digital labour operators to increase their overall control over workers' activities in a way that can be similarly effective to the control exercised by a devoted manager. Along the same lines, as Chapter 3 found, there is a recognition that the element of flexibility in the working schedules of many platform workers does not by itself prevent the presence of an employment relationship. That said, as this research highlighted, the ever-increasing number of victories of platform workers in front of national courts should not be seen as a panacea, especially when it comes to the protection of fundamental collective rights, recognised as human rights. As noted, the enjoyment of these rights should not be dependent on workers' ability to bring claims to courts. Such proceedings, furthermore, can require a long period of time and be very costly. Also, among other shortcomings,[1225] platforms have the capacity to unilaterally determine the terms and conditions of their contracts with clients and workers and, therefore, for those who will be employed under different agreements, new decisions by courts will be needed in clarifying their employment status.

Moreover, as Chapter 3 illustrated, several developments can be also traced in legislation. For example, a number of national legal systems via legislative acts, have adopted platform-specific measures with the purpose of offering or expanding the number of protections to platform workers, such as in the case of the so-called Riders Law, in Spain. The latter, among other things, includes a rebuttable presumption on the establishment of an employment relationship, as well as provisions on algorithmic transparency. The law at issue, however, as in the case of the majority of other platform-specific laws in other countries, has a rather narrow scope of application due

1224. Subsection 3.3.2.
1225. For instance, there are still some contradictory decisions even within the same country and despite the fact that working conditions can be similar.

to the fact that it only covers workers in the transport and delivery areas. Concomitantly, self-employed workers on platforms that, for example, offer cleaning and care services are excluded, let alone crowdworkers. Furthermore, as seen, some countries have attempted to introduce legislation or put in place other measures which attempt to combat misclassification issues in workplaces more in general. As noted, those developments can be equally relevant for platform workers. An example as such, for instance, can be traced to the adoption of the AB5 law in California, which provides for a broad range of elements for the determination of an employment relationship. To this extent, workers will no longer need to show that they are employed by a business; instead, they would be presumed to possess the employee status, except if the hiring entity succeeds in demonstrating that all three conditions of the ABC test are fulfilled. The optimism generated by this law with respect to platform workers, nonetheless, was evaporated shortly after the Prop 22 Referendum, which now excludes ride-hail and food-delivery app-based workers from nearly all employee rights under the law in question.

As many commentators admit, maybe the most important legislative development regarding platform work, at least at the EU level, constitutes the proposal to improve the working conditions of persons working through digital labour platforms. The instrument, albeit still in a draft form, encompasses a broad scope of application that captures all platform workers, including crowdworkers. On top of that, it enshrines a rebuttable presumption for an employment relationship, as well as important provisions that aim at mitigating the risks stemming from algorithmic management. As developed in Chapter 3, even though a significant step in the right direction, the proposed Directive, as it stands at the moment of writing, cannot be expected to solve all the challenges faced by platform workers, especially as collective labour rights are concerned.[1226] As developed, the indicators with respect to the rebuttable presumption are drafted in a rather stringent way. Workers, who will still have to present themselves in front of national courts, may find it difficult to satisfy some of the related criteria in order to fall into the realm of an employment relationship. Moreover, the instrument falls short of acknowledging the fundamental nature of collective labour rights in line with international standards and the CFREU. Along the same lines, it does not touch upon the threats that strict antitrust laws can pose for platform workers and other self-employed persons' collective labour rights and especially the right to collective bargaining.

As explained, the latter issue has been left upon the recent EU Guidelines on the application of Union competition law to collective agreements regarding the working conditions of solo self-employed persons. The Guidelines, by having as a point of reference competition law, stipulate the occasions in which EU competition law will not obstruct the conclusion of collective agreements signed by these workers. Such occasions, among other agreements, include those that are signed by persons who provide their services via the use of digital labour platforms. Once again, as this research explained, like in the case of other initiatives which attempt to regulate the

1226. Subsection 3.2.3.

relationship between competition law and labour law at a national level and developed above,[1227] such a development, albeit significant, is difficult to solve all the issues that vulnerable self-employed workers,[1228] including platform workers, are facing towards the effective exercise of their right to collective bargaining. The issued Guidelines, among other possible shortcomings, pay lip service to the nature of the right to collective bargaining as a fundamental human right and, simultaneously, they refrain from referring to the right to strike. The latter, as this research explained, is also recognised as an international human right, and according to international labour standards, it constitutes an indispensable component of the right to bargain collectively.

2.4 Platform Workers' Collective Mobilisation: Its Importance and the Limitations in Practice

As this research pointed out, the aforementioned recent changes and the growing focus on platform-mediated work, are not coincidental or a mere realisation on the part of regulators of the poor working conditions often faced by platform workers. In this regard, Chapter 4 illustrated the existence of mutual mechanisms tying workers' collective mobilisation and legal change in the context of platform work. Particularly, despite the presence of obstacles, both of legal and practical nature, trade unions have not been discouraged from seeking to organise and represent such workers. In their attempts, the experience they have acquired from the organisation of other atypical workers has played a key role. Of course, as seen, the representation of platform workers can be even more challenging due to the very nature of platform work. For example, the extraordinary ability of platforms to access a wide pool of workers (including many young and migrant workers), compared to other forms of atypical work, render the creation of a common collective identity and cooperation extremely puzzling. That said, the active involvement of institutional trade unions with platform workers and other workers in NSFE, *inter alia*, reflects their broader societal function as entities that do not solely act in their own best interest but are also concerned with the protection of workers beyond their membership.

As Chapter 4 demonstrated, the conclusion of collective agreements, or similar types of settlements, constitutes one of the main ways via which unions have attempted to tackle the problems stemming out of the platform economy. This development is exclusively observed in the context of on-demand, place-based work.[1229] In most of the cases explored, the content of such agreements resembles traditional collective negotiations in other sectors of the labour market. Among other

1227. For examples, as such (e.g., the Competition (Amendment) Act 2017 in Ireland), *see* Chapter 3.
1228. For instance, the provision enshrined in the Guidelines that that solo-self-employed persons have to earn the 50 per cent of their total annual income from a single principal can be problematic for certain workers who engage in a number of short-term contracts.
1229. As noted, crowdworkers have to operate in labour markets beyond the local level. As a result, their collective organisation is extremely challenging, not to mention the conclusion of collective agreements (*see* Chapter 4).

things, health and safety guarantees and a minimum remuneration are just some of the provisions included in these agreements. As seen, though, there are also a few examples, such as the Hermes collective agreement, that in addition to other elements, aimed at addressing some of the 'digital particularities' of platform work, such as the loneliness often experienced by these workers. Besides the conclusion of collective agreements, unions have also differentiated their strategies so as to extend their reach to platform workers. For instance, they have, in multiple cases, assisted platform workers in bringing misclassification claims in front of the courts. Important successes are observed in this respect. They have, moreover, used their resources to organise campaigns against the tactics used by platform giants, like Uber or to influence and push public authorities to adopt protective legislation and other measures. Not only this but on some occasions, they have also adopted 'modern' strategies that may differ from the classical resources of organisation, like collective bargaining and strikes. To this extent, this research referred to a cross-border initiative with the creation of a website that includes a rating system of working conditions on various platforms based on workers' reviews.

Importantly, this research pointed out that on numerous occasions, where traditional unions have not been as proactive, or the representation of such workers is considered impractical to occur through such unions, what is observed is there is an increased number of alternative organisations that represent platform workers' collective interests. These do not necessarily fit the traditional model of trade unions. Grassroots unions and other organisations of workers, which are usually comprised of young and migrant workers, have been decisive in addressing platform workers' specific challenges. In doing so, their efforts have been facilitated via the use of new technologies, such as online forums and social media, that function as labour campaigning tools. Moreover, all over the world, such unions have initiated many strikes, mainly against digital labour operators in transportation and food-delivery services. On top of that, they have used their resources to lobby for several pieces of legislation and proposals designed to ameliorate platform workers' conditions, like the AB5 law in California. Many of the protective measures adopted by platform companies during the COVID-19 pandemic, can be also attributed to those efforts.

Grassroots unions and traditional unions have been acting as one in many of the aforementioned developments, a cooperation that is indicative of solidarity unionism. Their collaboration, for instance, has led to the conclusion of a territorial-collective agreement in Bologna, which albeit not binding, also covers self-employed platform workers. It becomes evident, therefore, that platform workers, by using their fundamental collective labour rights have managed to win significant 'battles' and often achieve better labour protections. Of course, as this research claimed, several limitations continue to obstruct workers' collective action and interests. Among other things, as explained, most of the collective agreements identified in the context of the platform economy only cover employees. As a consequence, a considerable number of self-employed platform workers in a similar predicament to that of employees fall outside their protective scope. As noted, furthermore, even if some collective agreements for self-employed platform workers already exist, these have not followed the typical scenario of collective bargaining, as they have adopted a more 'diluted' version of collective bargaining or other agreements are not legally binding. An illustrative example is the Hermes agreement in the UK which, although it provides for important protections, it, nonetheless, fails to secure the collective representation of the couriers concerned. Also, as previously noted, the Bologna territorial-collective agreement lacks a binding force. Collective agreements for self-employed platform workers have also been materially undermined due to the intervention of national antitrust authorities, like in the case of the Hilfr agreement in Denmark.

Reflecting on these and other challenges analysed more in detail in Chapter 4, this research put forward a theoretical framework to advance the idea that fundamental collective labour rights should be applied to all workers, regardless of their employment status, including self-employed workers. This has been done through the adoption of a HRBA in labour policy. As noted, such an approach does not aim at forcing the requalification of workers who find themselves in a 'grey' zone between employment and self-employment, including many platform workers. It rather seeks to establish a protection floor for all workers, who, by exercising their fundamental collective rights, will be able to ameliorate their working conditions and produce adequate labour standards that will be dependent upon their employment status. As it was also noted, a HRBA has already been advanced by trade unions, which often enough are using the normative weight of human rights in order to enhance their claims inside and outside courtrooms.

2.5 A HRBA Towards Collective Labour Rights

The recognition of collective labour rights, as human rights through the language of international human rights and labour rights instruments, as well as the language of their respective supervisory bodies, constitute the normative references of this research. Both the rights to freedom of association and the right to collective bargaining have been included in numerous human rights instruments, such as the ICESCR, the ECHR, and the CFREU. The same can also be argued in relation to the right to strike. As noted, such rights are also part of the ILO Declaration on Fundamental Principles and Rights at Work, which, albeit not a human rights instrument, it has espoused a 'universalistic' approach that can equally be found in human rights law. Nowhere in these instruments is stipulated that such human rights should be only enjoyed by workers in an employment relationship.

By having human rights instruments and the ILO's international standards as a point of reference, this research, in turn, explored the possible benefits of a HRBA mainly, but not only from a legal point of view. Particularly, considering the shortcomings both in relation to the case law and legislation developed above, this research recognised that an approach as such moves away from a strict binary divide between employment and self-employment when it comes to the enjoyment of collective labour rights. This is because such a distinction is at odds with the principles and the universal application of fundamental human rights. This is also confirmed by the verdict of the supervisory bodies, which aim at securing the proper implementation of the international instruments at issue. For instance, both the CFA and the CEACR, have repeatedly pointed out that Conventions Nos. 87 and 98, should apply to all workers, regardless of the existence of an employment relationship, which is often non-existent. In a similar vein, the broad personal scope of the right to collective bargaining has also been confirmed by the ESC. The latter, in a recent case against Ireland, ruled that all workers should have the right to bargain collectively, including self-employed workers.[1230] It was mentioned that the purpose of competition law is not to restrict the rights to freedom of association and collective bargaining for those workers who may need it the most, due to their limited bargaining power compared to the providers of labour. Thus, an 'outright ban' on collective bargaining for all self-employed workers was found to be excessive as it was incompatible with Article 6 of the Charter.

Furthermore, a HRBA can be crucial in re-establishing the relationship between competition law and labour law. As it was pointed out, at the EU level, competition law's single-centred approach, exclusively focusing on consumer welfare and efficiency, can come into conflict with the social objectives pursued by the Union and incorporated in its Treaties. Along the same lines, a strict application of competition law can interfere with Article 28 CFREU (EU primary law), which provides for the protection of the right to collective bargaining. The CFREU, both in its Preamble and Article 52(3) makes an explicit reference to the ECHR and the ESC. In light of this, the rights contained in the EU Charter should be interpreted in line with these instruments and the verdict of their supervisory bodies. As explained, both the ECtHR and the ECSR, albeit with some differences identified in Chapter 5, have adopted a broad personal scope for the application of the rights to freedom of associations and collective bargaining, which also includes self-employed workers. The research also contented that, after all, collective bargaining and competition law should not always be conceived in opposite terms, as considerations about efficiency and the correction of democratic deficit(s) in labour markets, can constitute common ground for both fields. The recently issued EU Guidelines on the application of Union competition law to collective agreements for solo self-employed persons are expected to solve some of these issues, nonetheless, as noted, they should not be seen as a panacea, especially considering their soft law nature.

That said, a HRBA also becomes imminent considering the phenomenon of managerial prerogatives and their potential effect on workers. In the context of NSFE, including platform work, they can be further exaggerated. In this respect, a HRBA towards collective labour rights can be critical in limiting such prerogatives. It is by now well-established that collective bargaining, as an essential element of the freedom of association, as well as the right to strike, can be used as an extremely effective means in achieving a countervailing power towards employers, or the labour providers more in general. As such, a balance of forces can be re-established. Indeed, by using these rights, trade unions and other workers' associations have played a vital role in creating better jobs, increasing wages, and improving working conditions, more generally, in various aspects of working life.

1230. *Irish Congress of Trade Unions v. Ireland*, Complaint No. 123/2016.

As noted, moreover, the application of a HRBA towards collective labour rights can also be beneficial for the protection of other human rights at work, such as the right to privacy and the right to not be discriminated against. Against this background, as explained, collective labour rights and especially collective bargaining can offer *ex ante* protection towards workers' rights; something that is very important in the context of modern workplaces and the excessive use of new technological tools, like algorithms.

Finally, and not from a purely legal perspective, it was highlighted that a HRBA and a human rights narrative, more in general, can be useful in attracting the support of non-traditional partners, like consumers and civil society organisations. Such actors, considering the dominant position of businesses, such as in the case of platform giants, can constitute significant allies in the attempts of unions to raise awareness regarding the poor working conditions often faced by atypical workers. In a similar vein, the oratory of human rights can function as s a common language for workers with different occupational and even class characteristics; hence, limiting some of the practical impediments these types of workers face in organising their collective actions.

2.6 Looking into the Future

It can be suggested that the findings of this research contain some important observations about the future of trade unions, as well as the future of industrial relations, more in general, through the prism of a HRBA. As explained, the developments observed in the context of the platform economy constitute a valuable guide in this respect.

In contemporary times, trade unions have to cope with new realities. The workforce composition has endured major alterations in most countries, while the rise in the number of atypical work arrangements has generated a considerable number of issues for workers' collective representation and overall workplace unionisation. That said, among other problems, unions' adaptation to new challenges occurs within an environment where around the world, there is a significant drop in union membership or density. As a result, many have rushed, like multiple times in the past, to announce the trade unions' obituary. Contrary to such arguments, this research, by relying on platform workers' collective mobilisation, illustrated a number of occasions where trade unions, no matter the existence of legal and practical obstacles, have not solely actively defended the interest of their own members, but they have also shown a great interest in representing workers beyond their membership. In this context, labour activism has often been tailored to the particular features of atypical workers, such as platform workers.

As explained, the inclusion of platform workers and other workers with similar labour-related insecurities, in trade unions' actions, constitutes an important, but of course not the only prerequisite towards the latter's revitalisation efforts. As mentioned, through their engagement with platform workers, unions have the chance to regain their often-lost vitality and youthfulness and in turn to stay devoted to their wider commitments to equity and social justice. The synergies of institutional unions with grassroots unions, often representing platform workers, are also significant. Alternative unions' actions and practices can inform and update the methods used by traditional unions in extending their reach to workers within fissured and fragmented workplaces. On the other way around, such an interplay can also be particularly advantageous for grassroots movements, as they can take advantage of the experience, as well as financial resources and infrastructure that institutional unions have in their hands. As it was pointed out in Chapter 6, though, the effective protection of platform workers, including other workers in a grey zone between employment and self-employment, is also dependent upon another crucial factor, that is the readiness of national systems of industrial relations to effectively allow self-employed workers to bargain collectively, in line with the requirements that derive from a HRBA.

This research suggested that as a result of the way in which existing systems of industrial relations are presently structured, the effective application of a HRBA can be particularly challenging, even if we put restrictions stemming from competition law on the side. As noted, merely permitting collective bargaining for self-employed persons, as it currently happens in a number of countries, may not be enough to enable substantial bargaining activities in practice. By bringing the examples of countries like the UK and Belgium, this research indicated that national legislators did not have the self-employed in mind when drafting provisions related to laws on collective labour relations. High representation thresholds for unions' recognition, lack, or decline of multi-employer collective bargaining and the absence of statutory rights to compel employers to recognise collective agreements for self-employed workers, constitute only some of the impediments self-employed workers have to deal with when they attempt to exercise their right to bargain collectively. In practice, therefore, the latter takes the form of a 'mere liberty' rather than the form of an actual 'right', often enjoyed by employees.

As explained, the complications self-employed persons face in the conclusion of collective agreements can also be traced in the platform economy. Legal complexities have forced self-employed platform workers to proceed with collective negotiations that do not necessarily represent collective bargaining procedures of a traditional nature; they can be rather perceived as 'soft' or 'diluted version(s)' of collective bargaining. The Hermes agreement in the UK and territorial agreement via the establishment of the so-called Bologna Charter in Italy are illustrative in this respect. Such agreements are expected to proliferate, for as long as obstacles to collective bargaining for self-employed persist within national industrial systems. Albeit important in many respects, these types of agreements cannot be expected to have the same outcome(s) as agreements generated via collective bargaining processes of a traditional nature. In this sense, it is questionable whether such agreements point towards an effective application of a HRBA in practice. In this regard, this doctoral research in Chapter 6 has attempted to provide a building block for a 'future proof' labour law in relation to a growing number of self-employed workers in the labour market. In particular, by taking into account, the aforementioned complexities, this research came up with some requirements capable of facilitating in practice the exercise of collective bargaining for self-employed, including many platform workers:

- The first requirement provides that only for the purposes of unionisation and collective labour laws more broadly, an 'autonomous' notion of worker should be adopted in accordance with international obligations. This notion will be in line with, for instance, the ILO and the ESC that, via the language of their supervisory bodies, have embraced an all-inclusive notion of a 'worker' that included self-employed and is different and, or 'autonomous' from the notion of a 'worker' that employment and labour acts are currently using; or, a notion of a 'worker' that labour courts are typically referring to when have to decide whether an employment relationship exists *sensu stricto*. To this extent, national labour acts establishing the conditions for unions' recognition and the exercise of collective bargaining should insulate themselves from definitions found in other parts of legislation regulating employment and labour relations more in general, as well as labour courts' decisions on the existence of an employment relationship ('insulation approach').

- The second requirement is related to the facilitation and enabling of multi-employer negotiations. As explained, systems with multi-employer collective bargaining are in a better position to offer more inclusive labour protection, as they create minimum standards for payment and other work-related aspects in a specific sector or industry. To this extent, the coverage of collective bargaining agreements tends to exceed beyond trade union membership; something that is really important for workers providing their labour in fissured workplaces, where the identification of the formal employer(s) is always a challenge.
- The third requirement stipulates the facilitation and promotion of mechanisms that provide for the creation of communication channels, which will permit workers to communicate with each other and organise their collective actions. Such a suggestion is also included in the proposed EU Directive on platform work As seen, the lack of these mechanisms, like in the case of the Hilfr collective agreement in Denmark, has already undermined the impact of collective bargaining procedures for self-employed. Such a requirement can also correspond to countries' positive international obligations toward the facilitation of social dialogue.

Undeniably, the adoption of such recommendations or the implementation of any other possible transformation within national industrial systems will require quite some time and effort.

3 OVERALL RESPONSE TO THE RESEARCH QUESTION

This research relies on a series of socioeconomic, empirical, and legal studies, which show that self-employed platform workers often experience a labour protection gap. These workers share important features of flexibility and precariousness with other atypical work arrangements that are on the rise around the world, including an increased number of dependent self-employed persons.[1231] Self-employed platform workers, due to their employment status, are frequently excluded from the (protective) framework of employment and labour laws, including the exercise of their collective labour rights. This situation is particularly problematic as such (self-employed) workers often find themselves in a comparable situation to that of employees (with 'employment status') because of their weak negotiating position and economic dependency on their principals. As Chapter 2 explained, these exclusions can lead to the commodification of labour, a situation that, in turn, can put into question the key, or at least one of the key ideas behind the creation of labour law, namely, the notion that labour is not a commodity.

Based on the different chapters in this research, this research demonstrates that a HRBA towards collective labour rights is clearly capable of bridging the labour protection gap of platform workers with self-employed status. An approach as such forwards the idea that workers, regardless of their status, should be eligible to exercise their collective labour rights, also recognised as human rights. This notion becomes all the more relevant considering the importance and potential of such rights in practice, as developed in Chapter 4. By exercising their collective labour rights, platform workers, regardless of their employment status, have already achieved some important victories which have led to ameliorating their working conditions. Moreover, collective labour rights can have an immediate effect on workers' protection in contrast to legislative and judicial responses, which, as explained in Chapter 3, among other things, constitute much more time-consuming processes in bringing about the desired results. As seen nonetheless, self-employed platform workers continue to face legal restrictions (e.g., due to strict antitrust laws), which, for instance, among other things, often exclude them from the ambit of collective agreements. In light of this, a HRBA can generate several benefits. For example, as discussed in Chapter 5, this approach moves away from a strict dichotomy between employment and self-employment. This is also important for the field of labour law as a whole, as the allocation of fundamental collective labour rights to those who need it the most can assist the field in maintaining its normative coherence and integrity. Moreover, a HRBA can be utilised to re-establish the relationship between labour and competition laws. The nature of collective labour rights as human rights should guide this interplay. A HRBA towards collective labour rights can also be used as a shield of protection for the enjoyment of other human rights at work, like discrimination-related entitlements; it can, furthermore, help workers in solving some of the practical challenges are currently facing, such as the lack of a common identity. That said, as demonstrated in Chapter 6, the effective application of a HRBA is still away from being guaranteed in practice. This is to say that even if someone was placing competition-related issues on the side, there are still challenges stemming from complexions within national systems of industrial relations. As noted, in many instances, existing legal apparatuses for collective bargaining seem outdated and do not match the realities within the new world of work and the increase of

1231. Such workers, as explained, often find themselves in a comparable situation to that of employees due to their weak negotiating position and economic dependency towards their principals.

self-employed workers dependent upon their principals. Therefore, it remains to be seen how national systems of industrial relations will attempt to address such challenges and if their responses will be in line with the requirements of international labour and human rights instruments, as those illustrated in this research.

All in all, the recognition of fundamental collective labour rights as human rights applicable to all workers has not prevented restrictions on the effective application of these rights. Such limitations, nonetheless, should not discourage us from reiterating these rights' importance and status and trying to argue for their effective protection. These rights are essential for giving the platform economy a place where work is done in conditions of human dignity and an environment that is sustainable for labour rights guarantees.

Bibliography

Books

Aloisi, A. and De Stefano, V., *Your Boss Is an Algorithm: Artificial Intelligence, Platform Work and Labour* (Bloomsbury Publishing 2022).

Alston, P., *Labour Rights as Human Rights* (Oxford University Press 2005).

Anderson, E., *Private Government: How Employers Rule Our Lives and Why We Don't Talk about It* (Princeton University Press 2017).

Baccaro L. and Howell C., *Trajectories of Neoliberal Transformation. European Industrial Relations Since the 1970s* (Cambridge University Press 2017).

Bellace, J. and ter Haar, B. eds, *Research Handbook on Labour, Business and Human Rights Law* (Elgar Publishing 2019).

Comparato, F.K., *A afirmação histórica dos direitos humanos* (Saraiva 1999).

Cant, C., *Riding for Deliveroo: Resistance in the New Economy* (Polity Express 2019).

Chandler, A.D.J., *Scale and Scope: The Dynamics of Industrial Capitalism* (Harvard University Press 1994).

Cranford, C., Fudge, J., Tucker, E., Vosko, L.F., *Self-Employed Workers Organize: Law, Policy, and Unions* (McGill-Queen's Press 2005).

Daniels, G. and McIlroy, J. eds, *Trade Unions in a Neoliberal World* (Taylor & Francis 2009).

Davidov, G. and Langille, B. eds, *The Idea of Labour Law* (Oxford University Press 2011).

Davies, P. and Freedland, M., *Kahn-Freund's Labour and the Law*, (Stevens & Sons 1983).

Doellgast, V., Lillie, N. and Pulignano, V. eds, *Reconstructing Solidarity: Labour Unions, Precarious Work, and the Politics of Institutional Change in Europe* (Oxford University Press 2018).

Emery, F., *Characteristics of Sociotechnical Systems* (Tavistock Institute 1959).

Fabbrini, F., *Fundamental Rights in Europe* (Oxford University Press 2014).

Fenwick, C. and Novitz, T. eds, *Human Rights at Work, Perspectives on Law and Regulation* (Hart Publishing 2010).

Forsyth, A., *The Future of Unions and Worker Representation: The Digital Picket Line* (Hart Publishing 2022).

Freedland, M. and Countouris, N., *The Legal Construction of Personal Work Relations* (Oxford University Press 2011).

Friedman, M., *Capitalism and Freedom* (University of Chicago Press 1962).

Fudge, J., McCrystal, S. and Sankaran K. eds, *Challenging the Legal Boundaries of Work Regulation* (Hart Publishing 2012).

Gearty, C. and Mantouvalou, V. eds, *Debating Social Rights* (Hart Publishing 2011).

Gleason, S.E. ed., *The Shadow Workforce: Perspectives on Contingent Work in the United States, Japan, and Europe* (Upjohn Institute for Employment Research 2006).

Habermas, J., *Toward a Rational Society* (Beacon Press 1970).

Harvey, D., *A Brief History of Neo-liberalism* (Oxford University Press 2005).

Hendrickx, F. and De Stefano, V. eds, *Game Changers in Labour Law: Shaping the Future of Work* (Wolters Kluwer 2018).

Kestemont, L., *Handbook on Legal Methodology. From Objective to Method* (Intersentia 2018).

Kelly, J., *Rethinking Industrial Relations: Mobilization, Collectivism and Long Waves* (Routledge 1998).

Lipset, S.M. ed., *Unions in Transition: Entering the Second Century* (ICS Press 1986).

Marx, K., *Grundrisse: Foundations of the Critique of Political Economy* (Penguin 2005).

Moore, P.V. and Upchurch, M., U, M. eds, *Humans and Machines at Work: Monitoring, Surveillance and Automation in Contemporary Capitalism* (Springer 2018).

Patel, K. and Schweitzer, H. eds, *The Historical Foundations of EU Competition Law* (Oxford Scholarship Online 2013), available at: https://oxford.universitypressscholarship.com/view/10.1093/acprof:oso/9780199665358.001.0001/acprof-9780199665358.

Pinto, M., Smith, R. and Tung, I., *Rights at Risk: Gig companies' Campaign to Upend Employment as We Know It* (NELP 2019).

Polanyi, K., *The Great Transformation: The Political and Economic Origins of our Time* (2nd ed. Beacon Press 2001).

Posner, E.A., *How Antitrust Failed Workers* (Oxford University Press 2021).

Prassl, J., *Humans as a Service* (Oxford University Press 2018).

Prassl, J., *The Concept of the Employer* (Oxford University Press 2015).

Radin, M. J., *Contested Commodities* (Harvard University Press 1996).

Ratti, L., *In-Work Poverty in Europe: Vulnerable and Under-Represented Persons in a Comparative Perspective* (Kluwer Law International 2022).

Ravenelle, J.A., *Hustle and Gig: Struggling and Surviving in the Sharing Economy* (University of California Press 2019).

Rosenblat, A., *Uberland: How Algorithms are Rewriting the Rules of Work* (University of California Press 2018).

Schor, J. B., *After the Gig: How the Sharing Economy Got Hijacked and How to Win It Back* (University of California Press 2020).

Shostack, A.B., *CyberUnion: Empowering Labor Through Computer Technology* (Ebook, Routledge 2016), available at: https://www.taylorfrancis.com/books/

mono/10.4324/9781315292250/cyberunion-empowering-labor-computer-technology-arthur-shostack.

Slee, T., *What's Yours Is Mine – Against the Sharing Economy* (O/R Books 2015).

Smith, I. and Baker, A., *Smith & Wood's Employment* Law (11th ed. Oxford University Press 2013).

Srnicek, N., *Platform Capitalism* (Polity Press 2017).

Stammers, N., *Human Rights and Social Movements* (Pluto Press 2009).

Standing, G., *The Corruption of Capitalism: Why Rentiers Thrive and Work Does Not Pay London* (Biteback Publishing 2016).

Standing, G., *The Precariat: The New Dangerous Class* (Bloomsbury Academic 2014).

Standing, G., *Global Labour Flexibility: Seeking Distributive Justice* (Macmillan 1999).

Supiot, A., *Beyond Employment: Challenges in Work and the Future of Labour Law in Europe* (Oxford University Press 2001).

Supiot, A., *L' esprit of Philadelphie* (Seuil 2010).

Van Der Linden, M., *Workers of the World: Essays Toward a Global Labor History* (Brill Academic Publishers 2008).

Weiler, P., *Reconcilable Differences: New Directions in Canadian Labour Law* (Carswell 1980).

Wood, E.M., *The Origin of Capitalism: A Longer View* (Verso Books 2002).

Wouters, M., *International Labour Standards and Platform Work: An Analysis of Digital Labour Platforms Based on the Instruments on Private Employment Agencies, Home Work and Domestic Work* (Wolters Kluwer 2022).

Zweigert, K., and Kötz, H., *An Introduction to Comparative Law*, (Oxford University Press 1997).

Book Chapters

Adams, M. and Griffiths, J., *Against 'Comparative Method': Explaining Similarities and Differences* (Maurice Adams, M. and Jacco A. Bomhoff eds, *Practice and Theory in Comparative Law*, Cambridge University Press 2012).

Aloisi, A., Gramano, E., *A Solution in Search of a Problem? Collective Rights and the Antitrust Labour Exemption in Italy* (Shae McCrystal, Ewan McGaughey and Sanjukta Paul eds, *The Cambridge Handbook of Labor in Competition Law*, Cambridge University Press 2022).

Aloisi, A., Gramano, E., *Workers Without Workplaces and Unions Without Unity: Non-Standard Forms of Employment, Platform Work and Collective Bargaining* (Valeria Pulignano and Frank Hendrickx eds., *Employment Relations in the 21st Century: Challenge for Theory and Research in a Changing World of Work*, Kluwer Law International 2020).

Alvin, L.G., Corrada, L.R., *United States of America* (Frank Hendrickx ed., *International Encyclopaedia of Laws: Labour Law and Industrial Relations*, Kluwer Law International 2018).

Arthurs, H.W., *Labour Law after Labour* (Guy Davidov and Brian Langille eds, *The Idea of Labour Law*, Oxford University Press 2011).

Atkinson, J., *Human Rights as Foundations for Labour Law* (Hugh Collins, Gillian Lester and Virginia Mantouvalou eds, *Philosophical Foundations of Labour Law*, Oxford University Press 2018).

Blanpain, R., *Comparativism in Labor Law and Industrial Relations* (Roger Blanpain ed., *Comparative Labour Law and Industrial Relations in Industrialized Market Economies*, Wolters Kluwer 2014).

Bogg, A., Buendia, R., *The Law and Workers Voice in the Gig Economy* (Valerio De Stefano, Ilda Durri, Charalampos Stylogiannis and Mathias Wouters eds, *A Research Agenda for the Gig-Economy and Society*, Edward Elgar Publishing 2022).

Bogg, A., *Economic Coordination as Freedom of Association* (Shae McCrystal, Ewan McGaughey and Sanjukta Paul eds, *The Cambridge Handbook of Labor in Competition Law*, Cambridge University Press 2022).

Boto, M.J.M., *Collective Bargaining and the Gig Economy: Reality and Possibilities* (José M. Boto and Elisabeth Brameshuber eds, *Collective Bargaining and the Gig Economy a Traditional Tool for New Business Models*, Hart Publishing, 2022).

Bellace, J., Haar, B., *Perspectives on Labour and Human Rights* (Janice R. Bellace and Beryl ter Haar eds, *Research Handbook on Labour, Business and Human Rights Law*, Elgar Publishing 2019).

Butler, M., *Great Britain* (Frank Hendrickx ed., *International Encyclopaedia of Laws: Labour Law and Industrial Relations*, Kluwer Law International 2017).

Carinci, M. T., Dorssemont, F., *A Comparative Analysis* (Maria T. Carinci and Filip DORSSEMONT eds, *Platform Work in Europe: Towards Harmonisation?*, Intersentia 2021).

Casale, G., *The Employment Relationship: A General Introduction* (Giuseppe Casale G. ed., *The Employment Relationship: A Comparative Overview*, Hart Publishing 2011).

Cefaliello, A., Inversi, C., *The Impact of the Gig-Economy on Occupational Health and Safety: Just an Occupation Hazard?* (Valerio De Stefano, Ilda Durri, Charalampos Stylogiannis and Mathias Wouters eds, *A Research Agenda for the Gig-Economy and Society*, Edward Elgar Publishing 2022).

Collins, H., *Theories of Rights as Justifications for Labour Law* (Guy Davidov and Brian Langille eds, *The Idea of Labour Law*, Oxford University Press 2011).

Collins, H., *Is the Contract of Employment Illiberal?* (Hugh Collins, Gillian Lester and Virginia Mantouvalou eds, *Philosophical Foundations of Labour Law*, Oxford University Press 2018).

Compa, L., *Trade Unions and Human Rights* (Cynthia Soohoo, Catherine Albisa, Martha F. Davis eds, *Bringing Human Rights Home: A History of Human Rights in the United States*, Praeger Publishing 2008).

Compa, L., Gross, J.A., *Introduction* (Lance Compa and James A. Gross, *Human Rights in Labor and Employment Relations: International and Domestic Perspectives*, IL: Labor and Employment Relations Association Series 2009).

Countouris, N., *Uses and Misuses of 'Mutuality of Obligations' and the Autonomy of Labour Law* (Alan Bogg, Cathryn Costello, Anne C.L. Davies, Jeremias Prassl eds, *The Autonomy of Labour Law*, Hart Publishing 2015).

Countouris, N., *The Employment Relationship: A Comparative Analysis of National Judicial Approaches* (Giuseppe Casale ed., *The Employment Relationship: A Comparative Overview*, Hart Publishing 2011).

Canessa Montejo, M., *Labor Human Rights and the Jurisprudence of the Inter-American Court of Human Rights* (Janice R. Bellace and Beryl ter Haar eds, *Research Handbook on Labour, Business and Human Rights Law*, Elgar Publishing 2019).

Czarzasty, J., *Collective Bargaining in Poland: A Near-Death Experience* (Torsten Müller, Kurt Vandaele, and Jeremy Waddington eds, *Collective Bargaining in Europe: Towards an Endgame*, Vol. 2, ETUI, 2019).

Davies, P., Freedland, M., *Employees, Workers and the Autonomy of Labour Law* (Dieter Simon and Manfred Weiss ed., *Zur Autonomie des Individuums (Liber Amoricum Spiros Simitis)*, Nomos 2000).

De Stefano, V., Durri, I., Stylogiannis, C., Wouters, M., *Introduction* (Valerio De Stefano, Ilda Durri, Charalampos Stylogiannis and Mathias Wouters eds, *A Research Agenda for the Gig-Economy and Society*, Edward Elgar Publishing 2022).

De Stefano, V., Durri, I., Stylogiannis, C., Wouters, M., *Exclusion by Default: Platform Workers' Quest for Labour Protections* (Valerio De Stefano, Ilda Durri, Charalampos Stylogiannis and Mathias Wouters eds, *A Research Agenda for the Gig-Economy and Society*, Edward Elgar Publishing 2022).

De Stefano, V., Aloisi, A., *Fundamental Labour Rights, Platform Work and Human Rights Protection of Non-standard Workers* (Janice R. Bellace and Beryl ter Haar eds, *Research Handbook on Labour, Business and Human Rights Law*, Elgar Publishing 2019).

Dorssemont, F., *Collective Workers' Rights for Workers in the Gig Economy* (Maria T. Carinci and Filip DORSSEMONT eds, *Platform Work in Europe: Towards Harmonisation?*, Intersentia 2021).

Dorssemont, F., *The European Convention on Human Rights as a Fountain of Labour Rights* (Janice R. Bellace and Beryl ter Haar eds, *Research Handbook on Labour, Business and Human Rights Law*, Elgar Publishing 2019).

Drahokoupil, J., Fabo, B., *Outsourcing, Offshoring and the Deconstruction of Employment: New and Old Challenges* (Amparo Serrano-Pascual and Maria Jepsen eds, *The Deconstruction of Employment as a Political Question: 'Employment' as a Floating Signifier*, Spinger 2018).

Dukes, R., *Hugo Sinzheimer and the Constitutional Function of Labour Law* (Guy Davidov and Brian Langille eds, *The Idea of Labour Law*, Oxford University Press 2011).

Ewing, K., *Laws Against Strikes Revisited* (Catherine Bernard, Simon Deakin and Gillian S. Morris eds, *The Future of Labour Law*, Liber Amocorum Bob Hepple QC, Hart Publishing 2004).

Fox, E., *US and EU Competition Law: A Comparison* (Edward M. Graham and David Richardson eds, *Global Competition Policy*, Institute for International Economics 1997).

Franquet, V., Maisin, J.B., *Belgium* (Bernd Waas and Christina Hießl eds, *Collective Bargaining for Self-employed Workers in Europe: Approaches to Reconcile Competition Law and Labour Rights*, Kluwer Law International 2021).

Frege, C., Heery, E. & Turner, L., *The New Solidarity? Trade Union Coalition-Building in Five Countries* (Carola M. Frege and John Kelly eds, *Varieties of Unionism*, Oxford, Oxford University Press 2004).

Fudge, J., *Blurring Legal Boundaries: Regulating for Decent Work* (Judy Fudge, Shae McCrystal and Kamala Sankaran eds, *Challenging the Legal Boundaries of Work Regulation*, Hart Publishing 2012).

Fudge, J., *Labour as a 'Fictive Commodity': Radically Reconceptualizing Labour Law* (Guy Davidov and Brian Langille eds, *The Idea of Labour Law*, Oxford University Press 2011).

Fudge, J., *Constitutionalizing Labour Rights in Europe* (Tom Campbell, Keith D. Ewing and Adam Tomkins eds, *The Legal Protection of Human Rights: Sceptical Essays*, Oxford University Press 2011).

Gramano, E., Kullmann, M., *Algorithmic Discrimination, the Role of GPS, and the Limited Scope of EU Non-discrimination Law* (Valerio De Stefano, Ilda Durri, Charalampos Stylogiannis and Mathias Wouters eds, *A Research Agenda for the Gig-Economy and Society*, Edward Elgar Publishing 2022).

Hayter, S., *Unions and Collective Bargaining* (Janine Berg ed., *Labour Markets, Institutions and Inequality: Building Just Societies in the 21st Century*, Edward Elgar Publishing 2015).

Heißl, C., *National Approaches to Collective Bargaining for the Self-employed: Common Trends, Innovative Potential and Unresolved Problems* (Bernd Waas and Christina Hießl eds, *Collective Bargaining for Self-employed Workers in Europe: Approaches to Reconcile Competition Law and Labour Rights*, Kluwer Law International 2021).

Heinemann, F., *The Drivers of Deregulation in the Era of Globalization* (Peter Bernholz and Roland Vaubel eds, *Political Competition and Economic Regulation*, Routledge 2007).

Hendrickx, F., *Belgium* (Frank Hendrickx ed., *International Encyclopaedia of Laws: Labour Law and Industrial Relations*, Kluwer Law International 2022).

Hepple, B., *Factors Influencing the Making and Transformation of Labour Law in Europe* (Guy Davidov and Brian Langille eds, *The Idea of Labour Law*, Oxford University Press 2011).

Herod, A., *Theorising Unions in Transition* (John Pickles and Adrian Smith eds, *Theorising Transition: The Political Economy of Change in Central and Eastern Europe*, London, Routledge 1998).

Hughes, T.P., *Technological Momentum* (Merritt R. Smith, M.R. and Leo Marx, L. eds, *Does Technology Drive History?: The Dilemma of Technological Determinism*, The MIT Press 1994).

Hyman, R., *Changing Trade Union Identities and Strategies* (Richard Hyman and Anthony Ferner eds, *New Frontiers in European Industrial Relations*, Blackwell 1994).

Vogt, J., Bellace, J., Compa, L., Ewing, KD., Hendy, J., Lörcher, K., Novitz, T., *The Right to Strike Is Recognised as Customary International Law* (Jeffrey Vogt et. al., *The Right to Strike in International Law*, Oxford, Hart Publishing 2020).

Kozak-Maśnicka, M. and Pisarczyk, L., *Extending the Personal Scope of Collective Bargaining as a Chance for Gig Workers?: The Polish Case* (José M. Boto and Elisabeth Brameshuber eds, *Collective Bargaining and the Gig Economy a Traditional Tool for New Business Models*, Hart Publishing, 2022).

Kresal, B., *Collective Bargaining for Platform Workers and the European Social Charter* (José M. Boto and Elisabeth Brameshuber eds, *Collective Bargaining and the Gig Economy a Traditional Tool for New Business Models*, Hart Publishing, 2022).

Laagland, F.G., *The Netherlands* (Bernd Waas and Christina Hießl eds, *Collective Bargaining for Self-employed Workers in Europe: Approaches to Reconcile Competition Law and Labour Rights*, Kluwer Law International 2021).

Lehdonvirta, V., *Algorithms that Divide and Unite: Delocalisation, Identity and Collective Action in 'Microwork'* (Jörg Flecker, ed., *Space, Place and Global Digital Work*, London, Palgrave Macmillan 2016).

Leary, V., *The Paradox of Worker's Rights as Human Rights* (Lance Compa, L., Stephen F. Diamond eds, *Human Rights, Labor Rights and International Trade*, Philadelphia, University of Pennsylvania Press 1996).

Loi, P., *The Boundaries Between Collective Agreements and Statutory Legislation* (José M. Boto and Elisabeth Brameshuber eds, *Collective Bargaining and the Gig Economy a Traditional Tool for New Business Models*, Hart Publishing, 2022).

Lörcher, K., *The New Social Dimension in the Jurisprudence of the European Court on Human Rights (ECHR): The Demir and Baykara Judgment, Its Methodology and Follow-up* (Filip Dorssemont, Klaus Lörcher and Isabelle Schömann eds, *The European Convention on Human Rights and the Employment Relation*, Oxford and Oregon, Hart Publishing 2013).

Macklem, P., *The Right to Bargain Collectively in International Law: Workers' Right, Human Right, International Right?* (Philip Alston ed., *Labour Rights as Human Rights*, Oxford University Press 2005).

Mangan, D., *Ford, Taylor and the Gig: Workplaces in* Transition (Valeria Pulignano and Frank Hendrickx eds, *Employment Relations in the 21st Century: Challenge for Theory and Research in a Changing World of Work*, Kluwer Law International 2020).

Michaels, R., The Functional Method of Comparative Law, (Mathias Reimann, and Zimmermann, Reinhard eds, *The Oxford Handbook of Comparative Law*, Oxford, Oxford University Press 2006).

Mirtus, L., *Poland* (Bernd Waas and Christina Hießl eds, *Collective Bargaining for Self-employed Workers in Europe: Approaches to Reconcile Competition Law and Labour Rights*, Kluwer Law International 2021).

Misa, T.J., *Retrieving Sociotechnical Change from Technological Determinism* (Merritt R. Smith, M.R. and Leo Marx, L. eds, *Does Technology Drive History?: The Dilemma of Technological Determinism*, The MIT Press 1994).

Müller-Armack, A., *The Principles of the Social Market Economy* (Peter Kolsowski ed., *The Social Market Economy: Theory and Ethics of the Economic Order*, Springer 1998).

Pecinovsky, P., *The Right to Collective Bargaining for Economically Dependent Workers with a Self-Employed-Status* (Barry Cofler ed., *European Trade Unions in the 21st Century: The Future of Solidarity and Workplace Democracy*, St Antony's Series (e-book), Palgrave Macmillan 2018).

Perulli, A., *Subordinate, Autonomous and Economically Dependent Work: A Comparative Analysis of Selected European Countries* (Giuseppe Casale ed., *The Employment Relationship: A Comparative Overview*, Hart Publishing 2011).

Potocka-Sionek, N., *Crowdwork and Global Supply Chains: Regulating Digital Piecework* (Valerio De Stefano, Ilda Durri, Charalampos Stylogiannis and Mathias Wouters eds, *A Research Agenda for the Gig-Economy and Society*, Edward Elgar Publishing 2022).

Prassl, J., Risak, M., *The Legal Protection of Crowdworkers: Four Avenues for Workers' Rights in the Virtual Realm* (Pamela Meil and Vassil Kirov eds, *Policy Implications of Virtual Work*, Palgrave Macmillan 2017).

Rainone, S., *Labour Rights Beyond Employment Status: Insights from the Competition Law Guidelines on Collective Bargaining* (Tindara Addabbo, Edoardo Ales, Ylenia Curzi, Tomasso Fabri, Olga Rymkevich, Iacapo Senatori eds, *Defining and Protecting Autonomous Work*, Palgrave 2022).

Rainone, S., *Labour Law Beyond its Emancipatory Nature: What Is Left?* (Stafano Bellomo and Antonio Preteroti A. eds, *Recent labour law: Issues a multilevel perspective*, G. Giappichelli Editore 2019).

Rani, U., Gobel, N., Rishabh K.D., *Is flexibility and Autonomy a Myth or Reality on Taxi Platforms? Comparison Between Traditional and App-Based Taxi Drivers in Developing* Countries (Valerio De Stefano, Ilda Durri, Charalampos Stylogiannis and Mathias Wouters eds, *A Research Agenda for the Gig-Economy and Society*, Edward Elgar Publishing 2022).

Rosioru, F., *The Changing Concept of Subordination* (György Kiss ed., *Recent Developments Labour Law*, Akadémiai Kiadó 2013).

Sankaran, K., *Flexibility and Informalisation of Employment Relationships* (Judy Fudge, Shae McCrystal and Kamala Sankaran eds, *Challenging the Legal Boundaries of Work Regulation*, Hart Publishing 2012).

Schmidtchen, D., *Introduction* (Dieter Schmidtchen, Max Albert and Stefan Voigt eds, *The More Economic Approach to European Competition Law*, Mohr Siebeck 2007).

Schoukens, P., Barrio, A., De Becker, E., *Platform Economy and the Risk of In-Work Poverty: A Research Agenda for Social Security Lawyers* (Valerio De Stefano, Ilda Durri, Charalampos Stylogiannis and Mathias Wouters eds, *A Research Agenda for the Gig-Economy and Society*, Edward Elgar Publishing 2022).

Sedacca, N., *Domestic Work and the Gig Economy* (Valerio De Stefano, Ilda Durri, Charalampos Stylogiannis and Mathias Wouters eds, *A Research Agenda for the Gig-Economy and Society*, Edward Elgar Publishing 2022).

Swepston, L., *How the ILO Embraced Human Rights* (Janice R. Bellace and Beryl ter Haar eds, *Research Handbook on Labour, Business and Human Rights Law*, Elgar Publishing 2019).

Tyler, G., *Labor at the Crossroads* (Seymour M. Lipset ed., *Unions in Transition: Entering* the Second *Century*, ICS Press 1986).

Treu, T., *Italy* (Frank Hendrickx ed., *International Encyclopaedia of Laws: Labour Law and Industrial Relations*, Kluwer Law International 2020).

Vandaele, K., *Collective Resistance and Organizational Creativity Amongst Europe's Platform Workers: A New Power in the Labour Movement?* (Julieta Haider and Maarten Keune, eds, *Work and Labour Relations in Platform Capitalism*, Cheltenham, Edward Elgard 2021).

Weiss, M., *Re-Inventing Labour Law?* (Guy Davidov and Brian Langille eds, *The Idea of Labour Law*, Oxford, Oxford University Press 2011).

Weiss, M., *Challenges for Workers' Participation* (Tindara Addabbo, Edoardo Ales, Ylenia Curzi, Tomasso Fabri, Olga Rymkevich, Iacapo Senatori eds, *The Collective Dimensions of Employment Relations: Interdisciplinary Perspectives on Workers' Voices and Changing Workplace Patterns*, Palgrave Macmillan (eBook) 2021, available at: https://doi.org/10.1007/978-3-030-75532-4.

Ziller, J., *Hierarchy of Norms: Hierarchy of Sources and General Principles* (Ulrich Becker, Armon Hatje, Michael Potacs and Nina Wunderlich eds, *European Union Law' Verfassung und Verwaltung in Europa Festschrift für Jürgen Schwarze zum*, Nomos Verlagsgesellschaft 2014).

Journal Articles

Adams, Z., Deakin, S., *Institutional Solutions to Precariousness and Inequality in Labour Markets*, 52 British Journal of Industrial Relations 779 n. 4 (2014).

Adams-Prassl J., *What If Your Boss Was an Algorithm? Economic Incentives, Legal Challenges, and the Rise of Artificial Intelligence at Work*, 41 Comparative Labor Law & Policy Journal 123 n. 1 (2019).

Adams, R.J., *From Statutory Right to Human Right: The Evolution and Current Status of Collective Bargaining*, 12 Just Labour 48 (2008).

Addison, J.T., Siebert, S., Wagner J., Xiangdong W., *Worker Participation and Firm Performance: Evidence from Germany and Britain*, 38 British Journal of Industrial Relations 7 n. 1 (2000).

Ajunwa I., Crawford K., Schultz J., *Limitless Worker Surveillance*, 105 California Law Review 735 n. 3 (2017).

Aloisi, A., *Platform Work in Europe: Lessons Learned, Legal Developments and Challenges Ahead*, European Labour Law Journal Online Article (2022), available at: https://journals.sagepub.com/doi/pdf/10.1177/20319525211062557.

Aloisi, A., *Commoditized Workers: Case Study Research on Labour Law Issues Arising from a Set of 'On-Demand/Gig Economy' Platforms*, 37 Comparative Labor Law & Policy Journal, 653 n. 3 (2016).

Amber, D., 'Competition Law and Human Rights: A Complex Relationship', *Wirtschaft und Wettbewerb* Online Article (2021), available at SSRN: https://ssrn.com/abstract=3915662.

Andrias, K., *The New Labor Law*, 126 Yale Law Journal 1 (2016).

Arabadjieva, K., *Worker Empowerment, Collective Labour Rights and Article 11 of the European Convention on Human Rights*, Human Rights Law Review 1 (2021).

Baccaro, L., Howell, C., *A Common Neoliberal Trajectory: The Transformation of Industrial Relations in Advanced Capitalism*, 39 Politics & Society 521 n. 4 (2011).

Baldissone, R., *Human Rights: A Lingua Franca for the Multiverse*, 14 The International Journal of Human Rights 1117 n. 7 (2010).

Barnard, C., *Discrimination Law, Self-Employment and the Liberal Professions*, 12 European Anti-discrimination Law Review 21 (2011).

Barrow, C., *RMT v. United Kingdom [2014]: The European Court of Human Rights Intimidated into Timidity or Merely Consistent in Its Inconsistency?*, 3 European Human Rights Law Review 277 (2015).

Bednarowicz, B., *Delivering on the European Pillar of Social Rights: The New Directive on Transparent and Predictable Working Conditions in the European Union*, 48 Industrial Law Journal 604 n. 4 (2019).

Beerepoot, N. and Lambregts, B., *Competition in Online Job Marketplaces: Towards a Global Labour Market for Outsourcing Services?*, 15 Global Networks 236 n. 2 (2015).

Bellace, J., *The ILO and the Right to Strike*, 153 International Labour Review 29 n. 1 (2014).

Benassi, C., Vlandas, T., *Union Inclusiveness and Temporary Agency Workers: The Role of Power Resources and Union Ideology*, 22 European Journal of Industrial Relations 5 n. 1 (2016).

Benjamin, P., *An Accident of History: Who Is (and Who Should Be) an Employee under South African Labour Law*, 25 Industrial Law Journal 787 n. 5 (2004).

Berg, J., *Protecting Workers in the Digital Age: Technology, Outsourcing, and the Growing Precariousness of Work*, 41 Comparative Labor Law & Policy Journal 69 n.1 (2019).

Berg, J., *Income Security in the On-Demand Economy: Findings and Policy Lessons from a Survey of Crowdworkers*, 37 Comparative Labor Law & Policy Journal 554 n. 3 (2016).

Biasi, M., *'We Will All Laugh at Gilded Butterflies'. The Shadow of Antitrust Law on the Collective Negotiation of Fair Fees for Self-Employed Workers*, 9 European Labour Law Journal 354 n. 4 (2018).

Bimber, B., *Karl Marx and the Three Faces of Technological Determination*, 20 Social Studies of Science 333 n. 2 (1990).

Blackham, A., *We Are All Entrepreneurs Now': Options and New Approaches for Adapting Equality Law for the 'Gig Economy'*, 34 International Journal of Comparative Labour Law and Industrial Relations 413 n. 4 (2018).

Bodie, M.T., Cherry, M.A., McCormick, M.L., Tang, J., *The Law and Policy of People Analytics*, 88 University of Colorado Law Review 961 n. 4 (2017).

Bogg, A., *Square Pegs in Round Holes? Collective Bargaining and the Self-Employed*, 42 Comparative Labor Law & Policy Journal 409 n. 2 (2021).

Bogg, A., *Taken for a Ride: Workers in the Gig Economy*, 135 Law Quarterly Review 219 (2019).

Bogg, A., *Labour, Love and Futility: Philosophical Perspectives on Labour Law*, 33 International Journal of Comparative Labour Law and Industrial Relations 7 n. 1 (2017).

Bogg, A., *Subsidiarity or Freedom of Association? A Perspective from Labor Law*, 61 The American Journal of Jurisprudence 143 n. 1 (2016).

Bogg, A., Ewing, K., *The Implications of the RMT Case*, 43 Industrial Law Journal 221 n. 3 (2014).

Brand, O., *Conceptual Comparisons: Towards a Coherent Methodology of Comparative Legal Studies*, 32 Brooklyn Journal of International Law 405 Vol. n. 2 (2007).

Brandl, B. Bechter, B., *The Hybridization of National Collective Bargaining Systems: The Impact of the Economic Crisis on the Transformation of Collective Bargaining in the European Union*, 40 Economic and Industrial Democracy 469 n. 3 (2019).

Brudney, J.J., *The Right to Strike as Customary International Law*, 46 The Yale Journal of International Law 1 n.1 (2021).

Bryson, A., Ebbinghaus, B., Visser, J., *Introduction: Causes, Consequences and Cures of Union Decline*, 17 European Journal of Industrial Relations 97 n. 2 (2011).

Buch-Hansen, H., Wigger, A., *Revisiting 50 years of Market-Making: The Neoliberal Transformation of European Competition Policy*, 17 Review of International Political Economy 20 (2010).

Cartier, K., *The Transaction Costs and Benefits of the Incomplete Contract of Employment*, 18 Cambridge Journal of Economics 181 (1994).

Cengiz, F., *The Conflict Between Market Competition and Worker Solidarity: Moving from Consumer to a Citizen Welfare Standard in Competition Law*, 41 Legal Studies 73 (2020).

Clawson, D., Clawson, M.A., *What Has Happened to the US Labor Movement? Union Decline and Renewal*, 25 Annual Review of Sociology 95 (1999).

Cockayne, D.G., *Sharing and Neoliberal Discourse: The Economic Function of Sharing in the Digital On-Demand Economy*, 77 Geoforum 73 (2016).

Collins, H., *Regulating the Employment Relation for Competitiveness*, 30 Industrial Law Journal 17 n. 1 (2001).

Collins, H., *Independent Contractors and the Challenge of Vertical Disintegration to Employment Protection Laws*, 10 Oxford Journal of Legal Studies 353 n. 3 (1990).

Collins, H., *Labour Law as a Vocation*, 105 Law Quarterly Review 468 July (1989).

Compa, L., *Trade unions, NGOs, and corporate codes of conduct*, 14 Development in Practice 210 n. 1-2 (2004).

Culpepper, P.D., Thelen, K., *Are We All Amazon Primed? Consumers and the Politics of Platform Power*, 53 Comparative Political Studies 288 n. 2 (2020).

Davidov, G., *Collective Bargaining Laws: Purpose and Scope*, 1 International Journal of Comparative Labour Law and Industrial Relations 81 (2004).

Dagnino, E., Armaroli, I., *A Seat at the Table: Negotiating Data Processing in the Workplace. A National Case Study and Comparative Insights*, 41 Comparative Labor Law & Policy Journal 173 (2019).

Dagnino, E., *People Analytics: lavoro e tutele al tempo del management tramite big data*, 3 Labour & Law Issues 1 n. 1 (2017).

Dagnino, E., *Uber law: prospettive giuslavoristiche sulla sharing/on-demand economy*, 26 Diritto delle relazioni industriali 137 n. 1 (2016).

Daskalova, V., *Regulating the New Self-Employed in the Uber Economy: What Role for EU Competition Law?*, 19 German Law Journal 461 n. 3 (2018).

Dawkins, C., *Disciplining the Notion of 'Labour Rights as Human Rights'*, 13 Global Labour Journal 1 n. 1 (2022).

Deakin, S., Wilkinson, F., *Rights vs Efficiency the Economic Case for Transnational Labour Standards*, 23 Industrial Law Journal 289 n. 4 (1994).

Deakin, S., Lele, P. & Siems, M., *The Evolution of Labour Law: Calibrating and Comparing Regulatory Regimes*, 146 International Labour Review 133 n. 3-4 (2007).

Drahokoupil J., Jepsen M., *The Digital Economy and Its Implications for Labour*, 1. The Platform Economy, 23 Transfer 103 n. 2 (2017).

De Ruyter, M., Brown & Burgess J., *Gig Work and the Fourth Industrial Revolution: Conceptual and Regulatory Challenges*, 72 Journal of International Affairs 37 n.1 (2019).

De Stefano, V., *'Masters and Servers': Collective Labour Rights and Private Government in the Contemporary World of Work*, 36 International Journal of Comparative Labour Law and Industrial Relations 425 n. 4 (2020).

De Stefano, V., *Non-Standard Work and Limits on Freedom of Association: a Human-Rights Based Approach*, 46 Industrial Law Journal 185 n. 2 (2017).

De Stefano, V., *Labour Is Not a Technology: Reasserting the Declaration of Philadelphia in Times of Platform-Work and Gig-Economy*, 2 IUSLabor 1 (2017).

De Stefano, V., *The Rise of the 'Just-in-time Workforce': On-Demand Work, Crowdwork, and Labor Protection in the Gig-Economy'*, 37 Comparative Labor Law & Policy Journal 476 (2016).

De Stefano, V., *Casual Work Beyond Casual Work in the EU: The Underground Casualization of the European Workforce – and What to Do About It*, 7 European Labour Law Journal 421 n. 3 (2016).

Deutscher, E., Makris, S., *Exploring the Ordoliberal Paradigm: The Competition-Democracy Nexus*, 181 Competition Law Review 807 (2016).

Digennaro, P., *Subordination or Subjection? A Study About the Dividing Line Between Subordinate Work and Self-Employment in Six European Legal Systems*, 6 Labour &Law Issues 1 n.1 (2020).

Doherty, M., Franca, V., *Solving the 'Gig-saw'? Collective Rights and Platform Work*, 49 Industrial Law Journal 353 n. 3 (2020).

Dorssemont, F., *Les travailleurs de plateforme face au droit des relations collectives du travail. Les droits fondamentaux des travailleurs, one porte d'entrée?*, Journal of Social Law 111 n. 1 (2019).

Drahokoupil, J., Piasna, A., *Work in the Platform Economy: Beyond Lower Transaction Costs*, 52 Intereconomics 335 n. 6 (2017).

Duff, M.C., *ALT-Labor, Secondary Boycotts, and Toward a Labor Organization Bargain*, 63 Catholic University Law Review 843 n. 4 (2014).

Duhaime, B., Décoste, E., *From Geneva to San José: The ILO Standards and the Inter-American System for the Protection of Human Rights*, 159 International Labour Review 525 Vol. n. 4 (2020).

Duggan, J., Sherman, U., Carbery, R., McDonnell, A., *Algorithmic Management and App-Work in the Gig Economy: A Research Agenda for Employment Relations and HRM*, 30 Human Resources Management Journal 114 n. 1 (2020).

Durlauf, M., *The Commodification of Digital Labor in the Gig Economy: Online Outsourcing, Insecure Employment, and Platform-based Rating and Ranking Systems*, 7 Psychosociological Issues in Human Resource Management 54 n. 1 (2019).

Ebisui, M., *Non-Standard Workers: Good Practices of Social Dialogue and Collective Bargaining*, 1 E-Journal of International and Comparative Labour Studies 211, n. 3-4 (2012).

Encaoua, D., Hollander, A., *Competition Policy and Innovation*, 18 Oxford Review of Economic Policy 63 n. 1 (2002).

Estlund, C., *Rethinking Autocracy at Work*, 131 Harvard Law Review 795 n. 3 (2018).

Ewing, K., *Myth and Reality of the Right to Strike as a 'Fundamental Labour Right'*, 2 International Journal of Comparative Labour Law 145 (2013).

Ewing, K., Hendy, J., *The Dramatic Implications of Demir and Baykara*, 39 Industrial Law Journal 1 n. 1 (2010).

Ewing, K.D., *The Function of Trade Unions*, 34 Industrial Law Journal 1 n. 1 22 (2005).

Evans, M., *Trade Unions as Human Rights Organizations*, 7 Journal of Human Rights Practice 466 n. 3 (2015).

Evans, D.S., Padilla, A.J., *Designing Antitrust Rules for Assessing Unilateral Practices: A Neo-Chicago Approach*, 72 University of Chicago Law Review 73 (2005).

Fairbrother, P., *Rethinking Trade Unionism: Union Renewal as Transition*, 26 The Economic and Labour Relations Review 561 n. 4 (2015).

Forsyth, A., *Collectivising the Gig Economy in Australia*, 27 Journal of the International Centre for Trade Union Rights 28 n. 3 (2020).

Fox, E.M., *The Modernization of Antitrust: A New Equilibrium*, 66 Cornell Law Review 1140 n. 6 (1981).

Frankerberg, G., *Critical Comparisons: Re-Thinking Comparative Law*, 26 Harvard International Law Journal 411 (1985).

Fredman S., du Toit D., Graham, M., Howson K., Heeks R., van Belle J.P., Mungai P., Osiki A., *Thinking Out of the Box: Fair Work for Platform Workers*, 31 King's Law Journal 236 n. 2 (2020).

Freedland, M., *New Trade Union Strategies for New Forms of Employment – A Brief Analytical and Normative Foreword*, 10 ELLJ 180 n. 3 (2019).

Freedland, M., Dhorajiwala, H., *UK Response to New Trade Union Strategies for New Forms of Employment*, 10 European Labour Law Journal 281 n. 3 (2019).

Freedland, M., Prassl, J., *Employees, Workers and the 'Sharing Economy', Changing Practices and Changing Concepts in the UK*, 6 Spanish Labour Law and Employment Relations Journal 16 n. 1-2 (2017).

Freedland, M., Countouris, N., *Some Reflections on the 'Personal Scope' of Collective Labour Law*, 46 Industrial Law Journal 52 n. 1 (2017).

Frey, B.A., *The Legal and Ethical Responsibilities of Transnational Corporations in the Protection of International Human Rights*, 29 Minnesota Journal of International Law 153 (1997).

Frey, C.B., Osborne, M.A., *The Future of Employment: How Susceptible Are Jobs to Computerisation*, 144 Technological forecasting and social change 280 (2013), available at: https://www.oxfordmartin.ox.ac.uk/downloads/academic/The_Future_of_Employment.pdf.

Fudge, J., *The Future of the Standard Employment Relationship: Labour Law, New Institutional Economics and Old Power Resource Theory*, 59 Journal of Industrial Relations 374 n. 3 (2017).

Fudge, J., Jensen, H., *The Right to Strike: The Supreme Court of Canada, the Charter of Rights and Freedoms and the Arc of Workplace Justice*, 27 King's Law Journal 89 n. 1 (2016).

Fudge, J., *Constitutionalizing Labour Rights in Canada and Europe: Freedom of Association, Collective Bargaining, and Strikes*, 68 Current Legal Problems 267 (2015).

Fudge, J., *The New Discourse of Labour Rights: From Social to Fundamental Rights?*, 29 Comparative Labour Law & Policy Journal 29 (2007).

Garcia, J.A.L., *The Right to Strike as a Fundamental Human Right: Recognition and Limitations in International Law*, 44 Revista Chilena de Derecho 781 (2017).

Garden, C., *The Seattle Solution: Collective Bargaining by For-Hire Drivers and Prospects for ProLabor Federalism*, 12 Harvard Law and Policy Review Online 1 (2017).

Gartman, D., *Marx and the Labor Process: An Interpretation*, 8 Insurgent Sociologist 97 n. 2-3 (1978).

Georgiou, D., *The New EU Directive on Transparent and Predictable Working Conditions in the Context of New forms of Employment*, 1 European Journal of Industrial Relations (2022).

Gerber, D. J., *Constitutionalizing the Economy: German Neo-liberalism, Competition Law and the 'New' Europe*, 42 The American Journal of Comparative Law 83 n. 1 (1994).

Gerbrandy, A., *Rethinking Competition Law Within the European Economic Constitution*, 57 Journal of Common Law Studies 127 n. 1 (2019).

Gernigon, B., Odero, A., Guido, H., *ILO Principles Concerning the Right to Strike*, 137 International Labour Review 441 n. 4 (1998).

Graham, M. & Anwar, M.A., *Between a Rock and a Hard Place: Freedom, Flexibility, Precarity and Vulnerability in the Gig Economy in Africa*, 25 Competition & Change 237 n. 2 (2020).

Graham, M. and Anwar, M. A., *The Global Gig Economy: Towards a Planetary Labour Market*, 24 First Monday 1 n. 4 (2019).

Graham, M., Hjorth, I., Lehonvirta, V., *Digital Labour and Development: Impacts of Global Digital Labour Platforms and the Gig Economy on Worker Livelihoods*, 23 Transfer: European Review of Labour and Research 146 n. 2 (2017).

Gramano, E., Gaudio, G., *'New Trade Union Strategies for New Forms of Employment': Focus on Italy*, 10 ELLJ 242 n. 3 (2019).

Gumbrell-McCormick, R., *European Trade Unions and 'Atypical' Workers*, 42 Industrial Relations Journal 293 n. 3 (2011).

Habermas, J., *The Concept of Human Dignity: A Realistic Utopia*, 41 Metaphilosophy 462 n. 4 (2010).

Hamner, K. J., *The Globalization of Law: International Merger Control and Competition Law in the United States, the European Union, Latin America and China*, 11 Journal of Transnational Law & Policy 385 n. 2 (2002).

Hassel, A., *The Evolution of a Global Labor Governance Regime*, 21 Governance 231 n. 2(2008).

Hayter, S., Ebisui, M., *Negotiating Parity for Precarious Workers*, 5 International Journal of Labour Research 79 n. 1 (2013).

Hayter, S., Fashoyin, T., Kochan, T.A., *Collective Bargaining for the 21st Century*, 53 Journal of Industrial Relations 225 n. 2 (2011).

Healy, J., Nicholson, D., Pekarek, A., *Should We Take the Gig Economy Seriously?*, 27 Labour and Industry 232 n. 3 (2017).

Heery, E., *Unions and the Organizing Turn: Reflections after 20 Years of Organising Works*, 26 The Economic and Labour Relations Review 545 n. 4 (2015).

Heery, E., Williams, S., Abbott, B., *Civil Society Organizations and Trade Unions: Cooperation, Conflict, Indifference*, 26 Work, Employment and Society 145 n. 1 (2012).

Heiland, H., Brinkmann, U., *Liefern am Limit: Wie die Plattformökonomie die Arbeitsbeziehungen verändert*, 27 Industrielle Beziehungen 120 n. 2 (2020).

Hendrickx, F., *From Digits to Robots: The Privacy-Autonomy Nexus in New Labor Law Machinery*, 40 Comparative Labor Law & Policy Journal 365 n. 3 (2019).

Hendrickx, F., *Foundations and Functions of Contemporary Labour Law*, 3 European Labour Law Journal 108 n. 2 (2012).

Holmes, S., *Climate Change, Sustainability and Competition law*, 8 Journal of Antitrust Enforcement 354 n. 2 (2020).

Howson, K., Ferrari, F., Ustek-Spilda, F., Salem, N., Johnston, H., Katta, S., Heeks, R., Graham, M., *Driving the Digital Value Network: Economic Geographies of Global Platform Capitalism*, 22 Global Networks 631 n. 4 (2022).

Howson, K., Ustek-Spilda, F., Grohmann, R., Salem, N., Carelli, R., Abs, D., Salvagni, J., Graham, M., Balbornoz, M.B., Chavez, H., Arriagada, A., Bonhomme, M., *'Just Because You Don't See Your Boss, Doesn't Mean You Don't Have a Boss': Covid-19 and Gig Worker Strikes Across Latin America'*, 27 Journal of the International Centre for Trade Union Rights 20 n. 3 20 (2020).

Hua, J., Ray, K., *Beyond the Precariat: Race, Gender, and Labor in the Taxi and Uber Economy*, 24 Social Identities 271 n. 2 (2018).

Hyman, R., *What Future for Industrial Relations in Europe?*, 40 Employee Relations 569 n. 4 (2018).

Irani, L., *The Cultural Work of Microwork*, 17 New Media & Society 720 n. 5 (2013).

Jedličková, B., *Beyond the Economic Approach: Why Pluralism Is Important in Competition Law*, 37 U. Queensland LJ 41 n. 1 (2018).

Johnston, H., *Labour Geographies of the Platform Economy: Understanding Collective Organizing Strategies in the Context of Digitally Mediated Work*, 159 International Labour Review 25 n. 1 (2020).

Juravich, T., *Constituting Challenges in Differing Arenas of Power: Worker Centers, the Fight for $15, and Union Organizing*, 43 Labor Studies Journal 104 n. 2 (2018).

Kahn-Freund, O., *The Impact of Constitutions on Labour Law*, 35 Cambridge Law Journal 240 n. 2 (1976).

Kahn-Freund, O.O., *On Uses and Misuses of Comparative Law*, 37 Modern Law Review 27 n. 1 (1974).

Kalleberg, A.L. and Dunn, M., *Good Jobs, Bad Jobs in the Gig Economy*, 20 Perspectives on Work 10 (2016).

Katsabian, T., *Collective Action in the Digital Reality: the Case of Platform-Based Workers*, 84 The Modern Law Review 1005 n. 5 (2021).

Katsaroumpas, I., *De-Constitutionalising Collective Labour Rights: The Case of Greece*, 47 Industrial Law Journal 465 n. 4 (2017).

Keune, M., *Trade Union Responses to Precarious Work in Seven European Countries*, 5 International Journal of Labour Research 59 n. 1 (2013).

Koblen, K., *Labor Rights as Human Rights?*, 50 Virginia Journal of International Law 450 n. 2 (2009).

Kolasky, W. J., *What Is Competition? A Comparison of US and European Perspectives*, 49 The Antitrust Bulletin 29 n. 1-2 (2004).

Kovacs, E., *The Right to Strike in the European Social Charter*, 26 Comparative Labor Law & Policy Journal 445 n. 4 (2005).

Kranendonk, M., de Beer, P., *What Explains the Union Membership Gap Between Migrants and Natives?*, 54 British Journal of Industrial Relations 846 (2016).

Kullmann, M., *'Platformisation' of Work: An EU Perspective on Introducing a Legal Presumption*, European Labour Law Journal, Online 1 (2021), available at: https://journals.sagepub.com/doi/10.1177/20319525211063112.

Kullmann, M., *Platform Work, Algorithmic Decision-Making, and EU Gender Equality Law*, 34 International Journal of Comparative Labour Law and Industrial Relations 1 n. 1 (2018).

Lenaerts, K., Kilhoffer, Zachary, Z., Akgüç, M., *Traditional and New Forms of Organisation and Representation in the Platform Economy*, 12 Work Organisation, Labour & Globalisation 60 n. 2 (2018).

Lianos, I., Countouris, N., De Stefano, V., *Re-thinking the Competition Law/Labour Law Interaction: Promoting a Fairer Labour Market*, 10 European Labour Law Journal 291 n. 3 (2019).

Lianos, I., *Polycentric Competition Law*, 71 Current Legal Problems 161 n. 1 (2018).

Manokha, I., *The Implications of Digital Employee Monitoring and People Analytics for Power Relations in the Workplace*, 18 Surveillance & Society 540 n. 4 (2020).

Mantouvalou, V., *Labour Law and Human Rights*, 41 New Zealand Journal of Employment Relations 3 n. 2 (2016).

Mantouvalou, V., *Are Labour Rights Human Rights?*, 3 European Labour Law Journal 151 n. 2 (2012).

Marrone, M, and Finotto, V., *Challenging Goliath. Informal Unionism and Digital Platforms in the Food Delivery Sector. The Case of Riders Union Bologna*, 12 PACO 691 n. 3 (2019).

Maupain, F., *Revitalization Not Retreat: The Real Potential of the 1998 ILO Declaration for the Universal Protection of Workers' Rights*, 16 The European Journal of International Law 439 n. 3 (2005).

McCrystal, S., *Collective Bargaining Beyond the Boundaries of Employment: A Comparative Analysis*, 37 Melbourne University Law Review 662 n. 3 (2014).

Mezzaroba, O., Silveira, V.O.D., *The Principle of the Dignity of Human Person: A Reading of the Effectiveness of Citizenship and Human Rights Through the Challenges Put Forward by Globalization*, 5 Revista de Investigações Constitucionais 273 (2018).

Minter, K., *Negotiating Labour Standards in the Gig Economy: Airtasker and Unions New South Wales*, 28 The Economic and Labour Relations Review 438 n. 3 (2017).

Monti, G., *Collective Labour Agreements and EU Competition Law: Five Reconfigurations*, 17 European Competition Journal 714 n. 3 (2021).

Muldoon, J., Raekstad, P., 'Algorithmic Domination in the Gig Economy', European Journal of Political Theory 1 (2022), available at: https://doi.org/10.1177/1474 8851221082078.

Munck, R., *The Precariat: A View from the South*, 34 Third World Quarterly 247 n. 5 (2013).

Neilson, B., Rossiter, N., *Precarity as a Political Concept, or, Fordism as Exception*, 25 Theory, Culture & Society 51 n. 7-8 (2008).

Newlands, G., Lutz, C., Fieseler, C., *Collective Action and Provider Classification in the Sharing Economy*, 33 New Technology, Work and Employment 250 n. 3 (2018).

Nkabinde, B., *The Right to Strike, an Essential Component of Workplace Democracy: Its Scope and Global Economy*, 24 Maryland Journal of International Law 270 n. 1 (2009).

Norman, K., *ILO Freedom of Association Principles as Basic Canadian Human Rights: Promises to Keep*, 67 Saskatchewan Law Review 591 n. 2 (2004).

Ojeda Avilés, A., *The 'Externalization' of Labour Law*, 148 International Labour Review, 47 n. 1-2 (2009).

Paton, J., *Labour as a (Fictitious) Commodity: Polanyi and the Capitalist 'Market Economy'*, 21 The Economic and Labour Relations Review 77 n. 1 (2010).

Parker, G., Van Alstyne, M., Jiang, X., *Platform Ecosystems: How Developers Invert the Firm*, 41 Management Information Systems Quarterly 255 n. 1 (2017).

Paul, S.M., *The Enduring Ambiguities of Antitrust Liability for Worker Collective Action*, 47 Loyola University Chicago Law Journal 969 n. 3 (2016).

Pecinovsky, P., *EU Economic Governance and the Right to Collective Bargaining. Part 1. Standard and Extreme Governance and the Indicators and Limits of the Right to Collective Bargaining*, 9 European Labour Law Journal 374 n. 4 (2018).

Pichault, F., McKeown, T., *Autonomy at Work in the Gig Economy: Analysing Work Status, Work Content and Working Conditions of Independent Professionals*, 34 New Technology, Work and Employment 59 n. 1 (2019).

Pisarczyk, L., *The Crisis of the Collective Bargaining System in Poland*, 35 International Journal of Comparative Labour Law and Industrial Relations 58 n. 1 (2019).

Powers, M., *The Structural Organization of NGO Publicity Work: Explaining Divergent Publicity Strategies at Humanitarian and Human Rights Organizations*, 8 International Journal of Communication 90 n. 8 (2014).

Prahalad, C.K. and Hamel, G., *The Core Competence of the Corporation*, Harvard Business Review 79 n. March-April (1990).

Racabi, G., *Abolish the Employer Prerogative, Unleash Work Law*, 43 Berkeley Journal of Employment and Labor Law 79 n. 1 (2022).

Rani, U., Furrer, M., *Digital Labour Platforms and New Forms of Flexible Work in Developing Countries: Algorithmic Management of Work and Workers*, 25 Competition & Change 212 n. 2 (2021).

Rani, U., Dhir, K.R., *Platform Work and the COVID-19 Pandemic*, 63 The Indian Journal of Labour Economics 163 n. 1 (2020).

Rice, A.K., *Productivity and Social Organization in an Indian Weaving Shed: An Examination of Some Aspects of the Socio-Technical System of an Experimental Automatic Loom Shed*, 6 Human Relations 297 n. 4 (1953).

Rittich, K., *Between Workers' Rights and Flexibility: Labor Law in an Uncertain World*, 54 Saint Luis University Law Journal 565 n. 2 (2010).

Rosenblat, A., Stark, L., *Algorithmic Labor and Information Asymmetries: A Case Study of Uber's Drivers*, 10 International Journal of Communication 3758 (2016).

Rubery, J., Grimshaw, D., Keizer, A., Johnson.m M., *Challenges and Contradictions in the 'Normalising' of Precarious Work*, 32 Employment and Society 509 n. 3 (2018).

Schiek, D., Gideon, A., *Outsmarting the Gig-Economy Through Collective Bargaining – EU Competition Law as a Barrier to Smart Cities?*, 32 International Review of Law, Computers & Technology 275 n. 2-3 (2018).

Schnabel, C., Wagner, J., *Union Density and Determinants of Union Membership in 18 EU Countries: Evidence from Micro Data, 2002/03 1*, 38 Industrial Relations Journal 5 n. 1(2007).

Schor, J.B., Attwood-Charles, W., Cansoy, M., Ladegaard, I., and Wengronowitz, R., *Dependence and Precarity in the Platform Economy*, 49 Theory and Society 833 n. 5-6 (2020).

Schoukens, P., Barrio, A., *The Changing Concept of Work: When Does Typical Work Become Atypical?*, 8 European Labour Law Journal 306 n. 4 (2017).

Schubert, C., Hütt, M.T., *Economy-on-demand and the Fairness of Algorithms*, 10 European Labour Law Journal 3 n. 1 (2019).

Scolnik, F., *Grassroots Labor Organizations in Metropolitan Buenos Aires, 2003-2007*, 42 Latin America Perspectives 30 n. 2 (2015).

Scully, B., *From the Shop Floor to the Kitchen Table: The Shifting Centre of Precarious Workers' Politics in South Africa*, 42 Review of African Political Economy 295 n. 128 (2016).

Soriano, C.R., Cabanes, J.V., *Entrepreneurial Solidarities: Social Media Collectives and Filipino Digital Platform Workers*, 6 Social Media and Society n. 2 (2020), available at: 2056305120926484.

Spooner, D., *Trade Unions and NGOs: The Need for Cooperation*, 14 Development in Practice 19 n. 1-2 (2004).

Scruggs, L., Lange, P., *Where Have All the Members Gone? Globalization, Institutions and Union Density*, 64 The Journal of Politics 126 (2002).

Stammers, N., *Social Movements and the Social Construction of Human Rights*, 21 Human Rights Quarterly 980 n. 4 (1999).

Stanford, J., *The Resurgence of Gig Work: Historical and Theoretical Perspectives*, 28 The Economic and Labour Relations Review 382 n. 3 (2017).

Stone, K.W., *Flexibilisation, Globalization and Privatization: Three Challenges to Labour Rights in Out Time*, 44 Osgoode Hall Law Journal 79 n. 1 (2006).

Stone, V.W. K., *Legal Protections for Atypical Employees: Employment Law for Workers Without Workplaces and Employees Without Employers*, 27 Berkley Journal of Employment and Labor Law 253 n. 2 (2006).

Stylogiannis, C., *Freedom of Association and Collective Bargaining in the Platform Economy: A Human Rights-Based Approach and an Ever Increasing Mobilization of Workers*, 162 International Labour Review 1 n. 1 (2021).

Stylogiannis, C., *The Protection of the Right to Strike under the European Convention on Human Rights*, 6 UCL Journal of Law and Jurisprudence 142 n. 1 (2017).

Stucke, M., Maurice, E., *Should We Be Concerned about Data-Opolies?*, 2 Georgetown Law Technology Review 275 n. 2 (2018).

Supiot, A., *Labour Is Not a Commodity: The Content and Meaning of Work in the Twenty-First Century*, 160 International Labour Review 1 (2021).

Sutherland, W., Jarrahi, M.H., Dunn, M., Nelson, S.B., *Work Precarity and Gig Literacies in Online Freelancing*, 34 Work, Employment and Society 457 n. 4 (2020).

Tassinari, A., Maccarrone, V., *Riders on the Storm: Workplace Solidarity Among Gig Economy Couriers in Italy and the UK. Work*, 165 Employment and Society 35 n. 3 (2019).

Tattersall, A., *There Is Power in Coalition: A Framework for Analysing How and When Union-Community Coalitions Are Effective and Enhance Union Power*, 16 Labour and Industry 97 n. 2 (2005).

Teklè, T., *The Contribution of the ILO's International Labour Standards System to the European Court of Human Rights' Jurisprudence in the Field of Non-Discrimination*, 49 International Labour Review 86 n. 1 (2019).

Thomas, C., *Ride Oversharing: Privacy Regulation Within the Gig Economy*, 36 Cardozo Arts & Entertainment Law Journal 247 n. 1 (2018).

Todolí-Signes, A., *Algorithms, Artificial Intelligence and Automated Decisions Concerning Workers and the Risks of Discrimination: The necessary collective governance of data protection*, 25 Transfer: European Review of Labour and Research 465 n. 4 (2019).

Todolí-Signes, A., *The Gig Economy: Employee, Self-Employed or the Need for a Special Employment Regulation?*, Transfer: European Review of Labour and Research, Vol. 23, 193–205 (2017).

Tucker, E., *The Constitutional Right to Bargain Collectively: The Ironies of Labour History in the Supreme Court of Canada*, 61 Labour/Le Travail 151 (2008).

Van Kersbergen, K., Vis, B., Hemerijck, A., *The Great Recession and Welfare State Reform: Is Retrenchment Really the Only Game Left in Town?*, 48 Social Policy & Administration 883 n. 7 (2014).

Velyvyte, V., *The Right to Strike in the European Union after Accession to the European Convention on Human Rights: Identifying Conflict and Achieving Coherence*, 15 Human Rights Law Review 71 n. 1 (2015).

Waller, S.W., *Antitrust and Democracy*, 46 Florida State University Law Review 807 n. 4 (2019).

Weiss, M., *The Future of Comparative Labor Law as an Academic Discipline and as a Practical Tool*, 25 Comparative Labor Law & Policy Journal 169 n.1 (2003).

Weissbrodt, D., Kruger, M., *Norms on the Responsibilities of Transnational Corporations and Other Business Enterprises with Regard to Human Rights*, 97 American Journal of International Law 901 n. 4 (2003).

Wouters, J., Chanet, L., *Corporate Human Rights Responsibility: European Perspective*, 6 Northwestern University Journal of International Human Rights 262 n. 2 (2008).

Wood, A.J., Graham, M., Lehdonvirta, V., Hjorth, I., *Networked but Commodified: The (Dis)Embeddedness of Digital Labour in the Gig Economy*, 53 Sociology 931 n. 5 (2019).

Youngdahl, J., *Solidarity First: Labor Rights Are Not the Same as Human Rights*, 18 New Labor Forum 31 n. 1 (2009).

Zekić, N., *The Normative Framework of Labour Law*, Law and Method 1 (2019).

Reports and Papers

Aloisi, A. (2021), Demystifying Flexibility, Exposing the Algorithmic Boss: A Note on the First Italian *Case Classifying a (Food-Delivery) Platform Worker as an Employee*, Comparative Labor Law & Policy Journal, Dispatches.

Aloisi, A. (2020), *Hierarchies Without Firms? Vertical Disintegration, Outsourcing and the Nature of the Platform*, E-book 'Quaderni 8th Giorgio Rota Best Paper Award' 2020.

Aloisi, A. (2019), *Negotiating the Digital Transformation of Work: Non-standard Workers' Voice, Collective Rights and Mobilisation Practices in the Platform Economy*, EUI Working Paper No. 3. San Domenico di Fiesole, European University Institute.

Australian Government Productivity Commission, (2016), *Digital Disruption: What Do Governments Need to Do?*, Productivity Commission Research Paper, available at: https://www.pc.gov.au/research/completed/digital-disruption/digital-disruption-research-paper.pdf.

Barrio, A. (2020), *Contradictory Decisions on the Employment Status of Platform Workers in Spain*, Comparative Labor Law & Policy Journal Dispatches (No. 20).

Barenberg, M. (2015), *Widening the Scope of Worker Organizing: Legal Reforms to Facilitate Multi-Employer Organizing, Bargaining, and Striking*, Roosevelt Institute Report, available at: https://rooseveltinstitute.org/wp-content/uploads/2015/10/RI-Widening-Scope-Worker-Organizing-201510-2.pdf.

Berg, J., Furrer, M., Harmon, E., Rani, U., & Six Silberman M., *Digital Labour Platforms and the Future of Work: Towards Decent Work in the Online World*, Geneva, ILO (2018).

Boonstra, K., Keune, M., Verhulp, E. (2011), *Trade union responses to precarious employment in the Netherlands*, Amsterdam Institute for Advanced Labour Studies, available at: http://www.uvaaias.net/uploaded_files/regular/BARSORIReportTheNetherlands.pdf.

Caracciolo, A. (2015), *Right to Dignity into Contemporary New Humanism*, Conference Paper.

CIPD, (2017), *To Gig or Not to Gig? Stories from the Modern Economy*, Chartered Institute of Personnel and Development, London.

Clauwaert, S., Schomann, I. (2012), *The Crisis and National Labour Law Reforms: A Mapping Exercise*, ETUI Working Paper 2012.04, Brussels.

Clewlow, R. Mishra, G., *Disruptive Transportation: The Adoption, Utilization, and Impacts of Ride-Hailing in the United States*, Research Report (2017) UCD-ITS-RR-17-07, Institute of Transportation Studies, University of California, Davis.

Collier, R.B., Dubal, V. Carter, C., *Labor Platforms and Gig Work: The Failure to Regulate*, IRLE Working Paper (2017).

Countouris, N., Rainone, S. (2021), *Collective Bargaining and Self-Employed Workers: The Need for a Paradigm Shift*, ETUI Policy Brief.

Countouris, N., *Defining and regulating work relations for the future of work*, ILO, Geneva (2019).

Countouris, N., De Stefano, V., *New Trade Union Strategies for New Forms of Employment*. ETUC, Brussels, 2019.

Codagnone, C., Abadie, F., Federico, B., *The Future of Work in the 'Sharing Economy': Market Efficiency and Equitable Opportunities or Unfair Precarisation?*, JRC Science for Policy Report (2016) EUR 27913 EN, Institute for Prospective Technological Studies, available at: http://publications.jrc.ec.europa.eu/repository/bitstream/JRC101280/jrc101280.pdf.

Deakin, S., *The Contribution of Labour Law to Economic Development and Growth*, Centre for Business Research, Working Paper No. 478 (2016), Cambridge, University of Cambridge.

De Stefano, V., Taes, S., *Algorithmic Management and Collective Bargaining*, ETUI Research Paper, Brussels (2021).

De Stefano, V., Durri, I., Stylogiannis, C., Wouters, M., *Platform Work and the Employment Relationship*, ILO Working Paper, Geneva, ILO (2021).

De Stefano, V., Aloisi, A. (2018), *European Legal Framework for Digital Labour Platforms*, Luxembourg, Publications Office of the European Union.

De Stefano, V., '*"Negotiating the Algorithm": Automation, Artificial Intelligence and Labour Protection*', ILO Employment Working Paper N. 246, Geneva, ILO (2018).

De Groen, W.P., Kilhoffer, Z., Lenaerts, K., and Mandl, I. (2018), *Employment and Working Conditions of Selected Types of Platform Work*. Luxembourg, Publications Office of the European Union.

DeVault, I., Figueroa, M., Kotler, FB., and Maffie, MD., *On-Demand Platform Workers in New York State: The Challenges for Public Policy*, Report from the Worker Institute at Cornell University (2019).

Dolber, B., *Building Solidarity Among Gig Workers Through Digital Organizing*, Media, Inequality, and Change Center Report, University of Pennsylvania (2019).

Dunand, J.P., Mahon, P., *Switzerland*, (Daugareilh, I., Degryse, C., Pchet, P. eds, *The Platform Economy and Social Law: Key Issues in Comparative Perspective*, ETUI Working Paper, Brussels 2019).

Eichhorst, W., Schroeder, W., *The German Employment Model, the Trade Unions and 'Working 4.0.'*, Friedrich-Ebert-Stiftung, Bratislava, Friedrich-Ebert-Stiftung (2018).

Engels, S., Sherwood, M., *What If We All Worked Gigs in the Cloud? The Economic Relevance of Digital Labour Platforms*, European Economy Discussion Paper No. 099 (2019).

ETUC, (2021), *EU ends free ride for platforms*, Press Release, 9 December 2021, available at: https://www.etuc.org/en/pressrelease/eu-ends-free-ride-platforms.

ETUC, (2020), *Feedback on the Commission Inception Impact Assessment on Competition Law and Collective Bargaining for Self-employed*, Background Paper, February 2020, available at: https://ec.europa.eu/info/law/better-regulation/have-your-say/initiatives/12483- Collective-bargaining-agreements-for-self-employed -scope-of-application-EUcompetition-rules/F1567643_en.

ETUC, (2020), *National measures to protect non-standard workers including workers in the platform economy*, ETUC Briefing Note.

European Commission, (2020), *Study to gather evidence on the working conditions of platform workers*, available at: https://ec.europa.eu/social/main.jsp?catId = 738 &langId = en&pubId = 8280.

Eurofound, (2020), *Labour market change: Trends and policy approaches towards flexibilisation*, Challenges and prospects in the EU series, Publications Office of the European Union, Luxembourg.

Eurofound, (2020), *Platform economy: Developments in the COVID-19 crisis*, 3 July 2020, available at: https://www.eurofound.europa.eu/el/data/platform-economy/dossiers/developments-in-the-covid-19-crisis.

Eurofound, (2018), *Non-standard forms of employment: Recent trends and future prospects*, Dublin, Eurofound.

Eurofound, (2019), *Casual work: Characteristics and implications*, Luxembourg, Publications Office of the European Union.

Eurofound & International Labour Organization, (2017), *Working Anytime, Anywhere: The Effects on the World of Work 3*, Geneva, Publications Office of the European Union and the International Labour Office.

Eurofound, (2015), *Temporary compensation scheme for self-employed persons – measures in Denmark*, 15 April 2020, available at: https://static.eurofound.europa.eu/covid19db/cases/DK-2020-11_624.html.

Eurofound, (2015), *New forms of employment*, Publications Office of the European Union, Luxembourg.

European Parliament (2000), *Atypical Work in the EU,* Working Paper, Social Affairs Series, Luxembourg, available at: https://ec.europa.eu/social/BlobServlet?docId =2440&langId=en.

Ezrachi, A. (2018), *The Goals of EU Competition Law and the Digital Economy*, Oxford Legal Studies Research Paper No. 17/2018, Oxford.

Fairwork, (2019), *The Five Pillars of Fairwork: Labour Standards in the Platform Economy*, Fairwork Foundation, Oxford, UK, available at: https://fair.work/wpcontent/uploads/sites/97/2019/10/Fairwork-Y1-Report.pdf.

Fairwork, (2020), *Fairwork South Africa Ratings 2020: Labour Standards in the Gig Economy*, Cape Town, South Africa; Oxford, UK; Manchester, UK, available at: https://fair.work/wpcontent/uploads/sites/97/2020/03/Fairwork-South-Africa-2020-report.pdf.

Fairwork, (2020), *The Gig Economy and Covid-19: Looking Ahead*, Fairwork Foundation, Oxford, UK, available at: https://fair.work/en/fw/publications/the-gig-economy-and-covid-19-looking-ahead/.

Fulton L. (2018), *Trade unions protecting self-employed workers*, ETUC, Brussels.

Garben, S. (2017), *Protecting Workers in the Online Platform Economy: An overview of regulatory and policy developments in the EU*, European Risk Observatory Discussion Paper, Luxembourg, Publications Office of the European Union, available at: https://osha.europa.eu/sites/default/files/publications/documents /Protecting_Workers_in_Online_Platform Economy.pdf.

Gernigon, B., Odero, A., Guido, H., *ILO Principles Concerning the Right to Strike*, International Labour Organization (2000).

Global Commission on the Future of Work, (2019), *Work for a brighter future*, Geneva, ILO.

Hadwiger, F., *Realizing the opportunities of the platform economy through freedom of association and collective bargaining*, ILO Working Paper 80, Geneva, ILO (2022).

Haipeter, T., Owczarek, D., Faioli, M., Iudicone, F. (2020), *Don't Gig Up*, Final Report, available at: http://www.dontgigup.eu/wp-content/uploads/2020/04/Final-Report-3.pdf.

Harris, D., Krueger, A. B., (2015), *A Proposal for Modernizing Labor Laws for Twenty-First-Century Work: The 'Independent Worker'*, The Hamilton Project, Discussion Paper, http://www.hamiltonproject.org/assets/files/modernizing_labor_laws_for_twenty_first_century_work_kruegharris.pdf.

Hauben, H., Lenaerts, K., Waeyaert, W. (2020), *The platform economy and precarious work*, Publication for the committee on Employment and Social Affairs, Policy Department for Economic, Scientific and Quality of Life Policies, Luxembourg, European Parliament.

Heiland, H. (2020), *Workers' Voice in Platform Labour: An Overview*, WSI Study No. 21, Hans-Böckler-Stiftung, Wirtschafts- und Sozialwissenschaftliches Institut (WSI), Düsseldorf, available at: https://www.boeckler.de/de/faust-detail.htm?sync_id=9041.

Hermoso, M., (2019), *Spain. Case Study Report*, Don't Gig Up Project, available at: http://www.dontgigup.eu/wp-content/uploads/2020/05/Casestudy_ES.pdf.

Huws, U., Spencer, N.H., Syrdal, D.S., Holts, K. (2017), *Work in the European Gig Economy: Research Results From the UK, Sweden, Germany, Austria, the Netherlands, Switzerland, and Italy*, Foundation for European Progressive Studies Report, available at: http://unieuropaprojects.org/content/uploads/europeagig economy-longversionpdf.pdf.

Human Rights Watch, (2010), *A Strange Case*, Report, New York, Human Rights Watch.

ILO, (2022), *Social Dialogue Report*, ILO, Geneva.

ILO, (2021), *World Employment and Social Outlook 2021: The role of digital labour platforms in transforming the world of work*, ILO, Geneva.

ILO, (2020), *ILO Monitor: COVID-19 and the world of work*, Sixth edition, Geneva, ILO.

ILO, (2020), *World Employment and Social Outlook: Trends 2020*, Geneva, ILO.

ILO, (2018), *Digital labour platforms and the future of work: Towards decent work in the online world*, Geneva, ILO.

ILO, (2016), *Non-standard employment around the world: Understanding challenges, shaping prospects*, Geneva, ILO.

ILO, (2016), *Third item on the agenda: Information and reports on the application of Conventions and Recommendations*, Report of the Committee on the Application of Standards (2016) International Labour Conference 105th Session, Geneva, Provisional Record, May-June 2016 16(Rev) Part 2.

ILO, (2003), *Report V The scope of the employment relationship*, Geneva, ILO.

ILO, (1996), *Freedom of association: Digest of decisions and principles of the Freedom of Association Committee of the Governing Body of the ILO. Fourth (revised) edition. Geneva.*

ILO Committee of Experts, (2020), *Promoting employment and decent work in a changing landscape*, Geneva, ILO.

ILO Committee of Experts on the Application of Conventions and Recommendations, (2012), *Giving globalization a human face: General survey on the fundamental conventions concerning rights at work in light of the ILO Declaration on Social Justice for a Fair Globalization*, Geneva, ILO.

ILO Committee on Freedom of Association, (2018), *Freedom of Association. Compilation of decisions of the Committee on Freedom of Association*, Geneva, ILO.

ILO Committee on Freedom of Association, (2006), *Freedom of Association: Digest of decisions and principles of the Freedom of Association Committee of the Governing Body of the ILO*, Geneva, ILO.

International Trade Union Confederation (ITUC), (2019), *Organising and Collective Bargaining in Non-Standard Forms of Work*, Policy Brief 17 October 2019, available at: https://www.ituc-csi.org/Organising-CollectiveBargaining-in-Non Standard-Work.

Ilsoe, A., Jesnes, K. (2020), *Collective agreements for platforms and workers – two cases from the Nordic countries, Nordic Council of Ministers*, Copenhagen.

Insight2impact, (2019), *Africa's Digital Platforms and Financial Services: An Eight-Country Overview*, Johannesburg.

IPSOS, (2020), *High level summary of key findings*, Surveys commissioned by KU Leuven.

IRES, (2019), *Don't gig up!*, State of the Art Report, Institut de Recherches Économiques et Sociales.

Johnston, H., Land-Kazlauskas, C., *Organizing On-Demand: Representation, Voice, and Collective Bargaining in the Gig Economy*, Geneva, ILO (2019).

Katz, L.F., Krueger, A.B. (2016), *The Rise and Nature of Alternative Work Arrangements in the United States, 1995–2015*, NBER Working Paper No. 22667.

Kilhoffer, Z., De Groen, W.P., Lenaerts, K., Smits, I., Hauben, H., Waeyaert, W., Giacumacatos, E., Lhernould, J.-P., Robin-Olivier, S., (2019), *Study to Gather Evidence on the Working Conditions of Platform Workers*, Luxembourg, Publications Office of the European Union.

Lenaerts, K., Belbavy, M., Kilhoffer, (2017), *Government Responses to the Platform Economy: Where do we stand?, CEPS Policy Insights*, 27 July 2017, available at: https://www.ceps.eu/system/files/PI201730_Government%20Responses%20 to%20the%20Platform%20Economy.pdf.

Lane, M. (2020), *Regulating platform work in the digital age*, Going Digital Toolkit Policy Note, No. 1, available at: https://goingdigital.oecd.org/toolkitnotes.

Lodovici, M. (2018), *Independent Workers and Industrial Relations in Europe, the Role of Trade Unions*, Istituto per la Ricerca Sociale.

Moore, P.V., *The Threat of Physical and Psychosocial Violence and Harassment in Digitalized Work, ILO*, Geneva (2018).

OECD, (2020), *Distributional risks associated with non-standard work: Stylised facts and policy considerations*, OECD Policy Responses to Coronavirus (COVID-19), OECD Publishing, Paris.

OECD, (2020), *Organisation for Economic Co-operation and Development*, COVID-19: Protecting people and societies, OECD Policy Responses to Coronavirus (COVID-19), OECD Publishing, Paris.

OECD, (2020), *What have platforms done to protect workers during the coronavirus (COVID-19) crisis?*, OECD Publishing, Paris.

OECD, (2019), *Policy Responses to New Forms of Work*, OECD Publishing, Paris.

OECD, (2019), *Negotiating Our Way Up: Collective Bargaining in a Changing World of Work*, OECD Publishing, Paris.

OECD, (2018), *Issues note: The emergence of new forms of work and their implications* for labour relations.

Parminder, J.S. (2020), *Economic rights in a data-based society Collective Data Ownership, Workers' Rights, and the Role of the Public Sector*, Friedrich-Ebert-Stiftung, Global Policy and Development, available at: http://library.fes.de/pdf-files/iez/16034.pdf.

Pérez Del Prado, D. (2021), *The Legal Framework of Platform Work in Spain: The New Spanish 'Riders' Law'*, Comparative Labor Law & Policy Dispatch No. 36, Champaign, University of Illinois College of Law.

Pesole, A., Urzí Brancati M.C., Fernández-Ma*cías* E., Biagi, F., Gonz*ález* V*áquez* I. (2018), *Platform Workers in Europe: Evidence from the COLLEEM Survey*, Luxembourg, Publications Office of the European Union.

Perulli, A. (2003), *Study on Economically Dependent Work/Parasubordinate (Quasi-Subordinate) Work*, Brussels, European Parliament.

Prassl J. (2018), *Collective Voice in the Platform Economy: Challenges, Opportunities, Solutions*, ETUC Report, Brussels.

Rodgers, L., *Labour law and Kantian ideas of legality and citizenship*, University of Leicester School of Law Research Paper No. 14-07 (2014).

Rasche M. (2019), *Literature Review – Online Moderately Skilled Click-Work: Employment and Working Conditions*, Dublin, Eurofound.

Royo M.R.P., *Spain* Daugaeilh, I., (Degryse, C., Pochet, P. eds, *The Platform Economy and Social Law: Key Issues in Comparative Perspective*, European Trade Union Institute Working Paper, Brussels, 2019).

Schnabel, C. (2020), *Union Membership and Collective Bargaining: Trends and Determinants*, Discussion Paper Series, IZA Institute of Labor Economics.

Schroeder, W. (2016), Germany's Industry 4.0 strategy, Friedrich-Ebert-Stiftung Report.

Secretariat to the Expert Panel on Modern Federal Labour Standards, (2019), *Federal Labour Standards Protections for Workers in NonStandard Work*, Issue Paper, 4, available at: https://www.canada.ca/content/dam/esdc-edsc/documents/services/reports/SPAWID-SPLR-IssuePaper-Non-StandardWork-FINAL-EN.pdf.

Stylogiannis, C. (2021), *The 'Back and Forth' in the Protection of (Collective) Labor Rights under the ECHR Continues: The Holship Case*, Comparative Labor Law & Policy Dispatch No. 36, Champaign: University of Illinois College of Law.

Smith, R. (2018), *Marketplace Platforms and 'Employers' under State Law – Why We Should Reject Corporate Solutions and Support Worker-Led Innovation*, Policy Brief, New York, NELP.

Vandaele, K. (2018), *Will Trade Unions Survive in the Platform Economy? Emerging Patterns of Platform Workers' Collective Voice and Representation in Europe*, ETUI Research Paper, Brussels.

Vandaele, K. (2019), *Bleak Prospects: Mapping Trade Union Membership in Europe Since 2000*, ETUI, Brussels.

Visser, J., *Trade Unions in the Balance*, ILO ACTRAV Working Paper, Geneva (2019).

Williams, C.C., Lapeyre, F., *Dependent Self-Employment: Trends, Challenges and Policy Responses in the EU*, Employment Working Paper 228, Geneva, ILO (2017).

World Bank, (2020), *The Global Economic Outlook During the COVID-19 Pandemic: A Changed World*, 8 June 2020, Feature Story, available at: https://www.worldbank.org/en/news/feature/2020/06/08/the-global-economic-outlookduringthecovid19pandemicachangedworld#: ~ :text = Businesses%20might%20find%20it%20hard,by%20almost%208%25%20in%202020.

World Bank, (2016), *World Development Report 2016: Digital Dividends*. Washington D.C, World Bank.

Wouters, M. (2021), *Cheap and Flexible Labor For Non-Profits: How the Belgian 'Act On Auxiliary Income' Evolved Into an 'Act On Association Work*, Comparative Labor Law & Policy Dispatch No. 36. Champaign: University of Illinois College of Law.

Policy Documents and Memoranda

Article 29 data protection working party, (2014), *Opinion 8/2014 on the on Recent Developments on the Internet of Things*, 14/ENWP 223, 16 September 2014, available at: https://www.pdpjournals.com/docs/88440.pdf.

Austrian Chamber of Labour et al. (2016), *Frankfurt Paper on Platform Based Work*, Frankfurt.

European Economic and Social Committee (2017), *Opinion of the European Economic and Social Committee on 'Artificial intelligence – The consequences of artificial intelligence on the (digital) single market, production, consumption, employment and society (own-initiative opinion)*, Official Journal of the European Union, C 288, 31 August 2017.

European Commission, (2021), *Approval of the content of a draft for a Communication from the Commission – Guidelines on the Application of EU competition law to collective agreements regarding the working conditions of solo self-employed persons*, COM(2021) 8838 final, available at: https://ec.europa.eu/commission/presscorner/detail/en/ip_21_6620.

European Commission, (2017), *REFIT Evaluation of the 'Written Statement Directive' (91/533/ EEC) SWD 205 final*, European Commission, Brussels.

European Commission, (2017), *Commission Staff Working Document Impact Assessment Accompanying the Document Proposal for a Directive of the European Parliament and of the Council on Transparent and Predictable Working Conditions in the European Union' SWD (2017) 478 final*, European Commission, Brussels.

European Commission, (2021), *Questions and Answers: First stage social partners consultation on improving the working conditions in platform work*, Brussels, European Commission, available at: https://ec.europa.eu/commission/presscorner/detail/en/qanda_21_656.

European Commission, (2018), *Proposal for a regulation of the European parliament and of the council on promoting fairness and transparency for business users of online intermediation services*, Brussels, 26.4.2018.

European Commission, (2016), *Communication from the Commission to the Council. A European Agenda for the Collaborative Economy*, COM 356 final, Luxembourg, available at:
https://ec.europa.eu/transparency/regdoc/rep/1/2016/EN/1-2016-356-EN-F1-1.PDF.

European Parliament, (2020), *Data subjects, digital surveillance, AI and the future of work*, Panel for the Future of Science and Technology, European Union, Brussels, available at: https://www.europarl.europa.eu/RegData/etudes/STUD/2020/656305/EPRS_STU(2020)656305_EN.pdf.

ETUC, (2017), *ETUC Resolution on tackling new digital challenges to the world of labour, in particular crowdwork*, available at: https://www.etuc.org/en/document/etuc-resolution-tackling-new-digitalchallenges-world-labour-particular-crowdwork.

European Economic and Social Committee, (2010), *Opinion of the European Economic and Social Committee on new trends in self-employed work: the specific case of economically dependent self-employed work*, 29 April 2010, available at: https://www.eesc.europa.eu/en/our-work/opinions-information-reports/opinions/new-trends-self-employed-work-specific-case-economically-dependent-self-employed-work.

ILO Director-General, (1997), *The ILO, Standard Setting and Globalization*, ILO Doc. 2941/M.

Opinion of the Danish Competition and Consumer Authority, (2020), available at: https://www.en.kfst.dk/nyheder/kfst/english/decisions/20200826-commitment-decision-on-the-use-of-a-minimum-hourly-fee-hilfr/.

Opinion of Mr Advocate General Geelhoed delivered on 14 March 2002. – *A. G. Lawrence and Others v. Regent Office Care Ltd, Commercial Catering Group and Mitie Secure Services Ltd.*

Opinion of Advocate General Wahl delivered on 11 September 2014 – *Case C-413/13 FNV Kunsten.*

Blogs, News Articles and Other Online Sources

Aloisi, A., De Stefano, V., Six Silberman, M., *A manifesto to reform the Gig Economy*, Regulating for Globalization (1 May 2019), http://regulatingforglobalization.com/2019/05/01/a-manifesto-to-reform-the-gig-economy/.

Andrias, K., Sachs, B., *NDWA-Handy Pilot: Major Gains for Workers Long Excluded from Labor Law's Protections*, OnLabor (17 June 2021), https://onlabor.org/ndwa-handy-pilot-major-gains-for-workers-long-excluded-from-labor-laws-protections/.

Aloisi, A., De Stefano, V., *Delivering employment rights to platform workers*, il Mulino (31 January 2020), https://www.rivistailmulino.it/a/delivering-employment-rights-to-platform-workers.

Aranguiz, A., *Spain's platform workers win algorithm transparency*, Social Europe (18 March 2021), https://www.socialeurope.eu/spains-platform-workers-win-algorithm-transparency?fbclid=IwAR3cZoGEWJNveKMRScwpkUNnQUMHFAa9htj5-J5IxVxjPE2HsxqEL8SAhOc.

Aranguiz, A., *Platforms put a spoke in the wheels of Spain's 'riders' law*, Social Europe (2 September 2021), https://socialeurope.eu/platforms-put-a-spoke-in-the-wheels-of-spains-riders-law.

Bellon, T., *Uber Has Spent $19 Million on Coronavirus Financial Assistance for Drivers*, Reuters (21 May 2020), https://uk.reuters.com/article/uk-health-coronavirus-uber/uber-has-spent-19-million-on-coronavirus-financial-assistance-for-drivers-idUKKBN22X1XQ.

Berg, J., De Stefano, V., *It's time to regulate the gig economy*, Sheffield Political Economy Research Institute (18 April 2017), http://speri.dept.shef.ac.uk/2017/04/18/its-time-to-regulate-the-gigeconomy/.

Bertossi, E., *Riders in fila per il tampone rapido: "Torno a casa per Natale. Meglio perdere il lavoro che infettare qualcuno"*, Bologna Today (11 December 2020), https://www.bolognatoday.it/cronaca/tampone-rapido-covid-riders-autostazione-bologna.html.

Bostoen, F., *Abuse of Platform Power: Leveraging Conduct in Digital Markets Under EU Competition Law and Beyond*, PhD (2021), https://lirias.kuleuven.be/3439114?limo = 0.

Brennan, T., *Alibaba CEO talks 'power of the platform' at Davos*, Alizila 23 January 2020), https://www.alizila.com/alibaba-ceo-talks-power-of-the-platform-at-davos-2020/.

Brown, J., *Uber's rollout of living wage will put 'further pressure' on other gig economy firms to follow suit, experts warn*, People Management (17 March 2021), https://www.peoplemanagement.co.uk/news/articles/ubers-rollout-living-wage-will-put-further-pressure-on-other-gig-economy-firms?fbclid = IwAR0jngPs-ZHwO5G-BlrVmOjCTArLLPGCAXwwukzAGg9NKZrWfHi1IBpjFAw.

Bradshaw, T., *Just Eat offers hourly wages in UK gig economy shake-up*, Financial Times (9 December 2020), https://www.ft.com/content/352e3c09-7ce3-466a-b941-921f0d3906c7.

Brooks, C., *Meet the Militant Taxi Drivers Union That Just Defeated Uber and Lyft*, INTHESETIMES (5 August 2018), http://216.243.143.31/working/entry/21386/militant_taxi_drivers_union_uber_lyft_alliance_new_york_city.

Butler, S., *Uber to pay UK drivers minimum wage, holiday pay and pension*, The Guardian (16 March 2021), https://www.theguardian.com/technology/2021/mar/16/uber-to-pay-uk-drivers-minimum-wage-holiday-pay-and-pension.

Bursztynsky, J., *Instacart to provide workers with safety kits following strike over coronavirus protections*, CNBC (2 April 2020), https://www.cnbc.com/2020/03/27/instacart-updates-pay-safety-guidelines-as-workers-plan-monday-strike.html.

Castro, BV., Partenio, F., Cordero, K.H., *Pandemic Meets Precarity: The Case of Platform Delivery Work in Latin America*, DAWN (6 July 2020), https://dawnnet.org/wp-content/uploads/2020/10/CASTRO-PARTENIO-CORDERO_Pandemic-Meets-Precarity-The-Case-of-Platform-Delivery-Work-in-Latin-America.pdf.

Cant, C., *Precarious couriers are leading the struggle against platform capitalism*, Political Critique (3 August 2017) http://politicalcritique.org/world/2017/precarious-couriers-are-leading-the-struggle-against-platform-capitalism/.

Cellan-Jones, R., *Robots 'to replace up to 20 million factory jobs' by 2030*, BBC News (26 June 2019), https://www.bbc.com/news/business-48760799.

Countouris, N., De Stefano, V., *Collective-bargaining rights for platform workers*, Social Europe (6 October 2020), https://www.socialeurope.eu/collective-bargaining-rights-for-platform-workers.

Choudary, S.P., *The Dangers of Platform Monopolies*, Knowledge (8 May 2017), https://knowledge.insead.edu/entrepreneurship/dangers-platform-monopolies.

Compa, L., *Labor at a Crossroads: How Unions Can Thrive in the 21st Century*, The American Prospect (online 27 January 2015), https://prospect.org/justice/labor-crossroads-unions-can-thrive-21st-century/.

De Stefano, V., Aloisi, A., *European Commission takes the lead in regulating platform work*, Social Europe (9 December 2021), https://socialeurope.eu/european-commission-takes-the-lead-in-regulating-platform-work.

De Stefano, V., *Regulation is not an À la Carte menu: insights from the Uber judgment*, UK Labour Law Blog (2 March 2021), available at: https://uklabourlawblog.com/2021/03/02/regulation-is-not-an-a-la-carte-menu-insights-from-the-uber-judgment-by-valerio-de-stefano/.

De Stefano, V., *I now pronounce you contractor": Prop22, labour platforms and legislative doublespeak*, UK Labour Law Blog (13 November 2020), https://uklabourlawblog.com/2020/11/13/i-now-pronounce-you-contractor-prop22-labour-platforms-and-legislative-doublespeak-by-valerio-de-stefano/.

De Stefano, V., *Platform work and labour protection. Flexibility is not enough*, Regulating Globalization (23 May 2018), http://regulatingforglobalization.com/2018/05/23/platform-work-labour-protection-flexibility-not-enough/.

Doherty, I., *How Greek Delivery Riders Are Fighting the Gig Economy*, TRIBUNE (12 October 2021), https://tribunemag.co.uk/2021/10/how-greek-delivery-riders-are-fighting-the-gigeconomy#: ~ :text = Riders%20conducted%20a%20four%2Dhour,from%204.5%20stars%20to%20one.

Drimmer, J., *The Inter-American Court of Human Rights and the Gig Economy*, Lexology (11 February 2021), https://www.lexology.com/library/detail.aspx?g=e88aa8ad-447d-42d9-9f4a-650f3f1944ad.

Dukes, R. Streeck, W., *Putting the brakes on the spread of indecent work*, Social Europe (10 March 2021), https://www.socialeurope.eu/putting-the-brakes-on-the-spread-of-indecent-work.

Dubal, V., *AB5: Regulating the Gig Economy Is Good for Workers and Democracy*, LPEProject (3 October 2019), https://lpeblog.org/2019/10/03/ab5-regulating-the-gig-economy-is-good-for-workers-and-democracy/.

Espinoza, J., *Vestager says gig economy workers should 'team up' on wages*, (24 October 2019), https://www.ft.com/content/0cafd442-f673-11e9-9ef3-eca8fc8f2d65.

European Transport Workers' Federation, *3F secures ground-breaking national sectoral agreement for delivery riders*, (4 February 2021), https://www.etf-europe.org/3f-secures-ground-breaking-national-sectoral-agreement-for-delivery-riders/.

Eurofound, *Riders' Union Netherlands*, (19 May 2021), https://www.eurofound.europa.eu/data/platform-economy/initiatives/riders-union-netherlands.

Eurofound, *Deliveroo strike Spain*, (9 April 2021), https://www.eurofound.europa.eu/data/platform-economy/initiatives/deliveroo-strike-spain.

Eurofound, *GoOpti worker protest*, (22 January 2021), https://www.eurofound.europa.eu/data/platform-economy/initiatives/goopti-worker-protest.

Eurofound, *Registration of Amazon Flex deliverers*, (22 January 2021), https://www.eurofound.europa.eu/data/platform-economy/initiatives/registration-of-amazon-flex-deliverers.

Eurofound, *Mladi Plus*, (22 January 2021), https://www.eurofound.europa.eu/data/platform-economy/initiatives/mladi-plus.

Eurofound, *NIdiL and CGIL*, (22 January 2021), https://www.eurofound.europa.eu/de/data/platform-economy/initiatives/nidil-and-cgil.

Eurofound, *Safety Delivery Initiative*, (1 February 2021), https://www.eurofound.europa.eu/data/platform-economy/initiatives/safety-delivery-initiative.

Eurofound, *Riders' law*, (20 August 2021), https://www.eurofound.europa.eu/nl/data/platform-economy/initiatives/riders-law.

Fabian, S., *Pandemic's effects on online freelance work: distancing dividend or downscaling loss?*, On-line Labour Index: Covid-19 (2 April 2020), https://ilabour.oii.ox.ac.uk/pandemics-effects-on-online-freelance-work-distancing-dividend-or-downscaling-loss/.

Fairwork, *Fairwork Response to the European Commission's Proposal for a Directive on Platform Work*, Fairwork (9 January 2021), https://fair.work/en/fw/blog/fairwork-response-to-the-european-commissions-proposal-for-a-directive-on-platform-work/.

Forsyth, A., *What does collective representation look like in Australia's gig economy?*, Labour Law Down Under (27 October 2018), https://labourlawdownunder.wordpress.com/2018/10/27/what-does-collective-representation-look-like-in-australias-gig-economy/.

Georgiou, D., *An assessment of the EU's draft guidelines on the application of eu competition law to collective agreements of the 'solo self-employed'*, Competition Policy International (July 2022), https://www.competitionpolicyinternational.com/wp-content/uploads/2022/07/3-AN-ASSESSMENT-OF-THE-EUS-DRAFT-GUIDELINES-ON-THE-APPLICATION-OF-EU-COMPETITION-LAW-TO-COLLECTIVE-AGREEMENTS-OF-THE-SOLO-SELF-EMPLOYED-Despoina.pdf.

Gilbert, S., *COVID-19: A unique challenge for gig-sector businesses*, Lexology (8 April 2020), https://www.lexology.com/library/detail.aspx?g=d401d8ef-ffce-4769-b750-65bf7f18b627.

Groover, H., *Lengthy legal fight over Seattle's Uber unionization law comes to an end*, The Seattle Times (13 April 2020 (updated 14 April 2020)), https://www.seattletimes.com/seattle-news/transportation/lengthy-legal-fight-over-seattles-uber-unionization-law-comes-to-an-end/.

GMB Union., *Hermes and GMB in groundbreaking gig economy deal*, (4 February 2019), https://www.gmb.org.uk/news/hermes-gmb-groundbreaking-gig-economy-deal.

Guttuso, L., *In Pursuit of Cartels – a Critical Analysis of the Dynamics Between Public and Private Enforcement*, (Confirmation of PhD Candidature Document, The University of Queensland (2016).

Heikkla, M., Tamma, P., *Delivery companies unveil labor deal with Italian far-right union*, Politico (16 September 2020), https://www.politico.eu/article/delivery-companies-unveil-labor-deal-with-italian-far-right-union/.

Hiesse, E., *FO fully mobilized for bicycle deliverers working for the platforms (translation)*, FO's Coronavirus / Covid19 File (10 May 2020), https://www.force-ouvriere.fr/fo-pleinement-mobilisee-pour-les-livreurs-a-velo-travaillant?lang=fr.

IG Metall, Ombudsstelle für Crowdworking Plattformen vereinbart, available at: https://www.igmetall.de/download/2017_11_8_Presseinformation_OmbudsstelleCrowdworking_ef5ebcd3b52f834a38b64ec80377aee518d11009.pdf.

ITUC, Human and Trade Union Rights: https://www.ituc-csi.org/human-and-trade-union-rights#:~:text=The%20ITUC%20defends%20trade%20unionists,where%20these%20affect%20working%20people.

Jolly, J., Partridge, J., *Top UK fund refuses to invest in Deliveroo amid City concern over riders' rights*, The Guardian (24 March 2021), https://www.theguardian.com/uk-news/2021/mar/24/top-uk-fund-refuses-to-invest-in-deliveroo-amid-concern-over-riders-rights?fbclid = IwAR3ydNIWF7fWvckmLR0T-ugF14pgYLlvVIljDAVVhpwNKR0oPV8-StxXpD0.

Kaminska, I., *Davos: Historians Dream of Fourth Industrial Revolutions*, The Financial Times (20 January 2016), https://www.ft.com/content/17b90ed9-e57d-3940-90f4-d2d1699288b3.

Kaine, S., *All care and no responsibility: why Airtasker can't guarantee a minimum wage*, The Conversation (2 May 2017), https://theconversation.com/all-care-and-no-responsibility-why-airtasker-cant-guarantee-a-minimum-wage-76943.

Kasmir, S., *Precarity*, The Cambridge Encyclopedia of Anthropology (13 Mar 2018), https://www.anthroencyclopedia.com/entry/precarity.

Kelly-Lyth, A., Prassl, J., The EU's Proposed Platform Work Directive: A Promising Step, VERFASSUNGS (14 December 2021), https://verfassungsblog.de/work-directive/.

Kominers, S.D., Jin, L., *A Labor Movement for the Platform Economy*, Harvard Business Review (24 September 2021), https://hbr.org/2021/09/a-labor-movement-for-the-platform-economy.

Loffler, M., Tschiesner, A., *The Internet of Things and the Future of Manufacturing*, (1 June 2013), https://www.mckinsey.com/business-functions/mckinsey-digital/our-insights/the-internet-of-things-and-the-future-of-manufacturing.

Masige, S., *DoorDash and the Transport Workers Union have entered an agreement to support drivers during the pandemic, including financial help if they contract the virus*, Business Insider Australia (28 July 2020), https://www.businessinsider.com.au/doordash-transport-workers-union-agreement-delivery-drivers-2020-7.

Marshall, A., *Now the Courts Will Decide Whether Uber Drivers Are Employees*, Wired (1 March 2020), https://www.wired.com/story/courts-decide-uber-drivers-employees/.

Meneghello, R., *Gig Economy Business Model Dealt a Blow in California Ruling*, The New York Times (30 April 2018), https://www.nytimes.com/2018/04/30/business/economy/gig-economy-ruling.html.

Mitropoulos, A., *Precari-US?*, Tranversal (3 March 2005), https://transversal.at/transversal/0704/mitropoulos/en.

Moulds, J., *Gig workers among the hardest hit by coronavirus pandemic*, World Economic Forum (21 April 2020), https://www.weforum.org/agenda/2020/04/gig-workers-hardest-hit-coronavirus-pandemic/.

Muller-Heyndyk, R., *Hermes to offer drivers 'self-employed-plus' status*, Hrmagazine (4 February 2019), https://www.hrmagazine.co.uk/content/news/hermes-to-offer-drivers-self-employed-plus-status.

Nugent, C., *Migrants in Latin America Have Turned to Delivery Gigs During the Pandemic. But Drivers Say They're Facing Hostility and Mistreatment*, Time (10 April 2021), https://time.com/5953683/delivery-drivers-latin-america-migrants/.

Platform Revolution, *The Dark Side of Platform Monopoly*, Platform Revolution (2014), https://platformthinkinglabs.com/materials/the-dark-side-of-platform-monopoly/.

Pecinovksy, P., *Are national collective bargaining systems ready for solo, self-employed persons?*, Global Workplace Law & Policy (20 April 2022), http://global-workplace-law-and-policy.kluwerlawonline.com/2022/04/20/are-national-collective-bargaining-systems-ready-for-solo-self-employed-persons/.

Pskowski, M., Vilela, R., *They Aren't Anything Without Us': Gig Workers Are Striking Throughout Latin America*, Vice (12 August 2020), https://www.vice.com/en/article/jgxazk/they-arent-anything-without-us-gig-workers-are-striking-throughout-latin-america.

Pulignano, V., Mara, C., *Food-delivery riders, algorithms and autonomy*, Social Europe (21 January 2021), https://www.socialeurope.eu/food-delivery-riders-algorithms-and-autonomy.

Palmer, A., *How Amazon keeps a close eye on employee activism to head off unions*, (CNBC 24 October 2020), https://www.cnbc.com/2020/10/24/how-amazon-prevents-unions-by-surveilling-employee-activism.html.

Rainone, S., *Digital Transition: An Opportunity to Advance Labour Rights*, Global Workplace Law & Policy (1 February 2022), http://global-workplace-law-and policy.kluwerlawonline.com/2022/02/01/digital-transition-an-opportunity-to-advance-labour-rights/.

Rodríguez, R., *First collective agreement for platform workers in Spain*, Social Europe (13 January 2022), https://socialeurope.eu/first-agreement-for-platform-workers-in-spain?fbclid=IwAR0UoNfpKG3V8nqbVQUfiB5EvASfKieH45EnBp2TXV9un1WnQprxnyBYenw.

Rhinehart, L., McNicholas, C., *Collective bargaining beyond the worksite: How workers and their unions build power and set standards for their industries*, Economic Policy Institute (4 May 2020), https://www.epi.org/publication/collective-bargaining-beyond-the-worksite-how-workers-and-their-unions-build-power-and-set-standards-for-their-industries/.

Sachs, B., *Looks like the gig is up for Uber in California*, Onlabor (1 May 2018), https://onlabor.org/looks-like-the-gig-is-up-for-uber-in-california/.

Schaedel, J., Boughton, R., Xu, J., *California brings action against Uber and Lyft for misclassifying drivers*, (Lexology 20 May 2020), https://www.lexology.com/library/detail.aspx?g=b3b8b983-13b7- 4e61-99b8-8bdeb5962126.

Scheiber, N., Conger, K., *Uber and Lyft Drivers Gain Labor Clout, With Help From an App*, The New York Times (14 July 2020), https://www.nytimes.com/2019/09/20/business/uber-lyft-drivers.html.

Sciarra, S., *Modernization of Labour Law: A Current European Debate: a Public Lecture*, International Institute for Labour Studies (2007).

Solon, O., *Big Brother isn't just watching: workplace surveillance can track your every move*, The Guardian (6 November 2017), https://www.theguardian.com/world/2017/nov/06/workplace-surveillance-big-brother-technology.

Somovia, J., *ILO Director-General address to the European Parliament*, (14 September 2011), https://www.ilo.org/global/about-the-ilo/newsroom/statements-and-speeches/WCMS_162828/lang--nl/index.htm.

Staunton, B., *Grassroots action prominent in the platform economy*, Open Democracy (16 December 2018), https://www.opendemocracy.net/en/can-europe-make-it/grassroots-action-prominent-in-platform-economy/.

Sjåfjell, B., Jukka, M., *Corporate Purpose and the EU Corporate Sustain-ability Due Diligence Proposal*, Oxford Business Law (25 February 2022), https://www.law.ox.ac.uk/business-law-blog/blog/2022/02/corporate-purpose-and-eu-corporate-sustainability-due-diligence.

Taylor, D.B., *Instacart Shoppers Plan to Strike Over Coronavirus Protections*, The New York Times (28 March 2020), https://www.nytimes.com/2020/03/28/business/coronavirus-instacart-strike.html.

TUC, *Dignity at work and the AI revolution: a TUC manifesto*, Trade Union Congress (2021), https://www.tuc.org.uk/sites/default/files/2021-03/The_AI_ Revolution_20121_Manifesto_AW.pdf/.

The GREENS/EFA, *New EU Proposal Makes 4 Million Platform Porkers Eligible for Better Working Conditions*, Press Release (9 December 2021), https://www.greens-efa.eu/en/article/press/new-eu-proposal-makes-4-million-platform-workers-eligible-for-better-working-conditions.

The Gig Economy Project, *Gig Economy Project – Riders set to strike across Greece after viral #Cancel_EFood campaign*, Brave New Europe (18 September 2021), https://braveneweurope.com/gig-economy-project-riders-set-to-strike-across-greece-after-viral-cancel_efood-campaign.

UNI Global Union, Historic victories for Just Eat and Deliveroo workers in Europe, (5 January 2022), https://uniglobalunion.org/news/historic-victories-just-eat-and-deliveroo-workers europe?fbclid=IwAR3x3BJeUIuhBsICKGZCElYF3yeAYiT739oOAP2ZnKc4eyzC2ibv4JFF93s.

UGT, *The Labor Inspectorate should sanction digital platforms that threaten health (translation)*, (18 May 2018), https://www.ugt.es/la-inspeccion-de-trabajo-deberia-sancionar-las-plataformas-digitales-que-atentan-contra-la-salud.

Visser, J., Hayter, S., Grammarano, R., *Trends in Collective Bargaining Coverage: Stability, Erosion or Decline?*, Issue Brief No. 1 Geneva, ILO (2017).

Widner, J., *Gig economy un-gigged: collective bargaining agreement for bike couriers*, Lexology (18 December 2019), https://www.lexology.com/library/detail.aspx?g=0771b65a-6105-4128-a8a1-f384982f474d.

Worldometer, *Covid-19 Coronavirus Pandemic*, https://www.worldometers.info/coronavirus/.

Wood, A.J., Graham, M., *Networked but commodified: digital labour in the remote gig economy*, New Internationalist (28 February 2019), https://newint.org/features/2019/02/28/networked-commodified-digital-labour-remote-gig-economy.

White, B.J., *Uber CEO sees California ballot initiative as a model for other states*, Politico (11 May 2020), https://www.politico.com/states/california/story/2020/11/05/uber-ceo-sees-california-ballot-initiative-as-a-model-for-other-states-9424660.

Zamponi, L., *Bargaining with the Algorithm*, Jacobin Magazine (6 September 2018), https://www.jacobinmag.com/2018/06/deliveroo-riders-strike-italy-labor-organizing.

Table of Case Law and Administrative Decisions

European Court of Justice (CJEU)

European Court of Human Rights (ECtHR)

European Committee of Social Rights (ECSR)

ILO Supervisory Bodies

Other International Decisions

National Decisions

Table of Legislation

International Legislation

National Legislation

Belgium, Collective Labour Agreement Act 1968, Belgian Official Gazette 15 January 1969.

Belgium, Labour Relations Act 2006, 217, 224

Canada, Canada Labour Code, 111

Colombia, Colombia, Proyecto de Ley No, de 2019, Por medio de la cual se regula el trabajo digital económicamente dependiente realizado a través de empresas de intermediación digital que hacen uso de plataformas digitales en Colombia, 88–89

France, Loi n° 2016-1088 du 8 août 2016 relative au travail, à la modernisation du dialogue social et à la sécurisation des parcours professionnels, 87

Ireland, Competition (Amendment) Act 2017, 5, 179, 239

Italy, Decreto-Legge 3 settembre 2019, n. 101 disposizioni urgenti per la tutela del lavoro e per la risoluzione di crisi aziendali, 140

The Netherlands, ACM, Guidelines: Price Arrangements Between Self-Employed Workers (updated June 2020), 113, 114

The UK, The Employment Rights Act (ERA) 1996, 224

The UK, Trade Union and Labour Relations (Consolidation) Act 1992, 219

U.S.A., California Labour Code, 88

U.S.A., Clayton Antitrust Act 1914 15 US Code, 73

U.S.A., Iowa Code, 89

U.S.A., Utah Code, 89

Spain, Real Decreto-ley 9/2021, de 11 de mayo, por el que se modifica el texto refundido de la Ley del Estatuto de los Trabajadores, aprobado por el Real Decreto Legislativo 2/2015, de 23 de octubre, 87

Portugal, Lei n.° 45/2018 de 10 de agosto 2018. Regime jurídico da atividade de transporte individual e remunerado de passageiros em veículos descaracterizados a partir de plataforma eletrónica, 88

Ukraine, Закон України Про стимулювання розвитку цифрової економікив Україні, No. 1667-IX from 15.07.2021, 89

Slovenia, Zakon o inšpekciji dela (ZID-1) št. 19/14 z dne 17.03.2014, 90

BCLR - BULLETIN OF COMPARATIVE LABOUR RELATIONS

Vol. Author/Title/Year/ISBN

1. Roger Blanpain, *Individual Employment Contracts: Collective Agreements,* 1970.
2. Roger Blanpain, *Social Planning,* 1971 (ISBN 90-312-0018-2).
3. Roger Blanpain, *Guaranteed Income Funds,* 1972 (ISBN 90-312-0019-0).
4. Roger Blanpain, *Employee Participation at the Level of the Enterprise,* 1973 (ISBN 90-312-0020-4).
5. Roger Blanpain, *Vastheid van Betrekking: Staking en Bezetting,* 1974.
6. Roger Blanpain, *Labour Law and Industrial Relations (International Bibliography),* 1975 (ISBN 90-312-0023-9).
7. Roger Blanpain, *Multinational Enterprises,* 1976 (ISBN 90-312-0024-7).
8. Roger Blanpain, *Worker's Participation in the European Company,* 1977 (ISBN 90-312-0044-1).
9. Roger Blanpain, *Women and Labour,* 1978 (ISBN 90-312-0077-8).
10. Roger Blanpain, *European Conference on Labour Law and Industrial Relations: Multinational Enterprises,* 1979 (ISBN 90-312-0091-3).
11. Roger Blanpain, *Job Security and Industrial Relations,* 1980 (ISBN 90-312-0147-2).
12. Roger Blanpain, Greg Bamber & Russell Lansbury, *Technological Change and Industrial Relations: An International Symposium,* 1983 (ISBN 90-312-0205-3).
13. Roger Blanpain, James Janssen van Raay & A. Moulty, *Worker's Participation in the European Community: The Fifth Directive,* 1984 (ISBN 90-654-4187-5).
14. Roger Blanpain, *Equality and Prohibition of Discrimination in Employment,* 1985 (ISBN 90-654-4215-4).
15. Roger Blanpain, *Restructuring Labour in the Enterprise: Law and Practice in France, F.R. of Germany, Italy, Sweden and the United Kingdom,* 1986 (ISBN 90-654-4283-9).
16. Roger Blanpain & E. Kassalow, *Unions and Industrial Relations: Recent Trends and Prospect: A Comparative Treatment,* 1987 (ISBN 90-654-4294-4).
17. Roger Blanpain & Marco Biagi, *Trade Union Democracy and Industrial Relations,* 1988 (ISBN 90-654-4394-0).
18. Roger Blanpain & Jelle Visser, *In Search of Inclusive Unionism,* 1990 (ISBN 90-654-4439-4).
19. Roger Blanpain, *Flexibility and Wages: A Comparative Treatment,* 1990 (ISBN 90-654-4461-0).

20. Roger Blanpain, Stephen Frenkel & Oliver Clarke, *Economic Restructuring and Industrial Relations in Industrialised Countries,* 1990 (ISBN 90-654-4488-2).
21. Roger Blanpain & Friedrich Fürstenberg, *Structure and Strategy in Industrial Relations,* 1991 (ISBN 90-654-4559-5).
22. Roger Blanpain, Amira Galin & Ozer Carmi, *Flexible Work Patterns and Their Impact on Industrial Relations,* 1991 (ISBN 90-654-4572-2).
23. Roger Blanpain, *Workers' Participation: Influence on Management Decision-Making by Labour in the Private Sector,* 1992 (ISBN 90-654-4600-1).
24. Roger Blanpain, Brian Brooks & Chris Engels, *Employed or Self-Employed,* 1992 (ISBN 90-654-4613-3).
25. Roger Blanpain & Tiziano Treu, *Industrial Relations Developments in the Telecommunications Industry,* 1993 (ISBN 90-654-4642-7).
26. Roger Blanpain & Marco Biagi, *Industrial Relations in Small and Medium Sized Enterprises,* 1993 (ISBN 90-654-4696-6).
27. Roger Blanpain & Marco Biagi, *Participative Management and Industrial Relations in a Worldwide Perspective,* 1993 (ISBN 90-654-4769-5).
28. Roger Blanpain, Jacques Rojot & Hoyt N. Wheeler, *Employee Rights and Industrial Justice,* 1994 (ISBN 90-654-4804-7).
29. Roger Blanpain & Ruth Ben-Israel, *Strikes and Lock-Outs in Industrialized Market Economies,* 1994 (ISBN 90-654-4841-1).
30. Roger Blanpain, Kazuo Sugeno & Yasuo Suwa, *The Harmonization of Working Life and Family Life,* 1995 (ISBN 90-411-0064-4).
31. Roger Blanpain & Laszio Nagy, *Labour Law and Industrial Relations in Central and Eastern Europe,* 1996 (ISBN 90-411-0298-1).
32. Roger Blanpain, *Labour Law and Industrial Relations in the European Union,* 1997 (ISBN 90-411-0527-1).
33. Taco Van Peijpe, *Employment Protection under Strain,* 1998 (ISBN 90-411-0528-8).
34. Roger Blanpain, Takashi Araki & Ryuichi Yamakawa, *The Process of Industrialization and the Role of Labour Law in Asia,* 1999 (ISBN 9-041-1104-7-X).
35. Roger Blanpain & Marco Biagi, *Non-standard Work and Industrial Relations,* 1999 (ISBN 90-411-1117-4).
36. Roger Blanpain, *Private Employment Agencies: The Impact of ILO Convention 181 (1997) and the Judgment of the European Court of Justice of 11 December 1997,* 1999 (ISBN 90-411-1118-2).
37. Roger Blanpain, *Multinational Enterprises and the Social Challenges of the XXIst Century: The ILO Declaration on Fundamental* Principles *at Work, Public and Private Corporate Codes of Conduct,* 2000 (ISBN 90-411-1280-4).
38. Roger Blanpain, Ryuichi Yamakawa & Takashi Araki, *Deregulation and Labour Law: In Search of a Labour Concept for the 21st Century,* 2000 (ISBN 90-411-1370-3).
39. Roger Blanpain, *The Council of Europe and the Social Challenges of the XXIst Century,* 2001 (ISBN 90-411-1543-9).

40. Roger Blanpain, *On-Line Rights for Employees in the Information Society, Use & Monitoring of E-Mail & Internet at Work*, 2002 (ISBN 90-411-1626-5).
41. Roger Blanpain, *The Evolving Employment Relationship and the New Economy: The Role of Labour Law & Industrial Relations*, 2001 (ISBN 90-411-1691-5).
42. Roger Blanpain, *Involvement of Employees in the European Union, Works Councils, Company Statute, Information and Consultation Rights*, 2002 (ISBN 90-411-1760-1).
43. Michele Colucci, *The Impact of the Internet and New Technologies on the Workplace: A Legal Analysis from a Comparative Point of View*, 2002 (ISBN 90-411-1824-1).
44. Roger Blanpain, *White Paper on the Labour Market in Italy: The Quality of European Industrial Relations and Changing Industrial Relations*, 2002 (ISBN 90-411-1841-1).
45. Roger Blanpain, Russell D. Lansbury & Young-Bum Park, *Impact of Globalisation on Employment Relations: A Comparison of the Automobile and Banking Industries in Australia and Korea*, 2002 (ISBN 90-411-1850-0).
46. Roger Blanpain & Antoine Jacobs, *Employee Rights in Bankruptcy: A Comparative-Law Assessment*, 2002 (ISBN 90-411-1942-6).
47. Roger Blanpain, Takashi Araki & Shinya Ouchi, *Corporate Restructuring and the Role of Labour Law*, 2003 (ISBN 90-411-1949-3).
48. Roger Blanpain, *Collective Bargaining, Discrimination, Social Security and European Integration*, 2003 (ISBN 90-411-2010-6).
49. Roger Blanpain & Luis Aparicio-Valdez, *Labour Relations in the Asia- Pacific Countries*, 2004 (ISBN 90-411-2239-7).
50. Roger Blanpain & Ronnie Graham, *Temporary Agency Work and the Information Society*, 2004 (ISBN 90-411-2252-4).
51. Roger Blanpain, *The Actors of Collective Bargaining: A World Report*, 2004 (ISBN 90-411-2253-2).
52. Roger Blanpain & Michele Colucci, *The Globalisation of Labour Standards: The Soft Law Track*, 2004 (ISBN 90-411-2303-2).
53. Roger Blanpain, Takashi Araki & Shinya Ouchi, *Labour Law in Motion: Diversification of the Labour Force & Terms and Conditions of Employment*, 2005 (ISBN 90-411-2315-6).
54. Roger Blanpain, *Smoking and the Workplace*, 2005 (ISBN 90-411-2325-3).
55. Roger Blanpain, *Confronting Globalization: The Quest for a Social Agenda*, 2005 (ISBN 90-411-2381-4).
56. Roger Blanpain, Thomas Blanke & Edgar Rose, *Collective Bargaining Wages in Comparative Perspective: Germany, France, the Netherlands, Sweden and the United Kingdom*, 2005 (ISBN 90-411-2388-1).
57. Roger Blanpain & Anne Numhauser-Henning, *Women in Academia & Equality Law: Aiming High - Falling Short?*, 2006 (ISBN 978-90-411-2427-6).
58. Roger Blanpain, *Freedom of Services in the European Union: Labour and Social Security Law: The Bolkestein Initiative*, 2006 (ISBN 978-90-411-2453-5).
59. Roger Blanpain, Frans Pennings & Nurhan Sural, *Flexibilisation and Modernisation of the Turkish Labour Market*, 2006 (ISBN 978-90-411-2490-X).

60. Roger Blanpain & Boel Flodgren, *Corporate and Employment Perspectives in a Global Business Environment*, 2006 (ISBN 978-90-411-2537-X).
61. Roger Blanpain, Shinya Ouchi & Takashi Araki, *Decentralizing Industrial Relations and The Role of Labor Unions and Employee Representatives*, 2007 (ISBN 978-90-411-2583-3).
62. Roger Blanpain, *European Framework Agreements and Telework: Law and Practice: A European and Comparative Study*, 2007 (ISBN 978-90-411-2560-4).
63. Roger Blanpain, Jim Kitay, Leanne Cutcher & Nick Wailes, *Globalization and Employment Relations in Retail Banking*, 2007 (ISBN 978-90-411-2620-1).
64. Roger Blanpain, Russell Lansbury, Jim Kitay, Nick Wailes & Anja Kirsch, *Globalization and Employment Relations in the Auto Assembly Industry: A Study of Seven Countries*, 2008 (ISBN 978-90-411-2698-6).
65. Roger Blanpain & Michele Tiraboschi, *The Global Labour Market: From Globalization to Flexicurity*, 2008 (ISBN 978-90-411-2722-8).
66. Roger Blanpain, Michele Colucci & Frank Hendrickx, *The Future of Sport in the European Union: Beyond the EU Reform Treaty and the White Paper*, 2008 (ISBN 978-90-411-2761-7).
67. Roger Blanpain, Linda Dickens, *Challenges in European Employment Relations: Employment Regulation, Trade Union Organization, Equality, Flexicurity, Training and New Approaches to Pay*, 2008 (ISBN 978-90-411-2771-6).
68. Roger Blanpain, Hiroya Nakakubo & Takashi Araki, *New Developments in Employment Discrimination Law, 2008* (ISBN 978-90-411-2782-2).
69. Roger Blanpain, Andrzej Marian wiątkowski, *The Laval and Viking Cases: Freedom of Services and Establishment v. Industrial Conflict in the European Economic Area and Russia*, 2009 (ISBN 978-90-411-2850-8).
70. Roger Blanpain, William Bromwich, Olga Rymkevich, Silvia Spattini, *The Modernization of Labour Law and Industrial Relations in a Comparative Perspective*, 2009 (ISBN 978-90-411-2865-2).
71. Roger Blanpain, Juan Pablo Landa & Brian Langille, *Employment Policies and Multilevel Governance*, 2009 (ISBN 978-90-411-2866-9).
72. Roger Blanpain, European Works Councils; *The European Directive 2009/ 38/EC of 6 May 2009, 2009* (ISBN 978-90-411-3208-6).
73. Roger Blanpain, William Bromwich, Olga Rymkevich & Silvia Spattini, *Labour Productivity, Investment in Human Capital and Youth Employment: Comparative Developments and Global Responses*, 2010 (ISBN 978-90-411-3249-9).
74. Greg J. Bamber & Philippe Pochet, *Regulating Employment Relations, Work and Labour Laws: International Comparisons between Key Countries*, 2010 (ISBN 978-90-411-3199-7). General Editor: Roger Blanpain.
75. Roger Blanpain, Desislava Nikolaeva Dimitrova, *Seafarers' Rights in the Globalized Maritime Industry*, 2010 (ISBN 978-90-411-3349-6).
76. Roger Blanpain, Hiroya Nakakubo & Takashi Araki, *Regulation of Fixed- Term Employment Contracts*, 2010 (ISBN 978-90-411-3356-4).

77. Roger Blanpain, William Bromwich, Olga Rymkevich & Iacopo Senatori, *Rethinking Corporate Governance,* 2011 (ISBN 978-90-411-3450-9).
78. Roger Blanpain & Frank Hendrickx, *Labour Law between Change and Tradition: Liber Amicorum Antoine Jacobs,* 2011 (ISBN 978-90-411-3424-0).
79. Roger Blanpain, Thomas Klebe, Marlene Schmidt & Bernd Waas, *Trade Union Rights at the Workplace,* 2012 (ISBN 978-90-411-3460-8).
80. Roger Blanpain, William Bromwich, Olga Rymkevich & Iacopo Senatori, *Labour Markets, Industrial Relations and Human Resources Management: From Recession to Recovery,* 2012 (ISBN 978-90-411-4004-3).
81. Roger Blanpain, Hiroya Nakakubo & Takashi Araki, *Systems of Employee Representation at the Enterprise: A Comparative Study,* 2012 (ISBN 978-90-411-4080-7).
82. Roger Blanpain & Frank Hendrickx, *Temporary Agency Work in the European Union and the United States*, 2013 (ISBN 978-90-411-4769-1).
83. Roger Blanpain, Toker Dereli, Y. Pınar Soykut-Sarıca & Aslı en-Tabaı, *Emerging Patterns of Work and Turkish Labour Market Challenges under Globalization: Readings on Labour and Employment Relations*, 2014 (ISBN 978-90-411-4983-1).
84. Roger Blanpain, Pablo Arellano Ortiz, Marius Olivier & Gijsbert Vonk, *Social Security and Migrant Workers: Selected Studies of Cross-border Social Security Mechanisms*, 2014 (ISBN 978-90-411-4770-7).
85. Roger Blanpain & Nikita Lyutov, *Workers' Representation in Central and Eastern Europe: Challenges and Opportunities for the Works Councils' System*, 2014 (ISBN 978-90-411-4746-2).
86. Roger Blanpain, Ulla Liukkunen & Chen Yifeng, *China and ILO Fundamental Principles and Rights at Works*, 2014 (ISBN 978-90-411-4984-8).
87. Roger Blanpain, *The Use of Languages and Employment Relations*, 2014 (ISBN 978-90-411-5606-8).
88. Roger Blanpain, Hiroya Nakakubo & Takashi Araki, *Protection of Employees' Personal Information and Privacy*, 2014 (ISBN 978-90-411-5608-2).
89. Roger Blanpain, Jan Wouters, Glenn Rayp, Laura Beke & Axel Marx, *Protecting Labour Rights in a Multi-polar Supply Chain and Mobile Global Economy*, 2015 (ISBN 978-90-411-5662-4).
90. Roger Blanpain & Stefania Marassi, *Globalization and Transnational Collective Labour Relations: International and European Framework Agreements at Company Level*, 2015 (ISBN 978-90-411-4748-6).
91. Roger Blanpain, Frank Hendrickx & Petra Herzfeld Olsson, *National Effects of the Implementation of EU Directives on Labour Migration from Third Countries*, 2016 (ISBN 978-90-411-6257-1).
92. Roger Blanpain, Frank Hendrickx & D'Arcy du Toit, *Labour Law and Social Progress: Holding the Line or Shifting the Boundaries?* 2016 (ISBN 978-90-411-6747-7).

93. Roger Blanpain & Frank Hendrickx, *Reasonable Accommodation in the Modern Workplace: Potential and Limits of the Integrative Logics of Labour Law*, 2016 (ISBN 978-90-411-6258-8).
94. Roger Blanpain, Frank Hendrickx & Bernd Waas, *New Forms of Employment in Europe*, 2016 (ISBN 978-90-411-6239-7).
95. Roger Blanpain, Frank Hendrickx, Hiroya Nakakubo & Takashi Araki, *The Notion of Employer in the Era of the Fissured Workplace: Should Labour Law Responsibilities Exceed the Boundary of the Legal Entity?*, 2017 (ISBN 978-90-411-8470-2).
96. Elena Sychenko, *Individual Labour Rights as Human Rights: The Contributions of the European Court of Human Rights to Worker's Rights Protection*, 2017 (ISBN 978-90-411-8629-4).
97. William Bromwich & Olga Rymkevich, *Improving Workplace Quality: New Perspectives and Challenges for Worker Well-Being*, 2017 (ISBN 978-90-411-8628-7).
98. Sarah De Groof, *Work-Life Balance in the Modern Workplace: Interdisciplinary Perspectives from Work-Family Research, Law and Policy*, 2017 (ISBN 978-90-411-8630-0).
99. Sylvaine Laulom, *Collective Bargaining Developments in Times of Crisis*, 2018 (ISBN 978-90-411-8999-8).
100. Frank Hendrickx & Valerio De Stefano, *Game Changers in Labour Law: Shaping the Future of Work*, 2018 (ISBN 978-90-411-9953-9).
101. Ivana Palinkaš, *The Legal and Institutional Framing of Collective Bargaining in CEE Countries: Between Europeanisation and Decentralisation*, 2018 (ISBN 978-90-411-9199-1).
102. Jeremy Waddington, *European Board-Level Employee Representation: National Variations in Influence and Power*, 2018 (ISBN 978-90-411-9202-8).
103. Jan Pichrt & Kristina Koldinská, *Labour Law and Social Protection in a Globalized World: Changing Realities in Selected Areas of Law and Policy*, 2018 (ISBN 978-94-035-0093-5).
104. Matthew W. Finkin, *American Labor and the Law: Dormant, Resurgent, and Emergent Problems*, 2019 (ISBN 978-94-035-0654-8).
105. Giuseppe Casale & Tiziano Treu, *Transformations of Work: Challenges for the Institutions and Social Actors*, 2019 (ISBN 978-94-035-0891-7).
106. Miguel De la Corte-Rodríguez, *EU Law on Maternity and Other Child-Related Leaves: Impact on Gender Equality*, 2019 (ISBN 978-94-035-1452-9).
107. Valeria Pulignano & Frank Hendrickx, *Employment Relations in the 21st Century: Challenges for Theory and Research in a Changing World of Work*, 2020 (ISBN 978-94-035-1764-3).
108. Matteo Bottero, *Posting of Workers in EU Law: Challenges of Equality, Solidarity and Fair Competition*, 2021 (ISBN 978-94-035-2860-1).
109. Bernd Waas & Christina Hießl, *Collective Bargaining for Self-Employed Workers in Europe: Approaches to Reconcile Competition Law and Labour Rights*, 2021 (ISBN 978-94-035-2373-6).

110. Mathias Wouters, *International Labour Standards and Platform Work: An Analysis of Digital Labour Platforms Based on the Instruments on Private Employment Agencies, Home Work and Domestic Work*, 2022 (ISBN 978-94-035-4024-5).
111. Luca Ratti, *In-Work Poverty in Europe: Vulnerable and Under-Represented Persons in a Comparative Perspective*, 2022 (ISBN 978-94-035-4996-5).
112. Silvia Rainone, *The Role of the Court of Justice in EU Labour Law: A Case Study on the Transfer of Undertakings Directive*, 2023 (ISBN 978-94-035-2896-0).
113. Frank Hendrickx, Elena Gramano & David Mangan, *Privacy@work: A European and Comparative Perspective*, 2023 (ISBN 978-94-035-3106-9).
114. Elena Sychenko & Adalberto Perulli, *Employment Law and the European Convention on Human Rights: The Research of the Recent Jurisprudence of the ECtHR Related to Employment Law (2017-2021)*, 2023 (ISBN 978-94-035-3556-2).
115. Ilda Durri, *Casual Work Arrangements and Platform-Based Work: The Casual Work Agenda as a Way to Enhance the Labour Protection of Platform Workers*, 2023 (ISBN 978-94-035-3107-6).
116. Charalampos Stylogiannis, *Collective Labour Rights for Self-Employed Workers: A Human Rights-Based Approach of Platform Work*, 2023 (ISBN 978-94-035-0667-8).